AF249024

An Introduction
to Ukrainian History

Other works by the same author:

The Economic Factors in the Growth of Russia, Philosophical Library, New York, 1957

Old Ukraine, Its Socio-Economic History prior to 1781, Florham Park Press, Madison, N.J., 1963

The Ukrainian Economy, Shevchenko Scientific Society, New York, 1965

An Introduction to Russian History, Philosophical Library, New York, 1967

Ukraine and the European Turmoil, 1917-1919, Shevchenko Scientific Society and the Ukrainian Scientific-Historical Library, New York-Scranton, 1973 (co-authored with M. Stachiv and P. Stercho), 2 volumes

Philosophy in Economic Thought, Florham Park Press, Madison, N.J., 1972 (co-authored with V. Mott)

A History of the Russian Empire, Volume I, *Grand-ducal Vladimir and Moscow,* Philosophical Library, New York, 1973

On the Historical Beginnings of Eastern Slavic Europe, Readings, ed. by the author, Shevchenko Scientific Society, New York, 1976.

Philosophical Foundations of Economic Doctrines, Florham Park Press, Florham Park, N.J., 1977 (co-authored by V. Mott), second edition 1978

AN INTRODUCTION TO UKRAINIAN HISTORY

Volume I
Ancient and Kievan-Galician Ukraine-Rus'

by
Nicholas L. Fr.-Chirovsky
Seton Hall University

Philosophical Library
New York

To all those heroic Dissidents who gave their lives,
defending human rights and the right of all
nationalities, submerged by the Soviet Union, to have
freedom and national independence.

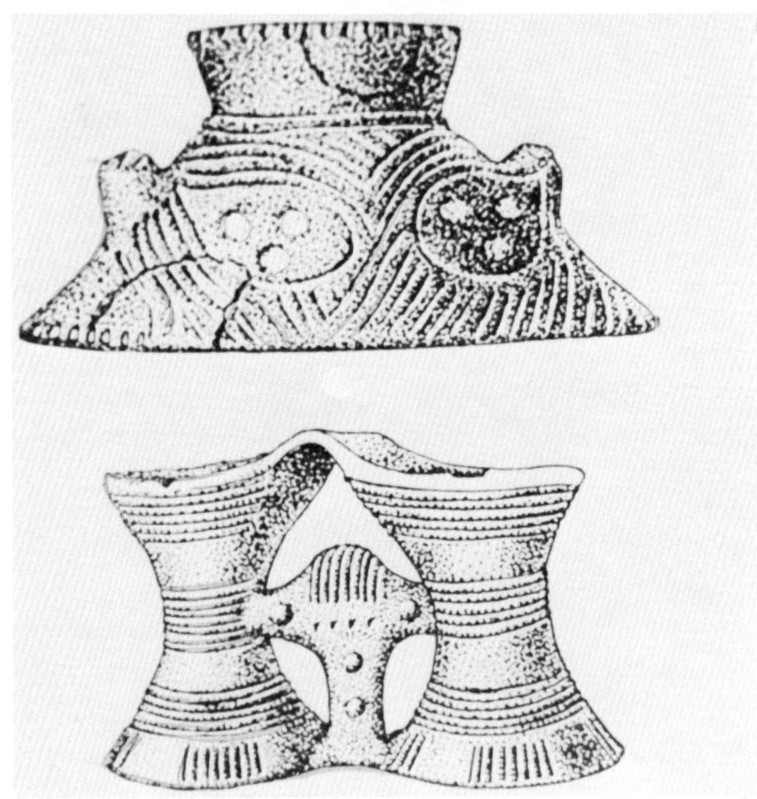

Tripillian pottery from southern Ukraine.

TABLE OF CONTENTS

A street scene from the city of Olbia, a Greek colony on the northern littorals of the Black Sea.

The fortification of the town of Bilhorod, from the tenth century.

PREFACE

The author's intention is to contribute to the knowledge of the East-European affairs in the Anglo-Saxon countries. In order to acquire a correct comprehension of the ethnical, national, racial, social, cultural and political developments and life processes, and the past and the present of all those different ethnical and national groups and communities of Eastern Europe living there, their individual lives for many centuries on their traditional and compact territories, one must study each and every community separately. Doubtlessly, historical studies must be the very beginning; the eye-opener. There have been many works published on Russia and Russian history. Yet, there has been definitely a shortage of such works in English about other nationalities in East Europe and their historical past. Of course, it would not be possible to tell the whole story about the non-Russian nationalities there by reading or studying the works on Russia, since there has not been enough time and space allocated to those nationalities, like the Ukrainians, Byeloruthenians, Lithuanians, Latvians, Estonians, Gruzians, Azerbaidzhanians, Tartars and others. Moreover, the Russian authors have not been particularly keen to publicize the very instance of the multi-national character either of the old Russian Empire or the present Soviet Union, although these facts could not have been and cannot be suppressed. Hence, the author has decided to write a work on only one aspect of this vast field, namely, to write a rather short version of a Ukrainian history; a history of the second largest nationality of East Europe.

Some thirty or more years ago there were but a very few books in English on Ukraine and Ukrainian history. Hence, the English speaking reader was confined to the books on Russian history or on any other Russian topic, as it was pointed out a while ago, to acquire his meager knowledge of Ukraine. These books, however, supplied only general information on Ukraine and Ukrainian people, and at times with a distorted interpretation to fit the Russian political ends. For a long time there was no adequate literature available to counteract that interpretation.

This situation has changed to a great extent. Presently there are various works published on Ukrainian history, such as M. Hrushevsky, *A History of Ukraine,* Yale University Press, New Haven, 1941; D. Doroshenko, *History of the Ukraine,* Edmonton, 1940; C. Manning, *The Story of the Ukraine,* New York, 1947; the same, *Twentieth Century Ukraine,* New York, 1951; W. Allen, *The Ukraine, A History,* Cambridge, 1940 (yet, Allen has accepted strictly the Russian interpretation of the East-European past); and more recently, I. Nahayevsky, *History of Ukraine,* Philadelphia, 1962 and subsequently, 1975, and some other minor works. Obviously, that list can never measure up to a long list of works on Russian history, published in English. There are also some general works on Ukraine in English, such as *Ukraine and Its People,* ed. by I. Mirchuk, Munich, 1949, and some books and pamphlets on Ukrainian geography and economy. In the area of the economic life of Ukraine, and specifically, about the Russian colonial exploitation of Ukraine, the following works were published in English: K. Kononenko, *Ukraine and Russia: A History of the Economic Relations between Ukraine and Russia, 1654-1917,* Milwaukee, 1958; N. Chirovsky, *Old Ukraine, Its Socio-Economic History Prior to 1781,* Madison, 1963; and the same, *Ukrainian Economy,* New York, 1965. J. Kolasky's *Two Years in Soviet Ukraine,* Toronto, 1970, exposed the Soviet terror measures in that country. The enumerating of the works in English on Ukraine and Ukrainian people is, of course, incomplete. L. Dobriansky, S. Horak, O. Pritsak, B. Kortchmaryk, I. Kamenetsky, M. Stachiv, P. Stercho, Ya. Bilinsky, N. Andrusiak, Z. Melnyk, M. Melnyk, I. Koropetsky and many many others have made recently a serious scholarly attempt to advance the knowledge of Ukraine in America and the Western world, in general, for which they certainly deserve credit.

Should a new book on the Ukrainian history be written and published? Of course. There is a need for new versions and presentations. First, because the existing ones are either incomplete (only to the First World War) or do not use recent historical and archeological research findings, which may require a new interpretation of the remote past. Furthermore, each historian (or author) has his own and specific approach. Hrushevsky prefers to emphasize the social aspects; Nahayevsky — religious and cultural ones; Allen accepted the Russian interpretation of the patterns of historical developments in Eastern Europe; Manning's presentation is too sketchy at times. Secondly, there are many works on Russian history with different approaches and interpretations, and new ones are still being written to present the Russian historical developments as comprehensively as possible. There is definitely a need to achieve the same end as far as the Ukrainian past is concerned. The author would like to contribute to that end with respect to Ukraine, although he is not pretending to present a perfect work; a revelation of its own or a masterpiece.

The Ukrainian historical past has been well reflected in the old primary sources. Their interpretation, however, was at times abused by some Russian and Soviet historians, who submitted to the pressure of the imperial plans of their governments, and talked rather of Russia as a monolithic concept and identical with East Europe as a whole. It was obviously not correct. Hence, a distortion of historical truth followed.

Long before the first Ukrainian-Rus'ian chronicle, the *Povist' vremennykh lit,* was written down in the eleventh century, the references to the early past of Ukraine-*Rus'* were made by the Greek, Latin, Norse and Oriental written sources; chronicles, travel accounts, descriptions or other works. It would be enough to mention only a few. Herodotus in the fifth century in his *Historiae* related on Ukraine and its early population. Ioannes Kedrenus (Kedryn) Skylitzes did the same in his *Historiarum Compendium* in the tenth century; Constantine Porphyrogenitus, in his *De Administrando Imperio,* in the tenth century; Procopius, in his *Historiae Bellarum,* in the sixth; Patriarch Photius in his *Letters* from the ninth century described the Rus'ian assault upon Constantinople; while Leo the Deacon referred in his *Historia* from the tenth century to the *Rus'* and their prince, Sviatoslav. The Arabic and Jewish merchants and travellers wrote a great deal about early *Rus'*-Ukraine, such as Ibn-Hawqal, Ibn-Dasta, Ibn-Jakob, Ibn-Fadlan, Masudi and others, in course of the ninth and tenth centuries, whose essays were well compiled by A. Garkavi, in his book entitled *Skazania muzulmanskikh pisatelei o slovianakh i russkikh,* St. Petersburg, 1870. *Rus'* was mentioned in the Norse sagas.

The Western historical sources, making all kinds of references to Ukraine-*Rus',* included among many others the letter of Bruno von Querfurt, who visited *Rus'*-Ukraine at the very beginning of the eleventh century. Tietmar von Merseburg wrote his *Chronicon* approximately at the same time, when he described the city of Kiev and the Pecheng threat. Jordanis in the sixth century referred to the Slavic tribes in Ukraine.

In the eleventh century, the *Primary Chronicle* or *Povist' vremennykh lit* was written. This first Ukrainian-Rus'ian historical work was subsequently amended, re-written and compiled in various ways by numerous authors and editors or groups of authors and editors. In this way the later versions of the chronicle writing, the *Laurentian Chronicle,* in the fourteenth century; the *Hypathian Chronicle,* in the fifteenth century; the *Galician-Volhinian Chronicle,* in the fourteenth century; and some others came into being, covering ever longer periods of Ukrainian history.

In addition, the Ukrainian-Rus'ian code of laws, the *Rus'ka Pravda* of the eleventh century, the lives of saints, the *Slovo o polku Ihoreve, The Lay of Ihor's Campaign,* the heroic epics about the Ukrainian struggle against the Cumans, the steppe nomads, supplied substantial information about the early Ukrainian past.

Some pertinent data about the Ukrainian history may be acquired from the later history writing of other nations and peoples, such as J. Dlugosz's *Historia polonica, Opera omnia,* from the fifteenth century, or V. Tatishchev's *Istoria Rossiiskaia,* from the eighteenth century, and some others, which might have been using some of the original historical source materials which might have been lost since, and were not available to the later historians. Furthermore, some original decrees and documents of the Ukrainian princes, as well as some of their coats of arms, were preserved to give witness to the past. Of course, the geology and archeology supplemented the needed data about the ancient times to complete the historical picture, whenever the written sources could not reach that far back.

One more remark, which might be fully superfluous because it is an obvious truth, is that a history of a people or a country is not only the rulers, kings, princes, wars and political developments, though they are its important components since they fundamentally affect the life of a people and country in all their evolutionary aspects. In fact, a history is the sum total of the developmental process of a people and a country, including all the political, social, cultural and spiritual, religious, economic and other aspects of human life on a certain territory. The author of this volume will sincerely attempt to present, though in brief, all these aspects of the past of the Ukrainian people from antiquity to the present day. A great deal of attention shall be paid to the economic life to show how the Ukrainian people lived then and how they earned their subsistence in the course of the changing times.

N.L. Fr.-Chirovsky

Maplewood, N.J.

XV

ACKNOWLEDGMENTS

The author wishes to express his deep appreciation to Messrs. Volodymyr Stoyko, Ph.D., of Manhattan College, and Vasyl Lencyk of Stanford College, for their most valuable suggestions toward improving the quality of the work as a possible textbook for college and university students. He also thanks Mr. Lubomyr Kalynych for drawing some maps for this publication and his advice in selecting the illustrations to reflect the Ukrainian civilization in the early era of the country's past.

Many thanks are also expressed to Mesdames Joan Driver, Doris Hayden, Dolores Condon and Marie Lauber for their tireless typing and retyping and making photostatic copies of the original manuscript to make it fit for typesetting. For the assistance in editing the book, I thank Mrs. Mary Pavlovsky, Mr. Stanley Strand and my son, John M. Fr.-Chirovsky.

N.L. Fr.-Chirovsky

Maplewood, N.J.

RUS'IAN TRIBES VIII-IX cc.
LITHUANIANS
POLES
DREGOVICHIANS
RADIMICHIANS
VIATICHIANS
SIVERIANIANS
DEREVLIANIANS
DULIBIANS
POLIANIANS
KYIV (KIEV)
KHORVATSIANS
ULYCHIANS
TIVERIANS
BLACK SEA
AZOV SEA
CRIMEA
Vistula
Buh
Prypiat
Don
Donets
Dnieper
Boh
Dniester
Pruth
Seret
Danube

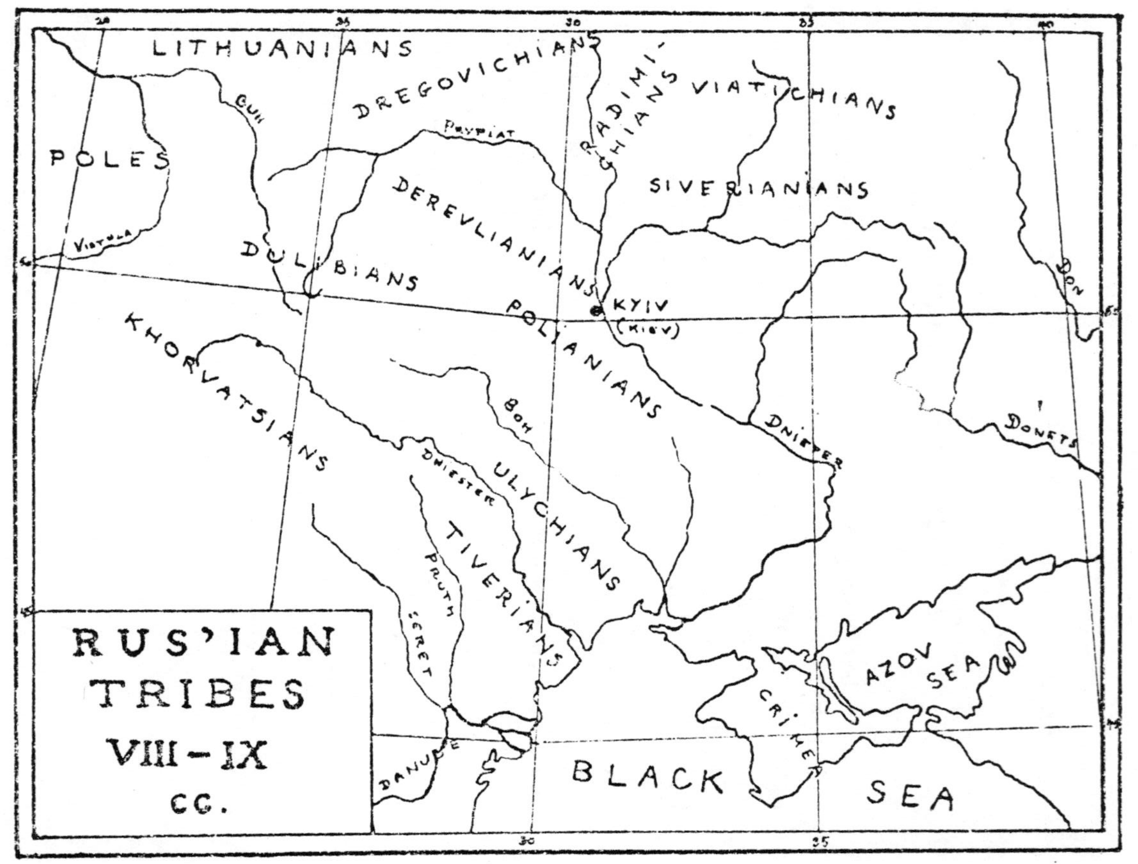

xviii

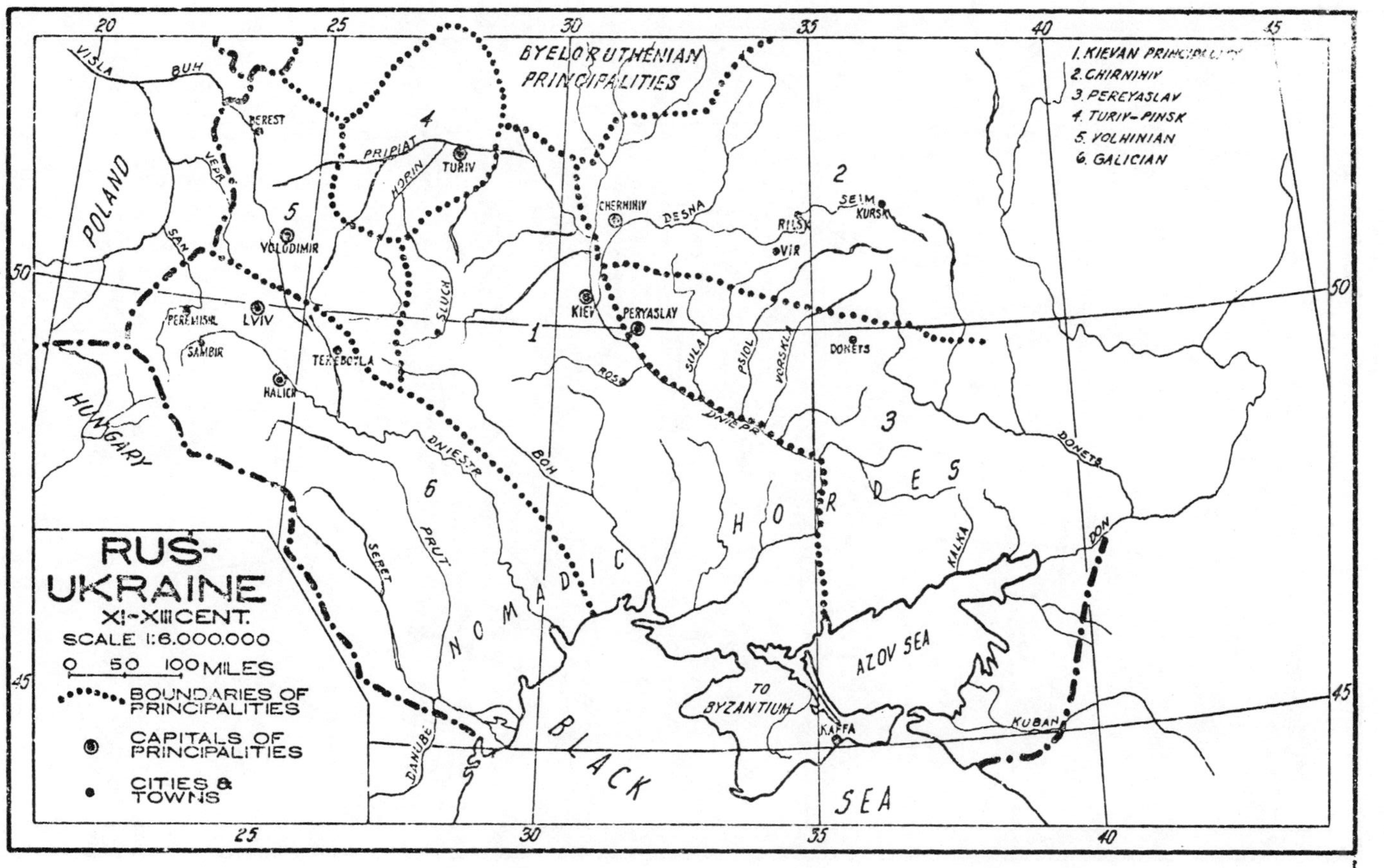
RUS-
UKRAINE
XI-XIII CENT.
SCALE 1:6.000.000
0   50   100 MILES
BOUNDARIES OF PRINCIPALITIES
CAPITALS OF PRINCIPALITIES
CITIES & TOWNS
1. KIEVAN PRINCIPALITY
2. CHIRNIHIV
3. PEREYASLAV
4. TURIV-PINSK
5. VOLHINIAN
6. GALICIAN
BYELORUTHENIAN PRINCIPALITIES
POLAND
HUNGARY
NOMADIC HORDES
BLACK SEA
AZOV SEA
TO BYZANTIUM
VISLA
BUH
BEREST
VEPR
SAN
PRIPIAT
HORIN
TURIV
CHERNIHIV
DESNA
RILSK
VIR
SEIM
KURSK
VOLODIMIR
SLUCH
KIEV
PERYASLAV
SULA
PSIOL
VORSKLA
DONETS
PEREMISHL
LVIV
SAMBIR
TEREBOVLA
HALICH
ROSS
DNIEPR
DNIESTR
BOH
SERET
PRUT
DANUBE
KALKA
DON
DONETS
KUBAN
KAFFA

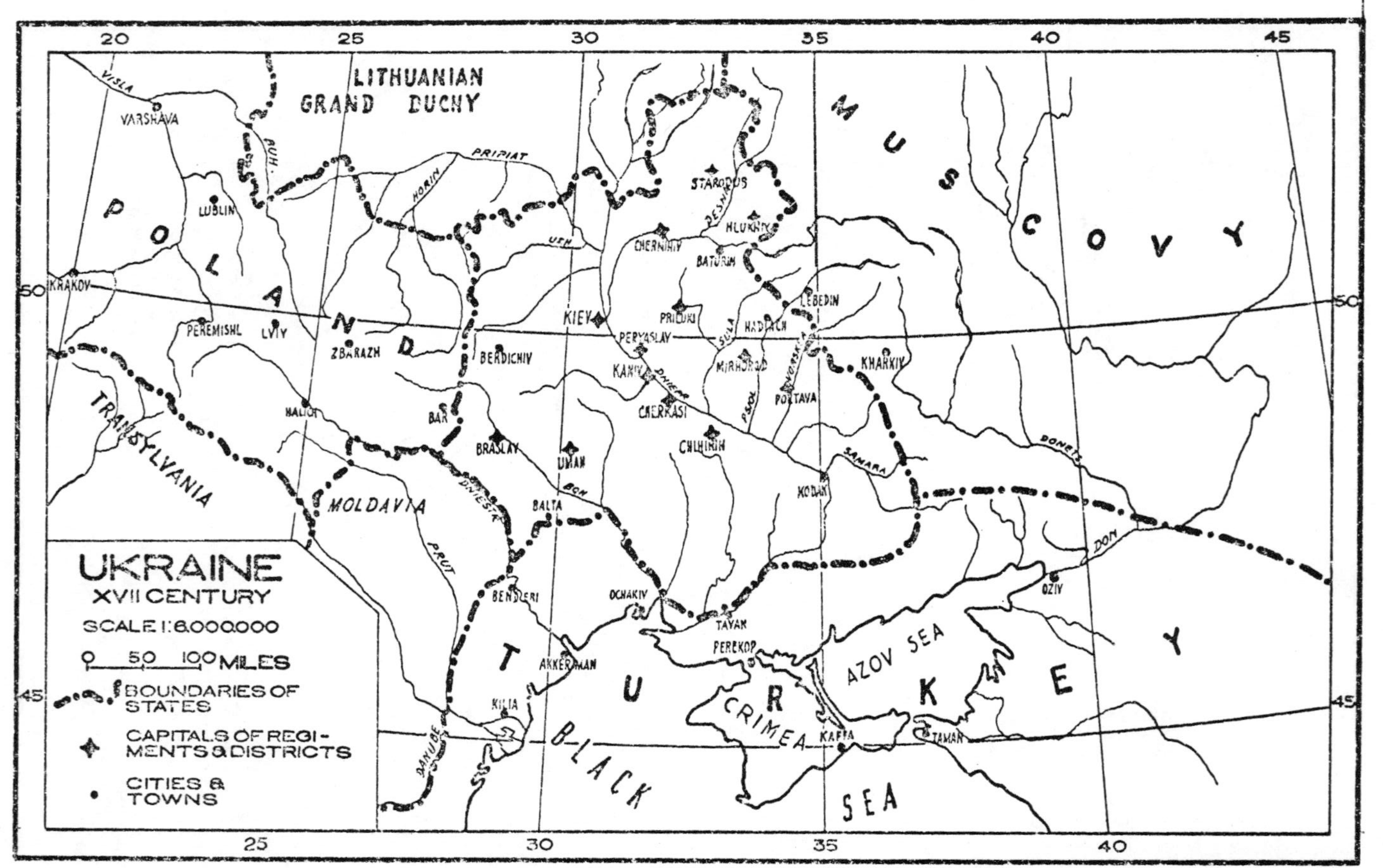

UKRAINE
XVII CENTURY
SCALE 1:6,000,000
0 50 100 MILES
BOUNDARIES OF STATES
CAPITALS OF REGIMENTS & DISTRICTS
CITIES & TOWNS
LITHUANIAN GRAND DUCHY
MUSCOVY
POLAND
TRANSYLVANIA
MOLDAVIA
TURKEY
CRIMEA
AZOV SEA
BLACK SEA
VISLA
BUH
PRIPIAT
HORIN
UFN
DESNA
STARODUS
HLUKHIV
CHERNIHIV
BATURIM
LEBEDIN
VARSHAVA
LUBLIN
KRAKOV
PEREMISHL
LVIV
ZBARAZH
BERDICHIV
KIEV
PRILUKI
PERYASLAV
HADIACH
SULA
MIRHOROD
POLTAVA
VORSKLA
PSOL
KHARKIV
KANIV
DNIEPR
CHERKASI
CHLHIRIN
SAMARA
DONETS
HALICH
BAR
BRASLAV
UMAN
BCH
KODAK
DNIESTR
PRUT
MOLDAVIA
BALTA
OCHAKIV
TAVAN
PEREKOP
BENDERI
AKKERMAN
KILIA
DANUBE
DON
OZIV
KAFFA
TAMAN

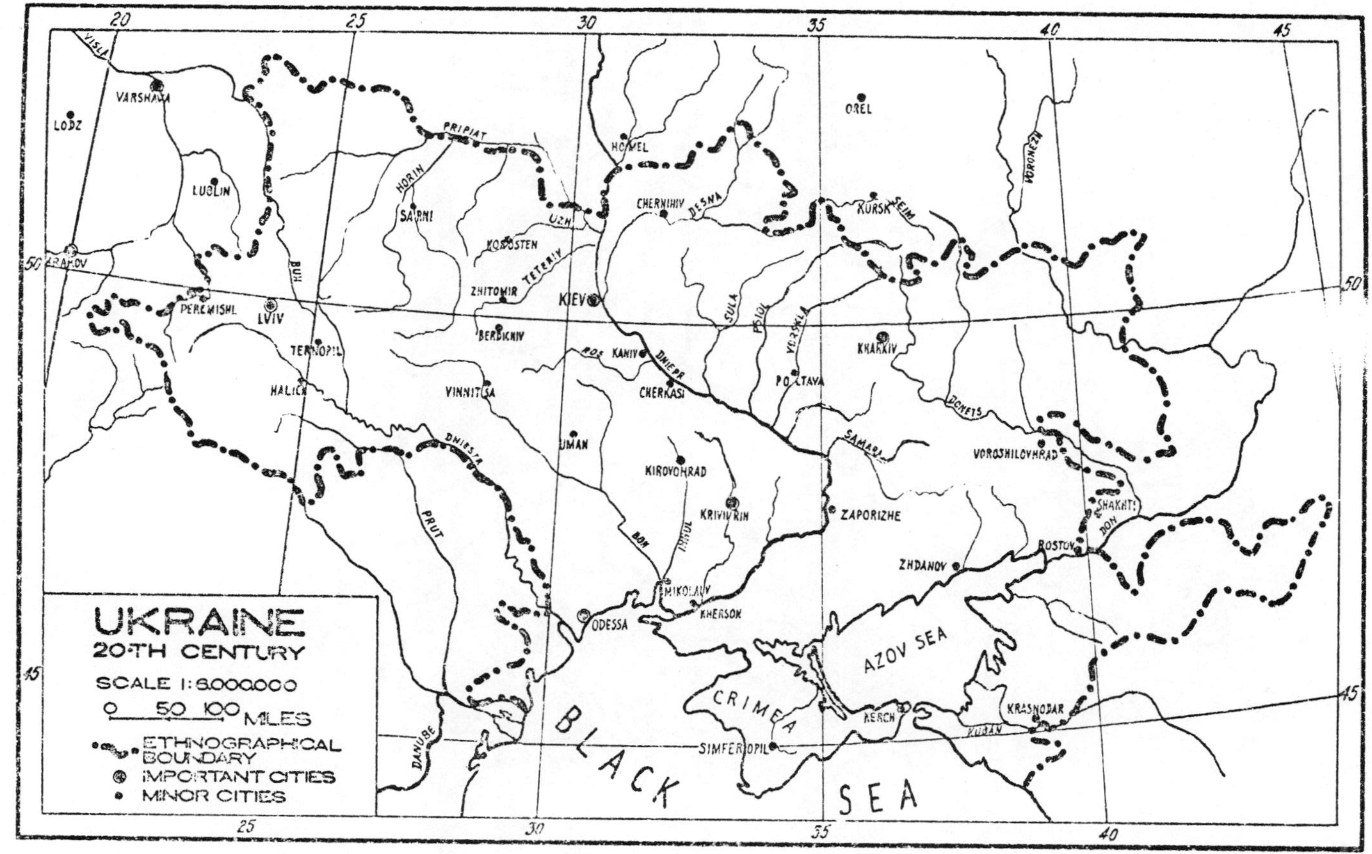

UKRAINE
20TH CENTURY
SCALE 1:6,000,000
0   50   100 MILES
ETHNOGRAPHICAL BOUNDARY
IMPORTANT CITIES
MINOR CITIES
VISLA
LODZ
VARSHAVA
LUBLIN
KRAKOV
PERE MISHL
LVIV
TERNOPIL
HALICH
BUH
SARNI
HORIN
PRIPIAT
KOROSTEN
ZHITOMIR
TETERIV
UZH
HOMEL
CHERNIHIV
DESNA
OREL
KURSK
SEIM
VORONEZH
BERDICHIV
VINNITSA
UMAN
DNIESTR
PRUT
DANUBE
ROS
KANIV
CHERKASI
KIEV
DNIEPR
SULA
PSIOL
VORSKLA
POLTAVA
KHARKIV
DONETS
SAMARA
VOROSHILOVHRAD
KIROVOHRAD
KRIVIVRIN
BOH
INHUL
ZAPORIZHE
SHAKHTI
DON
ROSTOV
ZHDANOV
MIKOLAIV
KHERSON
ODESSA
AZOV SEA
CRIMEA
KERCH
KUBAN
KRASNODAR
SIMFEROPIL
BLACK   SEA

A battle scene between the Rus'ian-Ukrainian and the Cuman warriors.

PART ONE

Introductory Matters and
the Pre-historic Era.

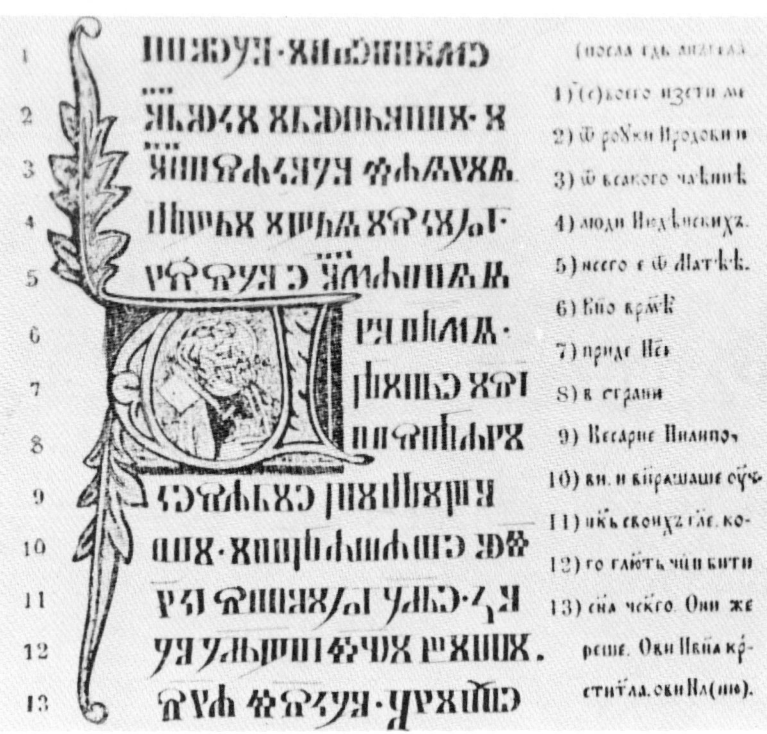

The old Hlaholytsian type.

Silver coins from the time of Prince Volodymyr the Great, with the heraldic insignia of the trident.

CHAPTER ONE

THE LAND AND THE PEOPLE

The name — The geographical and geo-political background — The people

The name of the country is Ukraine; its people are called Ukrainians. These terms are ancient, yet their use to designate this particular land and people was for centuries controversial. The violent opposition to the acceptance of these appellations was politically motivated and had no logical justification. History reveals that the ethnic-national community identified in the twentieth century as the Ukrainians bore in the past another ancient and traditional name, that of *Rus'*, a name used to designate both the land and the people.[1] Historians developed two major theories to explain the origin and the meaning of this archaic designation. The earlier speculation deduced the name *"Rus'"* from the Norse who conquered Ukraine in the ninth century and who were known as the Varengo-Rois; the latter attempted to derive the name of the whole country from the river Ros which flowed in the vicinity of Kiev,* the capital of *Rus'*-Ukraine. The

**Kyiv in Ukrainian, Kiev being the Russian pronunciation. We are using the name Kiev as more popular in the English-speaking lands.*

1

latter seems to be correct since the name *Rus'* was known in the Orient long before the arrival of the Northmen in Ukraine, and because Kiev and the banks of the Ros were cradles of the early political growth of the Ukrainian people.[2]

The original names of *Ukraine* and *Ukrainians*, *Rus'* and also *Rusichi*, were translated into Latin and other foreign languages as *Ruthenia* and *Rus'ia* to denote the country, and the terms *Ruthenians and Rus'ians* were employed to designate the people. The name *Rus'ia* was used in two ways: as a synonym for Ruthenia and also to designate medieval Ukraine. The Ukrainian people, however, were called *Ruthenians* or *Rusci* in the numerous medieval papal and secular documents and other historical sources, but never Russians. The names of *Muscovy* and the *Muscovites* were reserved as political and national designations of the land and the people that we know today as Russia and the Russians. The individual Northern territories were denoted separately as Novgorod, Suzdal, and Rostov. The old chronicles contained no implications which would include the Russians in the concept of *Rus'*, reserving as they did the name *Rus'* exclusively for the Ukrainian provinces.[3]

In the thirteenth century, it was customary to call the Duchy of Galicia and Volhinia (West Ukraine) *Rus'ia Minor* or *Little Rus'*. This designation did not apply then to the entire Ukrainian territory. In the early eighteenth century, the government at St. Petersburg officially conferred the name ''Russian Empire'' upon the Czardom of Muscovy, and thus the latter became modern Russia. At a later date the Muscovites came to be called Great Russians; the Ukrainians (Ruthenians), Little Russians; and the third East European Slavic nationality, the White Russians (Byeloruthenians). The entire Ukraine was officially renamed Little Russia. In 1713 and subsequently, Peter the Great issued imperial decrees to that effect.[4] This highhanded act of redesignation was characteristic of Tsarist arbitrariness and had little established historical precedent.

Apparently it was in the interest of Russian expansionism to confuse hopelessly the national designations of certain Eastern

European areas and peoples in order to obliterate the existence of three separate nationalities therein, and to create a false impression of homogeneity in the new Russian empire. The Ruthenians reacted by accepting a new and distinct name, one with certain historical tradition, in order to emphasize their national identity and to oppose the denationalization campaign of the Tsarist government. The name *Ukraine* was their spontaneous choice. It was soon adopted throughout the nation. At first, *Ukraine* did not designate the whole country and people but rather, according to its etymological sense, "Borderland" or "Frontierland," and its inhabitants. Actually the term *Ukraina* or *Vkraina* meant in the Ukrainian language about the same as "borderland." Already in 1187 and 1189, historical documents employed the designation *Ukraine* for Galicia and the eastern province bordering on the Cuman territories. The western districts, Berest, Vereshchin, Stolpne and Uhrovensk, were also called Ukraine by the 13th century. In the sixteenth century, the name *Ukraine* was first used in official documents and literature to designate the whole country. However, Galicia was at that time virtually excluded from the concept, and was consistently called "Ruthenian District." Finally, in the nineteenth century the appellation *Ukraine* became the national name of the entire ethnic territory populated by the Rus'ian stock.

The renaming of medieval *Rus'* (Ruthenia) as the modern *Ukraine* was an interesting although not isolated historical phenomenon produced by significant geo-political developments in East Europe. For example, Ukraine was the historical "borderland" of Western civilization. The historical mission of the Ukrainians was to intercept Asiatic nomadic invaders of Europe in almost constant warfare. Since the seventh century the Ukrainians battled the Avars, Khozars, Bulgars, Cumans, Torks, and Tartars. Their awareness of their mission and their sense of destiny found expression in Ukrainian folklore, folksongs, and poetry, and led to the adoption of the term "Borderland" or *Ukraine* as the distinct national name of the area.

Gradually the name was adopted by the Ukrainian scholars and politicians since, first of all, the new name contributed so much toward a clear-cut differentiation of Ukrainians from Russians and Byeloruthenians and, secondly, because the name *Ukraine* had been a symbol of the national self-assertion and independence movement since the time of the Cossack national wars against Poland and Muscovy-Russia.

The Ukrainian independence movement and national separatism were unacceptable to Russia and Poland, both of which claimed the Ukrainian territories. Since the term *Ukrainian* had become a symbol of that separatism, the official and scholarly circles in Warsaw and St. Petersburg made every possible effort to suppress first the name, then the Ukrainian national movement itself. The Poles were determined to retain at all costs the old name *Ruthenian* because it seemed to them to be neutral, hence less dangerous. The Russians tried to enforce the usage of the term *Little Russian* since this implied a national unity existing between the Great Russian and the Little Russian ethnic stocks. Thus, largely because of Russian and Polish hostility to the new name, the designations *Ukraine* and *Ukrainian* have only recently become acceptable to the free world's academic and political circles. During World War I when the national aspirations of the Ukrainian people were somewhat coinciding with the political interests of the German and Austrian-Hungarian Empires, Warsaw and St. Petersburg dismissed Ukrainian nationalism as just another Prussian intrigue lacking any real political significance. This attitude contributed considerably to the delay in the general acceptance of the new name.[5]

Objection has often been raised to the change of the national name from *Ruthenia* to *Ukraine* as unwarranted by any historical precedence. There is justification, however, for such a change. History reveals many changes of the national names of peoples and countries. New political developments, social and cultural changes, and new geo-political conditions may require a change in national designation from Muscovy to Russia, Gallia to France, Persia to Iran, Serbo-Croatio-Slavonia to Yugoslavia, and Wallachia and Moldavia to Rumania. A people have a right to decide what name they want to be called, just as they have a right to whichever form of government they prefer.

The Geographical and Geo-Political Background. The growth and development of any nation or people have always been conditioned by the geographical location of their homeland. The Ukrainian people are no exception. Their national growth, the development of their national culture and civilization, and the evolution of their own social, political, cultural, and economic institutions were largely a consequence of the geographical characteristics of their terrain and soil. Although Ukraine's geo-political position was unfavorable for herself, her proximity to the borders of Europe and Asia, her location in a straight wide gateway extending from the South-Siberian lowlands to the heart of Europe, was highly beneficial to the West. As a buffer state standing between two great civilizations, Occidental and Oriental, Ukraine absorbed much of the force of repeated tides of Asiatic armed invasions. The centuries-long struggle between the Orient and the Occident in religion, culture, politics, and warfare usually extended into Ukraine and projected with violent impact into the history of the Ukrainian people. Since the earliest times the Ukrainian territory has been the avenue for migrations of countless peoples, for the great marches of the Huns, Arians, Avars, Torks, and the Mongols of Genghis-Khan. Ukraine has no natural defensive fortifications such as great lakes, seas, mountains, or marshes, except the Black Sea and the Azov Sea in the South and the Polesian marshes in the North. This lack of defenses made the area a classic commercial and military route from East to West, and vice versa, and has obviously influenced Ukraine's historical development.

As if to compensate the Ukrainians for their highly vulnerable frontiers, Divine Providence provided them with a land rich in natural resources, a favorable climate, fertile soil and many minerals. Throughout the ancient period when nomadic cattle raising, hunting, and fishing were the foundations of the primitive economy, Ukraine, with its well developed water system, afforded outstanding opportunities for the economic growth of early communities. When agriculture became the leading medieval industry, Ukraine's black, fertile soil proved to be one of the richest. Slabchenko quotes sixteenth century West European travellers as saying that the fertility of this soil was so great that abundant crops were possible without fertilizers and with very little toil.[6] Furthermore, this fertile farmland was so abundant that it could be acquired by a simple act of homesteading and exploiting.

In addition, conditions for the development of commerce were highly favorable in Ukraine. Major trade routes extending from East to West and from North to South converged on Ukrainian territory. Moreover, the appreciable productivity of Ukraine's own economy could itself contribute substantially to an extensive volume of international trade. When the nineteenth century ushered in the industrial revolution, the rich mineral resources in the Donets Basin, the Krivyi-Rih and Zaporizha districts, and in West Ukraine, made possible such a rapid industrial development of the Ukrainian national economy that the whole territory assumed great international economic importance.[7]

Consequently, the Ukrainian people experienced constantly moving frontiers throughout their history. The core of their ethnographical territory was in the Northwest and included southern Polisia, Volhinia, and the Kiev and Chernihiv districts, the very locality where the ancient name *Rus'* and the modern name *Ukraine* had their origins. From there, ethnographic expansion through colonization continued whenever the political atmosphere was favorable. But whenever any external events developed unfavorably, the Ukrainian ethnic territory had a tendency to contract to its original ancient boundaries in the Northwest. Even by prehistoric times, the ethnographical territory of the Ukrainian people had expanded to the Carpathian mountains and the Black Sea steppes. At the time of the Kievan Empire, between 860 and 1240, the Ukrainian ethnographical territory was rather large, and the political power of the Ukrainians was at such a peak that the Empire included in its borderlands numerous national minorities, such as the Ugro-Finnic and North Slavic tribes in the distant Northeast, the Byeloruthenian tribes in the

Northwest (towards Lithuania and the Baltic littorals), and numerous nomadic tribes (of Turko-Mongol extraction) in the steppes of the Black and Azov Seas and in the Don-Volga Basin.

The impact of the Mongol-Tartar invasion in 1240 liquidated the Kievan Empire, and imposed Mongol rule over the Ukrainian people. The Ukrainian ethnographical territory was contracted at that time, especially in the South and in the East, and was reduced to its almost ancient and original territorial core, after having sought safety in the northwestern forests. The population left the unsafe southern steppes which were continuously exposed to the harassing and oppressing warfare and plundering expeditions of the Tartars.

After the invasion by the Golden Horde, the Galician-Volhinian Duchy in the Northwest was a strictly national Ukrainian state, which geographically shifted toward the West and the centers of Western civilization. The Lithuanian period in the following centuries experienced a new southward and eastward expansion of the Ukrainian ethnical area, made possible by the slowly declining power of the Mongols. The reconquest of the Ukrainian steppes lasted throughout the Polish and the Cossack-Hetman period, and until the second half of the nineteenth century, and culminated in an enormous expansion of Ukrainian territory. Soon the Donets and Don steppes became part of the Ukrainian national area, and filled the ethnic vacuum resulting from the disintegration of the Golden Horde. The political organism of the Ukrainian Cossack state was never able to cover more than two-thirds of the entire Ukrainian ethnographical territory, nor did the Ukrainian National Republic or the Ukrainian Soviet Socialist Republic ever include the entire Ukrainian national ethnic area. In the early nineteenth century the Ukrainians were populating areas as far away as the foot of the Caucasian mountains and the Volga steppes. In the twentieth century, as a result of policies of genocide and Russianization applied by the Bolshevik government of the USSR, the Ukrainian ethnographical territory again contracted both in the East and in the West.

Since the political boundaries of Ukraine did not include all the

Ukrainian ethnical territories in any historical period except that of the Kievan Empire, it seems more fruitful to study the social and economic history of the Ukrainian people than the history of the Ukrainian state. The latter approach might well be interpreted as an artificial political restriction of the scope of such a study which analysis restricted to the territorial limits of the contemporary Ukrainian Soviet Socialist Republic would do. A study undertaken along such lines, since it would automatically exclude other Ukrainian ethnic territories, would result in an inadequate treatment of the Ukrainian historical past.

For the sake of comprehensiveness this analysis should include the development of various segments of the Ukrainian people under different conditions—some within the political framework of the Ukrainian State, and others within the framework of the political organisms of such foreign powers as Poland, Czechoslovakia, and Rumania. This analysis should also include that large part of the Ukrainian ethnic territory under Russian rule in the nineteenth century, its smaller fragment under Austrian domination at the same time, and the peculiarities of both. The regional differences of the Ukrainian social, political, economic, and cultural evolution in the past had their origin in the artificial differentiations brought about by artificial political barriers and the distinctive political environments which resulted from the influence of foreign rules. These differentiations often resulted in interprovincial antagonisms and animosities among the southern and northern, eastern and western divisions of the Ukrainian people, making the overall process of building the national state all the more difficult. Nevertheless, these regional peculiarities, together with the developments in the central Ukrainian districts produced through the centuries that most interesting socioeconomic mosaic known as the Ukrainian people, an ethnic group determined to preserve its common cultural heritage in spite of formidable forces working to the contrary end.

Today the ethnographical Ukrainian territory covers the southern part of East Europe. More specifically, it extends approximately from 22° to 44° east longitude, and from 45° to 54° north latitude. This compact area excludes the ethnically mixed border-lands, and covers approximately 277,000 square miles of nor-mally broad lowland north of the Black and Azov Seas. During the twentieth century the Ukrainian ethnic area underwent a con-siderable contraction, especially after World War II, due to the forced deportation and compulsory recolonization of its popula-tion in its eastern and western borderlands. Because Soviet vital statistics are suspected of politically motivated distortions, the population of the smaller area can be estimated only at a maximum of 40,000,000. Many more Ukrainians live in South Siberia, Kazakhstan, Turkestan, and the distant districts of the Amur region, as a result of compulsory migration induced by the Russians, but since these Ukrainians have been separated from the ethnic-national core by great territorial distances, which have made it impossible for them to contribute to the organic evolution of the Ukrainian ethnic community, they are not included in the present analysis.

The People. The earliest information concerning the ancient Slavic tribes in Ukraine came from some Arabic travelers and merchants, such as Masudi, Ibn Dasta, and Ibn Jacob; the Greek Emperor, Constantine Porphyrogenitus; the legendary Ukrainian monk, Nestor (in his chronicle entitled *Povist' vremennykh lit*); the Hypathian and Laurentian chronicles of uncertain authorship; and many other, perhaps lesser known, authors and their written documents of the eleventh to fourteenth centuries. Nestor's *Povist' vremennykh lit,* apparently the oldest Ukrainian chroni-cle, contains much information about the ancient Slavs, their settlements, religious beliefs, and way of life, and the beginnings of the Kievan Empire, the second large-scale state organization of the Ukrainian Slavs, which as early as the eleventh century in-cluded all Eastern Slavs in its political framework. The chronicles enumerate several Slavic tribes inhabiting the East European area, and along with them, seven southern Slavic tribes which, according to the later historical studies, merged, and in the course of an ethnico-cultural evolution fused into a new national concept of the Ukrainian people. These Ukrainian tribes were the Polianians, Siverianians, Khorvatians, Derevlianians, Dulibians, Ulichians, and Tiverians. The Polianians settled on the banks of the river Ros and down the right bank of the river Dnieper. The Siverianians populated the area on the banks of the rivers Seim, Desna, and upper Vorskla. The Khorvatians were located on the banks of the upper Dniester and toward the foot of the Carpathian Mountains. The Dulibians populated the western, and the Derevlianians, the eastern part of Volhinia. The tribal area of the Ulichians extended along the banks of the lower Dniester, and the Tiverians settled in the area between the lower Dniester and Pruth rivers. The other Eastern Slavs, such as the tribes of the Dregovichians, Radimichians, Polotsians, Krivichians, Viatichians and Slovinians, lived in the northern part of East Europe, on the banks of the River Pripet and Berezina, and on those of the middle and upper Dnieper,* in the Volga-Klazma-Oka river system, and farther westward, toward the Baltic Sea. These Northwestern and Northeastern branches of the East Slavs, in later history, gave rise to two other Slavic nationalities, the Byeloruthenians and the Russians.

Since prehistoric times the Ukrainian southern Slavs were under potent influence of the Hellenic and Iranian civilizations. The Hellenic colonies on the northern coasts of the Black Sea (Pontus) radiated Greek culture in southern Ukraine as early as the eighth century before the Christian era. The ancient peoples of Ukraine, either the Scythians, the Sarmatians, or the immediate predecessors of the seven Ukrainian Slavic tribes, the Antes, were considerably influenced by the spiritual and material civilizations of ancient Greece through their commercial and social contacts with Hellenic colonies. Iranian culture influenced Ukraine from the time of Mithridates throughout the period of the Bosporan kingdom. Historical documents and archaeological studies distinctly established the influence of the Hellenic and Iranian civilizations on the cultural climate of Ukraine as a result

*Dnipro in Ukrainian, Dnieper being the Russian pronunciation. We are going to use the name Dnieper as more popular in the English-speaking lands.

of Slavic domination of Eastern Europe in the sixth and seventh centuries. Then began the cultural differentiation among the East Slavs, which process resulted in the formation of a distinctive Ukrainian culture quite different from the Russian. The spiritual origin of the latter culture must be sought in the Ugro-Finnic and Mongol elements of the European Northeast. Although Shakhmatov, Vozniak, Kuziela, and other Ukrainian and Russian students of East European history, languages, folklores, and literatures are convinced that the evolution of the Ukrainians, Byeloruthenians, and Russians into three separate ethnic groups was about completed by the eleventh century, the beginning of this process of differentiation no doubt took place in prehistoric times, certainly at a time prior to the migration of the Slavs to Eastern Europe.[8]

The seven Ukrainian tribes were assimilated into the new national-ethnic concept of the Ukrainian people in the course of the tenth and eleventh centuries, usually in a peaceful manner and without any considerable influx of foreign ethnic elements. The Ukrainians are relatively pure Slavic since they intermingled only very slightly with the Bulgar, Khozar, and Magyar rulers who dominated them from the eighth to the tenth centuries. The Khozars, for example, only levied a duty on the Eastern Slavs, and otherwise interfered but little in their tribal matters.

In the tenth century the Ukrainian tribes, with the help of Norse warriors, created the Kievan Empire. The original ethnic cell which initiated the growth of the Kievan state was the tribe of the Polianians. The political creation of the Ukrainians greatly advanced their national evolution in such areas as language, folklore, religion, and social, legal, and economic institutions. Minor tribal differences which formerly existed in customs, habits, and social institutions blended under the unifying influence of a common political organization. The Kievan *Rus'*, however, soon experienced an enormous territorial and political growth through the superior organizational skill of the Northmen who conquered Novgorod the Great and then came to Kiev. But, because of its extremely favorable location, and because the

Northmen cooperated with the more civilized Ukrainian Slavs in building the Empire, Kiev in a very short time assumed complete leadership and imposed a semi-colonial status upon the northern area. After Kiev had conquered and dominated vast areas of East Europe, and especially the European Northeast, the Empire lost all ethnical and racial homogeneity, and became a political melange of numerous nationalities, races, and religions. The Ukrainians amounted to at most a third of the entire population of the Kievan state, the total population of which at that time might have been some seven and a half million people.[9] Historians are agreed that there were very few Northmen in Kiev. The Byeloruthenian tribes, Russian tribes, the Mordvins, Merias, Cheremisians, Chuds, Volga-Bulgars, and many other tribes of prevailingly Ugro-Finnic and Mongol extraction, constituting a considerable portion of the population of the Ukrainian-Kievan state, were forced by the power of Kiev to join the Empire. Nevertheless, the southern Ukrainians retained and intensified their national individuality because of the following circumstances: the uniform living conditions, including geographic and climatic environment of their compact ethnical mass; the strong commercial relations with Byzantium; the immediate influence by Byzantine civilization; the considerable political and cultural connections with the West; the common language and religion; and the great distance which separated them from direct contact with the Ugro-Finnic ethnical communities. Moveover, the Ukrainians conducted themselves everywhere in the Empire as an elevated ruling caste, having little in common with the primitive subjugated tribes and clans. Shelukhin quotes much evidence of an antagonistic attitude especially of the northern Slavic (pre-Russian) communities toward the ruling and administrative elements immigrating from the South that were generally called *Rus'*.[10]

After the liquidation of the Kievan state by the Mongol-Tartar invaders of the thirteenth century, the process of crystallization of the Ukrainian nationality continued within the political framework of the Galician-Volhinian Duchy. The Galician-Volhinian state was a purely Ukrainian political entity which covered the Ukrainian cultural area to the exclusion of other ethnic groups. Because of the territories lost to the Mongols, this area was much smaller than that of the Kievan Empire. As rulers of this territory, the Galician-Volhinian dukes, in the fourteenth century, accepted and used the title of *"duces totius terrae Russiae,"* in order fully to express the national character of their duchy and to distinguish it from the Northeastern areas of Suzdal, Rostov, and Vladimir. By these elements the ethnic origin of the Ukrainian nationality was fully completed. Later developments, such as the Lithuanian-Polish rule, the increasing Western cultural influences, and the new political environment following the collapse of the Galician-Volhinian Duchy, merely westernized the Ukrainians to a greater extent.

Although the above account of the over-all ethnic national evolution of the Ukrainian people is comprehensive though brief, it is the specific subject matter of this analysis. Russian historians have given such a diametrically opposed interpretation of the ethnical developments of the medieval European Northeast that this account cannot be completed without a brief review of the Russian opinion on Ukraine as well as some notice of the origin of the Russian nationality, in order to clarify the controversy. As a matter of historical fact, three different ethnical-national processes developed in the Kievan Empire, resulting in the crystallization of three distinct nationalities: in the South, the Ukrainian people; in the Northwest, the Byeloruthenian people; and in the northeastern borderland of the Empire, the Russian people. The tribes of the Dregovichians, and partially, of the Krivichians, Radimichians, and Polotsians formed the Byeloruthenian nationality. The Byeloruthenian people have an historical past similar to that of the Ukrainians. The latter, however, were influenced by the Hellenic-Iranian civilization to a greater degree. After the collapse of the Kievan Empire, the Byeloruthenians joined the Grand Principality of Lithuania, while the Ukrainians lived in their own Galician-Volhinian state. Nevertheless, a century later both East Slavonic nationalities were merged in the political framework of the Polish-Lithuanian Empire.

Quite different was the third ethnic process which brought

about the crystallization of the Russian nationality in the far-distant forest areas of the Volga-Oka and Klazma regions. The Hellenic-Iranian influence did not directly extend to the ancestors of the modern Russians, whose culture, as a result, remained rather underdeveloped. These pre-Russian Slavic tribes of the Krivichians (partially), Viatichians, and Slovinians very early in pre-historic times came into contact with the Ugro-Finnic tribes in the area. The living conditions in the Northeast were very difficult. At first the Slavs fought the Ugro-Finns, but later they intermingled with their enemies in order to survive. This inter-mingling facilitated the process of amalgamation of Slavs and Ugro-Finns. The Northern Slavs and Finnic tribes found a common interest in their hostility toward their rulers, the more civilized southern *Rus'*. In the process of assimilation the Slavs gained a predominance, but the characteristics of the new ethnic alloy progressively alienated it from the Ukrainian South and the Byeloruthenian Northwest. The peculiarities of the severe climate and environment, especially the very hard struggle for economic survival in the poor forest areas of the Northeast, the great distance from the cultural centers of medieval Europe, and the impact of the Finnic ethnic characteristics produced the future Great Russian nationality. Outstanding Russian scholars and historians, like Shakhmatov, Platonov, Presniakov, and Pokrovskii, recognize to the fullest extent the role of the northern climate and of the Finnic ethnic element in the development of the Russian people, and accept the twelfth century as the time in which the process of the formation of the Russian nationality was completed. But, as it will be noted below, official Russian historians offer a different explanation.

By and large, the different ethnic processes, under completely different geographical and historical circumstances, culminated in the creation of three distinct East European Slavic nationalities, each possessing different national characteristics. Slavic Ukrainians, developing under more favorable conditions in the South, influenced by the free atmosphere of the steppes, and having been in the orbit of the Hellenic-Iranian spiritual radiation, became more individualistic, less ready to submit to authority, sometimes even anarchistic, and always broadly democratic-minded. Since they lived under less pressure from their natural environment, with its more favorable geographic and topographical conditions, they became, in contrast to the Russians, less consistent in thought and action, and at that time less stubborn, less cruel, and less determined to realize their ideas without regard for others, and without regard for the price to be paid for an eventual realization of those ideas.[11] On the other hand, the hardships of the northern life and the Ugro-Finnic national elements caused the Russian psychology to be more collective-minded, very well disciplined and ready to submit to authority, very consistent in thought and action, and cruel and inconsiderate in the realization of its own ideas. The autocratic system of Russian government throughout the centuries, a system never friendly to any democratic innovations, was a direct result of the nature of the people and of the adverse conditions under which they lived. The national characteristics of both peoples, the Ukrainians and the Russians, became even more different in consequence of the Mongol invasion in the thirteenth century. The Ukrainians were but briefly under Mongol rule. The Slavic Ukrainians, strongly influenced by Western civilization, did not develop a close relationship to their Mongolian conquerors. The Russians, on the other hand, already part Mongolian due to their absorption of Ugro-Finnic elements, collaborated more closely with the invaders of Genghis Khan. Then, too, Mongol rule extended over a longer period of time in the Northeast and resulted in considerable assimilation of Mongol blood by the Russian people. All classes of Russian society—aristocracy, country gentry and peasants—received an influx of Mongolian blood, either in the later period of the rule of the Golden Horde, or in the period which followed. All Russian national life, including social processes, governmental and administrative institutions, legal and financial systems, developed under the strong impact of Mongol institutions. These developments completed the evolution of the Russian national characteristics. The fact that the

Muscovites accomplished the building of their great empire is attributable to their Mongolian psychological characteristics. Some students of Russian history estimate that the Russians are eighty percent Mongolian. This might be an exaggeration, but no serious scholar could ever afford to deny the great significance of the Mongols in the development of the Russian nation and the Russian Empire.[12]

Russian official historiography, however, eventually came to an entirely different conclusion. At first, it fully disregarded the existence of three distinct nationalities of Slavic descent in East Europe, and accepted a theory of only one Russian people composed of three ethnic communities, namely, Great Russians, Little Russians, and White Russians. Before long this nationalistic historiography could not come to terms with the idea that the Kievan Empire was created by the Little Russians (Ukrainians). Finally, Pogodin and Sobolevskii elaborated a new approach, which was popularized by Kluchevskii, to the effect that the Kievan region since prehistoric times was populated by the Russians, and that during the Mongol invasion the Russians first emigrated to the Northeast, seeking safety, and that the Ukrainians only then came from the West and settled down in the Dnieper and Kiev area. Of course, any basic cultural and national differences between the Ukrainians and Russians were not admitted by Russian official historiography. Since there were no objective historical indications of any mass movements of population from the Kievan regions to the Volga-Oka areas at the time of the Mongol invasion, the Pogodin-Sobolevskii hypothesis proved to be a mere speculation. The hypothesis about the Northern emigration of the original Kievan Russians has been fully discredited by Maksymovych, Hrushevsky, and Presniakov, and at least doubted by others like Pokrovskii and Golubiev. But from the standpoint of Russian imperialism, it was undesirable to admit any national differentiation of European Russia. First of all, Russian aggression in Ukraine and Byeloruthenia, followed by Russian rule, could not easily be justified. Recently the Soviets have resorted to a new theory of prehistoric Russian nationality, which supposedly created the Kievan *Rus'*, Muscovite Grand Duchy, and the Russian Empire. According to this theory, the Great Russian people were the direct successors of the traditions of a pre-Russian nation, while the Ukrainians and the Byeloruthenians, having split from the Russian core under the Lithuanian and Polish rule, were declared to be a later product of some later centuries. Furthermore, the official view declares that there is a natural and organical trend among the three brotherly nationalities of the Russians, the Ukrainians, and the Byeloruthenians, to dissolve and to merge again into one homogenous nation and people. This time, however, Soviet-Russian historiography is referring to one Soviet people. Although this theory is refuted by the fact of ethnical-national differentiation in East Europe—a process which began in prehistoric times—it received the official approval of the Executive Committee of the Communist Party of the USSR on January 12, 1954, as the only one consistent with the Party Line.[13]

1. The name "Rus'" as the national identification of Ukraine seems to date back to the seventh and eighth centuries. Greek historical documents of the eighth century referred to "Rus'" or "Ros'" as an aggressive northern people. The Arabic, Persian and Jewish merchants and writers of the ninth and tenth centuries mentioned "Rus'": N. Chubaty, "The Meaning of 'Rus'' and 'Ukraine'", *Readings in Russian History,* ed. by S. Harcave, New York, 1962, pp. 9-21; B. Kortchmaryk, "Russian Interpretation of Ukrainian Historical Source Materials", *On the Historical Beginnings of Slavic Eastern Europe,* ed. by N. Chirovsky, New York, 1976, pp. 147-164; Yu. Sherekh, "Nazva 'Rus'", *Entsyklopedia Ukrainoznavstva,* Munich-New York, 1949, Vol. I, pp. 13-14; Ya. Rudnytsky and V. Sichynsky, "Nazva 'Ukraina'", *ibid.,* Vol. I, pp. 14-16.
2. M. Hrushevsky, *Istoria Ukrainy-Rusy,* New York, 1954, Vol. I, pp. 1-2, 366-394; M. Braichevsky, *Koly i yak vynyk Kyiv,* Kiev, 1963; also the same, "The Unification of the Old Rus' Lands around the Center of Kiev," *On the Historical Beginnings of Slavic Eastern Europe,* New York, 1976, pp. 53-81.
3. Kortchmaryk, *loc. cit.*
4. *Ibid.*; also, Chubaty, *op. cit.,* pp. 10-11.
5. M. Stachiv, N. Chirovsky and P. Stercho, *Ukraine and the European Turmoil, 1917-1919,* New York, 1973, Vol. II, pp. 351-405.

6. M. Slabchenko, *Orhanizatsia Hospodarstva Ukrainy*, Odessa, 1923, Part I, p. 1: "Ukraine was held for a golden country, a country of fabulous riches, where it was enough to kick slightly the earth to open the golden deposits."

7. K. Kononenko, *Ukraine and Russia, A History of the Economic Relations between Ukraine and Russia*, 1654-1917, Milwaukee, 1958, pp. 101-196.

8. D. Doroshenko, *Narys Istorii Ukrainy*, Munich, 1966, Vol. I, pp. 16-27 and 62-68; also, N. Chirovsky, *A History of the Russian Empire*, New York, 1973, Vol. I, pp. 5-11.

9. G. Vernadsky and M. Karpovich, *A History of Russia,* Vol. II, *Kievan Russia,* New Haven-London, 1951, pp. 104-105.

10. S. Shelukhin, *Ukraina,* Prague, 1936-37, introductory chapter.

11. I. Mirchuk, "The Basic Traits of the Ukrainian People," *Ukraine and Its People,* ed. by I. Mirchuk, Munich, 1949, pp. 35-42; also, A. Dombrovsky, "The Spiritual Trend of Ukraine in Antiquity", *Proceedings,* Shevchenko Scientific Society, New York-Paris, 1951, Vol. I, pp. 52-55; V. Shcherbakivsky, "Ukrainska Praistoria", *Nasha Kultura,* Warsaw, 1935-37, Vol. I.

12. Vernadsky, *op. cit.*, Vol. III, *The Mongols and Russia*, pp. 333-390; also, N. Trubetskoi, *Nasledie Jinghis-Khana*, Berlin, 1925.

13. "The Theses on the Three Hundredth Anniversary of the Unification of Ukraine and Russia", *Pravda*, January 12, 1954; Interpretation of the act: C. Manning, "The Kremlin's New Theses on Ukraine", *On the Historical Beginnings of Slavic Eastern Europe*, ed. by N. Chirovsky, New York, 1976, pp. 211-223.

CHAPTER TWO

THE BASIC TRAITS OF UKRAINIAN HISTORICAL DEVELOPMENT

Agricultural predominance — The nation of moving frontiers — Individualism — Vitality — Discontinuance of the historical evolution — Periods of Ukrainian history

Agricultural Predominance. Agriculture has predominated throughout Ukrainian economic history, and has profoundly affected the formation and development of Ukrainian cultural, social, and political institutions. In every period of Ukrainian history, farming, together with cattle raising, hunting, and fishing, was the basis of economic growth and the source of material wealth. Historians, however, have been somewhat confused by the highly commercialized economic growth of the Kievan Empire, so that Kluchevskii, Rozhkov, and certain others came to the conclusion that trade and commerce were actually the leading industries in Kievan Ukraine and formed the basis of her medieval economy, and that agriculture was only secondary. This hypothesis is not supported by the facts. First Grekov and then the majority of modern historians denied Kluchevskii's view. They stated that historical documents proved the predominance of agriculture in the national economy of the Kievan Empire.

Of course, trading and commerce were important to Kiev and they also developed in Ukraine in the later periods of her history. The late seventeenth century even witnessed a growth of modern manufacturing. These industries, however, were always secondary in importance.

There were two reasons for the predominance of agriculture: geographic environment and foreign aggression. In the first place, the extremely fertile soil and favorable climate were conducive to an agricultural economy. In the second, Ukraine's tremendous industrial potential of minerals, power, and labor could not be developed because of the intervention of external political and military factors. The Russian Tsarate, which for a hundred and fifty years ruled Ukraine, pursued a consistent policy of keeping the country agricultural, as a source of raw materials for an all-Russian market.

Thus, the predominance of an agricultural economy shaped the development of the Ukrainian people as did no other single factor. Country life, close to nature, influenced their character toward a deeply religious life, a strong faith in God, strict moral principles, consideration of others, and extreme individualism. Perhaps these qualities weakened the ability of the Ukrainians to resist the ruthlessness and cruelty of neighbors who repeatedly attempted to conquer their riches. It is enough to cite the Mongol raids, Russian inspired famines, and German genocides in Ukraine. The frequency of such invasions emphasized that the agricultural predominance of Ukraine's economy was indissolubly interwoven with its characteristic of being an economy of moving frontiers.

The Nation of Moving Frontiers. Since prehistoric times Ukraine has been a borderland, a frontier country. In the South and in the East stretched vast, largely unpopulated steppes, which, by their very character, invited settlement and colonization. The exposed position of the country constituted a door which swung in both directions; this facilitated both the expansion of the Ukrainian ethnic area and the invasion of Ukraine by her neighbors.

As a result, colonization of the borderlands took the form of voluntary, semi-military organizations and associations, which continuously conquered new areas for civilization. The voluntary character of these associations greatly strengthened the growth of individualism and the love of freedom among the Ukrainians.

This armed colonization movement was a permanent feature of the political and economic development of Ukraine and the Ukrainian people throughout their earliest history and the eras of the Kievan Empire and the Galician-Volhinian Principality, when the Black Sea steppes were penetrated by the *Rus'* in the face of opposition from the Asiatic Cumans. Furthermore, the entire Cossack period of Ukrainian history was an unrelenting process of armed colonization of the Black Sea steppes and the Donets Basin which lasted three hundred and fifty years. After the Russian Tsarate liquidated the Cossacks, the colonization of southern and eastern Ukrainian frontiers continued into the second half of the nineteenth century. The existence of vast, almost empty areas just beyond the borders had important repercussions on the entire history of the Ukrainian people. First of all, the bondage of serfdom seems to have been less oppressive in Ukraine than in central and western Europe, where because there were no frontiers the serfs had no opportunity to escape. The serfs of Ukraine, therefore, were treated better by the feudal lords and gentry than were those of the neighboring countries, just as the lot of the worker in early America was better than that of his European counterpart.[1] Thus the Ukrainian frontier existed as an alternative to servitude, and indirectly resulted in better treatment and higher wages even for those who did not accept its invitation. With the growing burden of bondage, peasants abandoned their homes and farms and escaped into the broad steppes in quest of greater freedom. The harsh punishment of recaptured fugitives did not prevent a continuous and ever increasing stream of illegal emigration to distant frontier lands. Serfdom and bondage did not exist in the frontier lands until the organized expansion of the state reached these borderlands. Then the process repeated itself, as successive waves of fugitive peasants escaped the bondage of

21

recently organized and "civilized" areas, and penetrated the even more distant frontiers. They created by this process the Ukrainian ethnographical territory, which continued to expand until modern times.

Another consequence of this process of expansion was the development of the free Cossack, who passionately loved his individual independence. The Cossacks became the symbol of national heroism for the Ukrainian people. Thus the Cossacks' faults and virtues soon became Ukrainian national characteristics.

Individualism had a profound influence on the development of the history of the Ukrainian people, particularly on the growth of their political, social, and economic institutions. Throughout their history the Ukrainians had been predominantly peasants. The soil was the principal source of their wealth and material growth. From love of the soil came the inspiration for Ukrainian art and culture. Even the upper classes, the old aristocracy and the modern intelligentsia, felt a strong attraction to the land. Always individualistic, the Ukrainian peasant relied on God, on nature, and on himself. Upon his farm or estate, the farmer or nobleman considered himself a sovereign lord, and resented any outside intervention or intrusion even in the form of communal activities for his own benefit.[2] The institution of the Ukrainian *hromada* was a voluntary and loose association of individuals who were ready to cooperate towards the realization of a definite goal. The *hromada* never resembled the Russian *mir,* that compulsory collective body to which the rights of individual peasants were subordinated. The *mir* was an organically collective institution whereas the *hromada* was a flexible organization without any sovereign rights.

Wide steppes, fertile soil, abundant space, and the remote Hellenic traditions inspired the individualistic philosophy of the Ukrainian people. This individualism, perhaps, was an indirect obstacle to the construction of the Ukrainian national state. The individualism of the Galician-Volhinian aristocracy indirectly contributed to the political collapse of the Ukrainian state organization. Developments in the Galician-Volhinian Principality were very much like the social-political situation in England at the time of the adoption of the Magna Charta. However, the insular character of England, which discouraged foreign intervention, enabled the English noblemen to establish the foundation of their parliamentarianism and democracy. The unfavorable geopolitical position of the Galician-Volhinian realm brought about its downfall. A foreign intervention utilized to its full extent the struggle between the despotic tendencies of the Galician rulers and the parliamentary tendencies of the *boyar* aristocracy. Had it not been for the Polish and Lithuanian intrusion, the Galician noblemen would probably have succeeded developing parliamentarianism, and then democracy, by way of a slow and organic evolution. The democratic arrangements in the Cossack period two and a half centuries later represent the real political trend of medieval Ukraine, although the individualism and love of independence of the Cossacks sometimes accentuated semi-anarchistic features that ruined the nation even while it was under construction. Appropriate examples are easily found in the history of Hetman Ukraine.[3] The recent history of the Ukrainian people shows some negative consequences of over-exaggerated individualism on political thought and action, in the attempt to establish a Ukrainian national state. In order to overcome the extremities of individualism, and to avoid at the same time the economically and socially destructive consequences of Communism, a strong nationalist movement was organized in Western Ukraine during the interwar period. However, because of the inborn Ukrainian individualism, and also because of the Russian-German intrigues, the strong national independence movement soon split into several fragments and immediately lost its initial power.

The most clear-cut economic projection of traditional Ukrainian individualism lies in the two principles of private property and individual initiative, which are inherent in the philosophy of the Ukrainian people. They always recognized and respected to the fullest extent both personal property and real property. The traditions of Hellenic civilization and Roman Law, which so deeply affected and influenced the early Ukrainian national development, contributed heavily to that feature of the social and economic evolution of the Ukrainians. The old Ukrainian code of laws, whether it was the official or private compilation of the eleventh or twelfth centuries, reflected very well the social and economic conditions of that time. The generally accepted name of this code was *Rus'ka Pravda*. *Rus'ka Pravda* specifically recognized the institution of private property and established its legal defenses.

Because of the individualist psyche of the ancient Ukrainians, the disintegration of the clan system in Ukraine had been almost accomplished in late prehistoric times. In early times, land had been held as private property by the free peasants, who acquired their lands after the disintegration of the communal clan ownership, by way of free physical occupation. The highly uneven distribution of land holdings among the peasants in Kievan *Rus'* seems to indicate very clearly that the process of appropriation had been brought about by individual initiative, without any organized communal action. Remnants of the ancient commune could be found in Kievan Ukraine only in the form of meadow, wood, and fishery rights. Shortly afterwards, the formation of the large-scale private landholdings of the *boyar* nobility and gentry developed, and gave rise to a Ukrainian type of quasi-feudalism. At the time of the Mongol invasion, communal property and communal economy revived in Ukraine. But it was a rather short-lived phenomenon, and it might be considered as an emergency measure organized to withstand the very difficult living conditions that accompanied foreign domination. After the situation improved, at least a little, holding of private property by peasants became the rule again.

Under Polish rule, however, the Ukrainian historical path experienced change. As the early Polish economy was based on large-scale land holdings and serf labor, the growing power of the Poles in Ukraine eliminated peasant ownership of land. Yet basically, the Polish social and economic constitution was individualist, and not collectivist like the Muscovite. The Ukrainian national revolution of 1648 resulted in a sudden revival of peasant private property rights, and in a recognition of the importance of soil as the main source of subsistence of the rural population. The Revolution partially destroyed the artificial Polish social order in Ukraine. For example, the latifundia of the Polish aristocracy and the landholdings of the gentry became free for peasant occupation and appropriation. But during the entire Cossack-Hetman period, a struggle between the principle of free peasant landholding and the principle of serfdom continued. Peasant property rights were tolerated, but their extent was subject to change, as a result of the growth of a social structure that was essentially a rigid class system. Thus the Cossack aristocracy and gentry, like the old Polish nobility, attempted by every means to restrict the individual rights of the peasants, and to turn the peasants into serfs.

In the political framework of Tsarist Russia, semifeudalism and serfdom prevailed, while the rural communities were collectively organized in the form of the so-called *mir*. Practically speaking, not much room was left for the rights of the peasant to private property under Russian rule. Deficiencies of the collectivist *mir* seemed to be overcome by Stolypin's reform, which aimed to abolish the communal-collectivist nature of the *mir* and the entire Russian agriculture, and to introduce individual farming. The reform was enthusiastically hailed in Ukraine, where it was considerably expedited. The ethnically Russian provinces, however, gave little support to the reform, since it was alien to the Russian collectivist psychology.[4]

A major clash between this collectivist philosophy of the Russians and the individualism of the Ukrainians first took place after the Bolshevik Revolution in the Russian Empire in 1917. The individualistic Ukrainians could not adjust to the idea of nation-wide collectivism, and their resistance to the socialization was so resolute and strong that the Kremlin resorted to an artificial famine in 1932 and 1933, primarily for the purpose of breaking down peasant opposition. This famine resulted in the death of six million peasants and crushed opposition to the collectivization of agriculture. The Ukrainian peasant had paid a terrible price for his individualism. The urban population, a minority of the Ukrainian people, who did not display the same degree of individualism, were partially saved from starvation.

Vitality. History offers distinct proof of the enormous vitality of the Ukrainian people. In the course of their historical past they have had periods of grave national tragedies, caused by their three deadly enemies: the Asiatic nomads, who settled in the South and East, in the Black Sea and Don-Volga steppes; the Poles, who settled in the West; and the Muscovite-Russians in the North. The Avars, Cumans, and Mongol-Tartars were the most hostile neighbors of the Ukrainian people. Under the impact of the Cuman attacks the Kievan Empire was weakened considerably. The Mongol invasion administered the *coup de grace*.

The constant warfare and plundering of the Mongols devastated the entire country over and over again in the course of the fourteenth to eighteenth centuries. These merciless raids threatened the entire Ukrainian nationality with extermination, and forced the Ukrainians during the fourteenth and fifteenth centuries to give up large portions of their ethnic territories. Only the enormous biological vitality of the Ukrainian people, their very high birth rate and amazingly large families, enabled them to overcome the catastrophic death rate resulting from the frequent bloody struggles in this area of the European frontier. There was, though, one important historical instance which greatly contributed to the national survival of the Ukrainian people. The Mongols were racially, religiously, and culturally so different from the Slavic, Orthodox, and westernized Ukrainians that there was no need for the latter to fear denationalization pressure from the Mongols or from the Moslems, Asiatic Tartars, and Turks. This preservation of their national identity helped the Ukrainians to become the victors in their struggle against the invaders. They soon rebuilt upon the ruins of society and economy, and also recaptured the lost ethnographical territories by means of armed colonization.

The Poles at the peak of their political power had also once represented a deadly threat to the integrity of the Ukrainian people. The Polish people, being Slavic, were culturally close to the Ukrainians. Denationalization rather than physical extermination threatened the Ukrainians under the rule of the Polish Crown. The Ukrainian western borders were shortened and pushed to the East by the pressure of Polish political and territorial expansion. Many square miles of Ukrainian ethnical territory were lost in this expansion. Under the influence of the Polish denationalization policies, almost the entire upper class of the Ukrainian society — both nobility and gentry — abandoned their fidelity to their country, people, and religion, and became Polish. Only a few remained Ukrainians. Several factors helped the Ukrainians to preserve themselves as a separate political nationality. First of all, the stock of the Ukrainian people, the peasantry, did not denationalize. The Orthodox Church and the Uniate Ukrainian Catholic Church, both somewhat different from Roman Catholicism (the ruling religion in the Polish kingdom), helped the Ukrainians to retain their national individuality and identity. Furthermore, the biological vitality of the lower classes again accounted for the ability of the whole people to withstand the influx of Polish culture. The lower classes produced a new Cossack nobility and gentry, and gave the people new leaders. The national state was reestablished after the National Revolution of 1648, and the Ukrainian people resumed their social and economic growth.

The Russians proved to be the most dangerous of all the enemies of Ukraine for many reasons. The Russians and the Ukrainians had a common national origin in the framework of the Kievan Empire. Also, from the second half of the eighteenth century up to the present day, the Ukrainians have been forced to join the same political organization, either under the name of the Russian Empire or under the name of the Union of Soviet Socialist Republics. Both nationalities have lived too long together in the framework of the same state organizations. Furthermore, both nationalities have been prevailingly Orthodox, and have been influenced by Byzantine culture. The Tsarist government used its Orthodox church very extensively to denationalize the Ukrainians. Then the Russians, without any historical justification, appropriated the Ukrainians' name, history, and civilization, and tried to reduce them to the ethnic status suggested by the term "Little Russians." Again, as in the past, the majority of the Ukrainian upper class denationalized but this time became Russian. The eastern Ukrainian ethnical frontiers contracted under the impact of Russian imperialism. In the first half of the nineteenth century, it seemed that Ukrainian nationality would be absorbed by Russianization. Police terror was also widely invoked in the form of deportation of Ukrainians, compelled to colonize Asiatic Russian possessions. As a matter of fact, the Tsarate in 1876 thought that it had realized its goal of total liquidation of the "Ukrainian Problem." Any official use of, or any printed publication in, the Ukrainian language was prohibited. However, a Ukrainian national rebirth came, again initiated by the Ukrainian peasant class, and again deriving its power and vitality, both physical and spiritual, from the native soil. The Ukrainian National Revolution of 1918, and the establishment of an independent Ukrainian state, proved that the Ukrainian people had again vigorously resisted the forces which aimed at their destruction and annihilation.

The Soviet regime then changed its tactics. Having profited by Tsarist experience, which showed that the Ukrainian question could not be settled politically as long as the Ukrainian people survived physically, the Soviets launched an extensive genocide policy in Ukraine. Mass murder, mass deportation to Siberia and Kazakhstan, three famines (1921-22, 1932-33, and 1946), and mass executions were aimed at depopulating Ukraine. The whole countryside, with its thousands of villages, was thus affected. Economic exploitation was carried out with great precision. Nevertheless, during the Second World War, in defiance of all Communist-Russian measures, the Ukrainian Insurgent Army started a war for independence throughout the nation, against both Russian and German invaders. The biological and spiritual vitality of the Ukrainian people overcame the genocide.

That enormous vitality of the Ukrainian people had been most strikingly proven by so-called Carpathian Ukraine (Hungarian *Rus'* in the past). The most south-western region of Ukraine has been separated by the Carpathian mountains from the main body of the land. Moreover, it remained under Hungarian rule and under a rather ruthless domination of Buda-Pest for a continuous seven hundred years, having been exposed to national and religious oppression, while also politically separated from remaining Ukrainian territories. Yet in spite of all those developments, this south-western region has stayed Ukrainian, and in 1939, when Czechoslovakia was disintegrating under the impact of Hitler's imperialism, Carpathian Ukraine declared its political independence and defended itself against the foreign Hungarian, Polish and Czech invaders.[5]

In the course of history, Ukraine was greatly depopulated and her cities and villages severely impaired during the Mongol invasion in the Middle Ages, during the National Revolution in the seventeenth century, and under the Russian-Communist rule in the twentieth century. Each time the population increased again, the lost ethnical areas were recovered, and the land was rebuilt to such an extent that the country was able not only to care for its own needs, but also to reenter foreign trade. The importance of this vital participation of Ukraine in foreign trade and commerce was evident during the Kievan Empire, under the Polish rule, in the Cossack-Hetman state, and in the framework of Tsarist international trade. Yet, despite this considerable commercial activity, a great deal of national energy was repeatedly directed toward rebuilding, again and again, social, political, and economic institutions. The Ukrainians were never discouraged, but as a result of such continual developments, the Ukrainian state survived only a relatively short time as a political sovereign unit.

Discontinuance of the historical evolution. As pointed out several times, there was a completely different course of events in the social and economic developments of the Russian and Ukrainian peoples. Their historical destinies have been diametrically distinct. Here the point must be stressed again, that the growth of the Russian nation was amazingly consistent and even.

The Mongol invasion was certainly a major disturbance. However, from the fourteenth century, when Moscow seized the national leadership, until the Bolshevik revolution in the twentieth century, the growth of the Empire was regular, nationally organic, and according to the established trends. This pattern is in sharp contrast to the uneven and irregular social and political development of the Ukraine.

The evolution of the Ukrainian social and political system began in the fourth century, during the Antian period, before Ukraine entered the historical-political arena of medieval Europe. This social, political and economic evolution continued in the Kievan Empire and the Galician-Volhinian Principality until 1349, the year of the liquidation of the Duchy by Polish and Lithuanian intervention. This event and the Mongol invasion brought to a violent end the organic evolution of Ukrainian parliamentary monarchism, the growth of the social classes, and the development of a predominantly agricultural economy and flourishing trade. After the Mongol invasion, a new phase of socio-political evolution began. A primitive economy of cattle raising, fishing, and hunting by the self-sufficient communal households followed in the second half of the thirteenth century, and succeeded the highly developed agriculture, trade, and commerce of the economically flourishing Kievan-Galician era. Moreover, primitive clan arrangements followed the strong state organization of Kiev, which was of an imperial stature. It was not one, but many steps backward in the overall evolutionary process.[6] The new period in the social and economic development of the Ukrainian people had still another distinct feature; namely, it was no longer purely Ukrainian nationally. The impact of Polish and Lithuanian social, political, legal, and economic institutions and influences on Ukrainian national life was enormous and challenging. Polish and Lithuanian institutions replaced many that were traditionally Ukrainian, or, at least, modified them considerably. The entire period featured a semi-feudal socio-economic structure of Ukrainian society, based upon serfdom and strict division into social classes. Transition from one class to the other was difficult, and eventually was legally prohibited. This lack of vertical mobility was distinctly a characteristic of the Polish socio-economic and political institutions, which by the end of this period had already reached a relatively high stage of development in Ukraine.

The national revolution of 1648 initiated a new national period of the social and political history of Ukraine. The rule of the Polish kings was succeeded by a rather democratic Ukrainian government. The old Polish structure was replaced by one with Ukrainian characteristics. Economically, the Cossack-Hetman period was an era of independent national economy that developed under a more favorable political atmosphere, and in a more balanced way; but it was still a continuation of the frontier land of Ukraine, constantly expanding toward the South and East. It was responsible for the growth of agriculture, commerce, and manufacturing. However, before the Ukrainian society and the Ukrainian economy developed fully in the sovereign state, by 1781, Ukraine was incorporated into the Russian empire.[7] Of course, there had not been enough time since 1648 and 1781 to permit the maturity of the Ukrainian national life, which was still predominantly an agricultural land of the frontier. With its inclusion in the all-Russian imperial market, Ukraine lost its relative independence, and was in the position of an exploited agricultural colony of the semi-mercantilist Russian empire.

Once more the progress of the socio-political evolution of the Ukrainian people was suddenly interrupted and directed to serve their conquerors. Mercantilism in the Russian Empire was succeeded by capitalism. Being politically a part of Russia at that time, Ukraine also experienced the transition, and became, especially after the abolition of serfdom in 1861, a semi-capitalistic colony of the semi-capitalistic Russian giant. The First World War and the National Revolution of 1918 produced a sovereign Ukrainian Democratic Republic. The period of a free Ukrainian nation in the twentieth century was too short, but it affected very deeply the evolution of social, political and economic institutions in Ukraine. Yet this brief national era was marked by a struggle between the old semi-capitalistic institutions and the socialist reform movement.

The Communist Revolution in the Russian Empire, 1917 to 1921, put Ukraine again under Russian rule. She soon became a Ukrainian Soviet Socialist Republic within the Soviet Union, with all the characteristics of radical socialist collectivism. The old class structure, capitalistic society, private property, and individual initiative were suddenly destroyed, repealed, and replaced by a new Communist society, new social classes, state ownership, and collective initiative. The process of building had to be started all over again from the social wreckage left behind by the Bolshevik Revolution. Indeed, the socio-political evolution of the Ukrainian people, even now, was to be anything but a steady and smooth growth.

Periods of Ukrainian History. For convenience in discussing the social, political and economic growth of the Ukrainian people, the whole evolutionary process will be divided into periods. Too significant and epochal events, and too fundamental changes took place in the course of these fifteen hundred years. These challenging events and changes are so distinct that they make the identification of individual periods a relatively easy task. The discussion of the unevenness and irregularity of the development of Ukraine has already established certain bases for a correct division of the history of the Ukrainian people into several periods of distinct characteristics. Seven different eras may thus be distinguished.

First period: the prehistoric, lasted from the remote times of the Slavic settlements of the Ukrainian territories, until 860 A.D. when Ukraine entered the historical-political scene of Europe. The Antian era and the existence of the Antian political organization, fifth-seventh century, was the peak of the period. The event of 860 A.D. was marked by the large-scale military expedition of the two Kievan chieftians, Askold and Dir, against Constantinople. In this period, Ukrainian nationality was formed, and its distinctive social and economic evolution began.

Second period: the Kievan-Galician era lasted from 860 until 1349, when the Galician-Volhinian realm was liquidated by Polish and Lithuanian intervention. It was an era of organic growth of medieval Ukrainian society and national economy. Within this period, three distinct phases of development can be distinguished, namely, the Kievan era, the Galician-Volhinian era, and the period of the Mongol rule in the Eastern Ukraine after 1240, the year of the Batu's conquest of Kiev.

Third period: the Lithuanian-Polish era continued from 1349 until the National Revolution of 1648-1649. The first phase of the period is the dark age of complete national ruin under the rule of the Mongols. The second phase is marked by a national revival within the framework of the so-called Lithuanian-*Rus'* state, which lasted until the Lithuanian-Polish Union of Lublin in 1569. In the Lithuanian-Ukrainian state, the Ukrainian social and economic institutions developed rather freely in spite of continuously growing Polish pressure. The Lublin Union which was preceded by the Polish annexation of most Ukrainian ethnical territories, formerly under Lithuania, initiated ruthless Polish rule in Ukraine. By this time the national character of the social and economic institutions in Ukraine had been almost entirely lost.

Fourth period: the Cossack-Hetman era lasted from 1648 until 1781, when Russian administration was introduced into Ukraine. At that time the political sovereignty of the Ukrainian people had been reestablished, and a new revival in the evolution of the Ukrainian society initiated. The Ukrainian national economy developed rather well. Two phases can be differentiated in this period. The first was characterized by national sovereignty in the complete sense of the term, a sovereignty that continued until the battle of Poltava in 1709. The second phase began with the period of growing Russian pressure initiated by Peter the Great.

Fifth period: the Russian Tsarist rule lasted from 1781 until 1917. The interests of the all-Russian imperialism and the political pressure of the Tsardom completely destroyed any essentially Ukrainian social, political and economic institutions, and turned Ukraine into an agricultural colony of the Empire in the course of the nineteenth century. Russian institutions and establishments were introduced throughout Ukraine.

Sixth period: the National Revolution and the era of the Ukrainian Democratic Republic extended from 1918 to 1921. This era, too short to have had any considerable effect on the social and economic evolution of the people, was brought to a violent end by the Communist domination of the Ukraine.

Seventh period: the Russian Soviet rule lasted from the Bolsheviks' conquest and domination of Ukraine in 1921 and 1922, and established there the radical socialist, political and economic order. From this time, Ukraine has been a colony of the Russians. Two separate phases of the Soviet rule in Ukraine can easily be identified. Until 1928, the era of the so-called New Economic Policy prevailed, in the course of which the Red regime was relatively tolerable. Ukrainization of the political and cultural life, and liberalization of the economic system were the marks of the time. Since 1928, the era has been one of ruthless collectivization of the country, and complete Russianization of all phases of Ukrainian culture and national development. The Five Year Plans had become the bases of the country's business management.

As anyone might expect who is conversant with the ways of history, the transitions from one of the above periods to another are neither immediate nor sharply defined. Such changes are often prolonged, as, for example, the Mongolian invasion, which links dramatically the second and third periods — the Kievan-Galician and the Lithuanian-Polish eras. Another example of such dynamically extended transition is the increasing pressure of Russian influence which culminated in the event of a complete annexation of Ukraine to the Tsarist Empire. Neither was the radical socialist order introduced overnight to Ukraine, as the subsequent detailed discussion should prove.

1.   C. Daugherty, *Labor Problems in American Industry*, Boston-New York-Chicago-Dallas-Atlanta-San Francisco, 1948-49, p. 38.

2.   I. Mirchuk, "The Basic Traits of the Ukrainian People," *Ukraine and Its People, Munich*, 1949, pp. 35-42.

3.   For example, the rebellion of Pushkar against Hetman Vyhovsky; the rebellions of individual otomans (commanders), such as Petryk and Palii, against Hetman Mazepa: M. Hrushevsky, *A History of Ukraine,* New Haven, 1970, pp. 310, 355-359.

4.   The anti-Stolypin attitude of the Russian general opinion, because of the collectivist and anti-individualist psychology of the Russians: E. Malaniuk, *Do problemy bolshevyzmu*, New York, 1956, pp. 78-79: "It was very indicative that a real sorrow after Stolypin's death covered Ukraine only; the masses of the peasantry were thankful to him..."; the Russian collectivist tendencies: H. Schwartz, *Russia's Soviet Economy*, New York, 1954, pp. 40-41; Russian socialists, like Tkachov, held the Russian *mir* institution (family collective) as an indication of the communist tendencies in Russian society: N. Chirovsky, *The Economic Factors in the Growth of Russia*, New York, 1957, pp. 139-140.

5.   P. Stercho, *Diplomacy of Double Morality, Europe's Crossroads in Carpatho-Ukraine, 1919-1939*, New York, 1971, pp. 1-25, 107-137.

6.   P. Lyashchenko, *History of the National Economy of Russia, to the 1917 Revolution*, New York, 1949, pp. 116-117; also D. Doroshenko, *Narys istorii Ukrainy*, Munich, 1966, Vol. I, pp. 97-98; N. Chirovsky, *Old Ukraine, Its Socio-Economic History Prior to 1781*, Madison, 1963, pp. 157-58.

7.   Chirovsky, *ibid.*, pp. 364-66; Doroshenko, *op. cit.*, Vol. II, pp. 268 and following; The idea of the discontinuance in the Ukrainian history was well reflected in the article by Pritsak and Reshetar: O. Pritsak and J. Reshetar, "Ukraine and the Dialectics of Nation-Building", *Slavic Review*, June, 1963, Vol. 22, No. 2, pp. 224-255, also reprinted in *On the Historical Beginnings of Eastern Slavic Europe,* ed. by N. Fr. Chirovsky, New York, 1976, pp. 165-210.

CHAPTER THREE

THE HISTORICAL PROLOGUE

The pre-historical legacy — The Hellenic colonies on the Black Sea shores — The impact of the steppes — The state of the Antes — The Slavic tribes of Eastern Europe.

The Pre-historical legacy. The cultural, social, economic and political development of any society is "organic" to the extent that any link in that development arises on the basis of the past achievements and mistakes. Nothing comes from nothing in the social evolution. Past developments have built the foundations of the present, and the present predetermines the future. However, evolutionary developments do not mean only a permanent growth; evolutionary ups and downs are historically interdependent, ever the causes and consequences of each other. Hence, in retrospect the remote prehistory of the European East, or rather, South-East, predetermined to some extent the developments in medieval Kievan *Rus'*, and the social and cultural growth of *Rus'* affected the course of events in the Lithuanian-*Rus'* state, while these two former social-political bodies, with their cultural atmosphere, influenced the growth of the Cossack-Hetman Ukrainian state. Then, in spite of the discontinuance of the historical course of the Ukrainian people due to the prolonged Russian

36

domination (1801-1917), the Cossack period inspired by a long shot the National Revolution of 1917-1921 and the establishment of the Ukrainian National Democratic Republic of the 1920s. The Soviet period has represented a complete break with the traditions of that nation, during which, however, the drive to national Ukrainian independence, resting on the traditions of the Cossack state and the Ukrainian Democratic Republic, was violently manifested by the Ukrainian nationalist and self-assertion movement before and after the Second World War, including the re-establishment of the Ukrainian statehood in 1941 and the ten-year long warfare of the Ukrainian Insurgent Army against Hitler's Germany and Stalin's Russia.

This should explain and justify the need of going deep into the past thousands of years, when studying the history of a country or people. Ukrainian history is no exception. In fact, a student of prehistory should go some 200 thousand years back, looking for traces of human existence in the territory of Ukraine.

The prehistoric legacy of the Ukrainian-*Rus'* people can largely be learned from archaeological excavations and the comparative archaeology of peoples living on similar cultural levels in different times. Yet, even that is not enough. There is no doubt that the life of man is remotely influenced by the stages in the formation of earth, which evolved over millions of years. The geological processes affected the topography and geography of the land, and the land, its shape and climate do directly influence the people living there. Hence, geology, in fact, must be the first discipline to be consulted, whenever one intends to research deeply and conscientiously the historical past of a people. The black soil, the humus, of Ukraine, the result of the geological process, profoundly influenced the course of the Ukrainian history and the formation of the spirit of the Ukrainian nation. On the other hand, the geological processes of thousands of years were deeply affected by the advancing and retreating glacier, which each time covered only northern parts of Ukraine, extending to the south differently in different parts of the country. Because of the meteorological and tectonic reasons, the glacier retreated finally further and further northwards, where it remained for a longer span of time, while in the South-East of Europe a milder climate developed. Consequently, man arrived at an earlier time to Ukraine than to any other parts of the European East, the Muscovite North-East, in particular, and there, in the Ukrainian South-East, human civilization also began to evolve at an earlier date, as well.

Once man appears in a certain region, then his history begins, but, as pointed out a while before, for that remote time, before written source materials were recorded, archeology and archeological interpretation are the only sources of information of man's very early whereabouts. Archeological excavations have uncovered early human dwellings, clothing, tools, foods and early primitive arts, which approximately illustrated the mode of living and the level of civilization of prehistoric peoples, while written sources of ancient times can only be used to supplement the knowledge of the later periods of prehistory, derived from the archeological studies. On the other hand, ancient written documents were too poetic and too biased, and clouded by guesswork and myths, in many cases, and only parts of them were reliable historical material, when projected against objective archeological findings.

For instance, the ancient Greek writers, who hated Slavs, called them "man-beasts, living like animals, eating all sorts of dirt." This did not properly reflect either the Slavic cultural level or the way of life at that time. As Lyashchenko said: "It would be, of course, entirely erroneous to see in this depiction of the Slavs . . . the reality of that low stage of social development. . . ."[1] Archeology has been a much more objective witness to the prehistoric past of the Slavs than the written source material. Yet, written history had become more and more reliable and useful as time progressed. Its reliability increased, with the rise of civilization; with greater competence in writing; with the increasing objectivity of the writers; and with the accumulation of literature enabling comparison and evaluation by discriminating historians.

Archeology revealed the existence of prehistoric man, his characteristics and ways of life through excavations, while geology provided a framework for the prehistory of the earth itself by dividing it into a number of evolutionary stages. Each stage of that geological development lasted, as pointed out, tens of thousands of years, largely before man came into being on earth. Then, upon that foundation of the geological evolutionary framework, archeology, after having located the first man on the globe, and, having followed its own scientific requirements and criteria, suggested its own theoretical system of man's struggle for survival and his struggle for the attainment of higher stages of civilization. Hence, according to man's changing mode of life and his use of bone, stone, and metal, archeology divided man's prehistoric past into the Old Stone or Paleolithic age, the New Stone or Neolithic age, the Copper and Bronze or Paleometalic age, and finally the Iron or Neometalic age. Each age constituted a number of eras in man's cultural evolution. Each era had had its impact on the prehistory of Ukraine.[2]

Traces of man's existence on the earth go back, perhaps, as far as the so-called Early Old Stone or Early Paleolithic age, some 400-200 thousand years before our era. The Old Stone or Paleolithic age of man's history can be divided into three eras: the Early, the Middle and the Late Old Stone or Paleolithic ones. During the Early Paleolithic time, Europe experienced its inter-glacial period, with its mild and humid climate, Mediterranean-like vegetation and huge animals, like the elephant, the hippopotamus and the mammoth. At that time the earliest traces of man in Europe, the so-called *Heidelberg man,* were scientifically established. There are archaeological evidences of man inhabiting the European East, or Ukraine in particular, during that time. The *Heidelberg man* lived at the lower stage of savagery in primitive herds. Tribes were yet unknown. Since the climate was mild, it seemed that he did not know how to build dwellings but he knew how to use caves for protection against changing weather conditions. He used extremely crude stone tools, as, for example, a crude hand-cleaver for hunting, which, perhaps, took a lifetime to make.

Then, the advance of glaciers changed the European climate

severely, also substantially changing the way of life of prehistoric man. Cold weather forced him either to invent or to perish. It forced him to advance "culturally." This new era in man's evolution is called the Middle Old Stone era. The more advanced prehistoric man of that era has been called the *Neanderthal man*. There is a strong archeological evidence available of human settlements in Ukraine, along the Dnieper and Donets river banks and in the Crimea during that time. Yet, there were no traces of the *Neanderthal man* identified in the European North-East, on the territory of Russia proper, using the modern terminology. Perhaps, he was discouraged by the harsh climate in the North-East. This might have explained (at least to some extent, and along with other contributory factors, like the impact of Greek culture upon Ukraine), why the cultural development of Ukraine was earlier and faster than that of Russia during the ancient era. Man arrived earlier in Ukraine and began to cultivate the area at the earlier date, too.[3]

The *Neanderthal man* learned to seek cover in caves and dug-outs and to dress in animal skins to protect himself against the cold and other dangers and inconveniences as well. Of course, hunting, trapping and fishing were still his main occupations and sources of livelihood, but his stone and bone appliances were improved, sharpened at the top, as, for example, spearheads and hand-cleavers. Economically, he advanced to some division of labor. He hunted for mammoth, bear and deer.

The *Neanderthal man* lived supposedly in large families of the pre-tribal stage, developed some religious beliefs and burial rituals, indicating, perhaps, an awareness of the immortality of the soul. This stage of man's evolution has been also referred to as the second era of savagery.

The further retreat of the glacier brought to South-Eastern Europe a new moderation of climate, initiating a new era. This was called the Later or Upper Old Stone age; the era of the *Homo Sapiens*, a rational, though still a savage human being. Although *Homo Sapiens* continued to use stone, bone and horn weapons and appliances, yet his workmanship became a far better one and the articles were substantially improved, indicating a constant, though a very slow, cultural evolution. He began to build permanent dwellings, huts, which sometimes were even equipped with heated chambers for cold seasons. His technique of division of labor and specialization was, for the time, quite advanced.

Socially, this man of the Upper Paleolith lived in tribes, while in many cases probably, matriarchy prevailed in the family, which was sedentary and less nomadic in any case. His religious life was more elaborate and quite deeper. Human settlements were scattered throughout the whole Ukraine at that time. Archeology uncovered many stone and bone tools and appliances, some of them being well ornamented. The richest findings so far have been identified in the Kiev, Mizen, Lubni and Kryvyi Rih regions. This was then apparently the era when man, having taken advantage of improvement of climate in Europe in general and in its North-East corner in particular, arrived and first settled on the territory of future Russia proper.

Then, sometime between 14,000 to 3,000 years B.C., the transition to a higher cultural stage was accomplished by man, differently in different parts of Europe. Man overcame at that time his savagery and reached the state of barbarism; he developed his civilization considerably when compared with previous eras. Hence, the new era was termed by archeology as a New-Stone or Neolithic age. During this period the continuous improvement of the climatic conditions apparently facilitated population growth, while that growing density of population in relation to primitive methods of production and means of survival, induced a more advanced mode of economic life. The Neolithic man in general, and by the same token in Ukraine, began to domesticate animals, like dogs, cats and horses; raise cattle, sheep and hogs; initiate farming by raising rye, oats and flax. He already drilled wells for water supply; improved production of appliances and weapons by polishing stones and boring holes, which took him many years of work. Horn and bone were still used to make useful things, but at the same time man also began to manufacture pottery and dishes from clay and beautify them with simple designs. Production was done collectively in primitive "shops." Simple trading and merchandise exchange by barter began to develop along the water routes.[4]

Blood relation and the tribal system became the foundation of the socio-economic organization in the Neolithic age; villages replaced the isolated settlements. Social differentiation into wealthy "nobility," free and unfree (slaves) members of the tribal society had already come into being. Religious life further developed and burial rituals became more complex. The Neolithic man extended his settlements further north, having taken advantage of the warming of the climate, on the one hand, and also because the increase of the population at that time in the South made the struggle for survival more difficult, having caused tribal strife and warfare, in result of which, as it is rational to assume, some clans and tribes were driven to the North in search of more peaceful surroundings.[5]

Finally, the Stone Age was over and the Metal Age had begun, while already at the end of the Neolithic era man learned in Ukraine how to extract metal ore from underneath the earth surface and the metal from ore, and how to make and use some metallic appliances and simple weapons, although the stone and bone utensils still remained most popular and were prevailingly employed by the barbarian forefather of the later Rus'ians-Ukrainians.

The Old Metallic or Paleometallic Age of Copper and Bronze, about 3,000 to 1,000 years B.C., was subsequently replaced by the New Metallic or the Neometallic Age of Iron. This transition was completed earlier in the South, in Ukraine and the Caucasian regions, than in the rest of Eastern Europe, having been substantially belated in the North, in the Muscovite or Russia-proper regions. The Metallic Age was distinctly marked by the use of copper and bronze, and ultimately, of iron to manufacture various utensils, appliances and weapons, and it represented tremendous progress toward the higher stage of "barbarism," leading directly to the epoch of "civilization," as Friederich Engels pointed out.

In Ukraine, from her western frontiers, bordering on Slovakia and the Balkan Peninsula, to the northern limits of the Chernihiv region and the eastern frontiers of the Slobozhanska Ukraine on the banks of the Donets River, down toward the South, to the banks of the Black Sea, during the times of the late Neolith and the Paleometal, a distinct cultural epoch, under the common name of the Tripillian Civilization, developed, having exhibited close similarities and relations to the almost contemporary at one time, so-called Aegean Civilization of the eastern Mediterranean region. The Aegean Civilization achieved its cultural heights in the island of Crete, having been protected by the naval power of the Cretan sea rulers and enriched by the vital sea contacts with Egypt, Syria and Asia Minor.[6]

The Tripillian Civilization, the name of which was derived from the village of Tripilla, the Kievan region, where significant archeological findings of that culture were located, was featured by large villages, constructed on the river banks, consisting of many wooden huts in the square form, covered with clay from the outside and largely painted in dark-red inside. The huts were normally divided into three or four rooms, with hearth and chimney. There were also in these villages the structures of a ritual nature, indicating a developed religious life and probably the faith in life after death. The excavation of all kinds of female statuettes point at a great respect paid by the Tripillian population to women, and perhaps, at the matriarchal social order of that civilization, as well.

The Tripillian people were largely agricultural, raising on their fields wheat, rye, millet, barley and other cultures, having used already primitive tools, like stone sickles and hoes, primitive ploughs, drawn by oxen; and along with farming, raising cattle on a large scale, like cows, sheep, hogs and horses. Hence, the material civilization of the Tripillians reached a high level of development in comparison with the previous ages. Yet, above all, the Tripillian population substantially developed the useful arts, ceramics, and painting and artistic textiles. They manufactured by hand only all kinds, big and small, of clay dishes, jugs, plates, animal and female statuettes in particular, dishes, jugs and plates which were beautifully painted, mostly in the standard manner; against the light-yellow background a dark-red spiral ornament being dominant. They also used two or three other colors and also painted on the jugs, jars and bowls some plant patterns and ornamented animal and human figures. The ox head with widespread horns, used to ornament the dishes, was one of the popular decorations. Along with the Tripillian ceramics, the Tripillian textile manufacturing with an artistic notion was also well developed.

The people of the Tripillian Civilization developed and maintained vital contacts with Asia Minor, Thessalonia, Transylvania, Caucasia and Transcaucasia, which only contributed to a further growth of their culture.[7]

With the advent of the metals in Ukraine, at first the copper tools, axes, chisels and hammers, apparently the over-all cultural level of the country declined under the impact of the invasions of the nomadic or otherwise barbarian hordes, the economic life of which was based primarily on cattle raising, while farming as a higher stage of material civilization disappeared for a while altogether in that area. The remnants of the ancient copper mines of that age were identified in the Donets River regions. Yet, for a long time in Ukraine, along with the copper, stone (flint) and bone tools and appliances were also in use, before the Metallic Age really took over. Subsequently, copper was mixed with lead, and a stronger alloy, called bronze, became the leading metal, employed for making weapons and appliances. At the end of the Bronze Age, the cultural level of the ancient population of Ukraine increased again. The bronze techniques reached a rather high level with several cultural centers in the upper-Dniester, Lviv, Rivne and Uman regions. The economic life was featured by primitive farming and cattle raising, while ceramics evolved further and achieved new artistic heights.

Approximately at that time, between 1,500 and 700 B.C., Ukraine was invaded and settled by new people, the Cimmerians, a Thracian ethnic group, which belonged to the Indo-European family of peoples, and meanwhile also, at the beginning of the first millenium B.C. the Iron Age (Neometallic era) came to South-Eastern Europe, when the use of copper and bronze was replaced by iron. According to Antonovych, iron came to Ukraine from Central Asia, and for that reason it spread in Ukraine sooner than it became popular in West and Central Europe. The era was featured by further progress in farming and cattle raising in the economic aspect, and the replacement of the matriarchate by the patriarchate, the priority of men over the women, in the social aspect. Rich archeological excavations of numerous burial grounds from that period give an ample proof of the iron civilization on the Ukrainian territory, uncovering widespread Hellenic, Central Asiatic and Siberian influences, with new forms of burial and new forms of arts, such as jewelry of Hellenic origin and rich ornamentations, made from bronze, gold, silver and bone, either coming from Asia or manufactured under the impact of the Asiatic influence.[8]

The older historical interpretation assumed that that cultural evolution, the transition from one cultural stage to another, in Ukraine was brought about by the coming of new peoples, new ethnic groups, either in the way of violent conquests or of peaceful colonization, who originated their native civilizations in their native lands or original settlements, then brought them to the new land of their subsequent colonization. Yet, the newer interpretation is that in reality the original ethnic substratum was actually accomplishing that entire evolutionary cultural process in Ukraine by its own spiritual and intellectual progression from one cultural stage to another, being aided by trade and cultural relations and contacts with other, either neighboring or distant, lands and peoples, as well as by merging with the waves of invading newcomers, who for a while dominated Ukraine and were a ruling stratum there, but subsequently were assimilated and absorbed by the original ethnic substratum, after adding to the evolving civilization of the land their own cultural acquisitions and peculiarities.[9]

When in Ukraine, the ethnic substratum of the Iranian and Thracian stock was essentially sponsoring the above cultural evolution with strong Aegean, Hellenic and Middle Eastern cul-

tural influences at its later stages, then the North-Eastern plain of Europe, the present Russia-proper, was occupied and inhabited by the Ugro-Finns, who in due process of time formed numerous tribes of Mongol extraction, the Ves', Meria, Chud', Mordva, Muroma, and further east, the Cheremisians, Permians and other related tribes, like the Voguls and Ostiaks, who migrated and subsequently extended their permanent settlements far beyond the Ural mountains. Later, the Bulgars of Turkish extraction arrived and settled in the Middle Volga Basin to affect the history of the North-Eastern plain quite distinctly from the historical developments in the Ukrainian South.

The Hellenic Colonies on the Black Sea Shores. It seems that so far historical writing definitely did not pay enough attention and did not properly evaluate the enormous impact of the Aegean, in particular of the Hellenic, and then, the Roman influences on the formation of the national characteristics and the historical fortunes of the Ukrainian people. By the way of numerous Greek colonies, which for many centuries existed as either independent or autonomous city-states on the northern banks of the Black Sea, in the Crimean Peninsula, and the banks of the Azov Sea, the Hellenic and then the Hellenistic culture, trade relations and institutions affected deeply and thoroughly the ethnic elements, which at different periods of ancient history were predominant in Ukraine, while its static ethnic substratum was permanently exposed to the Greek influences, which, according to the archeological and historical sources, reached territorially as far as the northern forest belt of the country. Each of those ethnic groups, the Cimmerians, Scythians, Sarmatians, Alans, Ostgoths, Antes or Slavs, was not free from the powerful effects of the Greek civilization. Yet, those influences never touched the European North-East to any substantial degree. The territorial distance was too great and the unfavorable topography was not conducive in that respect, either.

The first Greek settlers arrived at the northern shores of the Black Sea at the beginning of the Iron Age, and established there permanent colonies. Some of those colonies were established as early as the beginning of the seventh century B.C., others in the fifth century and even later. By the end of the sixth century the northern littorals of the Black Sea were covered by numerous, larger and smaller, more and less important, Greek settlements and towns, from which Tyras at the mouth of the Dniester River, Olbia on the banks of the Boh River, Chersones in the western part of the Crimean Peninsula, Theodosia in the eastern region of the Peninsula, Ponticapeion at the Kerch Straight, Phanagoris across the Straight, and Tanais at the northern end of the Azov Sea and the mouth of the Don River were the most important ones. Most of them were separate political entities, city-states, but culturally, religiously, socially and otherwise they were inseparable parts and components of the Hellenic world, which kept in close touch with the mother-cities, like Miletus, Delos and Athens, and the whole Greek community at large. They even took part in the all-Hellenic sports events.

Some of these colonies were big cities with several market places, paved streets, stone walls and fortifications, beautiful temples, public buildings and lavish private houses, sports stadiums; they were real cultural centers with scholars, writers and schools, disseminating the fruits of the Hellenic civilization as far as the town of Lubni in the Poltava region of today, where recently the ruins of the Greek temples of Dionysius, Apollo and Artemis were uncovered.[10] It is scarcely possible to assume that the Greeks reached only Lubni by some coincidence. There is evidence that they penetrated all over the southern regions of Ukraine and for many centuries, leaving a permanent imprint on the natives' historical fortunes.

These colonies were also ruled according to the Hellenic patterns as the city-state communities, largely by people's meetings and a senate of city's elders, and four archonautes at the top of administration. Of course, there were deviations from that constitutional standard structure of government. At times "tyrants," one-man rule, captured the city-state government in some Greek community and ruled it despotically, until they were forced to step down. There were also other modifications. Smaller colonies were at times overrun by large and powerful city-states, annexed by them and governed at will. Those city-states had well developed economies, based on manufacturing and trading, and in most cases they coined their own money of silver and gold to facilitate their large-scale commercial activities. Their economic significance for the Greek mother-land was enormous, since they were marketing middle-men between Greece and the "barbarian" peoples of the North. Since Greece proper was always short of food, the Black Sea colonies supplied the mother-land with grain, which they raised by themselves or bought from the "barbarians," fish and slaves, while selling to the northern "barbarians" the Greek products of wine, textiles, fine garments, cheap and costly, copper, gold and silver jewelry and weapons. Hence, those colonies shipped to Greece the "barbarian" produce of their primitive and extensive economies, while the "barbarians" were supplied by them with the products of the Greek or their own colonial advanced manufacturing economies. Whenever Greece, or Athens especially, was in dire need, the colonies either sold or gave her as a gift large supplies of grain to avert her troubles. Such was the case with Ponticapeion and the Bosphorian Kingdom assisting Athens with huge grain deliveries in several instances.

The city of Tyras was established by the emigrants of Miletus, which itself was a Greek colony in Asia Minor. For a long time it was a separate city-republic, while in the fourth century A.D. it was dominated by Rome politically, but protected by it very well otherwise. Roman emperors issued several privileges to facilitate the city's trading activities. In the neighborhood of Tyras there were several other minor Greek towns, such as Nikonion, Isiakion and Istrion, which at times were dependent upon the former. The city of Olbia was also established by Miletus, being sometimes called by the foreigners Boristen, because of its nearness to the Dnieper River, called Boristen in antiquity. It was one of the oldest and most important Greek colonies, a real center of the Hellenic civilization on the banks of the Black Sea and a very important trading market for the Greek-barbarian commerce. Its greatest development was achieved in the fifth and fourth centuries B.C. It had to defend itself against the onslaught of Zapirion, a general of Alexander the Great, and wage wars against the onslaughts of the steppe peoples, the Scythians, Sarmatians, Bastarnians and Getes. At one time it had to pay an annual tribute to the Sarmatian chieftains. Because of the continuous harassments by the steppe nomads, the survival of the community became very difficult, Olbia accepted the protection by Mithridates, king of Pontus. After Mithridates was defeated by Rome, the city, like most other Greek communities, was forced to submit to the Roman supremacy. Rome defended Olbia against the onslaughts of the steppe nomads and protected its trade.

On the Crimean Peninsula there were several Greek colonies, of which Chersones, established by the emigrants from Heracleia and Delos, sometime in the third century B.C., acquired great prominence. It made it, therefore, one of the younger colonies, but its historical fortunes were more impressive and of more lasting success. Because the city was gravely harassed by the "barbarian" Taurians, it was heavily fortified. Since it was a younger colony and initially rather unimportant, Herodotus did not even mention it in his writings. The remnants of the ancient paved streets, market places, water reservoirs, water installations, sewerage, ruins of public and private buildings, and temples have testified to the past greatness of the city of Chersones. Economic interests prevailed during its entire history as an independent or at times as politically dependent community. In order to maintain itself, Chersones had to wage continuous wars against the onslaughts of the Scythians, and other steppe hordes. In 110 B.C., Diophantes, Mithridates' general, helped the city to defeat a Scythian "king" Palak and his Roxolanian allies. Then, Chersones, along with other Greek communities, had to acknowledge Roman supremacy, which prevailed until the third century A.D. During the Byzantine supremacy in the Middle East, Chersones experienced a magnificent growth as the center of the Byzantine administration in Crimea and the Black Sea littorals. Of course, there was at times a strong movement among the Chersonesians to free themselves from the oppressive Byzantine dependence. In the eighth century A.D. the city and the region of Chersones were badly harassed by the growing power of the Khozars, who established a strong state of theirs at the mouth of the Volga River and its lower run.

Theodosia or Phedosia was still another Greek community in the Crimea. The time of its establishment is unknown. In the fourth century B.C. it was dominated by the Bosphorian state and continued to be quite unimportant. First in the fourteenth and fifteenth century it was dominated by the Italian city-state of Genoa, called Kaffa, and became a significant trading center. The city of Tanais at the mouth of the Don River became early the largest market for the "barbarian" trade from East Europe and Central Asia. Especially important was its fishing and fish trading. It was destroyed by Polemones, the ruler of the Bosphorian state in the first century, but then it recovered economically again. Phanagoris, according to Strabo, was a trading center of the Asian Bosphorians, where the goods were brought from the Caucasian and Sub-Caucasian regions for the Black Sea basin distribution.

The city of Ponticapeion, cited where presently the city of Kerch is located, according to historical sources, was already in the fifth century B.C. the capital of all Miletus colonies in the Black Sea area. Consequently, it must have been established much earlier, and its commercial significance was of a rather lasting nature. Its political constitution was at first of an aristocratic republic under the leadership of the family of Archeanakides. Subsequently, the dynasty of the Spartakides, of a foreign, non-Greek origin, took over, which conquered in the second half of the fifth century other neighboring Hellenic colonies, such as Phanagoris, Gorgipia and Theodosia, and established the so-called Bosphorian Empire. Having called themselves first only the archonates of Ponticapeion, the Spartakides then assumed the title of "emperors," and extended their rule even over some neighboring "barbarian" lands of the steppe hordes.

The Bosphorian Empire developed substantial fishing and fish processing industry, large trade volume, grain and wine production and cattle raising. It had for a long time enormous grain supplies at its disposal, either through its own farming or through the trade with the steppe peoples, and assisted Greece proper by food deliveries whenever needed there. Subsequently, the Bosphorian empire was exposed to the identical political fortunes as the other Greek colonies of the Black Sea basin. It was badly harassed by "barbarian" hordes. Its huge maritime fleet and commercial activities declined; it had to accept Mithridates' military protection to withstand the onslaught of the steppes and in the due course of the history, also the supremacy of Rome, having retained, however, its political autonomy. In the later centuries, the Bosphor again developed under the political supremacy of the Byzantinian Empire.

The Greek or Hellenic era in southern Ukraine left, as pointed out above, a lasting and indelible imprint on the Ukrainian people. The Hellenic culture, doubtlessly, fortified the growth of Ukrainian individualism, love for freedom, preference for the democratic way of life, and cultural creativity, which all crystalized later on. Then, the ancient familiarity with the Hellenic and Hellenistic civilizations and the Hellenic people facilitated the tendency of the Ukrainian-*Rus'* society of the ninth to thirteenth century to lean on and to absorb the Byzantine civilization, which in its own way had an enormous impact upon the evolution of the Ukrainian nation.[11]

The Impact of the Steppes. Another powerful force, which deeply affected the early history of the Ukraine, was the impact of the steppes, with all those numerous peoples who moved through the steppes in the course of the centuries, and left their imprints, either more or less penetrating, and contributed in various ways to shaping the national characteristics and cultural trends of the future Ukrainians. Their influence should neither be ignored, nor underestimated.

It is unknown what was the original ethnic substratum of Ukraine in grey antiquity. Yet, concluding from the later trends in the ethnic movements to and through Ukraine, known approximately, one may conclude that the fundamental ethnic stock in Ukraine for a great many centuries was Iranian-Arian, in contrast to the European North-East (Russia-proper of today) where the Mongolian ethnic substratum prevailed.

The first people known to history who came to Ukraine sometime in the second half of the second millenium B.C. to stay and to live there were, as mentioned, the Cimmerians of the Thracian ethnic stock. Their settlements spread from the Carpathian mountains and the mouth of the Danube River to the Kuban region, beyond the Azov Sea. They had rather strong political organizations with tribal "chieftains" of considerable power, built fortresses, and developed religious beliefs, indicated by burial rituals of their own. Their economy was based on a large-scale cattle raising, and during their stay the transition from the bronze to iron civilization was accomplished in Ukraine. During their bronze era, the Cimmerians developed ceramics with colored encrustinizations, and were involved in constant cultural and commercial relations with Caucasia, Transcaucasia, and Asia Minor in the East, and Selesia, in the West, and their civilization may be rightly considered for a continuation of the Tripillian culture. The Greek historian, Herodotus, wrote about the Cimmerians and their struggle against the invading Scythians around the year 700 B.C.

The Scythians, probably of Iranian stock, retreated from their original settlements under the pressure of Eastern hordes from Asia, and dominated the Ukrainian regions for some five hundred years. While the ruling horde of the Scythians was of Iranian extraction, there were then in Ukraine some minor hordes staying there for a while, which well might have been of Ugrian, Mongolian and even Slavic origin. Vernadsky reinforces this in his discussion of the question of the ethnical stock of the Scythians, and concludes that the names of the Scythian chieftains or kings, mentioned by Herodotus and other authors of antiquity, were definitely Iranian. At the time the Scythians dominated the Ukrainian steppes, the Greeks began to settle along the northern shores of the Black Sea, and develop their commercial and cultural centers there.

The civilization of Ukraine at Scythian times remained essentially Cimmerian, although considerable progress was achieved. Among the Scythians, a patriarchal system prevailed with already a substantial social differentiation, resulting in the development of wealthy noble families with social prestige and political influence. The Scythian religion continued to develop clearly on the Tripillian base with the admixture of the totem approach of the cattle raising societies. Also the burial rituals, either by cremation or by entombment, further evolved. The rituals were then taken over by the Antes and Slavs in Ukraine. The wealthy Scythians built the graves in the form of rather large structures.

The rich stratum of the Scythian society wore costly clothing with gold and silver ornamentations and possessed expensive arms and weapons. The Scythians lived in villages and towns, the latter being fortified for defense with walls. They developed the art of ceramics above the previous levels of achievement, with a strong Hellenic influence, manufactured large *amphoras* to keep water, wine and grain, manufactured beautiful dishes with the use of the potter's wheel and other utensils. Beautiful jewelry of copper, gold and silver was first produced for the Scythians by the Greek masters, depicting the scenes either from the Greek or the Scythian life-style while later on the Scythians themselves tried the art of making jewelry with success.

According to ancient writers, there were four distinct Scythian tribes: the Scythians-Cattlemen settled on the Boh River and their main occupation was cattle raising; the Scythians-Farmers lived between the Boh and Dnieper Rivers and raised wheat, millet, flax, barley, garlic and onions; the Scythians-Nomads moved around southwards of the former, while the Scythians-Imperials settled between the Dnieper and Don Rivers, and considered themselves the leading and dominant tribe among all the Scythians.[12]

Apparently by the fourth century B.C. the new invader had arrived in the Ukrainian steppes, and began either to force the

Scythians out of there or to dominate them. It was the people of the Sarmatians, being doubtlessly of Iranian extraction, hence related to the former. The Sarmatians were dominant in the area until the second century A.D. Although their stay in Ukraine was rather long, and although they gave the name for the land "Sarmatia" or "Savromatia" for a considerable length of time, the recent archeological studies substantially reduced their significance for the over-all historical process of Ukraine. Apparently the Sarmatians did not make any substantial cultural contribution. They, of course, harassed the Greek colonies, and in the fourth century they devastated the colony of Olbia. Foreign writers frequently confused the names of the Scythians with that of the Sarmatians, while Ptolemy, a Greek writer, consistently called Scythia "Sarmatia."

Around the first century A.D. one Sarmatian tribe, the Alans or Roxolanians, acquired some political prominence among the steppe peoples, and by their name overshadowed the others. They established themselves on the banks of the Azov Sea and then formed a political alliance which territorially extended as far as the Aral Lake, in Central Asia. Yet, it was short-lived. Subsequently, the Alans were defeated by the Huns and disintegrated into several tribal groups. One of them, called the Yazigians, migrated to the North-Caucasian area and became the forefathers of the later Osetens; the other one settled in the Crimean Peninsula.

The Sarmatian way of life was apparently featured by the high family and social position of women. This, again, became characteristic of the later Ukrainians as opposed to the Russians in their social life. The previous, old name of Ukraine, *"Rus'*," had been deduced by some students and historians of East Europe from the ancient name of the Roxolanians and their land "Rox" or "Roxolania." Both, the Sarmatians and the Alans, their ethnic branch, were nomads who did not know any farming and lived by hunting, fishing and raising cattle and horses.[13]

Then, during the first two centuries A.D., numerous barbaric and nomadic tribes of the Besses, Kostrobes, Karpes and Bastarnes (Bastarnai) of Celtic, Mongol and other ethnic origins, invaded Ukraine but never stayed long. In the third century A.D. the Goths of Germanic extraction came from the West and established a relatively strong state on the banks of the Dnieper River with its capital of Danparstadt, perhaps the city of Kiev of the later date.

Original settlements of the Goths were apparently on the banks of the rivers Vistula, Oder and Elbe, and then they migrated to the South, towards Thracia and Macedonia. Their eastern branch, the Ostrogoths or Ostgoths settled in Ukraine, between the Dnieper and Kuban Rivers, established their state after having destroyed the Bosphorian kingdom. The Ostrogoths achieved the greatest political prominence under their outstanding ruler, King Ermenrics (350-375 A.D.). The Scandinavian sagas have referred to the state of Goths and its political exploits many times. Having stayed for a considerable time in the Black Sea steppe regions, the Ostrogoths fell under the impact of the Pontian civilization and joined the Pontian cultural complex. Local craftsmen manufactured for the Gothic lords jewelry and artifacts from gold and silver, ornamented with precious stones, which were liked by the Goths very much. They have been falsely referred to as ''the Gothic style'' though not originated by them. Traditionally in these ornaments the animal motifs prevailed.

Having defeated the Goths in 375 in their march westwards, the Huns, the people of the Turkish-Mongol ethnic extraction, dominated Ukraine for a while, having established themselves between the Don and the Danube Rivers. The Hunnic pressure to the West was caused by the mighty Chinese offensive against their original settlements in Mongolia since the second century. The strong Hunnic state with its capital of Pannonia in particular in the fifth century accomplished the destruction of the Greek colonies on the littorals of the Black Sea and militarily harassed Byzantium, Italy and all of Central Europe. The peak of the political power of the Huns was achieved under their ingenious leader, Attila, and immediately after his death they began to disintegrate. Whatever was then left from the ethnic complex of the Huns in Ukraine was subsequently absorbed and assimilated by the dominant Slavic ethnic stock which populated these regions for very many centuries.[14]

In the sixth century the Avars or Obres, a nomad tribe of the Turkish origin, fell upon Ukraine. The Avars defeated the Alans and the Antes, captured the Antic prince, Mezamir, and finally dominated the Dulibians, another Slavic tribe, living in the Western part of Ukraine. The Avars or Obres succeeded to partially absorb the Slavs in their military formations and led them with themselves against the Byzantine emperor, Heraclios, who, however, defeated the Avars soundly. At the beginning of the seventh century, the Avar state achieved its largest territorial expansion: from the borders of the Kingdom of the Franks in Western Europe to the borders of the Byzantine Empire in the European South-East. Yet soon, a couple of decades later, the Avar State began to decline and the Ukrainian Slavs were gradually liberating themselves from the Avar domination, which according to the tradition, was a very oppressive one. Finally, they were badly beaten by Charlemagne and forced to retreat. Apparently, their retreat caused the migration of some Slavic tribes, which substantially affected the future ethnic composition of Ukraine.

Under the pressure of the Avar invasion, the Bulgars, a people of Turkish extraction, too, who lived at first at the lower Volga River, split into two parts. One branch passed through Ukraine in course of their migration to the South-West and ultimately settled in the Balkan Peninsula, establishing there the state of Bulgaria. The other branch went northwards, to the middle Volga, and organized there a state of its own, and subsequently achieved a political and cultural prominence between the ninth and twelfth centuries. The stay of the Bulgars in Ukraine was a rather short one; however, they were able to defeat several local tribes and semi-state formations.

A much more lasting impact upon the formation of the Ukrainian-*Rus'* nation of the future was made by the people of the Khozars, of a Turkish extraction, who came some time in the seventh century from Asia and settled at the mouth of the Volga River. By the eighth century they were able to have organized a powerful state there, which territorially stretched from the Dnieper and Desna Rivers in Ukraine to Dagestan in the Caucasian region. Several tribal communities of Ukraine, the Alans, the Siverianians and the Polianians, and some other Slavic tribes were subsequently dominated by the Khozars, although their rule was not rather oppressive. They demanded a tribute from the dominated peoples without interfering in their internal affairs at all. The conquered tribes were allowed to retain their self-government and to live their own social and political life.

The Khozars developed a substantial commercial civilization along with cattle raising and farming. Having settled at the mouth of Volga, they found themselves immediately in the center of trading activities, of which the river was the main route. Hence, they traded with the Bulgars, Scandinavia, the Arabs, Central Asian communities and Byzantium as well. The Khozars, having dominated the Ukrainian Slavs, naturally introduced them to well-developed trading activities, which apparently left an indelible imprint on the psychological predispositions of the future Rus'ians-Ukrainians. Historians also largely agree that the fact that various religions such as Christianity, Judaism and Moslem, freely developed in Khozaria, the Christianization of *Rus'*-Ukraine might have been favorably affected by it.[15]

Then, in the ninth century, the Finnic tribe of the Hungarns or Magyars settled on the banks of the Don River, next to the Khozars. Under the impact of the Pecheng invasion, the Hungarns moved to the West. For a short while they stayed in Ukraine, between the rivers of Dnieper and Boh, reached apparently with their settlements as far as the city of Kiev, and finally went further west, to the middle-Danube valley, the present day Hungary, and there established their permanent settlements and their state.

The Pecheng tribes of the Turkish extraction, definitely a nomad people, attempted to force their way to Europe in the eighth century, but the strong Khozar state (the Khozar *kahanate*) prevented them from achieving that. In order to stop the Pechengs, the Byzantine engineers constructed the fortress of Sarkel. Yet, at the beginning of the tenth century, after hard fighting with the Khozars, certain Pecheng detachments made their break-through and attacked the Ukrainian Slavs. The chronicle pointed out that "the Pechengs came to the *Rus'* land for the first time in 915," but did not stay there for long and moved further west.

First, after Sviatoslav, the Ukrainian-*Rus'* prince, destroyed the Kozar *Kahanate* in 965. The powerful deterrent for the Pecheng onslaught was gone. The Pechengs then came to the Ukrainian Black Sea steppes and established themselves there permanently, having presented for a while a permanent threat for the *Rus'* statehood in Ukraine.[16]

Of course, the powerful impact of the steppes upon the fortunes of the Ukrainian people did not terminate with the dissipation of the Pecheng threat. Later on the Torkmans, the Cumans, the Black Klobuks, and finally the Tartars established themselves in the Black Sea steppes, threatening for many centuries the Ukrainian people and their political organization with their onslaughts. Yet, these later hordes did not affect the ancient, pre-historic processes in the development of the Ukrainian nationality as its neighbors or over-lords. They were already the part of the recorded history of Ukraine and of the Ukrainian people to be discussed later on in a chronological order.

There cannot be any doubt about the deep and far-reaching impact of the steppes upon the formation of the Ukrainian nationality in antiquity. The cultures, civilizations, political organizations and ways of life of those ancient nomad or settled peoples, who stayed in Ukraine for any shorter or longer period of time in whatever capacity, were establishing distinct and separate layers, along with the Hellenic colonies on the littorals of the Black Sea, in the mosaics of the spiritual and cultural compositions of Ukraine.[17]

The State of the Antes. According to archeological findings, it may be assumed that distant forefathers or ancestors of the present-day Ukrainians had lived on their soil since the fourth or third millennium B.C., although their ethnic origin could not be identified with a degree of certainty. They had established their roots very deeply, which could not have been torn away from that soil by any prehistorical or historical cataclysms. The migrating peoples either came or went away or were assimilated and absorbed by the ancient ethnic stock of Ukraine. The specific and distinct funeral rituals uncovered by archeology in many regions of Ukraine from the end of the first millennium B.C. have strongly suggested their Slavic origin. The subsequent archeological excavations have indicated a certain cultural development of those people, largely identified as the so-called Cherniakhiv culture, from the name of the village in the neighborhood of which the remnants of that civilization were found, such as the burial grounds, some dishes and ornaments and weapons. It was apparently featured by considerable trade relations with the outside world, and the Roman provinces, in particular, suggested by large coin findings of the Roman origin. The people lived by settlements and built even some defense places, the *horodyshcha*. The excavations suggested their construction having supposedly taken place between two centuries B.C. and the second century A.D. The territorial extension of that cultural circle, sometimes identified by other names (Cherniakhiv, Zarubin and Korchuvate civilizations), in Ukraine was quite large.[18]

Then, since the seven century foreign historical sources, such as the writings of Hesiodes, Herodotus, Skylitzes, Pliny, Tacitus and others, began to refer to the Slavs, living in the North, somewhere between the littorals of the Baltic and Black Seas, calling them either Antes or Venedes. The Antes attracted the attention of Jordanis, a historian of the Goths, who identified southern Ukraine as their homeland, although according to other sources, their political organization had extended over a much larger area, from the Don River in the East to the upper Oder and Warta Rivers and the eastern parts of Bohemia, sometime in the fifth century of our era. Although not all historians agree as to the ethnic origin of the Antes, still most of them have considered them to be Slavs and the immediate predecessors of those Slavic tribes which a while later merged into and constituted the Ukrainian people of the future.

The Antes (or Antea) lived by small settlements or semi-villages on the banks of rivers and lakes, engaging in fishing, hunting and some farming for subsistence. Their funeral rituals resembled those from the time of the Cherniakhiv civilization. In order to defend themselves against an outside onslaught, several settlements jointly constructed fortresses. Braichevsky inclined to consider the so-called Trajan walls extending for tens of miles along the rivers of Krasna, Stuhna, Ros', Trubezh and Sula, for the Antian defense constructions.

Although the past and the culture of the Antes are not yet adequately researched, still quite a bit can be said about them and their political organization. Apparently their top ruling agent was the *viche*, people's meeting, of a democratic slant where all important matters were jointly decided. At the time of national emergency, they, like the early Romans, used to elect a leader or prince (*rex*), whose authority was fully respected at the time of his tenure. Though the Antes might have been a peace-loving nation, their fortunes were not that peaceful. They had to struggle against the foreign onslaughts of the Goths, Avars, and other invading hordes. Hence, they frequently organized strong political alliances, headed by outstanding leaders to avert the foreign aggressions. For example, "Prince" or "King" Bozh headed a rather large political alliance of the Antian tribes in 380 against Vinithar, a king of the Goths. Bozh lost the war. He, his sons and seventy Antian "elders," chiefs of individual tribes participating in the struggle, were either killed in action or taken prisoners and killed in reprisal. "Prince" Mezamir led a similar alliance in the five hundred-fifties against the Avar onslaught. Other more outstanding Antian leaders were Ardagast and Musoky. Subsequently, the Antes were involved in the wars against Byzantium. At first they only joined in the Byzantine campaigns of the Balkan Slavs, but later on they also undertook war expeditions of their own against Byzantium and its colonies. Jordanis and Procopius related about these joint assaults of the Huns (Bulgars), Slovens and Antes upon the Byzantine empire, which at one time repeated themselves every year.[19]

The political center of the Antian state-like formations was on the banks of the Black Sea. Kluchevskii, a Russian historian, considered the Antian statehoods for tribal associations, while other historians thought that they were simply temporary tribal alliances to resist foreign assaults. Yet, Jordanis, whose assertions cannot be easily dismissed, pointed out that among the Antes a hereditary royal system of government prevailed. Having considered the historical references to such instances as the ability of the Antes to gather the armies consisting of tens of thousands and even one hundred thousand men, to undertake distant war expeditions, as having been led by leaders, whose fame became international, like Bozh, Ardagast and Davrit; whose statehood persisted for almost three centuries, from the end of the fourth to the beginning of the seventh century, until it fell under the impact of the Avar aggression; having been ruled by ''kings'' and people's meetings, supported by substantial military forces; one must agree that their political organization was powerful for that time, resembling the constitutions of the huge West-European federations of the Franks under Charlemagne, of the Burgundians, Vandals and Goths, as Braichevsky asserted.

Hence, in the statehood of the Antes one may look for the political beginnings in Ukraine, the south-eastern corner of the European continent having actually been the very roots of the later Ukrainian-*Rus'* state of the ninth to thirteenth century. The very existence of the state of the Antes from the fourth to the seventh century, having been the first period of Ukrainian history, has proven unmistakably that the Kievan *Rus'* state was then a result of an organic and internal social and political process of the Ukrainian Slavic tribes, which gradually and consistently led to the formation of the Ukrainian nation; that the formation of the Kievan *Rus'* was definitely the product of the Ukrainian political genius, which might have been only aided and enhanced by the influx of foreign organizational, military and cultural elements, like the Norman military retinues in the service of the Kievan princes or the Byzantine spiritual and cultural influences, which affected the Ukrainian spirituality on the foundations laid by the Hellenic influences in course of the centuries of the grey antiquity. These historical facts have flatly denied the old, so-called Normanist theory of the beginning of the *Rus'* state with its capital in Kiev, which will be later on briefly discussed because of its traditional persistence. Braichevsky, an outstanding contemporary Ukrainian historian, put that idea very clearly across by asserting the following: "The Antian political union was an immediate political predecessor of the future *Rus'* state, and there the roots and origins of the old Rus'ian statehood are to be sought. Hence, the history of the old Rus'ian state began not in the middle of the ninth century with the arrival of the Normans, but at least some four or five centuries earlier; not with the mythical Norman colonization but in the sphere of the internal evolution of the eastern Slavs themselves."[20]

The Slavic Tribes of Eastern Europe. The state of the Antes was assaulted by the Avars in the sixth century, and it was fatal for the Antes. Their political organization collapsed. It is unfortunate that there is so little known about this period of Ukrainian history. The Antes came fully under the rule of the Avar overlords in the seventh century, and this was quite oppressive. Subsequently the name "Antes" was replaced by the name "Slavs" to designate those numerous tribes of a common origin who populated the most part of Eastern Europe, westward up to the Oder and Warta Rivers, Carpathian regions, Bohemia, Moravia, Transylvania and a substantial portion of the Balkan Peninsula included, having initiated the formation of various Slavic nationalities of the later date. By the seventh century the seven Slavic tribes of the eastern branch, the Polianians, Siverianians, Dulibians Derevlianians, Khorvatsians, Tiverians and Ulichians, which gave rise to the formation of the Ukrainian nationality, were already firmly settled in Ukraine, and later on only some minor shifts in their respective tribal territories took place. The oldest Ukrainian chronicle, *Povist vremennikh lit,* supposedly authored by monk

Nestor in the twelfth century, enumerated those Ukrainian Slavic tribes and even attempted to identify their territories, though highly inadequately. In order to acquire a more complete ethnic picture of Ukraine at that time, it is necessary to consult also other historical sources, the local ones as well as the foreign.

Hence, on the basis of the acquired historical data, the following distribution of the tribal settlements in Ukraine can be approximately identified: the Polianians, the tribe which played a leading role in the formation of the old Kievan *Rus'* state, lived in the middle Dnieper region, on the river's right banks, approximating the present-day Kievan land, *Kyivshchyna*. On the left bank of the Dnieper River, bordering on the Polianian lands, and in the basins of the Desna and Seim Rivers and other eastern tributories of the Dnieper, east of the Kievan land, the Siverianians settled. At one time a discussion went on among Ukrainian and Russian scholars with respect to the ethnic origin of the Siverianians. Most of the Russian scholars-historians were inclined to include that tribe among the north-eastern group of the Slavic tribes which, subsequently having merged with numerous Ugro-Finnic tribes of the Mongol extraction, built the Muscovite-Russian nationality. However, Hrushevsky proved by his article, ''Some debatable questions in old Rus'ian ethnography,'' published in 1904, that the above assumption was wrong, and that the Siverianians were definitely an Ukrainian tribe.[21] West of the Polianian land, south of the Prypiat River and in between the Horyn River in the west and the Dnieper River in the east, there lived the tribe of the Derevlianians, perhaps the most backward tribe within the south-eastern, Ukrainian tribal group. The tribe of the Dulibians was settled in the region of the upper Buh and Styr Rivers, west of the Derevlianian territory. The Dulibians, according to the chronicle, suffered greatly under the Avar oppression, but they overcame it successfully and at an early date developed on their territory a remarkable political organization, referred to by the Arab travelers as ''Valinana'' state. Later on apparently new names for the Dulibians came into use, applied to their three branches living in various parts of the Volhinia province; the Buzhanians, living on the banks of the Buh River, the Volhinians, settled around the town of Volyn' or Vai, as it was called by foreign visitors, and the Luchanians, who were settled in the region of the town of Luchsk or Lutsk. The Khorvatsians were settled south of the Dulibian territory, in the pre-Carpathian regions, the present-day Galicia. Their ethnic origin, according to the historians, might have been rather unclear. They might have been originally related to the other six south-eastern European Slavic tribes, which had constituted the base for the formation of the Ukrainian nationality. Some thought that the Khorvatsians in question were simply a remnant of a once large Slavic tribe, which subsequently migrated to the South of Europe. One must remember that presently the Croatians or Khorvatsians are a Slavic nation, which today, together with the Serbs, Slovenians, Macedonians and Montenegros, constitute the state of Yugoslavia. Others thought that the Khorvatsians were not a Rus'ian but a Western Slavic tribe.[22] The tribe of the Ulichians was originally settled between the rivers Dnieper and Boh. However, perhaps in the eighth century, probably under the pressure of the steppe nomads, they moved westward, and established themselves between the lower runs of the rivers Boh and Dniester. The Tiverians, the seventh of the Ukrainian tribes, were settled west of the Ulichian territory, between the Dniester and the Pruth Rivers and they reached with their settlements as far as the Black Sea.

Of course, this ethnic picture of Ukraine in the seventh to ninth centuries seems to be incomplete as far as the identification of individual tribal territories is concerned. It leaves a considerable part of Ukraine uncovered as if it was not populated, which can hardly be assumed. Hence, the interpretation of the historical data by various historians has implied that there must have been perhaps some other Ukrainian tribes which were settled in the Donets basin and on the left bank of the Dnieper River, south of the Siverianian tribal territory, or that perhaps the Siverianians populated much larger territory than it was originally assumed. It was assumed that perhaps, whenever the living conditions were more peaceful in the regions close to the Black and Asov Sea steppes, the Siverianians and the Ulichians spread their colonization toward the east and south-east, populating the regions mentioned above, and whenever the steppes became more dangerous, they retreated to the west. The Ulichians having moved from their original settlements to the area between the Boh and Dniester Rivers might have substantiated the theory to some extent. Furthermore, this prehistoric process would have been fully in accord with the over-all historical trend of Ukraine as having been a land of moving frontiers, as it was pointed out before.

The above seven south-eastern, Ukrainian tribes were but only a branch of the Slavic tribes in Eastern Europe. The other two branches were the middle one, the Byelorus'inian branch and the northern one, the Russian branch. Although for a considerable time there was a lack of general consent among the historians as to the point when those three branches were already differentiated ethnically and linguistically, having given rise to the subsequent development of the three East-European nationalities, the Ukrainians, the Byelorus'inians and the Russians, at the present there is but a little doubt about that. The above differentiation began as early as the third century A.D. in the original settlements of the Slavs and it took its definite shape in the seventh century. Recent archeological and historical studies, conducted by two outstanding Russian scholars, Tretiakov, an historian, and Rybakov, an archeologist, bear this out, as was suggested at the earlier date by Hrushevsky, Shakhmatov, Chubaty and others.[23] There have been no historical indications to accept as credible an assumption, once advanced by Russian historiography, that in remote antiquity there existed a common, pre-Rus'inian language for all East-European Slavs, from which supposedly later on three modern Slavic languages, Ukrainian, Byelorus'inian and Russian, developed. It has been proven that it was a political and unscholarly Russian maneuvering only to support the political and imperial ends, at first of St. Petersburg and, then, Moscow.[24]

The tribes of the Dregovichians, settled between the Pripet and Berezina Rivers, the Polotsians, on the banks of the middle West

Dvina, and the western segment of the Krivichians, originally settled at the upper-run of the Dnieper, West Dvina and Volga Rivers, and who were less affected by the Ugro-Finnic influx and impact than other northern Slavs, made up the Byelorus'ian nationality, having been substantially affected by their close neighborhood with the Lithuanian and Latvian tribes in their historical development.

The uppermost northern Slavic tribe of the Slovinians, living on the eastern banks of the Gulf of Finland and further east, towards the banks of the Ladoga Lake and along the Volkhov River, the eastern branch of the Krivichians, the tribe of the Radimichians, settled on the left bank of the Dnieper River, north of the Ukrainian tribe of the Siverianians, and the Viatichians, further north-east from the Siverianian tribal territory, having heavily merged with a score of the Ugro-Finnic tribal communities of the Ves', Iam, Meria, Murom, Meshchera, Mordva and many others, subsequently formed the Russian nationality. According to the chronicle relation, the tribes of the Radimichians and the Viatichians were actually of West-Slavic, Polish origin, supposedly descending from two Polish brothers, Radimko and Viatko, who for some reasons left their original settlements in the West and migrated to the East. Of course, not all Radimichians and Viatichians merged into the Russian nationality. Some branches of theirs joined the formation of the Byelorus'inian people, which has been evident in some Polish linguistic elements in the Byelorus'inian tongue. They certainly escaped the prevailing impact of the Ugro-Finns.

Whenever peace prevailed in the Black and Azov Sea steppes, as it was pointed out, the Ukrainian tribes used to settle and occupy the territories eastward, beyond the Don River, and southward, the littorals of the seas and beyond, the parts of the Kuban. In the ninth century there existed apparently in the western Crimea and on the eastern banks of the Kerch Straight, a strong and influential Rus'ian principality of Tmutorokan with its colonies in the Don basin. It had apparently its own Church organization. It soon collapsed, however, under the sway of the steppe hordes. The Tmutorokan political organization was formed most probably by a Ukrainian tribal branch of the Siverians or another tribe of an unknown origin. An educated guess was made by some historians that a Siverian princely dynasty was ruling in Tmutorokan, where the spiritual and commercial life was quite developed.

The Ukrainian Slavs had organized a commercial center at Oleshia at the lower run of the Dnieper River. There were numerous Ukrainian colonies in the Crimean Peninsula, in the city of Korsun.

1. P. Lyashchenko, *History of the National Economy of Russia*, New York, 1949, pp. 35-36.

2. M. Hrushevsky, *Istoria Ukrainy-Rusy,* New York, 1954, Vol. I, pp. 21-83; also, G. Vernadsky and M. Karpovich, *A History of Russia*, Vol. I, *Ancient Russia*, New Haven-London, 1952, pp. 15 and further.

3. N. Polonska-Vasylenko, *Istoria Ukrainy*, Munich, 1972, Vol. I, pp. 41-49.

4. The cultural social, economic and political levels in the development of any ethnic group represent an accumulation of achievements and experiences of all their preceding generations from earliest times. Every detail is there important, such as how early man arrived in the given area and how early, after having gotten used to the given environment, he began to create new spiritual and material values there; M. Arkas, *Istoria Pivnichnoi Chonomorshchyny,* Toronto, 1969, pp. 17-220.

5. Pre-history: Lyashchenko, *op. cit.,* pp. 17-34; Vernadsky, *op. cit.,* pp. 14-48; Hrushevsky, *loc. cit.;* Arkas, *ibid.;* Ya Pasternak, *Arkheolohia Ukrainy,* 1961; *Istoria Ukrainskoi RSR,* I. Artemenko, ed.-in-chief, Kiev, 1977, Vol. I, pp. 23-120.

6. W. Ferguson and G. Bruun, *A Survey of European Civilization*, Boston, 1958, p. 23.

7. Polonska-Vasylenko, *op. cit.,* Vol. I, pp. 49-55: Tripillian Culture; V. Shcherbakivsky, *Formatsia ukrainskoi natsii*, Prague, 1941, pp. 13-14, 27-31, 40-43; the same, *Kamiana doba v Ukraini*, Munich, 1947.

8. Polonska-Vasylenko, *op. cit.*, Vol. I, pp. 54-56.

9. M. Hrushevsky, "Ethnographic Categories and Cultural-Archeological Groups in Contemporary Studies of Eastern Europe", *On the Historical Beginnings of Eastern Slavic Europe*, ed. by N. Chirovsky, New York, 1976, pp. 39-53.

10. O. Povstenko, *Istoria ukrainskoho mystetstva*, Nuerenberg-Fuerth, 1948, Vol. I, p. 24.

11. M. Rostovtsev, *Yllinstvo i iranstvo na yuge Rossii*, Petrograd, 1918; the same, *Davno-mynule nashoho pivdnia*, Petrograd, 1916; Hrushevsky, *Istoria Ukrainy-Rusy*, 1954, Vol. I, pp. 84-104: on the Greek colonies.

12. Polonska-Vasylenko, *op. cit.*, Vol. I, pp. 57-58; Hrushevsky, *op. cit.*, Vol. I, pp. 107-116.

13. M. Viazmitina, "Sarmaty", *Narysy z starodavnoi istorii URSR*, Kiev, 1957; Polonska-Vasylenko, *op. cit.*, Vol. I, pp. 60-61.

14. Shcherbakivsky, *Formatsia ukrainskoi natsii*, Prague, 1941, pp. 110-112; E. Reischauer and J. Fairbank, *East Asia, the Great Tradition*, Boston, 1960, pp. 94-95.

15. Hrushevsky, *op. cit.*, Vol. I, pp. 227-230, 395-397.

16. Polonska-Vasylenko, *op. cit.*, Vol. I, pp. 65-66.

17. Shcherbakivsky, *op. cit.*, pp. 1-117.

18. M. Braichevsky, "Starodavni skhidni sloviany," *Narysy z starodavnoi istorii URSR*, 1957, pp. 315-327.

19. M. Braichevsky, *Koly i yak vynyk Kyiv*, Kiev, 1963, pp. 132-134; the same, "The Unification of the Old Rus'ian Lands Around the Center of Kyiv", *On the Historical Beginnings of Eastern Slavic Europe*, ed. by N. Chirovsky, New York, 1976, pp. 57-61.

20. *Ibid.*, p. 58.

21. English translation of the article in *On the Historical Beginnings of Eastern Slavic Europe,* as above, pp. 13-38.

22. *Ibid.*, pp. 30-31.

23. N. Chirovsky, *A History of the Russian Empire,* New York, 1973, Vol. I, p. 10, also, N. Chubaty, *Kniazha Rus'-Ukraina ta vyneknennia triokh skhidnioslovianskykh natsii,* New York-Paris, 1964.

24. C. Manning, "The Kremlin's New Theses on Ukraine", *On the Historical Beginnings of Eastern Slavic Europe*, as above, pp. 211-223.

CHAPTER FOUR

THE SOCIAL AND POLITICAL HERITAGE OF THE PREHISTORIC PERIOD

Origin of early political organizations — Social structure — Early economic development — Agriculture — Commerce — Religious beliefs.

Origin of Early Political Organization. Since man is naturally social, the individual knows and feels that he can best develop both spiritually and materially when living together with other human beings as a member of a community. This fact was already recognized and analyzed more than two thousand years ago by Aristotle. However, the forms of social organization have been subject to a continuous evolution which has gone on through the remote centuries of prehistoric and ancient times, eventually culminating in the highest stage of socio-political organization, the state or nation. In primitive times, only instinct and psychic spontaneity were at work producing such communities as the family, the clan, the tribe, or simple tribal, semi-state organizations. Perhaps the ancient states grew out of blood relations and the patriarchal principle. Later, when civilized men began to analyze the significance of socio-political associations, states were thought to originate by social contract. The conscious building of political organizations by social agreements does not rule out the spontaneous establishment of social groups. The state is rather a culmination of rational as well as intuitive comprehension by the mind of man of the need of individuals to live and grow within the framework of an orderly arranged society. It must be stressed, however, that neither the state nor any other form of social organization is an end in itself, but rather the means toward realizing its prime objective, the most effective development and growth of the individual personality. If one applied the obverse philosophy and regarded the State as an end in itself, the road to totalitarianism would be already paved.

The Ukrainian Slavs, like other races and peoples at their primitive and prehistorical stages of national development, instinctively and spontaneously aimed to form social organizations and quasi-state organisms. The idea of a social contract to create a state appeared very early among the Eastern Slavs. The chronicles of the time tell of an invitation extended to the Norsemen by the Slovenians, asking them to rule over the Slovenian lands.[1] The arrival of Askold and Dir at Kiev may also suggest the possibility of a social contract in the growth of the old Kievan empire. Later on, at the time of a higher level of the social and cultural evolution of the Ukrainian people, there were no traces of any totalitarian trends, such as despotism, absolutism, or dictatorship. Thus, the ancient political organizations of the Ukrainians in the eighth and ninth centuries emerged, originating as they did from the family and blood relationships. Nevertheless, reminiscences of the distant past existence of the strong state formations of the Scythians, Roxolianians, Iazygians, Sarmatians, and Goths in Ukrainian territories in the remote prehistoric age, indirectly contributed to the desire of the Ukrainian Slavs to have a state organization of their own. Moreover, the experiences of hardships they suffered under the Avar and Magyar rule extremely intensified that desire.

Originally, the entire organized life of the ancient Ukrainians developed merely in the form of a self-sufficient household economy, and from that original cell of human organization, the growth of the Ukrainian nation began. The very ancient Ukrainian family, at the Tripillian era might have been founded on the matriarchal principle, where the mother was the center of the family and enjoyed their respect and authority. This resulted in the monogamous marriage and the relatively high morality of the sexual life of the Ukrainian Slavs later on. Polygamy prevailed among the Polianians. Later the matriarchal principle was replaced by the patriarchal family constitution, so that in the earliest Ukrainian legal codification, *Rus'ka Pravda,* the latter alone prevailed. The reminiscence of the old matriarchial system survived probably in the elevated position of Ukrainian women in the family and society under the Kievan empire, and afterwards, throughout the centuries up to the present day. This high social position of women in Ukraine directly contrasted to their status in Muscovy-Russia and Poland.[2] On the eve of the historical period, the Ukrainian family was already patriarchal, for the father had extensive authority, especially with respect to managing the communal efforts to provide subsistence. The family was a most natural form of cooperation toward common survival, as based on blood relation. The prevailing severity of the environment necessitated, on the other hand, a strong patriarchal rule. The eldest of the family regulated social life within the household, organized economic activities, and also acted as judge in family quarrels. His position in the family, however, was never as absolute and despotic as among the other peoples. The elevated position of mother and wife in the family, the rather democratic constitution of clan and *verv,* and the inborn Ukrainian individualism prevented the ''paterfamilias'' from becoming a despot.

Out of the ancient family there developed the clan system, which, still having been to some extent agnatic, can doubtlessly be regarded as a surrogate of the later state organization and as a further step in that direction. The clan, especially, in the final development of its constitution, profoundly influenced the permanent settlements of the Ukrainian Slavs. The clan settled down regularly in a compact way, and gave rise to the old Ukrainian village. Clan villages were communities of collectively organized labor, production, dwelling, and consumption. Clan communities owned pasture lands, woods, beehives, and fisheries, and collectively raised cattle, cultivated soil, and participated in trading, which was a very important occupation especially among Polianians, who became the most civilized and most powerful among the Ukrainian tribes and actually initiated the building of the Kievan Empire. The clan was governed and regulated by a chieftain, called *starosta* (the eldest). His authority, however, was neither despotic nor unlimited. There existed a clan council, composed of all family heads, which retained a supervisory power and restricted the authority of the chieftain in many respects. Although the power of the council was often more comprehensive than that of the chieftain, practically speaking, the personality of the latter was usually the deciding factor, since it largely determined the extent of his real authority. The economic constitution of the clan was communal, as pointed out, but not communistic, in the modern sense of that term. The clan owned properties, but its members could not own property, so that there was no institution of inheritance. But at the same time, pauperization of individuals was impossible, since a clan as a whole took a moral and material care of all its members, protecting them against any misfortunes. The clan constitution was predetermined by environment. It was hard for the individual to survive in the virgin woods or vast steppes. Even a small family was not able to survive. Therefore, the ancient Ukrainians lived in their clans numbering as many as fifty or sixty persons. Dwellings and farms of the clan were often fortified for protection against all kinds of human and animal enemies, and were called *dvorishche* in the old Slavonic language. Of course, not all clans enjoyed the same social and economic status; there were poor and insignificant clans, as well as wealthy and powerful ones. This difference was determined by the size of the clan, its collective initiative and effort, and the leadership of its chieftain and council. By and large, the clan performed in miniature all the functions of the state: protection, defense, social care, and regulation of the communal economy. And above all, the clan was a community of production and consumption. But by the eleventh century, the clan organization completely disintegrated under the impact of growing individualism.

Several reasons contributed to the disintegration of the clan. First, the inborn Ukrainian individualism asserted itself persistently with only slight changes to conform to new environmental factors. Thus new forms of cooperation were found to replace compulsory collective institutions based upon blood relationships. Secondly, flourishing trading activities and growing wealth made each participant think more independently as he came into contact with foreign cultures. Moreover, commerce and trade, requiring a great deal of individual initiative, did not fit into collectivism. Furthermore, in the tenth and eleventh centuries, the powerful Kievan state organization already existed to solve the problem of collective security formerly left to the clans. Once they no longer required clan protection the individualistic Ukrainians took full advantage of the newly formed state to repudiate the clan restrictions. Finally, when outside pressures diminished somewhat, there was no great need for clan life in the fortified *dvorishche*.

In the prehistoric period of the socio-political evolution of the Ukrainian people, the clans had formed a number of tribes by the process of confederation; and in the political framework of the Kievan Empire, the tribes melted down into the Ukrainian nation, while the clans disintegrated and disappeared. The chronicles named, as pointed out, seven Ukrainian Slavic tribes: the Polianians, Derevlianians, Dulibians, Khorvatians, Siverianians, Ulichians, and Tiverians. The individual tribes had soon developed their own political organizations — the tribal states. On the eve of the historical period, tribal communities were no longer based on any blood relation, although in a few cases there were among them the memory of a famous ancestor and common origin. Tribes were rather territorial and ethnic groupings. They differed among themselves in customs, way of life, and religious beliefs.[3] Ethnically the seven tribes were rather similar. Geographical conditions and natural environment formed separate tribes as specific communities of interest. The individual tribal interests originated, of course, specific tribal economies. Accordingly, the Polianians developed agriculture and trading; the Derevlianians and Dulibians, forest economy; and the Ulichians and Tiverians, cattle and horse raising, because of the closeness of the steppes. The topography of the tribal lands was a very important element in determining the individual tribal traits and characteristics, their customs, and their principal occupations, and largely contributed to the origination of the first tribal political organizations. Later on, however, under the impact of the unifying power of the central government of Kiev, those differences were reduced, but in some distant geographical areas of Ukraine, like the Carpathian Mountain provinces, the individualities of the old tribal traditions were retained until the second half of the twentieth century.

The first state-like political organizations were created by the separate tribes along tribal principles. Neither strong nor durable, only a few of these tribal states gained any degree of power. The chief, elected to his office, was at first called "thousander," *tysiatsky*, then prince. His political position became stronger and more lasting through the gradual adoption of the principle of heredity. But some references in the old chronicles imply that sovereign rights were still vested in the people, who could confirm or expel their princes. There was no tradition of absolutist forms of government among the ancient Ukrainians.

The prince ruled with the advice and consent of the peoples' meeting, a body composed of all free and adult males of the tribe, summoned to consultation at regular intervals, or whenever it was necessary or expedient. This body considerably limited the power and authority of the princes, but here again the personality of the prince usually was the deciding factor in the division of authority between the two sources of political power. In only a few cases did the prince succeed in reducing the authority of the peoples' meeting to any considerable degree.

These peoples' meetings were, according to Beztuzhev-

Riumin, the core of the democratic rule of the old Slavic tribes. The meeting was composed of the eldest of the tribe. Usually the tribal princes called the meetings to decide some important question, but there is ample evidence of meetings without dukes, called to order in special cases, mostly to oppose the duke or even to organize action against him, to expel or even to kill him, and then to introduce a new one. The sovereignty of the people and the spirit of democracy were here distinctly evident still in the historical times.

The origin of the institution of the above tribal dukes is historically not clear. The chronicles mention various tribal rulers, like Kyi, Shchek, and Khoryv among the Polianians, and state that the Derevlianians had their own dukes, as Mal, for example, as also the Dregovichians and Slovinians (Hipatian Chronicle). The ancient documents, however, do not indicate anything about the origins and character of these tribal rulers, whether they were hereditary or electoral.[4]

A fortified town served as the political and economic center of the tribal state structure, and the capital of its territorial administration. The territorial administrative units were called *vervy*. Historical documents name numerous "towns" in Ukraine in the ninth and tenth centuries, such as Cherven, Peremyshl, Volyn, Lubetch, Terebovla, Peresechen, Turiv, Kiev, Peryaslav, and many others, the majority of which must have been capitals of some kind of political organisms in the remote prehistoric era. Ancheological studies implied the existence of about a thousand such fortified "towns" at various periods prior to the organization of the Kievan realm in the ninth century. These towns indicate, of course, the relatively advanced development of architecture and construction among the ancient Ukrainian Slavs. The new administrative unit of the *verv* probably developed in the interest of efficiency when the tribal-state organization was still composed of clans. A *verv* was formed strictly according to territorial and geographical principles and without any reference to blood relation or common ancestry. After the disintegration of the clan system, its importance increased considerably. Expediency produced the *verv* organization. The council of the elders of the particular *verv* territory seemed to carry the most weight. The *verv* community had actually two main responsibilities: to provide the people with protection, and to collect tribute payments and service owed to the tribal prince or other rulers.

Already in the early period, the political evolution of the Ukrainians progressed to the point of large-scale, if temporary political formations. These state formations grew beyond the limit of the tribe, and were developed strictly according to geographical factors and political expedience. Masudi reported that in the ninth century there existed a strong, semi-political and semi-military federation in the area of present day Volhinia (West Ukraine), which he called *Valinana*. The name may resemble the modern terminology and may be simply an Arabic distortion of the original Slavic name. The Valinana federation was ruled by the Dulibian dukes and it was formed, probably, for the purpose of overthrowing foreign rule and providing a more adequate defense against the hostile tribes. The historical documents of the sixth century reported a most intolerably harsh Avar rule over the Dulibian tribe. The suffering of the Dulibians might have taught them how to build a strong political organization of their own, in order to defend and to preserve their freedom. They might have been exposed also to attacks of the Moravians, who succeeded in the eighth century in establishing a powerful empire, and who certainly dominated some western borderlands of Ukraine. In this way they became the political neighbors of the Dulibians. Their relationship must not have been very pleasant and peaceful for the Dulibians, who then created a federation for mutual defense. Territorially, *Valinana,* or Volhinia, extended far beyond the tribal limits of the Dulibians and covered, at least, a major part of East Galicia. The western Galician areas were under Moravian rule. Ibn Dasta, another Arabian traveler-merchant, relates of a Slavic city *V-a-i,* situated about a ten days' journey from the Hungarian borders. This reference might have pertained to the city of Volyn, the probable capital of the Dulibian federation.

Another large political federation, also in Western Ukraine, was known under the name of the "Red-Towns," *Chervenski-Horody*. The Red-Towns area was for a long time the major political issue, and a continuous source of quarrels between the Ukrainians and the Poles. Also, the Derevlianians succeeded in creating a strong political organization, which later caused much trouble for the Kievan duke Ihor (Igor) and his wife, Duchess Olha (Olga, Helga), when they tried to establish Kievan supremacy to lay the foundations for the Kievan Empire. The Derevlianians' duke, Mal, was singled out by the chronicles for his stubborn opposition to Kiev. No doubt, the Polianians also had a relatively strong state organization reinforced by their commercial wealth and higher civilization, before the Kievan Empire had been formed. The beginnings of the political organization of the Polianians were associated by the chronicles with the name of Kyi, the mythical founder of Kiev, and his two brothers, Shchek and Khoryv, and their sister, Lebed. Archeological studies revealed, however, a very ancient origin of Kiev, long before the Slavic era in Ukraine, and perhaps at the time of the Gothic settlements in the third century A.D.[5] Kyi, Shchek, and Khoryv were probably the most outstanding among the Polianian rulers. Or perhaps they gained their fame by rebuilding the city after its destruction, or after some historical cataclysm. Although the older historiography regarded those names and the entire story about the foundation of Kiev, given by the chronicles, as legendary, today they are considered reminiscent of true and factual developments.

Prince Kyi most probably was the founder of the rather influential dynasty of the Polianian tribe, which, according to Rybakov, must have originated in the sixth century, Kyi himself having been possibly a contemporary of the Byzantine emperor Justinian. There are some references in the chronicle compilations of a later date to Kyi's military expeditions against Byzantium and Volga Bulgars, and to his assumed founding of the town of Kievets on the Danube River. Kyi's dynasty might have ruled for some two and a half centuries in the Polianian principality, of which, however, there are no written historical relations. The last descendants of the dynasty might have been the two, already well known by historical sources, princes of Kiev, Askold and Dir, although the *Povist' vremennykh lit* referred to them as Normans. Kyi must have waged some warfare with some other Ukrainian tribes, and with the tribe of the Derevlianians.

Apparently, after Kyi's death, the Polianian principality, along with other tribal lands in Ukraine, was dominated by the Khozars.

The Arab writers of the tenth and twelfth centuries, having written about the past, made several references to three political centers of *Rus'*, Kuiaba, Slavia and Arsania. Kuiaba might have been the distorted name of Kiev; Slavia might truly have referred to Novgorod the Great in the land of the Slovinians; and Arsania was most probably identifying Tmutorokan at the mouth of the Kuban River. There have been, however, other attempts of interpreting those relates by Istarkhi, Ibn-Hawqual and Idrisi.[6]

All these historical references, as Braichevsky asserted, have doubtlessly reflected the long process of political consolidation of the Ukrainian Slavs, which was steadily taking place long before the Normans, under the name of the Varangians, appeared in the land of the Polianians, and organically led to its culmination point in the form of the Kievan *Rus'* state in Ukraine, the southeastern corner of the European continent.

Political life in the ancient tribal state organizations was neither peaceful nor quiet. First of all, hostile foreigners constantly harassed the ancestors of the modern Ukrainians. The chronicles and other historical documents supply abundant information about the Khozars, Avars, and other neighboring peoples, who extended their rule over the Slavic territories. The Slavs had to pay a heavy tribute to the Khozars, a Turkish people. They soon tried to rid themselves of foreign domination and its heavy economic burden. On the other hand, within the autonomous Slavic tribes a continuous struggle for power was going on. Especially strong was the struggle between monarchic principles, represented by the princes, and democratic and parliamentary democratic principles, represented by the people. The tribal chiefs, or the Norman outsiders, because they frequently sought to seize an absolutist rule, were frequently expelled by the people. The echo of these developments was distinctly marked in the chronicles, when the *Povist' vremennykh lit* related the previously mentioned event of the expulsion of the intruders by the Slovinians. Then the Slovinians began to rule themselves, but proved unable to maintain order. Consequently, they invited the Normans to return and resume their rule. Analogical developments of expulsion of dukes by noblemen and people occurred often in medieval Ukraine whenever these dukes exhibited any despotic tendencies. These historical events are indicative of the traditional hatred of arbitrary rule by the ancient and medieval Ukrainians, a trait which still characterizes their descendants.

Social Structure. The ancient, prehistoric man felt his full and complete dependence upon nature and natural elements, and was acutely conscious of their power and his own weakness. Natural forces were actually the model and framework according to which the primitive man formed his way of life. Kept in constant contact with the natural phenomena which predetermined his physical and social existence, the ancient human being, when he only began to think and to perceive reality, saw over all in his environment differentiation and inequality. Accordingly, he also began to differentiate his social position. Anybody who succeeded in gaining more power or prestige in some way, either because of his physical strength, skill, or mind, or by accumulated wealth, at once attempted to dominate the weaker, or at least gain an elevated social and political status.

Social differentiation had its deep psychological motivation; therefore it was deeply rooted in the human social constitution. The typical man is self-centered and egoistic, at least to a certain extent. He usually thinks better of himself, and he likes to be better than and different from others. Consequently, he tends to take advantage of every available opportunity to place himself above others, or at least differently from others. These two powerful factors, man's own psychology and the physical environment, originated social differentiation and the evolution of social classes among the most primitive and also civilized societies. Moreover, the more primitive the civilization level of given societies seemed to be, the more drastic and sharp their social differentiation and stratification tended to develop, as the result of their lack of understanding of the dignity of man as an image of God, and of the original plans of God. Spiritual and mental degeneration and deterioration also produced sharp social stratifications. Social studies have recognized two principal forms or types of social differentiation: caste stratification and class differentiation. A caste society is constituted by a very rigid stratification into a number of exclusive and tightly closed and separate segments (castes), where each and every caste has different legal status and position in the entire social structure, different rights and obligations. A transition from one caste to another, either upward or downward, is almost impossible. The caste system is frequently based on religious beliefs; it is strictly hereditary and is deeply permeated by the principle of blood relationship and blood differentiation. The old Hindu caste system of the Brahmins and the ancient Egyptian society would be distinct examples of such a social constitution. A class society, on the other hand, is a more liberal social differentiation, without any religious notion forming its basis. Medieval Europe can serve here as an example, with its four distinct and separate classes of the nobility, the clergy, the townspeople, and the peasantry. The true origin of class stratification was rather the old professional and economic differentiation of ancient society rather than any principle of blood relation. Later developments, however, brought on the element of blood relation, and differentiated legal status of individual classes, as well. The transition from one class to another was not always easy, but at least possible. As a matter of fact, in the majority of cases, a West European class society was featured by dynamic changes in the composition of its individual classes, by which some members of the upper classes were reduced to a lower status, and at the same time, the newcomers from the lower strata were raised to the ranks of the nobility or gentry.

The social structure of medieval Ukrainian society was analogous to that of Western Europe, although it was still much more liberal and much less rigid. Mobility from one class to another was not at all difficult. Even the transition from the status of a slave to that of a free man was relatively easy. This might indicate a relatively high cultural level in the pre-Kievan and Kievan society of the Ukrainians. The oldest social stratification of the Ukrainian Slavs distinguished actually only two principal classes: the free people and the slaves. The free enjoyed the fullness of the legal and economic status of the clan or tribe citizenship, being endowed with all the civil and political rights. They owned properties, either individually, after disintegration of the clan system, or collectively, through their being fully privileged members of the clan community. According to Kluchevskii's historical interpretation, the differentiation into free and unfree came in Ukraine as a result of conquest and war. By and large, the free were the Slavic conquerors, the unfree were the original non-Slav inhabitants of Ukraine, made slaves by the law and custom of the conquering newcomers. Then, the wars among the individual Slavic tribes added the Slavic element to the slave class in the form of prisoners of war. Originally, the defeated and the prisoners were killed by the conqueror. Later on, however, when their value as labor force was recognized, their lives were spared, but socially all rights were denied to them as punishment for their resistance and opposition. Along with their possessions and wealth, the vanquished were deprived of their freedom.

It seems, however, that the Slavic conquerors were socially differentiated already before their arrival in Ukraine. There were among them wealthier and poorer elements. At that time, during which the economics of primitive man prevailed — hunting, fishing, and cattle raising — the surest way to acquire wealth and recognition was by trading and mercantile activities. Thus, merchants among the ancient Ukrainian Slavs soon became the monied people, who also enjoyed a high social status because of their economic power. A class of wealthy merchants appeared very early among the Ukrainian Slavs, especially among the Polianians and Siverianians. Those merchants of necessity had to become warriors, since they had to defend their goods and their wealth against all kinds of enemies at home, as well as on their travels to commercial centers.[7] After the migration and the final settlement of the Eastern Slavs in Ukraine, these powerful merchant-warriors probably took from the original population the majority of their territory by armed force, thereby considerably increasing their own wealth. There is, however, some historical evidence which leads us to assume that some of the more prominent persons among the conquered tribes soon managed to improve their position and join the upper class of the wealthy. Hence, their wealth, including the acquired landed properties, and their warrior capacity made those merchant-warriors a retinue or *druzhina* (guard or guard-team) of the dukes. Already in prehistoric times, some kind of early aristocracy emerged from these, characterized by higher social status, greater economic power, and high political position. The old legend of the chronicles about the three brothers, Kyi, Shchek, and Khoryv, who built and operated a ferry on the River Dneiper, gained recognition, accumulated wealth, and then were assumingly elected to be the rulers of the Polianians, seems to indicate clearly the commercial background and economic motivation of the early class differentiation among the Ukrainian Slavs. Perhaps even the princes were chosen from the ranks of the wealthy merchants.

Thus, there were basically three social classes among the ancient Ukrainian Slavs, and there are convincing indications that the social cleavage among them was considerable, although not insurmountable. The wealthy upper classes of the land owners and merchants, because of their riches, acquired certain conceptions of superiority and did not like to intermingle with the common people. The criterion of freedom distinguished the common people from the slaves, and was sufficient enough to separate these two classes. Racially and nationally, the old Slavic nobility was not homogeneous, and especially later, the princely retinue, *druzhina* was a real melting pot of the Slavic, Allan, Antic, and Scandinavian ethnic elements. Thus it was not the national, but rather the economic and social status that determined the issue of social stratification. Slavic elements, as has been pointed out, not only joined the upper class, but were also among the slaves, as a consequence of intertribal conflict or crimes. On the other hand, a common man could become a grandee by acquiring riches or by performing a heroic deed, while a slave could gain freedom. It seems that already in the prehistoric age some forms of slave liberation existed and that these forms were more developed only later on under the impact of Christianity, and therefore made more numerous and more dignified.

Early Economic Development. The early economic development of the Ukrainian Slavs was a process of evolution from the most primitive to one of the more advanced forms of production and distribution. When the Slavs came to Ukraine they were nomadic barbarians engaged in a hunting and fishing economy.[8] The flora and fauna of the area afforded the newcomers excellent opportunity for abundant hunting and fishing and for rapid progress toward the pastoral and agricultural economies. This does not mean that during the hunting and fishing periods, the Ukrainian Slavs did not engage in other occupations. As archaeological excavations have disclosed, they traded extensively. However, hunting and fishing were their principal activities and the basis of their economy. Since such a food-gathering economy required about one square mile of land for each mouth to feed, it was capable of supporting only a relatively small population.

Originally the Ukrainian northern forest regions and southern steppes were ideally suited to this way of life. They contained numerous animals which provided meat and skins, rivers and lakes full of all kinds of fish, and useful plants of many varieties. The chronicles and other written reports of this early period support archaeological findings that prove the existence at the time of large numbers of wild animals such as ureoxes, bears, leopards, wolves, foxes, deer, lynxes, elks, martens, beavers, otters, cattle, wild horses, and wild goats in Ukraine. Rivers and lakes contained a great variety of fish, including sturgeon, sheathfish, crucion pike and carp, all of which contributed in large measure to the diet and trade of the people. From hunting and fishing, the ancient Ukrainians derived their basic means of subsistence, as well as skins and furs for clothing against the severe winter. Furs, obtained through hunting and trapping, were also an important article of trade and the means of paying taxes even in remote times.

How profoundly important furs were for the early people can be seen from the early use of fur as a kind of commodity-money for the limited exchange among the eastern Slavic tribes.[9] More specifically, marten skins were widely used as a medium of exchange and as a means of paying debts. Later on, at the time of the Kievan Empire, when metallic money had come into use, one of the basic monetary units was called "marten," as a reminiscence of the older tradition. This tradition was not exceptional since it was common for the members of a primitive society to select a certain basic commodity, produced by their economy, as a measure of value and wealth and as a generally acceptable medium of exchange, and to make it their substitute for money. Furthermore, furs were the major commodity used for paying tributes and other tax-like contributions either to invaders and conquerors or to the Slavic rulers themselves.

Hunting, trapping, and fishing were carried on within the framework of the self-sufficient household economy of the clan, and initially, on a collective basis without any particular division of labor, although they remained the primary masculine occupations. Hunting was performed by pursuing animals either on foot or horseback, by extending huge nets among the trees, or, frequently, by placing traps to bar the animals' escape. Birds were caught by means of small nets and snares. The first form of division of labor was arranged according to sex. Women spun and wove cloth, while men tailored the clothes and twisted ropes for nets that were extensively used in hunting, trapping, and of course, fishing. Initially, there was little distinction in the type of work performed by freemen and slaves. Perhaps slaves did only more menial labor, such as taking care of the scanty livestock, twisting ropes, making nets, and performing repair work around the household, while the free men did actual hunting, trapping, and fishing, some major jobs in the household, as well as some trading. Probably a limited amount of farming was also done by the slaves. As long as the collectivism of the clan system prevailed, hunting was performed on communally owned areas, and fishing on communally controlled rivers and lakes, or on unclaimed land as long as it was still available. However, even after the clan organization disintegrated, hunting and fishing rights still continued for a long time to be the communal property of every village population.

In time, with the increase of the density of the population, and the parallel decline in reserves of animals, birds, and fishes as free gifts of nature, a cattle raising economy came into being among the Ukrainian Slavs. Wild animals, such as cows, oxen, horses, hogs, and goats were caught, tamed, and domesticated. The animals were at first raised to supply food, meat, milk and milk products, and some raw materials like horns and skins. Even horses were originally raised for food until their value as draft animals and for military purposes was recognized and exploited. With the growing significance of cattle-raising the Ukrainian economy moved toward the pastoral stage, which, however, never gained so great a degree of economic predominance in Ukraine as among the Oriental peoples.

At any rate, animal husbandry became a distinct and important profession, divided into several classes, probably differentiated even in their social status, according to the types of animals produced. Horse-breeding developed partially as a result of domesticating wild horses called *tarpans*, but more generally from horse trading and the importation of horses from Asia.

This importation came about through the exchange with the Khozars, Cumans, and other steppe people, who maintained extensive commercial relations with the Central Asiatic markets, and were also excellent horse breeders. Horse-breeding and cattle-raising, according to Kulisher, were practiced in Ukraine since the earliest prehistoric era.[10] The vital importance of these industries is well illustrated by a passage in the writings of Emperor Constantine Porphyrogenitus, when he says: ''Rus' en-

deavors to keep peace with the Cumans, because it receives livestock, horses, and sheep from them, and this enables Rus' to live
better and more conveniently."[11] The economic significance of
the early Slavic trading is also clearly indicated here.

Another important branch of early Slavic business was bee-
keeping for honey and wax, especially in the forest areas of
Ukraine. Honey was served as an almost daily meal, and wax
was used to make candles. Both articles became important export
items, imported especially by Byzantium. Because of the importance of honey and wax production, early customs became established laws that afforded strict protection to the property rights to
the beehives of the clans, and, later, of the individuals. Since
immemorial time, furs, honey, wax and slaves were the most
important parts of the Ukrainian economy, and were synonymous
with wealth and opulence.

Separate crafts were developing out of the somewhat
specialized production of homes, home appliances, and tools for
hunting, trapping, and fishing within the framework of the family
household. Among the most important crafts, which eventually
experienced their first full growth in the Kievan Empire, were
weaving, spinning, the production of linen from flax and hemp,
procurement of garments as early tailoring, making hunting and
fishing nets, carpentry, tanning, and pottery ceramics. The tanning craft was well developed even prior to the Kievan period, as
was clearly indicated in the story of a tanner, Kuzhumiaka, who
saved his city from a dragon and from the Cumans. Tanners
probably enjoyed much social esteem. In the forest areas, still
another trade developed, namely the lumber industry, and in
connection with it, the production of tar and potash. All home
appliances and tools were produced by various groups of early
craftsmen from wood also. The crafts were still clumsy and inefficient during the prehistoric times, but progress had been
achieved by the ninth and tenth centuries. The craftsmen were
gradually concentrating in the early villages and towns, the latter
becoming a new class of townspeople. which differed from the
peasants in the matter of specialization. It seems to be quite

certain that the skilled trades were first brought into Ukraine by the Iranian and Arabic craftsmen. Then, in the later centuries, the Iranian and Arabic masters and the Oriental patterns were replaced by the Greeks and Germans and their trade skills.

Finally, some metallurgy, primarily the iron industry, was also developed although to a very limited degree. Iron ore was extracted in the northern areas of Ukraine as early as the era of the Antes, while the Polianians and Derevlianians continued the traditions of mining and processing of the ore, chiefly for military purposes. Primitive foundries existed in the tribal territories of the Polianians, Derevlianians, and the Siverianians, already in the eighth and ninth centuries. Along with the extraction and processing of iron ore, the craft of blacksmithing and weapon production emerged very early in Ukraine. In the western areas of Ukraine, the later Galicia, salt mining was an important industry, but the eastern Ukrainian provinces had to rely largely on the importation of salt from the Crimean Peninsula and the Don-Volga area.

Agriculture. During the pastoral age agriculture was already developing on a limited scale, but because of its secondary character it was left largely to women and slaves. Nevertheless, as a result of a gradual economic evolution of the Ukrainian Slavs, agriculture finally superseded cattle raising by the time of Ukraine's appearance upon the European historical scene. Some authors consider a developed agricultural economy to have been the primary occupation and the basis of the national wealth in some later period of the Kievan supremacy, possibly in the twelfth or even the thirteenth century, but linguistic studies of the old Slavic language in Ukraine, as well as archaeological excavations afford irrefutable proof of an ancient tradition of farming among the Ukrainians. Since remote times rye, wheat, oats, barley, millet, and spelt were cultivated as food for people and domestic animals. Buckwheat came into use sometime later.

Even the primitive agricultural period represented great progress in the production, consumption, and standard of living of the old Ukrainians, compared to the previous economy of hunting, fishing, and cattle-raising. The cultivation of orchards was widely prevalent as early as the Iranian era. The production of apples and cherries was especially widespread. Foreign travelers reported the existence of numerous orchards and great quantities of fruit in this area.[12] There was, however, little gardening and vegetable production; it was not until the time of the Kievan Empire that an extensive vegetable cultivation came into being and became an important branch of farming.

Farming was practiced by way of large and small landed estates operated on the basis of private ownership and control. There is no valid reason to attribute any collective agricultural system to the ancient Ukrainian Slavs, since agriculture developed as one of their leading industries only after the disintegration of the communal clan constitution. This development, however, produced a labor problem, first, because collective cultivation was out of the question, and secondly, because farming was a much more intensive way of production than cattle-raising, requiring much more labor. The individual household could not supply the needed manpower, especially when the latifundia system began to emerge. Hence, the growing use and increasing importance of slavery in the agricultural economy came about as a direct result of these developments.

Farming methods were primitive. At first, only freely available soil was used, for the elimination of the forests was not yet necessary. At that time fertilizer was unknown. Later, when the decreasing availability of free land for cultivation paralleled a rapid increase in population, deforestation was made necessary. Woods were burnt to make way for farmland. Experience proved that the resultant ashes when plowed into the soil, made an excellent fertilizer. Animal manure came into use much later.

There was initially no rationality in the utilization of the fields; neither field rotation nor crop rotation was practiced. After two or three years' cultivation, the given area was left to lie fallow for an indefinite time, or a quest for new land was made. This system, called *pereloh* in Ukrainian, was both extensive and inefficient. But as long as land was abundant it sufficed. Under the pressure of a growing demand for food caused by population increases, it became necessary to adopt the systematic two- and three-field rotation of crops.

In the wooded areas, when the lands were left without cultivation for several years, certain patches were again covered, as Vernadsky said, with a new growth of bushes and young trees which were burned anew to fertilize again the soil for growing crops for the next year or two. In the steppes a similar method was used; that is, leaving once plowed and cultivated plots to lie fallow and to become covered with grass and other steppe growth while other areas were farmed.

In cultivating the soil, the Slavs used the simple method of breaking up the land with a hoe or other primitive tools made from wood or stone. The work was done by the men, principally by the slaves. Very early, however, a wooden plow was introduced, at first pulled by men, later by horses or oxen. The wooden plow was a traditional agricultural tool of the ancient Scythians. Among the primitive implements used in farming were, first of all, wooden tools, like a wooden harrow, rake, shovel, flail, and fork; thereafter, a shovel with an iron blade, a scythe, a sickle, and an iron fork came into use, but probably not before the historical era. The productivity of this simple type of agricultural economy was obviously low, since the wooden implements did a poor job in plowing and cultivating.

With the transition of the Slavic economy from the pastoral stage to the agricultural, the Ukrainian village emerged. Originally the clans lived on their farms isolated from each other. With the growth of the population, the married children could no longer remain with the clan, and were compelled to build their own homesteads, consisting of dwellings, shelters for domestic animals, and primitive barns for storage. These homesteads of the blood-related clans were arranged close to each other, yet outside the old clan bounds. Thus the primitive Ukrainian village emerged as a number of individual households. Later on, ''strangers'' also came to the village, and after a period of adjustment, were accepted into the community with full rights and privileges.

With the passing of time and the amalgamation of more strangers, the ancient village became exclusively an administrative and organizational unit within the framework of the *verv,* losing its tradition of a blood-related community.

The development of the Ukrainian village was preconditioned by the severity and uncertainty of the environment. People preferred to live close together in order to increase their security, to defend themselves more effectively against such dangers as thieves, robbers, and enemies, and to protect themselves and their cattle from wolves, bears, and lynxes. Originally the villages were built without any plan. Soon three leading forms of villages developed: the group village, the one-street-village, and the chain village. The group villages were very populous and were somewhat irregularly built, with many streets running in all directions and with houses arranged centrally and close to each other. This was the oldest and most popular type. The one-street village was the most regular form of settlement; it was found primarily in the northern areas. Homes were built on both sides of a solitary street and immediately behind them extended fields and meadows. The chain-village was the latest type of Ukrainian settlement from the thirteenth and fourteenth centuries and was the out-growth of the traditions of the Magdeburg law and German colonization. It developed along a main street, but less regularly than the one-street village, with some side roads, and with the homesteads located at various distances from the main street. The village became the center of the agricultural economy of the Ukrainian people.

Commerce. Those villages which, because of their proximity to ancient pagan places of worship or to the fortified residences of tribal dukes, afforded opportunities for mass meetings and business transactions, soon developed into the early trading centers in the form of towns. The areas surrounding the ducal residences were especially conducive to the growth of towns, since the dukes could guarantee protection and safety. Their castles were usually constructed in almost inaccessible places, or on the trading routes, to secure for the dukes themselves either easy defense or profitable business, or both.[13] Among the most ancient towns in Ukraine, as it was pointed out previously, were Kiev, Iskorosen, Turiv, Pereschen, Volyn, Pereyaslav, Cherven, and many others, which from their beginnings as fortified places, soon developed into substantial commercial centers. Not infrequently the dukes themselves established new towns either at the crossroads of commercial routes or elsewhere for defense as was indicated by the *Lavrentivska Litopys'*, for example.

At first there was literally no difference between the mode of life of the village and of the town. The countryside peasants engaged in some trading, aside from their farming and cattle raising, and the townspeople cultivated the soil and bred cattle, aside from their trading. But the growing specialization required by the expanding market and growing density of population, finally brought on a clear-cut difference between the village and the town. This growth of the town was initiated and accomplished among the Polianians and Siverianians sooner than among any other Ukrainian tribe.

Politically, the growth of towns resulted in the increasing importance of people's meetings, which in many cases became much more powerful than the tribal princes, and decided the leading problems of their tribes and territories, sometimes completely ignoring the princes. It seems, therefore, that the development of towns and commercial activities contributed to the growth of the democratic constitution of the ancient Ukrainian tribes, which was, however, a little weakened in the Kievan era. As a matter of fact, when commerce evolved among the Ukrainian Slavs in the most distant prehistorical period, it was conditioned primarily by the geographic topography. First of all, the geographic differences of the northern forest and the southern steppe areas necessitated exchange and commercial trading between the two parts of the country. Secondly, the growing production specialization of the village and of the town demanded reciprocal exchange. And finally, the location of Ukraine at the crossroads of the major commercial routes of medieval East

Europe decisively contributed to the increase of commercial activities on the part of the Ukrainian Slavs.

The considerable development of early Ukrainian trade has been fully recognized by historiography. Some historians even went so far in their speculations as to accept the predominantly commercial character of the ancient Ukrainian economy, without giving credit to agriculture as the real foundation of the country's economy.[14] There is no doubt, however, that the economic evolution of Ukraine already reached the agricultural-commercial stage at the time of the Kievan Empire, considerably ahead in time of the West European countries. Archaeological excavations have revealed the very ancient character of Ukrainian trading activities. Numerous Roman, Greek, Arabic, and Persian coins from the first and third centuries after Christ were found all over Ukraine from the river Dniester to the Don, and from the Crimean Peninsula to Novgorod the Great, proving the vital commercial activity between Ukraine and distant lands. These vital quantities of foreign coins also furnished proof of the accumulation of relatively great wealth as a result of commerce.

Domestic commerce was not equally developed in the various regions of Ukraine, and similarly the participation of the individual tribal areas in foreign trading was not of the same extent and volume. This difference was largely determined by the economic convenience of the geography of the given territory. It was stressed before that the Polianians and Siverianians excelled others in this respect, while the Derevlianians, living in their forests and marshes, were far behind the former in their economic evolution. Domestic exchange was largely carried on in the form of direct trading between the producer and consumer, at first predominantly by way of barter. Very early, however, foreign coins came into use even in domestic trading, which was mainly transacted in the public market places. Regular weekly, semi-monthly, monthly, or, later, yearly, trading fairs were held to bring the sellers and buyers together. The tradition of the fairs had grown considerably in importance by the time of the Kievan

Empire, and these fairs, especially the semi-annual and annual ones, became a major mercantile event. Retail stores, which appeared relatively early in Ukraine, for a long time played only a secondary and supplementary role, and their owners also traded their merchandise at the fairs. Foreign goods were sold mainly in the market places.

In their foreign trading the Ukrainian merchants traveled as far as Greece, Bohemia, Hungary, Caucasia, Persia, the Balkan Peninsula, and the lower-Volga area, and as early as the seventh and eighth centuries. The three major commercial routes in East Europe made Ukraine an important intermediary for transit and trade between East and West on the one hand, and North and South on the other. Furthermore, as a consequence of being the commercial middleman, Ukraine soon became a very important trading partner in the medieval international exchange of Europe, and an important consumer of foreign products.

The first of these routes, and the most important in its political aspects and consequences, was the so-called "Varango-Greek Route," connecting Scandinavia and Byzantium through the Baltic Sea, the Ladoga Lake, the River Volkhov, and the tributaries of the River Dnieper, down the Dnieper, and through the Black Sea. The Varango-Greek Route channeled from Greece and the East to Ukraine, gold, silver, copper, bronze, silk, spices. wines, fruits, carpets and perfumes, and it was the outlet for Ukrainian furs, wax, honey, and slaves to the Greek, Persian, and Arabic markets. Commerce showed the way, and by that route the Northmen came to Ukraine, and advanced her political consolidation. The second trading channel was the so-called "Iron Route," along the River Dnieper, the Black Sea, the River Danube, and into the heart of the Balkan Peninsula. The Iron Route connected Ukraine with the important commercial centers of Southeast Europe. The commercial potentials of the Balkan lands later on induced Prince Sviatoslav to wage wars against the Bulgarians and the Greeks. The third, the so-called "Salt Route," extended to the mouth of the River Don, through the Azov Sea, to the Crimean Peninsula, and the ancient Greek Black

Sea colonies. By the Salt Route the early Ukrainian Slavs imported salt and Oriental goods, and came into early direct contact with the Greek and Iranian civilizations, which profoundly influenced Ukrainian culture. Still another route led toward the Khozar commercial centers, especially to their capital, Ityl, from which horses, cattle, and Oriental merchandise were brought. By means of the Ukrainian-Khozar trade, the Ukrainian Slavs were in touch with central Asia. The tenth century seems to mark the peak of the commercial development of the ancient Ukrainian Slavs, which declined after Sviatoslav of Kiev destroyed Ityl and Bulgar, two important commercial centers of East Europe. The Khozars also tutored the Ukrainian Slavs in commerce, being themselves very successful merchants.

The rather primitive economy of Ukraine of that time exported only a little variety of the produce of her forests and steppes. Wood, wooden articles, especially wooden boats, honey, wax, furs, and numerous slaves were the main export items. Ukrainian merchants of the tenth century traveled as far as Bagdad and Syria, and later as far as Daghestan in the East, and Prague and the islands of Rugia in the West. They brought home a great variety of merchandise, as mentioned above, like wines, tropical fruits, spices, salt, carpets, velvets, silks, china, silver, gold, copper, other metals, metal goods, arms, fine linen, woolen materials, sheep, horses, and cattle. The slave trade was a very important branch of commerce, and it continued throughout the prehistoric era on a large scale in the entire Orient. In the eighth and tenth centuries female slaves of Slavic extraction were widely known. Slaves were, according to Hrushevsky, the chief article which attracted the Arab merchants and induced them to visit and to travel in Ukraine. The origin of the slave trade in Ukraine seems to be Oriental, probably the remnant of the extensive Iranian influence in the early centuries, even from the pre-Slavic era of Ukraine.

The standards of consumption of the early Ukrainians followed the natural character of Slavic economy, which featured hunting, fishing, farming, and trading. The Ukrainian diet included various kinds of meat, such as beef, lamb, veal, and poultry; milk and milk products, such as cheese and butter; a variety of porridges prepared from millet, barley, and wheat; a few vegetables; honey, both as food and as drink; and, of course, a variety of fish. The wealthy classes of merchant-warriors and the princely families no doubt consumed important luxuries not available to the average citizen. Clothing, both garments and shoes, was mainly produced from skins and furs. Linen from flax and hemp was used considerably later, perhaps on the eve of the historical era. Woolen materials were little known in the early times. Home appliances were largely made from wood and clay. Glass was rarely used, and certainly not among the common people, since there were no glass works in ancient Ukraine. But commercial activities were the source of much wealth, and of a relatively high standard of living among the upper classes of the *Rus'* society. Arabic travelers recounted the riches of the Ukrainian Slavs. Ibn-Dasta, Ibn-Hawqal, and others said that the *Rus'* were constantly trading, had numerous rich and large cities, and lived in plenty, and that even the men wore golden bracelets while the women wore heavy golden chains and costly necklaces, and that their households were abounding in luxurious furnishings, carpets, and rugs. Their garments were of Byzantine fabrics and Oriental silks, and their furs were costly sables and beavers.[15] These reports indicate a great difference and cleavage between the rich and the common people among the old Ukrainian Slavs.

Religious Beliefs. In order to learn at least in broad outlines the way of life of the Eastern Slavs as a basis for the historical growth of Ukraine, it is necessary to cover briefly the religious beliefs, which were the expression of their spiritual and cultural life. These had a significant bearing on their history.

The Slavs were pagans whose body of beliefs was still immature and on a much lower level of spiritual evolution than that of such civilized people as the Hindus, Greeks, Romans and Germans. At the time of the introduction of Christianity to Ukraine, furthermore, Slavic paganism had assimilated Oriental and Greek religious elements.

Slavic paganism was polytheistic; it was based on belief in a plurality of gods. In this respect, it represented a religious regression when compared to the old monotheistic Finnic religion. This was, however, a normal course of spiritual evolution of ancient man from his original belief in one Supreme Being to a polytheistic religion of many gods, lesser gods, demons, fairies and nymphs, living in the woods, on the mountains and in the seas. Christianity reintroduced belief in one God to the European continent.

The Slavs then believed in a number of gods, related to various forces of nature, the marvel of which they could explain only through the intercession of a supernatural power. In their pantheon the leading gods were Svaroh, Dazhboh, Khors, Striboh, and then Perun, Volos (Veles), Mokosh and Div. References to these deities have been scattered throughout various historical source materials, such as chronicles and travel descriptions, writings about the lives of saints and old poems, which originated a little later, in the Christianized Kievan state of the tenth century. It is highly possible that this pantheon of gods may represent a later fusion of the two different religious systems of the *Sclavenis* and Antes, since it seems that there was no logical connection between Svaroh, Dazhboh, Khors and Striboh, who were related to each other in Slavic beliefs, on the one hand, and Perun and Volos, on the other. Mokosh, apparently, was a female deity, a lesser goddess of Finnic origin, whose meaning in the cult is not clear. Khors, whose divine capacities were similar to those of Perun, was introduced into the northern Slavic religious body by the Scandinavians. The adoration of Mother Earth for her fertility had an Indo-Iranian background, and was absorbed into the paganism of the Slavs.

Svaroh, apparently the chief deity among the Slavs, was the god of the heavens and of light and fire. It can be assumed on the basis of historical references that three other gods, Dazhboh, Khors and Striboh, were related to Savaroh, presumably having been his sons or embodiments of his specific qualities. Dazhboh was the creative god of the sun, a living deity, who blessed nature with fertility.[16] He was definitely a helping god and friendly to man. Striboh was the god of winds, while Khor was considered the god of sunlight, akin to Svaroh. These three gods were sometimes referred to as the *Svarozhichi,* being in Svaroh's family.

Perun and Volos were not in Svaroh's family. Perun, a powerful and widely adored deity, was the god of storms, thunder and lightning, while Volos was the divine protector of cattle, money and commerce. It has been suggested by some students of Slavic history that even the cult of Volos developed under Scandinavian influence.

Along with these major deities the old Slavs revered rivers, trees, nymphs, fairies, and other spirits or the reincarnation of spirits. Their belief in evil spirits or demons was definitely of foreign, primarily Oriental, origin.[17]

The religion of the Slavs was closely related to nature. This is illustrated by its rituals and festivities with a yearly and seasonal cyclic character. Those rituals and festivities survived much longer than paganism in Eastern Europe. After the introduction of Christianity, for more than two centuries a form of religious dualism prevailed, a religious mixture of paganism and Christianity. During that era, the people, having kept their traditional customs and rituals, gave them a Christian counterpart: they identified St. Ellias with Perun and St. Vlasius with Volos; they celebrated Christian holy days with paganish festivities. Some remnants of Slavic pagan rituals and customs can be found even today among the village folk throughout the European part of the Soviet Union.

The old Slavs evidently did not build temples and had no priests. Later, however, perhaps under foreign influence, especially the Finnic one, and due to further evolution of their religion, temples were constructed and priests, called *Volkhvy,* took charge of religious rites in the most northern part of Ukraine.

Idols, however, mostly made from wood and sometimes from stone, and pictures of deities were known among the Slavs. The remnants of those idols have been found in various places.

The Slavs must have believed in, or at least subconsciously admitted the immortality of the human soul. First of all, they had elaborate burial rituals either by inhumation or by cremation. Vernadsky states that the cult of Perun, as God of lightning, must have been connected with cremation, while inhumation of the dead must have been the ritual of the Svaroh cult.[18] Secondly, the worship and adoration of clan ancestors, bringing them milk, bread, meat and honey as offerings on certain religious days, to invoke their protection for the clan, was an ancient custom among the Slavs. These customs persisted beyond the pagan era, deep into the thirteenth century. These two facts indicate the Slavic belief in a life after death. The burial rituals among the Slavic tribes were described at length by the Arabic travelers, Ibn-Fadlan and Ibn-Dasta.[19]

To be sure, these religious beliefs of the South-Eastern, Ukrainian Slavs were, during their later development, considerably different from those of the North-Eastern, Russian Slavs, since the former were greatly affected in their spiritual and cultural evolution by Hellenic and Iranian spiritual and cultural trends, and the latter — by the Finno-Ugrian ones, as it was indicated before. The adoration of the female goddesses, such as Lado, the goddess of beauty and love, and Vesna, the goddess of mystery of life, might have been the example of that Hellenic influence, while the belief in the wicked and evil gods and goddesses might have illustrated the Oriental spiritual impact upon the Ukrainian Slavs, and those gods were completely unrelated to the original Slavic family of divinities. That belief in evil divinities like god Div, the protector of night and the nightly fear, or goddess Khmara, the sponsor of rain, and finally the belief in wicked half-gods, such as devils, witches and vampires, was of a later date.

Although the religious belief of the ancient Slav was rather primitive and poorly developed, it still penetrated his whole life, close within the framework of a yearly ritual; the winter, spring, summer and fall cycles, marked by proper holidays, customs and holy day rituals with proper dances, songs and celebrations, like the winter holy day of *Kolada,* or summer holy day of *Kupalo*. Consequently, with the advent of Christianity, that primitive paganism, without a developed organization, priests and temples, rather easily, without any violent struggle, gave in, while many of its rituals and customs of beauty were adopted and built into the Ukrainian brand of Christian rites and system of holidays.[20]

1. *Povist' vremennykh lit*, po Lavrentievskomu spisku, St. Petersburg, 1910, year 862, p. 20.

2. G. Vernadsky and M. Karpovich, *A History of Russia*, Vol. II, *Kievan Russia*, New Haven-London, 1951, pp. 154-157: the authors stressed there the difference in woman's social status in old Ukraine, on the one hand, and in old Suzdal-Muscovy, on the other: also the monogamic and matriarchal traditions in Ukraine: V. Yaniv, "Ukrainska rodyna," *Entsyklopedia ukrainoznavstva*, Munich-New York, 1949, Vol. I-III, pp. 1134-1136; compare the elevated position of the Ukrainian woman in the old Rus'ian code of law, the *Rus'ka Pravda*.

3. M. Hrushevsky, *Istoria Ukrainy-Rusy*, New York, 1954, Vol. I, pp. 357-358: "But this (agnatic element) in the ninth and tenth centuries was only an echo of the past. . . . The tribes were already too big, and territorially too extensive in the tenth and eleventh centuries, as to be able to retain any traditions of a common genealogy. . . . On the new territories they were doubtlessly formed under the impact of the geographical circumstances" (358).

4. M. Braichevsky, "The Unification of the Old Rus'ian Lands around the Center of Kyiv", *On the Historical Beginning of Eastern Slavic Europe*, ed. by N. Chirovsky, New York, 1976, pp. 57-65.

5. The thesis is mainly represented by German and Scandinavian historiography on the basis of the legend of Jordanis, a Gothic historian: L. Schmidt, *Geschichte der deutschen Stämme bis zum Ausgange der Völkerwanderung*, 1904, p. 99; D. Doroshenko, *Narys istorii Ukrainy*, Munich, 1966, p. 30: "The Goths established their empire on the banks of Dnieper, with its center in the city of Danparstadt, which has been identified by some with Kiev." Other authors accept an even more ancient origin of Kiev, than the Gothic era in Ukraine, however, always associating its growth with its convenient location on the cross-roads of commercial routes.

6. Braichevsky, *op. cit.*, pp. 63-64.

7. V. Kluchevskii, *Istoria soslovii v Rossii*, Moscow, 1913, pp. 41-42.

8. A rational division of the economic evolution into a number of cultural stages: F. List, *National System of Political Economy*, New York, 1904, Bk. II, p. 143.

9. Primitive hunting and fishing in old Ukraine: I. Krypiakevych, "Pobut," *Istoria ukrainskoi kultury*, Winnipeg, 1964, pp. 40-42.

10. J. Kulischer, *Russische Wirtschaftsgeschichte*, Jena, 1925, Vol. I, pp. 88-89.

11. Constantine Porphyrogenitus, *De Administrando Imperio*, Chapter IX.

12. The Jewish traveler, Ibn-Jacob, and the Greek Emperor, Mauricius, noted "all types of fruit stacked in piles". Mauricius wrote in the sixth and Ibn-Jacob in the tenth century.

13. P. Lyashchenko, *History of the National Economy of Russia*, New York, 1949, p. 73: "The social division of labor and the rise of the town were gradually progressing"; the emergence of the primitive town: Hrushevsky, *op. cit.*, Vol. I, pp. 361-365.

14. The commercial nature of the Slavic economy: V. Kluchevskii, *Boiarskaia duma drevniei Rusi*, Moscow, 1909, p. 13; Kulischer, *op. cit.*, Vol. I, pp. 103-105 and 118-157; and many other authors and historians.

15. A. Garkavi, *Skazania muzulmanskikh pisatelei o slovianakh i russkikh*, St. Petersburg, 1870, pp. 221, 268, 85; the relations of Ibn-Hawqal, Ibn-Dasta, Ibn-Fadlan, and others.

16. Broadly on the Slavic mythology: Krypiakevych, *op. cit.*, pp. 64-66; Yu. Fedoriv, *Istoria tserkvy v Ukraini*, Toronto, 1967, pp. 7-11; V. Mansikka, *Die Religion der Ostslaven*, Helsinki, 1922.

17. Vernadsky, *op. cit.*, Vol. II, pp. 48-56: The Religion of the Eastern Slavs.

18. *Ibid.*, p. 55.

19. Garkavi, pp. 85-102, 262-270.

20. Fedoriv, *loc. cit.*; also, V. Petrov, "Obriadovyi folklor narodno-kalendarnoho tsyklu yak metodolohichna problema," *Naukovyi zbirnyk Ukraiskoho Vilnoho Universtetu*, Munich, 1948, Vol. V, pp. 149-154.

PART TWO

The Kievan-Galician Era

Prince
Sviatoslav
the
Conqueror

Prince Volodymyr
the Great

CHAPTER FIVE

THE RISE AND FALL OF KIEVAN RUS'

The rise: the first princes — Sviatoslav the Conqueror —
Volodymyr the Great — Yaroslav the Wise — The fall: the
confederated state — Volodymyr Monomakh — The disintegration of the empire — The Mongol-Tartar invasion.

The Rise: The First Princes. The state organization of the
Antes and the similar state organizations of the Slavic tribes in
Ukraine, such as *Valinana, V-a-i,* and *Chervenski Horody* represented the historical prologue of the political process of the
development of the powerful political formation of the Ukrainian
Slavs of the ninth to thirteenth century under the name of Kievan
Rus' or the Kievan *Rus'* realm. Probably one of the earliest written references to *Rus'* could be found in the *Bertinian Chronicle*
in the year 839, which concerned the difficulty of returning home
of the *Rus'* envoys from Byzantium to their homeland, since
''some barbarian and extremely cruel tribes'' dominated the regions through which the said envoys had to travel. Further
analysis of the above reference can only lead to the following
conclusion, that the *Rus'* state was then a well-organized political
formation, having diplomatic relations with the Byzantine Em-

pire, and that also the Normans were in service of the *Rus'* rulers, because these envoys were apparently "Swedish," as the chronicle testified.[1] Otherwise the process of organization and growth of the *Rus'* state proceeded without being noticed by the Byzantine and West-European historical records, until the new power made its forceful entrance into the European political developments in the year 860.

This year, according to the Byzantine sources, during the absence of Emperor Michael III from the capital, a huge *Rus'ian* naval force of some 6,000 to 8,000 men and 200 ships, under the leadership of Prince Askold, attacked the capital of Byzantium and its vicinity. The capital was not taken by the *Rus'ian* forces, but the vicinity was thoroughly plundered. Apparently the city was miraculously saved by a sea storm, which badly damaged the *Rus'ian* navy. The assault was not a simple barbarian expedition for booty, but a revenge of the *Rus'* upon the Greeks for their violations of international law and unfair trade practices, according to Patriarch Photius testimony and other Greek sources. The war led to some kind of a treaty between *Rus'* and Greece with religious and commercial connotations. The *Rus'* chronicle *Povist' vremennykh lit* gave a little different date of the campaign and set it at 866, while the treaty must have been negotiated later on, perhaps in 874.

In the wake of the above war, the Christianization of *Rus'* under the auspices of Prince Askold was accomplished. The Prince became Christian, and upon his request, the emperor sent a bishop and priests to Kiev, the capital of *Rus'*. Only later a relapse into paganism took place under the impact of unfavorable developments, such as a too rapid conversion, subsequent wars dominating all attention and the new Normanic dynasty taking over the rule of the country. Hence, some one hundred and twenty years later a new Christianization process of *Rus'* had to be undertaken by Prince Volodymyr, the Great. The Christianization of *Rus'* under Askold was corroborated by the testimony of Patriarch Photius and other sources.[2] Furthermore, Photius pointed out, that *Rus'* had dominated other neighboring lands. This reference, together with other historical sources, might only have indicated an advanced stage of political evolution of *Rus'* toward a power.

Povist' vremennykh lit talks about two princes, Askold and Dir, which seems to be incorrect, as far as their common expedition against the Greeks was concerned. Dlugosh, an early Polish historian, who could have used some historical material, long lost since, asserted that the Kyi dynasty ruled for a long time the Polianian land, and that Askold and Dir were the Kievan princes of that dynasty. Masudi, an Arab traveller, stated that Dir ruled before Askold. Consequently, Askold must have been the last of the Kyi dynasty, then replaced by a new Norman one. Of course, it is presently impossible to ascertain the timing of the Dir's and Askold's reigning, unless some new historical sources should be discovered. According to the tradition, Dir and Askold had been buried in two different and quite distant places in Kiev. This would not have been the case if they would have ruled together and waged war against Byzantium together, and were killed by Oleh, a Norman leader, at the same time, as the *Povist'* erroneously implied. Yet, those two last members of the ancient Slavic dynasty accomplished apparently a great deal during their separate, but following each other, reigning tenures with respect of consolidating the young *Rus'* state. According to chronicles, they waged wars against the Polotsians, Krivichians and Bulgars in order to expand the central rule of Kiev. Only then, the grand war expedition against Byzantium and the treaty with the Greeks, which entered *Rus'* on the scene of the European political relations, could have been possible.[3]

Yet, because of serious loopholes in historical sources, there is also another version about Askold's and Dir's rule. *Povist' vremennykh lit* asserted that the Kyi's dynasty was terminated in 852 by the arrival of two Norman noblemen, Askold and Dir, from the North, who assumed the princely rule in Kiev. They were supposedly the members of Ruryk's retinue, who seized power of Novgorod the Great in the land of the Slovenians, the tribe which subsequently merged into the Russian nationality.

According to that chronicle, in 882, another Norman, Oleh or Oleg, the guardian of Ruryk's son, Prince Ihor or Igor, having heard of Kiev's wealth, arrived there with the child Ihor, with a great force, composed of the Norman, Chud', Slovenian, Meria, Ves', and Krivichian warriors, seized the city, over-powered Askold and Dir and executed them as supposedly the usurpers of the princely throne to which they were not entitled, since they were not of princely origin.[4] In both cases quite a large number of the Norman warriors came to Ukraine with their leaders. *The Bertinian Chronicle* referred indirectly to that instance, as it was pointed out before.

On the basis of the assertion of the *Povist' vremennykh lit* the so-called Normanistic theory of the beginnings of the *Rus'* state was developed. It was initiated by three eighteenth century historians of German descent, Bayer, Schlözer and Müller, who, in their historical works, insisted on a Germanic or Normanic political origin of *Rus'*. Taking into consideration the account of events in the *Povist'* and the ancient presence of a large number of Norman-Varangians in Novgorod the Great, Rostov, and then, in Kiev, testified by numerous historical documents of the time, these historians concluded that actually the Normans initiated, organized and maintained early political organizations (states) in Eastern Europe. They concluded, that the Slavs were unable to rule themselves, as the wording of the said *Povist'* admitted, and that the Germanic people had to help them in this respect. The theory had certain elements of inborn German chauvinism, featured by contempt for the Slavs, and it was originated by Germans, residing in Russia. At first, the Normanistic interpretation of the origin of *Rus'* was uncritically accepted. Yet, soon a reaction to the above one-sided interpretation developed. Above all, it was a direct insult to the national and patriotic sentiments of the Ukrainians and Russians, instigated by German-originated insinuations, which attempted to prove that the Normans were the only state-building force in the East, and that the Slavs lacked such qualities. Prominent Russian and Ukrainian historians, like Lamanskii, Gedeonov, Ilovaiskii and Hrushevsky, who uncovered several weak points in the Normanistic interpretation, opposed it. First of all, they came to the conclusion that the wording of *Povist' vremennykh lit* cannot be taken literally and on full face value. However, most important was the historical fact of the ancient existence of a strong and well developed Slavic political organization, attesting to the state-building qualities of the Eastern Slavs. Furthermore, the Slavic *Rus'* in the Ukrainian South was well known to foreign travellers and writers long before the Norman-Varangian arrival in Kiev. Hence, the above historians concluded that the Normanic ethnic element might have helped the political evolution of the *Rus'* state at its later stage, but it was not the only state-constructing factor, as the German originators of the Normanistic theory preferred to see. The Normans, called Varangians or *Variahy* in Ukraine, might have been valuable servants in the service of the Slavic-originated Kievan *Rus'* realm.[5]

Povist' vremennykh lit related in a very colorful manner, mixed with legendary elements, the event of Oleh's arrival to Kiev and taking over the city in the name of Ruryk and his minor son, Ihor. Politically important here was only the instance of termination of the rule of the Kyi dynasty, and the beginning of the rule of the new Ruryk dynasty in *Rus'*, which remained in power in Eastern Europe or its parts for a number of centuries. In Ukraine, until 1340, and in Muscovy, until 1598. Prince Oleh was apparently the regent, who ruled from 882 to 912 in the name of Prince Ihor, but he certainly acted very independently and accomplished a great deal with respect to expansion and consolidation of the Kievan state. In fact, he accomplished so much, that some historians assumed that the chronicle was mistaken again by talking of one Oleh. They assumed, that there were in reality two princes of the same name, who reigned at different times; perhaps one after the other. But this is only a hypothesis.

He originally ruled, in the name of Ihor, over the Slovenians, the Chud', Meria, Ves' and other Finnic tribes, and the Krivichians, whose warriors joined his invasion army, which he then brought upon Kievan *Rus'*. After having dominated Kiev, he

extended his reign over the Polianians, Siverianians, Derevlianians and Radimichians, and waged wars against the Ulichians
and Tiverians, apparently without subjugating the two latter
tribes. The wars against the Siverianians and Radimichians,
brought Oleh into war with the Khozars. As a result of this war,
he plundered the littorals of the Caspian Sea. Even the western
Khorvatsians joined his war exploits, suggesting his influence
over the western regions of Ukraine as well.

Politically, Oleh introduced a great change in the constitutional
structure of the Kievan state. Under Askold and Dir it was a
largely ethnically homogeneous state, which consolidated Ukrainian tribes, while under Oleh, it became a multinational empire,
extending its indefinite borders far to the North, East, South and
West, populated with the Ukrainian, pre-Russian and Finnic
tribes and ethnic communities. He was a gifted statesman and a
shrewd politician. He treated all dominated peoples alike, no
matter whether they were his old allies, such as the Slovenians,
Krivichians and Finnic tribes, who helped him to get hold of
Kiev, or the newly subjugated communities, like the Polianians
or Derevlianians. He levied heavy tributes on the former as on the
latter. He did not dismiss or kill the original tribal chieftains after
the new territories were dominated, but kept them as his governors to administer the newly acquired provinces and let them
participate in the country's government process. By doing so, he
was able to consolidate his empire well, and in consequence of
these measures as a strong ruler, he could in 907 undertake his
grand war expedition against Byzantium. The war was, like the
previous campaign led by Askold, commercially motivated.

Again the colorful description of the campaign by the chronicle
suggested certain relevant strategic aspects. Byzantium and its
vicinity were unexpectedly attacked from the side of the sea and
the land. The vicinity was plundered but not the city. His military
force must have been huge, since it was joined by warriors from
all subjugated lands. The Byzantines were impressed and
yielded. A very favorable treaty was negotiated, which shed a
great deal of light upon the causes of war and the nature of the
Ukrainian economy at that time.

The treaty was commercial throughout, aiming at every possible trade advantage for the Ukrainian-*Rus'* merchants. The Ukrainian goods were admitted to Greece duty free and the merchants were supplied by the Greeks with whatever shipping supplies were needed; loss of a ship, international crime, flight of a slave, living of the Ukrainian merchants in a special section of the capital when staying there (Rus'ian *ghetto*), their maintenance at Greek expense for six months, and other matters were legally regulated. The treaty had been a very important historical document, which underscored an over-all international recognition of *Rus'* as an equal partner of the Byzantinian Empire.

Although the *Povist'* talked about two Rus'ian war expeditions against Byzantium, in 907 and 911, in reality there was only one successful campaign of Oleh. Then a few years later, after concluding the above treaty with Greece, Prince Oleh died apparently from being bitten by a poisonous snake in 913, opening the way to Ihor to assume belatedly the throne, to which he was entitled. Apparently, Oleh was such a strong personality as a regent that by his great authority he kept Ihor from claiming his right to rule over *Rus'* too long.

Ihor ruled from 913 to 945, when he met his violent death. He inherited a powerful and a rather well cemented empire, which during his life he attempted to enlarge and to strengthen even more. He finally conquered and annexed the territories of the Tiverians and Ulichians, incorporated the area between the rivers Dniester and Danube, and undertook two war expeditions on the littorals of the Caspian Sea, in 913 as an ally of the Khozars and in 943 against Berdah, where he acquired a great booty, but no political gains. He seemed still to be a Viking-Norman and not a calculated statesman in those cases.

The commercial relations with Byzantium seemed to be a perennial problem for the *Rus'* society, aggravated by the relations with the Greek colonies on the littorals of the Black Sea and the fishery rights in those areas. Byzantium then associated itself with the Pechengs, the new horde which arrived from Asia into the Black and Azov Sea steppes and began to harass the Ukrainian southern frontier regions. To stop the Byzantinian harassments, Prince Ihor undertook a war expedition against Constantinople in 941. Yet, the Greeks used some kind of an explosive material, called by the Rus'ians the "Greek fire," and destroyed many ships of Ihor's navy, ending the project in failure for *Rus'*. Ihor undertook another expedition, which forced the Byzantine to yield again. A new treaty was concluded, but it was not so advantageous as the previous one, negotiated by Oleh. *Rus'* had to give up her plans of expansion in the Black Sea and Dnieper mouth areas, to pay duties for trading with Greece and Greek colonies, and to assist Byzantium militarily.[6]

However, the treaty is important for another reason too. It enumerated the names of various members of the dynasty, various princes, noblemen, *boyars,* and merchants, some Slavic, some Scandinavian, indicating that some cosigners were pagan and some Christian on the *Rus'* side of the agreement, shedding light upon the social relations in the Kievan Empire of those days.

It seems that Ihor's realm was not yet fully consolidated and cemented. Some tribes resisted the central pressure of Kiev and refused to pay taxes, in particular the Derevlianians. Prince Ihor had to go there and quell the opposition. Nevertheless, he was not careful enough. He was ambushed by the Derevlianian warriors, and then cruelly murdered. It was the tragic outcome of the centralist tendencies of Kiev and the centrifugal tendencies of individual tribes, which preferred their tribal autonomy.[7]

With Ihor's death, his wife, Princess Olha or Olga, assumed the regency in the name of her minor son, Prince Sviatoslav. Her reign lasted approximately from 945 to 964. The history of her descent is not yet certain. She might have been Oleh's daughter of noble origin, and this might explain Oleh's lasting rule, since Ihor might not dare to resist his father's-in-law authority and prestige. She might have been a noble woman from Pskov, as the *Povist'* related; nevertheless a legend persists of her common origin. However, no matter what her family origin might have been, she was an extraordinary woman, very clever and a very good diplomat. The Norman retinue recognized her authority fully and the conquered tribes, in spite of their centrifugal tendencies, also largely submitted to her rule, although there still persisted a hostile feeling among the Slavic tribes towards the Scandinavian dynasty.

First of all, according to the law of revenge, binding the land, Princess Olha carried out her revenge for the murder of her husband upon the revolting Derevlianians. She executed the Derevlianian envoys, who came from their tribal prince, Mal, to suggest a marriage between him and Olha. Then, she led a punitive war expedition against their land, during which many Derevlianians perished, set fire to their main fortress of defense, the town of Iskorosten, and killed 5,000 Derevlianians during the post-mortem reception to honor Prince Ihor. *Povist' vremennykh lit* described at length the tortures applied to the Derevlianians. Probably, the intensity of revenge induced other tribes, which desired autonomy from the Kievan centralism, to think twice before starting any opposition, and it may be one of the reasons why the rest of Olha's reign was rather peaceful.

Olha was an able administrator, for whom the chronicles could not offer enough words of praise. She travelled throughout the huge empire extensively, visited the newly annexed tribal territories to prevent any uprisings, regulated the system of taxes and tributes, introduced what might have been considered an attempt to separate the state treasury from her private princely one; regulated hunting rights and the rights of bee-keeping, and the production of honey and wax by issuing laws, which were differently called, according to the matters they regulated, the *ustavy, uroky, broky* and *dani*. Fur skins became a kind of money. During her reign a considerable assimilation of the Normanic ethnic element into the Slavic main population body was accomplished. The Scandinavian names began to disappear, being replaced by the Slavic ones. Her own son was called Sviatoslav, not a Scandinavian name, like his father and mother and, perhaps, both of his grandfathers.

Christianity was centuries-old in Ukraine, and the Ukrainian Slavs were well acquainted with it, especially since Askold's attempt to baptize the whole country. The relapse into paganism with the advent of a new dynasty could not stop its spreading for long. Some historians expressed an assumption that Ihor might have been secretly a Christian. Olha at the latter part of her reign decided to become Christian, too, although it is not certain exactly where and when she was baptized. Most probably, she received Christianity in Kiev around 955, and thereafter she travelled to Constantinople, maybe even twice, for religious and political reasons. She might have desired to obtain some Byzantine support in bringing Christianity to *Rus'*, and also had some commercial reasons to repair relations with Constantinople, which deteriorated during Ihor's reign. The *Povist'*s story about Olha being baptized in Constantinople and the emperor being her godfather is hardly credible, because the Byzantine sources, which related comprehensively Olha's stay in Byzantium, do not mention her baptism at all.

She arrived at Constantinople with great pomp and a great many people in her escort, so that even the Byzantines were impressed. She was given a royal reception throughout. The emperor conferred with her about state matters, and he might even have asked her for military assistance. The fact is that in 961 the Rus'ian warriors were fighting as allies on the emperor's behalf.[8]

However, no matter how glamorous was Olha's arrival in Constantinople and her reception by the imperial family, Olha was not happy. Upon her return to Kiev, she dispatched envoys to Otto I, asking him to appoint and send to *Rus'* a bishop. Apparently she did not trust the Byzantine emperor, and wanted to establish an autonomous Rus'ian church organization. Bishop Adalbertus arrived belatedly in Ukraine, and his mission was not a success. The first Ukrainian chronicle was written down later on, when *Rus'* was fully under the Greek ecclesiastic influence, so it did not even mention Olha's envoys in Germany in the church matters as offensive for the Orthodox of that time. On the other hand, it fabricated the story of Olha's baptism in Constantinople and the Emperor's being her godfather, apparently to strengthen the ties between Kiev and Constantinople and to raise the former's political and spiritual prestige.[9]

Sviatoslav the Conqueror. Princess Olha was certainly outstanding as a ruler and as a woman. The historical sources had but only praise for her. After her son, Prince Sviatoslav, reached a proper age, she transferred her authority to him, and he assumed the reign, which lasted from 964 to 972. The transition of authority was peaceful, which again pointed to Olha's greatness. Sviatoslav, although carrying a Slavic name, was a typical Viking on the throne, an adventurous and daring leader, fully in love with warfare. He spent his whole life waging wars, conquering new lands and looking for new commercial and other advantages for his retinue and people. According to Hrushevsky, he resembled a Cossack on the throne by his personal traits of a courageous and noble man. Sviatoslav completed the unification of all Eastern Slavs under one Kievan rule and then he indulged in an endless chain of foreign wars to enlarge his realm and his fame. Yet, he had actually very little attachment to *Rus'* as his homeland; he was ready at one point to trade her for a Balkan home; this, indeed, underscored his Viking character. His sons and grandsons were different; they were truly Ukrainian rulers who greatly cared for their dominions.

In his drive to submit all Eastern Slavs to Kiev's authority, he waged a war against the Viatichians, who were still paying tribute to the Khozars, and were quite unwilling to exchange the mild Khozar rule for submission to the growing empire, led by an energetic prince. Subsequently he moved against the Finnic tribes, and forced them under his authority. The war against the Finnic tribes brought him into a war conflict with the Volga Bulgars in 964; he beat them and destroyed their capital, the city of Bulgar, a very important commercial center of North-East Europe at that time. Sviatoslav's booty must have been very substantial. From there, he moved his forces immediately against the Khozars, and in 965 captured and destroyed their centers, Ityl, the capital and commercial intermediary with Central Asia, Sarkel, a fortress of defense against the threat of Asiatic hordes, and Semender. His exploits were definitely of a dubious success. In the short run, Sviatoslav might have captured rich booty and annihilated a commercial rival. Yet, in the long run, as pointed out, it was a military-political blunder of a grand scale. Through the destruction of the Bulgar and Khozar states, the European bulwarks against the onslaughts of the Asiatic nomad hordes, at first of the Pechengs, and then, of the others, the Torks and Cumans, were leveled off, and from then on the *Rus'* realm was directly exposed to recurring tides of barbarians from the Orient, which eventually in the middle of the thirteenth century spelled out the irrevocable end of the Kievan Empire. Yet, Sviatoslav was still a Viking adventurer and not a statesman of stature. Although the Pecheng hordes harassed Ukraine to a minor extent before the Bulgar and Khozar states were destroyed, their devastating onslaughts came just after that event. Immediately following those exploits, Prince Sviatoslav carried his war expedition to the Kuban and Caucasian regions, and defeated the tribes of the Kosygians and Osetians, extending his rule over the Taman Peninsula and Tmutorokan *Rus'*, but not for long. The Byzantine intrigue averted his attention from the Eastern project and left it unfinished and without any apparent gains for *Rus'*.

Byzantium had its problems with its northern neighbor, the Balkan Bulgarians, and followed its traditional policy to turn dangerous neighboring peoples against each other to preserve its own peace and safety; this time Constantinople instigated Sviatoslav against the Bulgarians. In 968, he moved against the Balkan Bulgarians and defeated them, conquered many of their towns, and decided to transfer there, to the town of Pereyaslav, Pereslava today, his capital and to live there, having cared but little about Kiev. He supposedly had said that all the riches come to Pereyaslav from all over the world and that he liked to stay there.[10] The Bulgarians accepted him as their ruler by compromise. But, the Greeks did not like that, to have close to their borders a dangerous and warlike Rus'ian "barbarian." Hence they conspired with the Pechengs, and sent them against Kiev.

The Pechengs attacked Ukraine, besieged Kiev and almost captured Olha with her grandchildren. Sviatoslav was persuaded by the Kievan messengers to return to Ukraine and to free her from the Pecheng onslaught. However, having defeated and driven away the enemy, he immediately returned to Bulgaria to resume his project of assaulting the Greeks and of driving them out of Europe. Perhaps, he had a grand dream of becoming a *Rus'* -Bulgarian ruler with Byzantium under his heel. Yet, the Greeks did not wait for that and undertook a powerful offensive and defeated Sviatoslav, in spite of his considerable forces and desperate fighting. The defeat forced him to accept an unfavorable treaty with Byzantium, after which he met personally with Emperor Johannes Tzimiskes upon his own request. Then, he began his march back to Kiev, nursing a plan, however, to gather new forces and to come back to accomplish his original project of living in Bulgaria and ruling over a vast empire. Nevertheless, when approaching home, he was attacked by the avengeful Pechengs, perhaps sent there by the Greek diplomatic maneuvering, and having been assaulted unexpectedly, he was killed in action, in 972.

This was the end of a great military genius and a true noble knight, who never attacked anybody without a formal declaration of war, by stating: "I move against you." His great personality and his devoted governors and generals preserved the Kievan realm, in spite of the lack of his own devotion to *Rus'* herself as a nation and many centrifugal tendencies of various lands and tribes. His age was the time of full relapsing of Rus', and in particular, of her leading class of noblemen and retainers, into paganism. Sviatoslav himself did not want to think of Christianity, supposedly because of the opposition of his retinue, *druzhyna,* which, as he said, might have laughed at him if he would have become Christian.[11]

Sviatoslav, having three sons, divided his realm among them, as the custom deemed proper. He gave Kiev to Yaropolk; Ovruch with the land of the Derevlianians to Oleh; and Novgorod the Great in the land of the Slovenians — to Volodymyr. Since all his sons were rather young, he appointed for them wise and experienced advisors. Sveneld, a tested and faithful advisor to Ihor and

Olha, was supposed to assist Yaropolk in Kiev; Dobrynia, who had been praised by the ancient songs, *bylyny,* and sagas, went to Novgorod to guide the actions of Volodymyr. However, the brotherly love did not prevail too long among the three princes. A conflict immediately developed due to some kind of rivalry or jealousy. Oleh killed Lut, Sveneld's son, when the latter was hunting on the former's territory. Sveneld, then, instigated Yaropolk to punish his brother. During the encounter Oleh perished. Maybe it was Yaropolk's scheme of gathering all his father's lands. Anyway, Volodymyr thought so and out of fear went to Scandinavia to build up his military strength in order to settle the account with Yaropolk, who meanwhile was able to unite in his hands his father's territorial inheritance and rule as a grand prince from 972 to 979.

Prince Yaropolk was unlike his father, not a Viking but a *Rus'ian* statesman, who aimed at strengthening his realm and raising its international prestige. Internally, the realm was unified; tribal princes of centrifugal tendencies disappeared almost entirely; people's meeting lost constitutional and political importance. Yaropolk's retinue, *druzhyna,* the military basis of princely power, was no more prevailingly Norman but consisted of the Slavic-Ukrainian, land- and office-holding noblemen. Internationally, Prince Yaropolk, maybe as a Christian of Roman rite, secretly, however, assumingly baptized by a Western monk, maintained vital relations with the German court and the Pope of Rome, sending envoys and receiving envoys in an attempt to raise the prestige of his realm and dynasty. He was apparently an able leader of his lands, but subsequent developments did not allow him to continue his good work. Maybe, his pro-Western orientation hurt him. Prince Volodymyr meanwhile organized a powerful military force out of the Normans and north-eastern tribes; soon he recaptured Novgorod the Great, moved against Yaropolk and defeated him. The latter was then treacherously killed.[12]

Volodymyr the Great. Grand Prince Volodymyr, who could rightly be called that, although he apparently did not use the title, reigned from 980 to 1015. His era could be truly identified as the *Golden Age* of the *Rus'*-Ukrainian realm, along with the reign of his later successor, Yaroslav, the Wise, from 1019 to 1054, although a political decline of Kievan *Rus'* began during his reign.

Volodymyr took rule over a huge empire, which included some twenty different lands, three emerging East-Slavic nationalities of the Ukrainians, Russians and Byelorus'ians, as they were later called, and many Finnic ethnical communities, which were being gradually assimilated by war and peace by the North-Eastern Slavs. There was very little in common among these ethnic entities, and only the authority of the prince or of the dynasty of Ruryk produced an uneasy unification. The new prince was soon tested by the centrifugal forces. First of all, the Viatichians, who kept their tribal autonomy longer than other communities, rose against Kiev. Hence, in 981 and 982, Volodymyr had to move against that tribe to force it to submission. A tribute was levied anew against the Viatichians. In 984, the Radimichians, who rendered a substantial resistance, had to be pacified and to be forced to submit and pay tribute, which burdened them long, deep into the twelfth century, according to the chronicle. There were also other uprisings which Volodymyr had to quell.

In the course of the anti-Yaropolk campaign, Volodymyr conquered anew the land of the Polotsians, who also exhibited a centrifugal and autonomous tendency. He killed their prince Rohvolod and annexed their territory. In 981, he carried the warfare westward, against the Bohemians, who meanwhile had dominated the Ukrainian western and Carpathian regions, where the tribe of the Khorvatsians lived, and annexed the regions of Peremyshl, Cherven', Buzhsk, Belz and Volyn. *Povist' vremennykh lit* referred to those towns as having been "Polish" at that time. It is an obvious mistake. At that time the Polish state had not such a territorial extension, having been barred by the enormous growth of the Bohemian realm, and the chronicler simply confused the political situation of his time, when Bohemia had declined and Poland expanded to the West, with the situation in the second half of the tenth century. These western Ukrainian

119

territories were apparently already under Oleh's domination a century before and were lost by Kiev during Sviatoslav's reign, who was interested in other political projects, and not in western regions. In 992, Volodymyr annexed the so-called Carpathian *Rus'*, beyond the Carpathian Mountains, to compensate himself for the losses in the southern and eastern steppe regions, where the Pechengs settled themselves firmly, and interrupted the *Rus'ian* salt importation. Salt could have been gotten in these western Ukrainian regions also, and from the western lands as well. In 983, Volodymyr fought against the Yatvingians, the Lithuanian-related tribe in the North-West, extended his territory there, too, and established a town of Volodymyr, not far from the Buh river, later on called Volodymyr Volynsky, to strengthen his grip over the area. In 993, he moved against Poland to assert himself in the West. It was the time of the most far-reaching extension of the Kievan realm in the West.[13] His war expedition against the Volga Bulgars did not apparently bring any conquest, but resulted in some peace treaty. However, most war projects of Kiev were not directly carried out by Volodymyr himself. Rather his generals were in command. He stayed in the capital, attending the state affairs as a true statesman of stature, unlike his father.

Much of his attention was absorbed by the constant struggle against the Pechengs, menacing Ukraine and Kiev itself. To stop their annoying and destructive onslaughts, Volodymyr ordered defense walls and fortresses constructed along the rivers of Stuhna, Desna, Sula, Trubezh and others for miles and miles, with defensive towers and gates, in a snake-like fashion, somewhat resembling the ancient Roman wall, the *limes,* as Polonska-Vasylenko asserted.

Internally, the consolidation of the realm continued, but at a rather slow pace. The importance of the Normans constantly declined, although Volodymyr used them extensively. At one point he got tired of them and their demands; he refused to pay them and sent them to Constantinople to render their mercenary services. The government machine had been progressively Slavicised, as the names of the leading men had indicated. The tribal designations were disappearing, like the Polianian or Siverianian lands, having been replaced by territorial designations, derived from the urban centers, such as the Kievans, Chernihivians, Smolenskians. No traces of traditional tribal chieftains had remained, and only sons and governors of the Kievan prince ruled respective lands as his viceroys. Yet, the centrifugal tendencies, due to the considerable conglomeration of different ethnical and racial entities, continued to exist, and at times the differences were so strong, that even Volodymyr's viceroys, and in particular, his own sons, attempted to reject the loyalty to Kiev and to serve the local interest. Such were the cases with the Polotsian land, which had its own prince; while Volodymyr's sons, Sviatopolk in the land of the Derevlianians, and Yaroslav in Novgorod the Great, were readying uprisings against their father, having intended to denounce any allegiance to the capital of Kiev. Sviatopolk was even ready to fight against his father with the foreign assistance of the Polish prince, Boleslav, his father-in-law. These developments brought ample proof that the Empire was not yet well cemented.

It was either Volodymyr's own or his advisers' idea to use Christianity, a new religion but well known in Ukraine, as a unifying force. Volodymyr, who initially was outwardly a devoted pagan, although Christianity was made probably dear to him by his grand-mother, Princess Olha, made a final move in that respect of a lasting consequence. Askold's Christianization of *Rus'* of a one hundred and twenty years before was only an ephemeral happening. Furthermore, all European powers of that time were Christian, and it seemed to be the only way to become a member of that exclusive political community. The Eastern wing of Christianity, of the Byzantine rite was better known, and as a matter of fact, known for centuries in Ukraine. It was also in the minds of men of that time associated with the might and glamor of the Byzantine Empire. It was the very reason why Volodymyr decided to baptize *Rus'* in the Byzantine rite of Christianity. The colorful story of *Povist' vremennykh lit* about Volodymyr's sending envoys all over to find out which religion was the best to accept, was simply the chronicler's legendary ornamentation of the whole narration, which had little to do with the real developments.

Volodymyr might have become Christian earlier, but it was kept secret. Again because of the scarcity and little reliability of the available historical resources, there have been two versions of how Ukraine-*Rus'* became Christian. The older and more widely accepted version is the "Greek" one. Prince Volodymyr wanted to make the event highly significant. Hence, he managed to draw the Byzantine court into the whole development. He asked the Greek emperors that they permit him to marry their sister, Anna, and that she should introduce Christianity to her new country. According to the proud tradition of the Byzantine court, it was an insult that a "barbarian" would marry a Greek princess of the imperial dynasty. At first, having been threatened by an uprising of Varda Phokas, one of their generals, emperors Basil and Constantine agreed to the proposal in exchange for Volodymyr's military assistance of 6,000 men. After Phokas was defeated and executed, the emperors did not want to keep their part of the agreement. Volodymyr went to war against the Greeks, captured the Crimean colony of Chersones and prepared an assault upon the capital of Constantinople itself. Then, the emperors yielded. Volodymyr married Princess Anna, who brought with herself priests, books, icons (holy pictures) and church vestments to Ukraine-*Rus'*. Later Volodymyr returned his conquests to the emperors. Subsequently, he carried out the baptism of his realm, starting with the capital of Kiev. According to the chronicle, he ordered all Kievans to get in the waters of the Dnieper River and be baptized. All supposedly were very joyous. In reality, however, the whole procedure was not so peaceful. Force was applied, especially in the distant regions, and the images of the pagan deities were destroyed by force, too.

Nevertheless, some additional historical sources suggested that the Christianization of *Rus'* was actually accomplished by the way of Bulgaria. In the town of Okhrida in Bulgaria there was at one time a patriarchate, independent upon Constantinople. And a great many scholars accepted the theory that from there Christianity was accepted; that the Bulgarian bishops and priests, books, vestments and icons arrived first in Ukraine; and that the similarity of languages and books, written in old Slavonic, largely facilitated the success of the Christianization of *Rus'*. Above all, the Byzantinian sources did not mention such an important event as the baptism of the huge northern empire, and the event was too grand to be ignored, if it really had taken place. Only some one and a quarter century later, after the Eastern schism, and after a prevailing Greek influence established itself throughout southern *Rus'*, the Ukrainian chronicles forged the whole story, by giving the Christianization event the "Greek" interpretation and suppressed its Bulgarian origin.[14] *Povist' vremennykh lit,* as it was pointed out before, has been full of such inaccuracies or direct misinformation. Also its story of a complete change of Volodymyr's character after he accepted Christianity, from a rough and cruel man to a noble and saintly one, deserves little credibility, as well.

Volodymyr was truly a great ruler. In order to assert himself in the religious matters, and according to Olha's tradition, he kept vital contacts with Rome, exchanging envoys in 988 and 994. Hrushevsky stated that it was quite possible that Volodymyr received a royal crown from the Pope of Rome. In order to assert himself internationally and to maintain relations with the countries of the Western civilization, he assumed diplomatic relations with Bohemia and Hungary and other lands, and strengthened dynastic relations, having married his sons and daughters with members of foreign ruling houses of Poland, Sweden, Hungary, Bohemia. He himself, having been married to Anna, a sister of the Byzantine emperors, no doubt, elevated the prestige of the house of Ruryk. The marriages with Westerners doubtlessly advanced the favorable relations with the Western wing of Roman Christianity. The arrival in Ukraine of Bishop Bruno of Querfurt in 1006 or 1007, a relative of Emperor Heinrich II, and his official welcome in Ukraine, were the indications of that friendliness with Rome and Germany. During the Chersones campaign,

Pope John XV sent to *Rus'* a holy gift, the head of St. Clemens, once Pope of Rome, who was greatly venerated by the *Rus'*-Ukrainians.

Prince Volodymyr constructed churches, towns, fortresses, palaces and defense walls, coined the currency, issued laws, called *ustavy,* to regulate the church organization, settled people in the frontiers of his realm, raised his country's culture and morals through Christianization. In some places schools were established. In order to increase his popularity and overall good-will among the people, he gave tremendous banquets, to which people of all walks of life were invited. He died in July of 1015, leaving behind a most favorable memory, having been praised by the sagas and *bylyny,* by average men in the street, as well as by leading personalities, like Metropolitan Ilarion, monk Nestor and others, popularly called, Volodymyr, *Yasne Sonechko,* the Glaring Sun.[15]

The Kievan Empire of *Rus'* reached its widest territorial extension under Volodymyr's reign: from the mouth of the Danube river, along the frontiers of the southern and eastern steppes of the Black and Azov Seas, reaching the Kuban valley and Tmutorokan, and then northwards, across the upper Donets and Don river systems, toward the Oka-Klazma-upper Volga water system, towards the White Sea, but not quite, and the Ladoga Lake, and then westwards, to the banks of the Baltic Sea, its borders touching the Chud', Latvian and Lithuanian lands on the banks of that sea; and from there, southwards, running near the Vistula river to the Carpathian mountains, enveloping West Ukraine (Galicia and Carpathian Ukraine) and present-day Bessarabia, toward the mouth of the Danube river. It was much larger and much more powerful than the empire of Charlemagne, yet sharing in the near future a similar fate. The former split into three distinct nations; Ukraine, Beyloruthenia and Russia, while the latter split also into three ones, Germany, France and Italy, all of them having subsequently distinct national life processes.

Yaroslav the Wise. It took about four years after Volodymyr's death until the permanent government under his son

Yaroslav was finally established. The constitutional system of the realm was not yet mature, and it did not provide any smooth transition of sovereignty. The customary approach of dividing the realm among all sons of the deceased monarch, perhaps under supremacy of the oldest one was a poor constitutional scheme, especially for a realm which consisted of many nationalities and races, being at the same time territorially huge and internally not well cemented. The symptoms of future trouble were visible during Volodymyr's life time. His sons, Sviatopolk and Yaroslav, were affected by those centrifugal tendencies, were either planning to or rising against the central authority of their father, while other sons were not exactly submissive, either.

Apparently Sviatopolk, one of the older sons, aspired to inherit the entire realm after father's death, and immediately proceeded with eliminating other contenders to the throne. He engineered the assassination of two younger brothers, Borys and Hlib, who resided as viceroys in the northern regions of the empire, and Sviatoslav, who governed in the Derevlianian land. Other brothers were paralyzed with terror and submitted, while Yaroslav, who governed in Novgorod the Great, soon gathered substantial forces and moved against Sviatopolk. Sviatopolk was defeated badly in the battle of Lubech in 1016, but did not yield. He went to Poland and asked his father-in-law, Prince Boleslav I, for military assistance. Boleslav, leading Polish, German and Hungarian warriors and mercenaries, assisted by Sviatopolk moved against Yaroslav, defeated him and captured Kiev in 1018, having been greeted there as victors. Returning back to Poland, Boleslav captured the West-Ukrainian regions of *Chervensky Horody* and other towns, which had seemed to become the bone of contention and a source of continuous warfare between Poland and *Rus'*. Taking Kiev by Boleslav's and Sviatopolk's troops was given by them an international resonance to establish the latter as an undisputed ruler of *Rus'*. Yet, Sviatopolk's victory was a short lasting one. Yaroslav gathered new forces, defeated his brother resoundingly and drove him out of Ukraine. His father-in-law did not come a second time to rescue him, and so, Sviatopolk was forced to run to the west, and died running somewhere "between the Bohemians and the Poles," perhaps persecuted by Yaroslav's agents. Supposedly for bringing foreigners (the Poles) upon Ukraine-*Rus'*, posterity denounced him by calling him Sviatopolk, the Sinner, *Okaianyi*. In fact, the subjects, to please Yaroslav, called the former a Sinner, Tomashivky asserted.

By 1019, Yaroslav was firmly occupying the Kievan throne. However, he was not actually a sole heir and ruler of the vast empire. His brother Mstyslav ruled in Tmutorokan and fought energetically against the Caucasian tribes. Subsequently, a war developed between the two brothers, which lasted for some three years. In 1026, a peace treaty was negotiated; Yaroslav kept under his scepter the regions on the right bank of the Dnieper river, with Mstyslav on the left one, and from that time on there was peaceful cooperation between them until Mstyslav's death, in 1036. From 1036 to 1054, Yaroslav was sole ruler of *Rus'*, after having eliminated his brother Sudyslav of Pskov, whom he kept in prison for many years. Only the land of Polotsk continued to maintain its political autonomy under a separate prince of a different branch of the House of Ruryk, most probably, however, recognizing Kiev's supremacy in some degree.

The matter of the West-Ukrainian regions, annexed by Boleslav, became an important political issue. After Boleslav's death, Yaroslav immediately took advantage from some Polish difficulties, and in 1030 and 1031 undertook two war expeditions against Poland; captured the town of Belz, the *Chervensky Horody* and other towns and regions and reincorporated them to the *Rus'* realm. At that time, he brought many Poles as war-prisoners and settled them in various Rus'ian fortresses along the Pecheng borders. He did not succeed in recapturing Carpathian Rus', which, during the struggle after Volodymyr's death among his sons, was conquered by Hungary and remained under Hungarian occupation almost uninterruptedly.

In connection with the Polish political affairs, Yaroslav waged a war against the Yatvingians in 1038 and against the Lithuanians in 1040 and the Mazovians, a Polish tribal community, in 1041 and again in 1047. Yaroslav was deeply involved in the Polish matters of succession, and in that connection, supporting subsequently Casimir, Boleslav's son in his bid for the throne, he negotiated an alliance with Heinrich II, emperor of Germany's Holy Roman Empire. After having put Casimir on the throne, he married him to his daughter, and his son Iziaslav to Casimir's sister. Having related his dynasty to the Polish dynasty of the Piast, Yaroslav unwisely assisted Poland in getting out of political troubles and becoming a stabilized and strong state. In a few decades, however, Poland became one of the worst enemies of Ukraine-*Rus'*.[16]

Yaroslav was also deeply interested in the expansion and strengthening of his realm in the North. He fought against the Chud' and other Finnic tribes, and in order to establish himself there, he founded a city of Yuriiv, after his Christian name, Yurii, to control the area. Presently the city, situated in Estonia, carries the name of Tartu. His governor, Ulyb, led another war expedition in the territories of the Northern Dvina river in 1032, while ten years later his son, Volodymyr of Novgorod, carried a war expedition in the territories of the Yam river to subject the other tribes. In both cases the results were dubious, however.

The northern conquest projects were definitely related to Yaroslav's Scandinavian policies, in which he was deeply involved. His court was always full of Scandinavian mercenaries, who participated in most of his war projects. In his court there lived for some time the members of the royal Scandinavian families, and close dynastic ties between the House of Ruryk and the Scandinavian ruling families were established. Yaroslav himself was married to a daughter of the Swedish king. Yaroslav's court had been mentioned many times in the sagas. Two sons of the English king, Edmund, stayed for a while in Kiev. The northern conquests served apparently as an avenue to connect *Rus'* more closely with Scandinavia.

Otherwise, Grand Prince Yaroslav maintained close diplomatic and dynastic connections with Germany, France and other West-European powers. He closely cooperated with the German emperor in the Polish affairs, as it was mentioned. Intermarriages were frequent and many among the Ukrainian and German princely and noble families. Yaroslav's daughter, Princess Anna, was married to Henry I, king of France, and according to the documents of that time, she played important roles in France's political matters.

On the other hand, Yaroslav must have been cool towards Byzantium for a few reasons. In 1043, Yaroslav's son, Prince Volodymyr, led a war expedition against Constantinople, which again was probably commercially motivated, like the previous wars from the time of Askold on. A Ukrainian merchant was killed in Constantinople. This was the last straw to kindle the war. The troubled situation must have been evolving for a long time. The Ukrainian forces were badly defeated in the war, while the Byzantines took many war-prisoners and blinded the Ukrainian general, Vyshata. A treaty was negotiated, unfavorable for the Ukrainian side. In order to smooth the strained situation, Yaroslav's son, Vsevolod, was married to Anna Monomakh, the emperor's daughter. Yaroslav was definitely unhappy with the Byzantine interference in the church matters of *Rus'*. Being friendly with the West, he did not want to submit the Ukrainian Church to the decisions of the Patriarch of Constantinople, who according to the Eastern *caesaropapistic* doctrine was fully submissive to the emperor in church affairs, as well, making it the avenue of political penetration. Yaroslav was, therefore, behind making Ilarion, a Ukrainian, the Metropolitan of Kiev and All-*Rus'*, with a strong trend towards ecclesiastic independence. Constantinople did not like it at all. It normally made a Greek a metropolitan for Ukraine-*Rus'*.

Diminishing the Pecheng threat, which harassed Ukraine from the South-East, was a significant development. They were pressed from the East by the new oriental hordes of the Torks and Cumans that spelled danger for Ukraine in the long-run, however. The last Pecheng assault took place in 1036, having threatened even Kiev, but badly beaten by Yaroslav's troops, the horde of the Pechengs dissipated, and its majority went westwards, to

Hungary. On the place where the Pechengs were ultimately beaten and repulsed, Yaroslav had constructed a beautiful Cathedral of St. Sophia in Kiev, which was supposed to reflect the grandeur of the *Rus'* Empire, just as a similar Cathedral of St. Sophia in Constantinople had been reflecting the might and the cultural greatness of Byzantium.

Yaroslav, called the Wise by posterity, tried to complete the organization of the Church and make it independent of the Patriarch of Constantinople to some extent; he constructed towns, churches, palaces, fortresses; promoted the development of culture and economy, and of trade, in particular; enlarged the capital of Kiev and made it a real center of the vast realm in all respects, and a unifying force for all lands and peoples. He gathered around himself the blood and intellectual elite of the realm and with their assistance he ruled the land wisely. The codification of the Rus'ian common law into a book of *Rus'ka Pravda,* the Rus'ian Law, became another cementing force of the Empire. It was a glorified result of the intellectual effort of Yaroslav and his esteemed advisors.[17] His vast realm, perhaps of the same territorial extent as of his father's, built one Church metropolis, with five dioceses, where truly Christian civilization was fast rising and expanding. Schools were organized; libraries established; church architecture flourished.[18]

Yaroslav the Wise died in February 1054, leaving behind a testament by which he divided his Empire among his sons according to the principle of seniorate. Three older sons received larger provinces as separate principalities; Iziaslav received the Kievan land with Novgorod, Pskov, Turiv and Derevlianian provinces; Sviatoslav — the Chernihivian and Siverianian lands, with Tmutorokan and the territories of the Radimichians and Viatichians; Vsevolod received Pereyaslav, southern Siverianian land, Rostov-Suzdal and other towns of the Oka-Klazma-Volga regions. The two younger sons received according to the testament; Ihor — Volhinia; Viacheslav — the Smolensk land. The Polotsk principality was ruled by Prince Vseslav, Iziaslav's grandson, while Galicia and *Chervensky Horody* were apparently given to

Prince Rostyslav, Yaroslav's grand-son. Grand Prince Yaroslav, while dividing his realm among the heirs, demanded that they should live in peace and love, and honored the oldest heir, Prince Iziaslav, as if he were their father, who apparently was supposed to be the supreme ruler or sovereign.[19] It was the essence of the seniorate principle. Yet, although the seniorate was customary at that time, it was the fatal beginning of the end of the *Rus'* Kievan realm; the permanent source of domestic and dynastic wars, quarrels and misunderstandings, which eventually terminated the grand Kievan era of the history of Ukraine. It is surprising that Yaroslav, having the knowledge of internal wars among the sons of Sviatoslav, his grandfather, and Volodymyr's, his father's, in which he himself unluckily participated, was so short-sighted and believed that his sons would act differently. His testament lacked any executive power. Hence, Yaroslav's death terminated the "Golden Age" of Kievan *Rus'*, and the time of decline began.

The Fall: The Confederate State. Not only was the principle of seniorate a fatal decision to make, but it seemed that with Yaroslav's death the political genius and statemanship of the Ruryk dynasty were exhausted for a while, at least of its southern branch. There were no more political giants, like Sviatoslav the Conqueror, Volodymyr the Great, and Yaroslav the Wise. Except Prince Volodymyr Monomakh, at the beginning of the twelfth century, only mediocre personalities occupied the Kievan throne for a short time, who were incapable and not able to afford to have anything grand done. Hence, the mediocrity of the ruling princes was, perhaps, the more significant cause of the Kievan decline than the seniority principle itself. Of course, the permanent threat of the steppes, the Cumans and, subsequently, the Tartars, who settled in the Black and Azov Sea steppes, and who uninterruptedly assaulted Ukraine by their rapacious raids, like the Pechengs did before, from the eleventh to the eighteenth century, contributed as the third cause to the decline and fall of Kievan *Rus'*, this very defense wall of Europe against the onslaughts of Asia. Understandably, there were still other causes of trouble, perhaps of a minor nature, but having been still contributory ones, like the particularism of individual lands or provinces of Ukraine, the struggle between the monarchistic principle of the princely rule, the aristocratic principle of the oligarchic rule of the nobles, the *boyars,* and the democratic principles of the rule of the people through the people's meeting, the *viche*.

After Yaroslav's death, five princes reigned in Kiev. Iziaslav, who according to the testament was supposed to be the Kievan sovereign "in place of the father," ruled in Kiev from 1054 to 1068, then, from 1069 to 1073, and finally, from 1077 to 1078; his brother Sviatoslav, from 1073 to 1076; third brother, Vsevolod, from 1078 to 1093; Iziaslav's son, Sviatopolk, from 1093 to 1113; and finally, Volodymyr Monomakh, Vsevolod's son, who succeeded in recovering for a short while the splendor of the capital of Kiev and the *Rus'* realm. It was the first period of a decline, but not yet a menacing one.

Iziaslav's frequently interrupted reign was well meant, but poorly carried out. No doubt, he was Western-oriented at the time, when the schismatic rupture was accomplished between Rome and Constantinople, and the latter's influence and impact upon the spiritual and otherwise aspects of life of the Kievan society were ever deeper penetrating in the *Rus'* soil. It certainly contributed to a clash between the prince of Kiev and members of the dynasty and the broad classes of the population. Furthermore, Iziaslav lacked ability and was a poor tactition.

Actually from the very beginning of the seniorate system there was no harmonious cooperation among the brothers. At first the three older brothers cooperated, but acted one-sidedly towards other members of the dynasty. In 1057 they committed injustices towards Viacheslav's sons, eliminating them from the rightful succession to their father's lands and making them the *izgoii,* the social outcasts, without a proper place in the *Rus'* social structure. They freed some relatives from prison, while putting others into the prison, as they deemed advantageous for themselves. At first, all three of them fought jointly against the new invaders from Asia, the Torks and the Cumans. They defeated the former but were defeated by the latter in the early 1060s. The Cuman onslaught resulted in a formal rebellion of the Kievan population against their prince, to whom he refused to give arms and organize an anti-Cuman war expedition. Iziaslav apparently did not trust his people because of some earlier conflicts. The rebels expelled Iziaslav from Kiev and proclaimed Vseslav the Grand Prince. Iziaslav went to Poland, and in a few months returned supported and assisted by Boleslav the Daring. Iziaslav recaptured the capital, while his son cruelly punished the rebels. The *viche* was put under princely supervision. Obviously, the way in which Iziaslav and his son dealt with the rebels did not spell any future friendly developments.

Meanwhile, after a short lull in matters, a serious conflict, concerning the territorial division of lands among the princes, erupted among the three older brothers. Iziaslav lost Kiev again, and then went to Poland and Germany to look for help. The conflict among the brothers was soon related to the prolonged Western political-ecclesiastic struggle between Emperor Heinrich IV and Pope Gregory VII, into which Poland and other countries were drawn, including other Iziaslav's brothers. Iziaslav, not having received any assistance from Heinrich, turned for assistance to the Pope, having sent his son Yaropolk to Rome. It was the era of intense diplomatic relations of *Rus'* and the West, including the papacy. Pope Gregory, though not helping Iziaslav militarily, issued a letter, by which the former was confirmed as the ruler of the *Rus'* Kingdom. The move certainly antagonized the pro-Byzantine and Orthodox feelings of the Kievan society at that time and did not help the prince in the long run, although at a certain point the monks of the Kiev-Pechera Monastery, the most influencial religious congregation in Ukraine for a long time, came in defense of Iziaslav's rights to the throne, and against his brother Sviatoslav, who occupied the Kievan throne illicitly for a short while.

The third term in Iziaslav's Kievan rule was equally unfortunate. Iziaslav got involved in continuous struggles with the *izgoii* princes, to whom he denied either directly or indirectly the rights to their respective princely lands, the *udily*. He was killed during this domestic warfare, into which the foreign and barbarian Cumans were drawn for the first time. The Cumans from this point on knew very well how to get involved into Ukrainian domestic affairs to their own advantage and toward weakening the *Rus'* state.[20]

Although it seemed that Sviatoslav was the most able of all brothers and tried to unite under his scepter most lands, his reign of three short years in Kiev was not eventful. He was, perhaps, more interested in books and intellectual matters than in political affairs. He had a large library and upon his advice a literary collection, called *Zbirnyk Sviatoslava,* was published.

Vsevolod, the third son of Yaroslav, being in Kiev, united under his rule many lands again, Kiev, Chernihiv, Smolensk, Pereyaslav, Oka-Klazma-Volga watershed regions and other provinces and principalities of the realm, having dreamt of the restoration of the old splendor and might. Yet, it produced numerous and continuous conflicts with many *izgoi* princes, who just did not want to yield and give up their inheritance rights. The most notorious conflict of succession was with Princes Volodar and Vasyl of Galicia, sons of Prince Rostyslav, who insisted on their right to retain their land in their family and their possession. The most tragic aspect of these struggles for succession between the Kievan prince and the *izgoii,* princes forced out of their fathers lands and having no home and no social status, was the instance of the *izgoii* on bringing the Cumans into the picture. They undertook many booty expeditions under the pretext of aiding the *izgoii,* and by so doing, devastated and ruined the Ukrainian cities and countryside. The townspeople and the peasants suffered especially, since their trade and farming were falling apart.

Vsevolod might have been well educated, might have known many languages, might have increased the dynastic and diplomatic connections with the West-European courts and powers, and might have maintained good relations with Constantinople, having been married to Anna Monomakh, the Emperor's daughter, yet his reign could not be considered a glorious era in the history of Ukraine-*Rus'*, because of these numerous dynastic and domestic warfares, which impoverished the country, and in which there was neither an end nor a victor. Chaos was spreading. Yaroslav's principle of seniorate clearly did not work. No prince was really willing to respect and obey the senior prince of Kiev and there was no orderly succession to the senior princely throne or the patrimonial throne of the father in a separate land, but an armed and bloody struggle, in which the princes, nobles, townspeople and peasants, villages, towns and castles perished in smoke, fire and ruin. With Vsevolod's death, the rule of the first generation Yaroslav's sons came to an end, and the throne of Kiev, with the consent of Vsevolod's son, Prince Volodymyr Monomakh, was taken over by Sviatopolk, Iziaslav's son, who ruled for twenty years, a troubled era.

It was the time of the most devastating Cuman raids and assaults, which ruined the Kievan and Pereyaslav lands, and devastated even parts of Chernihiv and Siverianian principalities. Under the impact of those assaults, the Ukrainian ethnic element began to retreat to the north-eastern provinces of the country, looking for safety and more peaceful living conditions. That progressively reduced the Ukrainian ethnic territory in the southern and south-eastern frontiers. The most dangerous was then the Cuman Khan Boniak, who uncompromisingly devastated Ukraine at the background of the unceasing dynastic quarrels and warfares of the princes of the Ruryk house. Even numerous intermarriages and family ties between the Ruryk and Cuman princes and princesses did not moderate the situation. The bloodshed continued. Ultimately, Grand-Prince Sviatopolk married a Cuman princess, daughter of Tuhor Khan, to acquire peace, but all efforts were in vain. Soon, an alliance of three Cuman Khans, Boniak, Kuri and Tuhor, assaulted Ukraine by a most vicious and devastating war raid. The population of the borderlands was fleeing in masses to the more safe northern regions of Ukraine.

According to the chronicle, the wise noblemen, the *boyars,* were persuading the princes to stop their nonsensical dynastic fighting, to unite in a common effort and to finish up the Cumans for saving the fatherland. Finally, the Ruryk princes arranged a convention at Lubech, in fall 1097, near Kiev to resolve the tragic situation. The most important agreement, reached by the Ukrainian princes at Lubech, was actually the abrogation of the seniority principle and adopting in place of it the patrimonial principle, after nearly fifty years of the unsuccessful application of the former. From now on, no more was the senior prince supposed to go to the capital of Kiev to exercise his grand-princely authority of somewhat centralist flavor over other princes of the dynasty. It was the root of envy and constant conflict. It had been agreed that in the future all princes would hold to their patrimonial principalities or *udily;* in the particular land, the son should rule after his father and so on. It was definitely replacing centralism by decentralism, and so *Rus'* was becoming a federated or confederated state of the Ruryk dynasty. Furthermore, the convention agreed to place the responsibility for honoring the principle jointly upon all princes. And finally, it was agreed to build an alliance of all princes against the Cuman threat, prohibiting at the same time individual members of the dynasty to negotiate individual and private alliances with the Cuman enemy for their individual ends.[21]

Nevertheless, the articles of the Lubech convention were not honored for long. An intrigue was manufactured, Prince Vasyl of Terebovla was blinded by Sviatopolk and a three-year war among the princes resulted, from 1097 to 1100, into which the foreign powers, Poland and Hungary, were drawn. The princely convention of Vytechiv, in 1100, to deal with the problem, did not produce any worthwhile result. Yet, during the war turmoil the ancient constitutional role of the people's *viche,* to supplement the inadequate authority of the prince, the people, the nobility and the Church, began to affect the political developments. The popular voice, for instance, persuaded Volodymyr Monomakh not to start a war of revenge against Sviatopolk to punish him for blinding Vasyl, from which only the Cumans could have had an advantage. The Lubech and Vytechiv agreements had a positive aspect after all, since they established the practice of periodic princely meetings, the so-called *snemy*, where all kinds of dynastic and political problems were discussed and at times resolved, including the common action of the Ruryk princes against the Cuman onslaught. Prince Volodymyr Monomakh became the hero of the victorious Cuman wars, while Sviatopolk's position as the senior Kievan prince was fading away.

Prince Sviatopolk was not popular with the people at all. He and his close associates were mixed up with some shady monetary deals, illicit business operations and illicit confiscations of properties to their advantage; hence, his death unleashed a bloody riot in Kiev during which many of his cronies, including some princely officials, perished. Frightened by the developments, the people's *viche* of Kiev asked Volodymyr Monomakh to accept the grand-princely throne, although constitutionally he had no apparent right to do so. Yet his personality and his fame were more important, and finally, after a few requests from the *viche*, he agreed and came to the capital of the realm.

Volodymyr Monomakh. Monomakh's fame was great before he assumed the Kievan throne. During the time of his predecessors, the Cuman raids were getting more cruel and devastating as a revenge or response to the limited Ukrainian defense measures. Finally, due to Volodymyr's initiative, in 1111 a common action of the Ruryk princes was undertaken to pacify the rapacious Cumans. In the battle at the Donets river, the Cumans were badly defeated, and much booty and many prisoners were taken by the Ukrainians. Khan Otrok left the Ukrainian steppes and went with his horde to Gruzia, in the Caucasian regions. The battle received a great resonance all over Europe, in all its capitals, including Rome. Volodymyr's prestige was record high, while Sviatopolk was left completely in the shadow of his cousin.

Volodymyr was given a surname of Monomakh, since he was a son of a Greek princess, Anna Monomakh, and Grand-Prince Vsevolod. He was a skillful diplomat, and by diplomatic maneuvers he kept a relative peace among the princes of the dynasty, but at the same time he succeeded in enlarging his realm by annexing the Turiv-Pynsk and Volhinian lands. At the peak of his reign, he actually ruled over three-fourths of the traditional imperial lands of *Rus'* from the time of Volodymyr the Great and Yaroslav the Wise. At one time he attempted to expand his domination over some towns on the Danube river by diplomatic measures and a limited military action, but did not succeed. As the tradition deemed proper, Monomakh continued close dynastic ties with the European courts, which certainly enhanced Kiev's prestige. He himself was married to Gita, daughter of Harold II, King of England. His son, Mstyslav, was married to Kristine, daughter of the king of Sweden, while his daughter, Yevphimia, was married to Koloman, king of Hungary. There were also other matrimonial ties.

Volodymyr ruled successfully with the assistance of his sons, who respected him and obeyed his orders. The place of the seniority of the Kievan throne was certainly recovered again. In the consequence of the said revolt of 1113, Monomakh added some new articles to *Rus'ka Pravda,* the celebrated book of laws, to regulate money lending and interest rates in order to protect people against rapacious loan sharks and their usury. What kind of ruler Volodymyr Monomakh was or intended to be, or expected or wanted his sons to be, could be deduced from his literary work, entitled *Pouchennia ditiam, Advice to Children.* It was a partially autobiographical work where, on the basis of his own life, Volodymyr suggested to his sons what kind of men and princes they should be. The work is permeated by high moral standards of love, charity and justice, telling how children should be raised, and then, as adults, how they should be charitable to the poor, respect their officials and advisors, guard themselves against being unjust or unfair to anybody. As princes, they should not kill anybody, neither the guilty nor the innocent. It was a splendid manifestation of medieval humanism, supposedly based on an English pattern, written by a bishop, but it was of a much higher intellectual and moral level than the supposed original.[22]

Volodymyr respected and advised others to respect foreigners and merchants, probably having in mind the advantages coming to his country through the mercantile intercourse with foreign lands.

Grand-Prince Volodymyr Monomakh was peacefully succeeded by his son, Prince Mstyslav, who reigned in Kiev from 1125 to 1132, continued to some extent his rule according to his father's tradition. He was respected and obeyed by other princes in the junior towns and principalities, while successfully dominating and annexing to his *patrimonium* the Polotsk land and large parts of Byeloruthenia or Byelorussia. His authority and influence was also felt in Novgorod the Great, the important northern commercial center. Kiev still continued to preserve its prestige of the true capital of all *Rus'*. Mstyslav, assisted by other princes, continued to fight against the Cumans, who harassed Ukraine, but not so cruelly as before. Particularism still yielded to centralism.

Nevertheless, in spite of a superficial lull, the quarrels among the princes continued, energetically participated in by Mstyslav himself, who on the other hand attempted to strengthen and extend the dynastic ties with Sweden, Norway, Denmark, Greece, Hungary, Bohemia and other lands with success. Because of his struggle against the Cumans and relative prestige among the princes and various branches of the Ruryk dynasty, Mstyslav sometimes was called the Great, while the Orthodox Church included him among its saints, along with Olha, Volodymyr the Great, Borys, Hlib and others.

The Disintegration of the Empire. After Mstyslav, the Kievan throne was ascended by his brother, Prince Yaropolk, who reigned from 1132 to 1139, a short seven year period. He lacked ability and prestige and his rule was filled with all kinds of internal dynastic conflicts and strifes, which not only continued to impoverish the broad classes of population, but also resulted in heavy territorial losses for Kiev, while the separatist tendencies of individual principalities and lands manifested themselves vehemently. Polotsk, Minsk, Galicia and Novgorod the Great made themselves almost entirely independent of the Kievan senior prince, whose prestige declined to a record low level. In particular, Novgorod exhibited a drive for independence. Here also the prestige of the local prince declined, while the "democratic" rule of the people began to take over.

During the one hundred years, from 1139 to 1240, during a real disintegration process of the once powerful and glamorous empire, as Polonska-Vasylenko asserted, the Kievan throne was occupied for a longer or shorter period of time by 25 different senior princes. Consequently, Kiev experienced then forty-eight separate ruling periods; one lasting 13 years; one six years; two for five years; four four years long; three three years long; seven only two years long; and 36 ruling periods lasting only one year or even shorter.[23] A few of the more outstanding of them, but not great ones at all, were Vsevolod, 1139-1146, Ihor, 1146, Iziaslav, 1146-1154; Yurii the Longhanded, 1154-1157, with interruptions; Rostyslav, 1158-1167, Mstyslav, 1167-1170, Sviatoslav, 1175-1194; and Ruryk, 1194-1215. Strifes, conflicts, dynastic wars, bloodshed and devastation of the land, of which there was endless number and apparently no end, and during which some foreign powers were also involved in the domestic encounters, fully exposed the internal weakness of the realm, caused by irresponsible members of the once splendid dynasty.

Rather intense and heavy in consequences was the conflict between Iziaslav and Yurii the Longhanded, who persistently fought for the domination and retention of the Kievan throne, forcing out of and replacing each other on it for two or three times. Iziaslav was liked better by the people, seriously mourned by them when he died, while Yurii, who came from northern Suzdal, was deeply hated by the southern Ukrainian population. At his death, an open rebellion erupted in Kiev, during which time Yurii's courts and palaces in the city and in the suburbs were pillaged and ruined, while his "Suzdal *boyars*" and other associates, including his son, Vasyl, were mercilessly annihilated. It was actually the first and openly pronounced manifestation of a national conflict between the Ukrainians, the southern builders of the Kievan realm, and the northern colonial people, who were in the process of merging with the Ugro-Finnic ethnic element and of laying the foundations for the formation of the future Muscovite-Russian nationality. At the very moment of the rule and death of Yurii the Longhanded, Dolgorukii, the hegemony of Ukraine was eventually breaking down, and the hegemony of Russia in East Europe was just in the process of being conceived.

Yet, Yurii the Longhanded, was still feeling some allegiance to Kiev, and his ambition was to acquire the senior Kievan throne as the expression of the supreme authority in *Rus'*. However, after his death, the northern Suzdalian throne was succeeded to by his son, Prince Andrei Bogolubskii, who was completely alien to Kiev. When he was brought south by his father, he clearly showed his hostile attitude towards the Ukrainians and the Ukrainian branches of the Ruryk house. He was also deeply despised by them all, as well. In 1154, Yurii made him prince of Vyshhorod, a town in the vicinity of Kiev. Andreii could not stand the conditions there and soon left the place secretly, without his father's knowledge, and went back to the North, Suzdal and Vladimir on Klazma, which he liked. He took with him to the North treasured holy pictures, *icons,* Church books, vestments and vessels, including the *icon* of the Holy Mother of Vyshhorod, which was later greatly revered throughout all Russia.

Andrei moved the capital of his Suzdalian principality from Suzdal to Vladimir on Klazma to make himself politically more independent, following from the very beginning the political blueprint for the principality's expansion, as it was set up by his father. He went even further than that. He dreamed of its greatness and a "senior" position among the northern petty principalities, paraphrasing and completely twisting the old myth of Kiev. Having suppressed democratic institutions, the *viche* and the *boyar duma,* council, in his land and having established himself as an autocrat, he decided to destroy Kiev and to knock out its power for several reasons. First of all, Andrei intended to ruin Kiev so severely that it would lose any attraction as a "senior" city of the old realm. In this way he intended to elevate Vladimir as its political successor in the "new" realm because of the latter's factual power which it began to wield. Andrei's later action in 1169 proved to be his original intention. Second, Kiev's ruin would force its traditionally flourishing trade to disappear and East-European commerce would necessarily have established its center in political safe Vladimir on Klazma, in the Suzdalian principality. Third, by damaging Kiev's power and prestige, he thought, he would eliminate it as Vladimir's contender with respect to political supremacy over Novgorod the Great, which always looked for a powerful protector. The domination of Novgorod seemed to Yurii and Andrei to be a necessary prerequisite for strengthening Suzdal's and Vladimir's position in developing their Occident-Orient trading, Novgorod being somewhat a "window to Europe." Then, the Kievan and Novgorodian questions were linked inseparably in Andrei's mind. Finally, the fourth reason for Andrei's animosity to Kiev was, of course, anchored in its Ukrainian national character as opposed to Vladimir's incipient Russian one.

To carry out these motives and without any historically clear *casus belli,* Andrei sent his armies under his son's command against Kiev at the beginning of 1169. Some princes of the Ukrainian and Byeloruthenian branches of the Ruryk house joined the Suzdalians and Vladimirians in the seige, and eventually the conquest, pillage and merciless destruction of the ancient city and capital. The chronicle asserted that such merciless looting and ruining of the capital had never been witnessed before.[24] For many decades many contenders to the Kievan throne fought for the city, conquered and, then, left it. However, in most cases, with one serious exception, they had rather intended to preserve its splendor. Andrei Bogolubskii meant to destroy it once and for all. Andrei's invasion and pillaging left a permanent scar; Kiev never recovered. The era of what can be called the Muscovite-Russian hegemony and supremacy had begun in East Europe. From that time on Andrei considered himself to be the "senior" prince in the Ruryk dynasty, with his capital in Vladimir on the Klazma in the North-East. In his self-styled capacity of "a Grand

Duke,'' he began to dispose of Kiev and other Ukrainian principalities and cities as his vassal possessions. He placed his candidates as junior princes there or ordered them out at will, and continued to interfere in Ukrainian affairs from his northern and alien capital, causing more chaos, confusion and dynastic strife. He invited Cuman raids upon Ukraine which aimed directly at the further weakening of Kiev and the Ukrainian South. Andrei suddenly in 1174 stopped Vladimir's interference in the Kievan *Rus'* matters for a while. This lull lasted until his younger brother, Vsievolod, emerged from the Suzdal-Vladimirian dynastic wars as a victorious contender, and placed himself on the Vladimir throne.[25]

Vsievolod, although interested in Kievan and southern political affairs, never intended to visit there or to become militarily involved in Ukrainian domestic and dynastic warfares, as his father Yurii or his brother Andrei had done. He simply used political and diplomatic maneuvers and intrigues to stimulate and to intensify these warfares by setting one prince of the southern branches against the other and by encouraging the Cumans to assault and to devastate the Ukrainian provinces. Vsievolod utilized the resulting chaos to enforce his grand-ducal will in Kiev to the advantage of the pre-Muscovite north. Many centuries later a Polish historian, J. Lelevel, who dealt with the issue of the Suzdal-Vladimir-Moscow relation toward Ukraine-*Rus'*, made the following assertion: "Moscow is a Muscovite place, a degenerate and illegitimate daughter of mother *Rus'* against whom it raised its criminal hand. Historians of the German Reich are no longer interested in Switzerland and Holland because of their separation from the Reich. And those new lands, after the organization and formation of their own states, never raised their hands against neighboring Germany. This is unlike Moscow, which, with an empire of its own and fully separate from *Rus'*, has always sought to dominate *Rus'*. The absence of a clear distinction between Muscovy and ancient *Rus'*, unjustifiably encouraged by certain historians, has resulted in a complete misunderstanding of

Rus' beginnings. This in turn resulted in the denial of another nationality's existence."[26]

The formation of the Muscovite-Russian nationality in the northern colonial borderlands of the Kievan *Rus'* empire definitely affected the process of the latter's disintegration because of the arising national-ethnical antagonism. An entirely new national entity was developing in the North, which had by no means any interest in the preservation of an alien, multi-racial and multi-national realm. Similar national alienation was going on in the north-western regions of the empire, with enhanced territorial particularism and hostility toward Kiev's centralism. Ethnically the pre-Russian Novgorodian commonwealth, which had for centuries exhibited centrifugal tendencies, as it was pointed out before, during the reigns of Volodymyr the Great and Yaroslav the Wise, successfully then separated itself from Kiev's protection. Also, the Polotsian and the Smolenskian lands, being ethnically, prevailingly Byeloruthenian or Byelorussian, took full advantage of Kiev's growing weakness and separated themselves as independent principalities of an ethnically monolythic character. In the far North-East, the Murom land, still prevailingly Ugro-Finnic, though under the rule of the princes of a branch of the Ruryk house, equally alienated itself from Kiev, with which it had literally nothing in common.

Yet, the decentralization process was proceeding further than the national differentiation of the *Rus'* empire. Even the ethnically monolythic Ukrainian territories in the South and South-West of the realm, due to the dynastic particularism of the separate branches of the Ruryk house, were alienating themselves from each other. In particular, the Galician and Volhinian principalities, soon unified under one dynasty, traditionally displayed politically separatist ambitions. Then, after the complete fall of Kiev, the fate designated the Galician-Volhinian principality to inherit from Kiev the tradition of Ukrainian statehood, and to continue it for some one hundred years. The fortunes of the Galician-Volhinian state, the ethnically monolithic Ukrainian

143

political organization, which at one time was enabled to unify almost all Ukrainian provinces, including Kiev, but with exception of Chernihiv and Pereyaslav, must be discussed in a separate chapter. North-east of Kiev, the Chernihivian principality, the land of the ancient Siverianians, was alienating itself from Kiev, trying to live a separate political life under the Sviatoslav branch of the Ruryk dynasty. The Chernihiv princes were often allying themselves with the Cumans to defend their autonomy, and equally they often also joined the unified war projects of the Ukrainian princes against the Cuman onslaughts. The city of Chernihiv was the seat of the senior prince of the land, while minor towns, such as Novhorod Siversky, Kursk, Briansk and Trubchevsk housed some junior princes of the princely branch. Of course, dynastic conflicts were also going on, splitting the land into many petty principalities, struggling for the "senior" throne of Chernihiv, and weakening the land substantially.

North-west of Kiev, the Turiv-Pynsk land with mixed Ukrainian and Byeloruthenian population, had separated itself from the Kievan supremacy since the 1150s, which was splitting into petty principalities. The land subsequently had to defend its autonomy against the Galician-Volhinian principality's domination, since the latter was by far more powerful, and against the Lithuanian assaults. Finally, south-west of the Kievan land, the Pereyaslav territory, once connected with the Chernihiv land, was subsequently separated from it, and served for some time as a transitionary principality, a stepping stone toward acquiring the Kievan "senior" throne. The Pereyaslavians soon began to aspire to more independence, not having been happy to live in Kiev's shadow, and invited the Suzdalian princely branch to rule over them to underscore in this way their opposition to the ancient capital of *Rus'*. The Pereyaslav land suffered badly from the Cuman assaults, having been close to the Cuman territories. At first its borderlands were devastated and depopulated in the east and south-east, but in the twelfth century, due to the constant anti-Cuman wars, a part of the lost territories toward the Vorskla river and beyond were regained again.

Of course, after the individual lands separated themselves politically from the Kievan supremacy, the proper Kievan principality was reduced apparently to the original land of the Polianians, the very original *Rus'* of the late eighth and early ninth century, and forced to live its own territorial political life. Doubtlessly, it was the most populated and urbanized province of Ukraine with many towns, such as Vyshhorod, Bilhorod, Vasyliv, Trepol, Torchesk, Yuriev and others, while the southern borderland was defended by a series of fortresses. After the territorial particularism took over and overpowered fully Kiev's centralism, the class of the *boyars,* nobles, acquired a strong political position, and heavily influenced the choice and selection of individual princely branches and individual princes, who were seated on the Kievan throne. The people's meeting also gained more power and influence in the political course of events. It was pointed out before, that even earlier, when Kiev was still the capital of *Rus'*, the common people and the *boyars* at times affected the princely successions or openly showed their displeasure with some princes, like Sviatopolk in 1113 and Yurii Dolgorukii in 1157. Frequently, the prince had to consult the *viche*, according to the chronicle. Yet, because of its senior position as the seat of the grand prince, which frequently passed from one branch of the Ruryk house to another, the Kievans were actually unable to acquire for themselves one steady dynasty, a particular branch of the Ruryk house, which would have had a special attachment to and would have paid a special attention to and particularly cared for the Kievan principality and the city itself, as is the case in other territories, or lands. On the other hand, the Kievans at times searched for princes to come and to rule over them, since according to the political conceptions at that time, a prince had to rule over a community, and a regular way of life of a community could have hardly been imagined without a prince of a Ruryk dynasty in any part of *Rus'*. Nevertheless, in spite of its political decline, the city of Kiev still remained an important cultural, religious, economic and political center of Ukraine, or the ancient *Rus'* proper, during this entire period.

This was the general state of the political affairs in Ukraine-*Rus'* on the eve of the fearful Mongol or Tartar invasion, which knocked the Kievan realm completely out of existence.[27]

The Mongol-Tartar Invasion. Until the thirteenth century, when Temudzhin Genghis Khan succeeded in building his vast Mongolian empire, various Mongol tribes, along with the related Tartars, Merkits, Keraits, Naimans and some others, were building numerous semi-political organizations of ephemeral character. "Empires" were quickly organized by more outstanding chieftains and then just as quickly dissolved on the death of those chieftains, whose personal abilities were the only foundation of power of those "empires." In the eleventh century the chieftain of the Mongol tribe, Kabul Khan, became an important political figure among nomadic rulers in Mongolia. Esugay Bagatur, Kabul's grandson, was an unimportant tribal chief. However, because of the tradition of his clan and his personal qualities, he was held in esteem by his people. Then, Temudzhin, Esugay's son, elevated his tribe to the level of a world-wide political and historical prominence. The impact of Temudzhin's historical mission was so great that the name of the Mongols, one ethnic community of tribes, had since been generally applied to identify all nomadic tribes of Mongolia, including the Tartars.

Having united all related tribes, the Mongols, the Tartars, the Merkits, the Keraits, the Naimans and others around 1211, Temudzhin invaded North China. Between 1212 and 1220, he conquered the provinces under Chinese supremacy, Manchuria and Chinese Turkestan, and later on the Moslem states of Central Asia. He soon reached and overran Transcaucasia. Through the passages of the Caucasian Mountains, his armies suddenly appeared in the Black and Azov Sea steppes and attacked the Cumans in 1222. The Cumans asked the Ukrainian princes to help them against the new and unknown but terrible invader. The princes of the Ruryk house, having been related by many marital ties with the Cuman khans, resolved to assist militarily the Cumans in their struggle against the Mongols. However, a bloody battle at the Kalka river in 1223 became a major defeat of the Cuman and the allied Ukrainian-*Rus'* armed forces. Then, suddenly the Mongols, apparently not yet ready to continue their European conquests and considering the penetration of the Ukrainian steppes as a strategic raid to get the "feeling" of the European battleground, withdrew to Asia, making no attempt to invade the territories further north. Things quieted down for a while.

In 1236, the Mongols, or the Tartars, as they were popularly called, reappeared but from the North. Khan Batu crossed the Ural Mountains from Asia with his armies of some 50,000 Mongols and 100,000 Turks and other auxiliary troops, followed by masses of people, old and young, women and children. It all seemed like a mass migration. Batu invaded the lands of the Volga Bulgars with the definite purpose of keeping them, and there were other territories he hoped to conquer permanently for his people to settle or to roam around in. Consequently, Batu's invasion resembled, as stated, a migration of people looking for new homes, preceded by vast armies to annihilate any opposition by the native population of the conquered countries. In 1237, the capital of the Volga Bulgars was destroyed as a symbol of conquest.

Then, immediately Batu proceeded with the conquest of the North-Eastern, pre-Russian principalities, which, having been involved in domestic quarrels, were not ready for the onslaught, at all. The main encounter between Yurii II, prince of Vladimir, and Batu's forces took place on the banks of the Sit River in March 1238. The Vladimirian army was outmaneuvered and completely beaten. The Mongol victory was complete. After the battle on the Sit River, the entire Russian North-East was open to the Mongols. The junior principalities were no serious military opposition to Batu's invasion forces. Neither had Novgorod the Great, great commercially but weak militarily, scarcely any hope of stopping the Mongol victorious march.

While Batu operated in the North, Khan Mongka fought in the Caucasian and Pontic areas, slowly approaching the Ukrainian frontiers, and then, the capital of Kiev. Perhaps Mongka's progress was not sufficiently rapid, and perhaps his forces were inadequate to accomplish the job of conquering the Ukrainian

South. Batu, therefore, brought his forces, operating in the Russian North, to a sudden halt some 65 miles east of Novgorod and ordered them to march south. His march southward was rather uneventful. In 1239 only some minor military projects were accomplished, except for the one against the Cumans. In the summer of 1240, Batu began the conquest of Ukraine. Mongka seized, pillaged and devasted Pereyaslav and Chernihiv lands and demanded the submission of Kiev. But his envoys were killed. The Mongols were vengeful. Under the supreme command of Batu, they moved against the city and took it in December 1240. The city's population was slaughtered mercilessly and the city was looted, burned and ruined. Subsequently, other provinces of Ukraine were dominated by the Mongol hordes, and the Ukrainian princes following the Russian example, submitted to Batu's and Great Khan Ugedey's supremacy. Only a few resisted, but with no success. Prince Danylo of Galicia tried to outsmart Batu, but eventually he also had to submit. Hungary was the next object of Batu's invasion, and soon, parts of Poland, Silesia and Hungary were overrun by Mongol troops.

The Polish-German forces were completely put to rout by the Mongols in the battle of Lignica, in Silesia; the Hungarian army was fully defeated in the battle on the banks of the Tisa and Solona Rivers in April 1241. *En route* to Hungary, the Mongol forces, which fought in Poland, invaded Moravia and Bohemia, looting as they went.

Actually, the death of Great Khan Ugedey in distant Mongolia, in December 1241, saved Central Europe from the distraction experienced by East-European nations, Ukraine having been again, as at the time of the Pecheng and Cuman threat, a wall protecting Western civilization, upon which the terrible waves of the Asiatic invasions were breaking their powerful impacts. When the news about the death of Ugedey reached Batu's camp in 1242, all Mongol military operations were stopped and Batu himself and his troops marched back to his *ulus,* his territory, now west of the Ural Mountains.[28]

On his return from the Central Europe campaign and *en route* to Mongolia, Batu established the Khanate of Kipchak or the state of the Golden or White Horde with its capital of the new city of Sarai on the banks of the lower Volga River. As a good administrator, he immediately introduced order and efficient government in his new state, which stretched west of the Ural Mountains, and which in the future was designated as Muscovy, Ukraine, Byeloruthenia and the Don-Volga steppes, down to the shores of Black and Azov Seas and the Caucasian Mountains.

Although it seemed at the beginning of Batu's invasion that all of Western civilization would perish under the overwhelming impact of the Asiatic hordes, this severe fate was, in fact, reserved for the three East-European nations, the Ukrainians, the Muscovites-Russians and the Byeloruthenians, whom the Mongols were to keep under their rule for some time, with a mixed consequence for each one separately. The invasion had a lasting consequence in the development of the Muscovite-Russian people. First of all, the emerging Russian nationality, already prior to the Tartar conquest, was a racial ally of the Slavic and Ugro-Finnic ethnical components with their biological and psychological features, as was broadly explained in the introductory chapters. Hence, it was much easier for the north-eastern Rostovians, Suzdalians, Vladimirians, Riazanians, Permians and others, to adjust to "peaceful" coexistence with the Mongol suzerain; to accept his rule, and eventually to develop friendly relations with him. Secondly, the less developed culture of the north-eastern community, with more Mongol and Oriental elements than that of the Ukrainian and Byeloruthenian nationalities, made it more susceptible to Mongol social, political, legal, economic and other influences than its western and southern, ethnically different neighbors. Thirdly, the prolonged Mongol rule over the Muscovites, some 250 years, together with Moscow's partial adoption of the culture of the Golden Horde, inevitably left a permanent impression upon Russian national psychology, as well as on Russian national institutions. The harsh lessons taught by the Tartars and their techniques, which were adopted by the Muscovites-Russians, made them capable of building an empire and successfully overrunning the Ukrainians and the Byeloruthenians, as Batu's hordes had done earlier.

On the other hand, in Ukraine and Byeloruthenia there was almost no Mongol tradition. Both countries were culturally more advanced, hence less susceptible to Mongol influences. They remained under Tartar rule for only 100 years or even less. They did not develop, therefore, any far-reaching or lasting contacts or relations with the Mongols. Soon being included in the political framework of the Lithuanian-*Rus'* (Ukrainian) Grand Duchy and the Polish-Lithuanian Commonwealth, the Ukrainians and Byeloruthenians were again, as at the time of the Kievan and Galician realms, more intensely drawn into the sphere of Western and Roman Catholic civilization. For these reasons, both nationalities successfully resisted the impact of the Mongol institutions upon their national life, and became, therefore, even more alienated from the Russians as a result.

There is, of course, another theory concerning the origin of the three East-European nationalities. A majority of Russian historians, either consciously or unconsciously following the imperial political tendency, in particular Pogodin and Sobolevskii, in order to build an ethnical basis for the Russian domination of Ukraine and Byeloruthenia, implied that originally Ukraine was populated by the Russians, and that as a result of the Mongol invasion the original Russian population migrated in masses away from the unsafe Ukraine to the safe northern Muscovite regions, and that subsequently the first Ukrainians came from the West, assumingly, from Galicia. That theory was supposed to establish the claim that in fact the Russians and not the Ukrainians have been the builders of the Kievan realm. However, there are no historical sources available that would support that claim, at all. Moreover, the testimony of Plano de Carpini, papal envoy to the Mongols, who passed through Ukraine at that time, did not mention anything about any supposed migration of people away from Ukraine because of the devastations. Just to the contrary, his testimony rather sponsors an assumption that the usual economic life then, including farming and commerce, was proceeding according to plan and pattern.[29]

The Mongol intention was to keep a close check on East Europe, including Ukraine, in order to secure for the Horde revenues by way of tribute collections, and supply of auxiliary armed forces for Sarai's military undertakings. Therefore, immediately after having established the state of Golden Horde (Khanate of Kipchak), Batu summoned the Ukrainian and North-Eastern princes to the lower Volga to receive from his hand the *yarlik,* the official Mongol confirmation of their rights to rule in their respective lands by the grace of the khan, on paying homage to him as their suzerain. Initially, the Khanate of Kipchak was only a component territory of the Mongol commonwealth, therefore Batu's confirmation was not a sufficient act to establish a full-fledged *yarlik.* This was especially significant at the time of Great Khan Guyuk, when some princes had to travel to Karakorum, in Mongolia, to receive their *yarlik.* Some North-Eastern princes, like Alexander Nevskii and his brother, Andrei, were particularly instructed by Batu to go to Karakorum, since Guyuk had been determined to exercise his supremacy over the Golden Horde, which did not please Batu at all. After Mongka became the Great Khan, he delegated full suzerain authority in European affairs to Batu, his close political associate and friend. Since that time, all Ukrainian princes were in general not required any more to undertake the exhausting journey to Karakorum to see the Great Khan. The *yarlik* was granted by Sarai. Initially, the Ukrainian princes were tempted to react to the Mongol rule in different ways. Most of them, overwhelmed by Sarai's might, cooperated with it; others accepted it passively; a few, like Danylo of Galicia, tried to resist but in vain. Eventually all of them had to recognize and fully honor their vassal relationship to Sarai, to promise the Khan military assistance and tribute and payment as signs of submission. Batu and his immediate successors regarded Ukraine as a mere province of the Golden Horde, for a while, at least. Some princes, who were lax in tribute payment, were punished by a Tartar looting raid, or were ousted, or even killed, their principalities given to some other princes, or left without the princes and to be ruled "democratically" by the *viche* or the people's elderlies or Tartar appointees, under Sarai's direct supremacy through its field officials. The existence of these princeless "free" communities, which governed them-

The Church of the Tithe in Kiev, western facade (989-996).

The St. Sophia Cathedral in Kiev, a model (1037).

selves "democratically," represented certainly a negative phenomenon from the constitutional and political points of view of the Ukrainian life process of that time, when the monarchistic systems prevailed all over Europe. It, therefore, irked the Ukrainian princes, who in addition thought that only the members of the Ruryk house could be princes. The so-called "Tartar communities" were a break with a tradition and customary system of government. Hence, whenever it was possible, the princes undertook punitive actions against the "Tartar communities" for their "revolutionary" attitude, and tried to get them back under their princely authority. That at times angered the Mongols, who liked the princeless communities, where their authority was direct. Consequently, the Khan at times punished the princes for fighting against and "pacifying" these communities. It multiplied chaos, which was in favor of strengthening the Tartar grip over Ukraine. Prince Danylo of Galicia, in particular, fought against the "Tartar people," the so-called "Bolokhiv communities," which brought him at odds with Sarai.[30]

On the other hand, the Mongol *yarlik* changed to some extent the constitutional position of the prince in Ukraine, whose authority from that point was actually unlimited. He could disregard the *boyar duma,* the council of nobles, and the *viche,* the people's meeting, which were rather important state institutions in the Kievan realm, especially during the period of its disintegration process. Yet, the Mongol supremacy weakened the power of princes, since the latter's authority was strictly dependent upon the whims of the Khan and the intrigues in Sarai. The princes could have been removed, replaced or have received another assignment at any time at the Mongol's will.

The impact of the Mongol invasion upon Ukraine was enormous in the negative sense. The ruthless invasion, conquests, pillaging, ruining and burning of the Ukrainian cities, towns and villages, the repetitive devastating punitive actions, atrocities and raids for booty completely impoverished the land and forced a regression in its spiritual, cultural and social life. Politically, central Ukraine and its eastern and southern borderlands actually became the Tartar territory for a number of decades, with only some degree of local autonomy. It does not mean that every walk of life was wiped out, and that the population emigrated to other and more safe regions of East Europe, as Pogodin and Sobolevskii, suggested. By no means. According to historical sources, everyday life began to go ahead immediately after the invasion in Ukraine, but on a substantially reduced scale; the peasants were doing their farming, having been encouraged by the Mongols "to sow wheat and millet," the merchants resumed their trading on a small scale; the artisans worked on their particular crafts, at times having been invited to sell their services to the Mongols and to go to distant Mongolia or other parts of the vast Mongol empire. Spiritual and cultural life suffered most. The invasion and the prolonged consequences of the general devastation and uncertainty were not conducive for a spiritual and cultural process. Churches and schools were ruined. The Metropolitan of Kiev and all *Rus'* left Kiev and went to Suzdal, looking for more safety. That left the Ukrainian Orthodox Church without leadership for some time, followed by a general decline of the religious life. Paganism, "dual belief" and superstitions were on the rise. The only positive aspect of the invasion, for Ukraine, was the dissipation of the Vladimirian principality, later called Muscovy, which would subsequently be exerting imperialistic pressure to the South and attempting to dominate Ukraine. The Suzdal-Vladimir and neighbor principalities were also dominated by the Mongols, and their political ambitions were curbed for some time.

It is clear that the Mongol invasion really terminated the political existence of the *Rus'* realm, but its complete down-fall was caused by many reasons which weakened its might and made it a rather easy prey of foreign aggression. These reasons were mentioned before, but to conclude the chapter, they must be summarized here. First of all, the realm was territorially too vast to be kept strongly centralized and under tight control of Kiev, considering absolutely inadequate overland roads due to thick and extensive forests, almost jungles, marshes, unpassable rivers and difficult transportation conditions, especially in late fall, winter and early spring months because of weather. Communication was even poorer. It was surprising that the realm was able to continue to exist for four hundred years. Secondly, for most of the same reasons, as listed above, strong centrifugal and decentralization tendencies, at first tribal and then territorial, continually contributed to the disintegration process, whenever the senior prince in Kiev was not a strong personality. Thirdly, the realm was enormously differentiated in racial and ethnical respects. The Ukrainian tribes were already greatly differentiated from the Russian and the Byeloruthenian ones, and they all had nothing in common with numerous and also greatly differentiated Ugro-Finnic tribes of a large number. The national antagonism among all of them was continuously growing and getting more intense. Bogolubskii's pillage and burning of Kiev might have served as an example of such antagonism between the Ukrainian South and the Russian North, which was on the rise. Fourthly, the Ruryk house was unfortunately very fertile and speedily multiplying, contributing to a ridiculously minute division of the realm into many and too small principalities, which were getting progressively, economically poor and politically and militarily weak and not able to resist any strong outside pressure. Fifthly, unfortunately the relations among the princes of the Ruryk house were extremely hostile, intensified by the territorial antagonisms, accompanied by endless dynastic bloody strifes, conflicts and open wars, which, as described above, devastated, impoverished and weakened the realm in all possible respects. In addition, especially among the southern Ukrainian branches of the ruling house, there were no great princely personalities born, who might have overcome all odds and difficulties and might have united all Ukrainian lands in a strong Ukrainian state. The Russian North was in a much more fortunate situation, where there were strong princely personalities before and after the Mongol invasion and they succeeded in constructing a powerful principality, at first the Vladimirian, and then its political successor, the Muscovite principality, such as Andrei Bogolubskii, Vsievolod the Big Nest, Alexander Nevskii, Ivan 1, Kalita, and Dimitrii Donskoi.[31]

Fortunately, however, the tradition of Ukrainian statehood was preserved for the next 110 years by the Galician-Volhinian principality. The chapter should be closed with a quotation from Vernadsky's work, in which he gave the characteristics of the old Kievan *Rus'*, in order to acquire an approximate understanding of the history of that empire. He said the following: "There must have been something in Kievan Russia (he erroneously identified Ukrainian *Rus'* with Russia, having followed the standardized and politically motivated Russian interpretation) which made people forget its negative side and remember only its achievements. That 'something' was the spirit of freedom — individual, political, and economic — which prevailed in Russia of that day and to which the Muscovite principle of individual's complete obedience to the state was to present such a contrast."[32] Perhaps this underscores effectively the psychological difference between those two East-European Slavic nationalities, so clearly visible in their two respective political organizations, the Ukrainian *Rus'* realm and the Russian Muscovite principality.

1. *Annales Bertiniani in usum scholarum,* Hannover, 1883, ct. 19-20.
2. Photii's sermons were published several times. For example, *Fragmenta historiae graecea,* ed. by Miller, 1870, or *Zapiski petersburgskoi akademii nauk,* St. Petersburg, 1906.
3. M. Braichevsky, "The Unification of the Old Rus'ian Lands around the Center of Kyiv," *On the Historical Beginnings of Eastern Slavic Europe,* ed. by N. Chirovsky, New York, 1976, pp. 73-74.
4. *Ibid.,* p. 71, having quoted *Povist' vremennykh lit.*
5. On the Normanistic and Anti-Normanistic approaches: N. Riasanovsky, *A History of Russia,* New York, 1963, pp. 25-30; M. Hrushevsky, *Istoria Ukrainy-Rusy, New York, 1954, Vol. I, pp. 602-624;* Braichevsky, *op. cit.,* pp. 53-55; M. Vasmer, "Wikingenspuren in Russland," *Sitzungsberichten,* Preussische Akademie der Wissenschaften, Phil.-Hist. Klasse, Berlin, 1931.
6. Princes Oleh and Ihor: Natalia Polonska-Vasylenko, *Istoria Ukrainy,* Munich, 1972, Vol. I, pp. 95-99; D. Doroshenko, *Narys istorii Ukrainy,* Munich, 1966, Vol. I, pp. 42-43; Hrushevsky, *op. cit.,* Vol. I, pp. 429-446; the same, *A History of Ukraine,* New Haven, 1970, pp. 47-58.
7. *Provest' vremennikh let,* ed. P. Adrianovaia-Perets, articles and commentaries by D. Likhachev, Moscow-Leningrad, 1950, Part I, The Years for Oleh, Ihor and Olha; Braychevsky, *op. cit.,* p. 76-78.
8. *Lavrentievskaia letopis,* Moscow, 1910, p. 61; B. Grekov, *Kievskaia Rus',* Moscow, 1953, pp. 458-459.

9. *Povest'*, year 955.

10. *The Russian Primary Cronicle*, ed. by S. Cross and O. Sherbowitz-Wetzor, Cambridge, 1953, pp. 86-87.

11. I. Nazarko, *Sviatyi Volodymyr Velykyi, volodar i khrystytel Rusi-Ukrainy*, Rome, 1954, pp. 38-39.

12. Polonska-Vasylenko, *op. cit.*, Vol. I, pp. 107-108.

13. *Povest'*, year 981.

14. Yu. Fedoriv, *Istoria tserkvy v Ukraini*, Toronto, 1967, pp. 45-48.

15. About Volodymyr the Great: Hrushevsky, *Istoria Ukrainy-Rusy*, Vol. I, pp. 478-538; Polonska-Vasylenko, *op. cit.*, Vol. I, pp. 110-122; Doroshenko, *op. cit.*, Vol. I, pp. 44-46; G. Vernadsky and M. Karpovich, *A History of Russia*, Vol. II, *Kievan Russia*, New Haven, 1951, pp. 56-74.

16. Polonska-Vasylenko, *op. cit.*, Vol. I, pp. 125-126.

17. V. Sergeievich, *Russkaia Pravda v cheteriokh redaktsiakh*, St. Petersburg, 1904; Zimin, A., *Pamiatki prava Kievskavo gosudarstva, Russkaia Pravda prostrannoi redaktsii*, Moscow, 1952.

18. Hrushevsky, *op. cit.*, Vol. II, pp. 9-46; the same, *A History of Ukraine*, New Haven, 1970, pp. 76-79; Polonska-Vasylenko, *op. cit.*, pp. 124-134.

19. *Povest' vremennikh let*, Part II, pp. 388-390.

20. Iziaslav's reign: Polonska-Vasylenko, Vol. I, pp. 134-137.

21. The Lubech convention: Hrushevsky, *Istoria Ukrainy-Rusi*, Vol. II, pp. 90-91; S. Soloviov, *Istoria otnoshenii mezhdu kniaziami Rurikovo doma*, Moscow, 1847, on Lubech.

22. *Povest' vremennikh let*, Vol. II, pp. 425-457.

23. S. Tomashivsky, *Istoria Ukrainy, starynni viky i seredni viky*, Munich, 1948, p. 72; also Polonska-Vasylenko, *op. cit.*, Vol. I, p. 153.

24. Hrushevsky, *op. cit.*, Vol. II, pp. 196-197; *Ipatievska litopys'*, year, 1169.

25. Hrushevsky, *ibid.*, Vol. II, pp. 216-219.

26. J. Lelevel, *Polska, Rzeczy i Dzieje Jej*, Poznan, 1863, Vol. V, pp. 26-28.

27. Soloviov, *op. cit.*; the individual lands before the invasion: Hrushevsky, *op. cit.*, Vol. II, pp. 126-505; briefly: Polonska-Vasylenko, *op. cit.*, Vol. I, pp. 156-175.

28. The Mongols and the Mongol invasion: N. Chirovsky, *A History of the Russian Empire*, New York, 1973, Vol. I., pp. 153-184; also very comprehensively, Vernadsky, *op. cit.*, Vol. III, *The Mongols and Russia*, New Haven, 1953, pp. 1-200.

29. Chirovsky, *loc. cit.*, pp. 164-166.

30. N. Dashkevich, *Bolokhovskaia ziemla i ieia znachenie v russkoi istorii*, Kiev, 1878; the same, *Noviisheie domysly o Bolokhove i Bolokhovtsiakh*, Kiev, 1884; briefly Doroshenko, *op. cit.*, Vol. I, pp. 90-91.

31. The Pogodin-Sobolevskii theory: *Ibid.*, pp. 63-68; A. Krymsky, "Filologia i Pogodinskaia hipoteza," *Kievskaia Starina*, Kiev, 1898, Books Vi, VII and IX; 1899, Books I and II.

32. Vernadsky, *op. cit.*, Vol. II, *Kievan Russia*, p. 18.

Prince Lev I of
Galicia Volhinia

King
Yurii I
of
Galicia-
Volhinia

158

CHAPTER SIX

THE GALICIAN-VOLHINIAN REALM

— The Galician Principality — The Galician-Volhinian principality: Prince Roman — Danylo and Vasyl — The last Galician-Volhinian rulers — The Polish-Lithuanian takeover.

The Galician Principality. The western borderland, the Sub-Carpathian Galician area, originally settled by the tribe of the Khorvatsians, joined the Kievan realm most probably during Oleh's time, though the relation might have been a very loose one. The Khorvatsian warriors were taking part in Oleh's Byzantine campaign, according to historical sources. This might have been the indication of the submission of the Galician province to Kiev. It bordered on Poland and Moravia, and at one time it was under the domination of the powerful Moravian realm. Boleslaw, a Polish ruler, when helping Sviatopolk, the Sinner, his son-in-law, in his bid for the Kievan throne against Yaroslav the Wise, annexed the province in question to the Polish state. Yet, immediately after Boleslaw's death, Yaroslav the Wise undertook a war expedition against Poland, and taking advantage from temporary chaos there, claimed Galicia, or its part, the "Red-Towns," and incorporated it into the Kievan *Rus'* realm. It has been assumed that at his death bed in line with his testament he gave Galicia to his grandson, Prince Rostyslav, who, however, died early. Then, because of the seniority principle, established by Yaroslav, and the notorious warfare among the princes to acquire the Kievan throne, resulting from that principle, which was grossly abused by the warring factions, Rostyslav's sons, princes Ruryk, Volodar and Vasyl, became the *izgoii,* the outcasts. Yet they did not want to yield and to give up their rights to their father's inheritance. After a few years of hard struggle, and wandering through Ukraine as far as Tmutorokan, in 1084, the three brothers were able to regain their patrimonial share and settle for good. Ruryk, however, soon died, while Volodar ruled in Galicia's western part with the capital of Peremyshl, and Vasyl, popularly called Vasylko, in the eastern part with the capital of Terebovla. The brothers lived in harmony and ruled in Galicia jointly. The year of 1084 must be considered the beginning of successful and progressive splitting and separation of Galicia from the Kievan center; for one of the earliest centrifugal trends away from the Kievan imperial multinationalism and towards the ethnically Ukrainian statehood in the west of the Empire.[1] A little later the north-eastern Oka-Klazma-Volga region began to get away from Kiev and tend toward its own, ethnically Muscovite-Russian statehood. Not before long these two new political centers began to compete for the domination of Kiev, which has remained ethnically Ukrainian through the subsequent centuries and hostile to the northern and for many centuries rather Oriental Muscovy, while leaning toward the Westernized Galicia and Volhinia. Of course, the princely conventions in Lubech and Vytechiv, which abolished the principle of seniorate and introduced the principle of patriomoniate, greatly enhanced the separatist tendency of Rostyslav's two sons, Volodar and Vasyl, and strengthened their ruling positions in Galicia. The immediate attempts of the grand princes of Kiev to recover and to extend their supremacy over Galicia did not succeed.

The chief goals of Volodar's and Vasylko's external policy was securing the safety of their land from any threat from abroad, and in the way of military operations and diplomatic measures they neutralized the assaults, intended by the Polish, Hungarian and Kievan neighbors to dominate totally or in part Galician regions. In order to protect themselves from the side of the Black Sea steppes, the princes utilized every peaceful opportunity to settle the lower Dniester and the sea littoral, the *Ponyzzia,* with the Pecheng and Torkman war captives, who subsequently assimilated and extended the Ukrainian ethnic territory to the south.

Galicia soon began to flourish economically for two or three main reasons. First, since there were rather ample deposits of salt, and salt was in great demand throughout the whole of Ukraine-*Rus'*. In particular, its significance increased after the nomads cut off Ukraine's salt supplies from the East and South. Second, through her southern, Sub-Carpathian regions there ran important commercial routes from the East to the West, having made out of Galicia an important commercial middleman for all sorts of goods. And three, the growing political might of the land simply aided and promoted a successful growth of its business and economy.

After Volodar's and Vasylko's death, the Galician principality was divided among their sons, but soon, after a few years of internal struggle, Volodar's son, Prince Volodymyr, popularly called Volodymyrko, an able but completely unscrupulous ruler, was capable of uniting almost all Galicia under his sceptor, with the exception of the region of Zvenyhorod.

Prince Volodymyr was an outstanding statesman, full of energy and ambition but without any moral principles, who used bribes, slander, killing and broken oaths, to achieve his political objectives. Intrigues and bribes were also within his diplomatic measures, used preferably by him. Volodymyr of Galicia conducted wars to dominate and to keep Volhinia under his scepter. While fighting against the Kievan grand prince to assert his sovereignty, he associated himself with Suzdal, the arch-enemy of the Ukrainian south. Taking in account all his character flaws, it must be admitted that Volodymyr was the founder of the Galician-Ukrainian political might.

At this time, social-political trends began to develop and grow in Galicia, which made it different from the rest of Ukraine *Rus'*. Namely, the class of the *boyars,* the nobility, was growing very strong, which made the Galician developments of that time similar to the English ones before and after the adoption of the *Magna Charta Libertatum*. Only the Galician geo-political environment was different, and that trend contributed to its collapse some two hundred years later. Also, the townspeople, due to the commercial growth of the land, became very strong. At one time, with the consent of the townspeople, antagonized by Volodymyr's ruthlessness, Prince Ivan of Berlad, as he was subsequently called, *Berladnyk,* attempted to unseat Volodymyr and to dominate Halych, which was made the capital of Galicia by Volodymyr, but did not succeed. Berladnyk was defeated and forced to stay in the town of Berlad in the south, between the rivers Pruth and Seret, though always in strong opposition to Volodymyr.

Volodymyr died rather suddenly during one of his military operations, while the chronicle ascribed his death to the punishment by God for a broken oath, and was succeeded by his son, Prince Yaroslav, the Eight-Senses, *Osmomysl,* who ruled from 1153 to 1187, after having received from his father a rather powerful state. He lived up to his responsibilities and great abilities, and might be considered a most powerful ruler among all princes of Ukraine of that time. Because of his abilities, he was called the Eight-Senses, *Osmomysl,* and he was greatly praised by the outstanding literary creation of medieval Ukraine, *Slovo o polku Ihoreve,* the *Lay of Ihor's Campaign*. Yaroslav's great achievement was in colonization of the southern borderlands of his principality, reaching down as far as the Danube River, and the rich development of commerce and economy of the land, which obviously contributed to the strength of the merchant class and its clash with the nobility.

The above mentioned clash culminated in Yaroslav's family

affair. The prince dismissed his legally married wife, daughter of Yurii Dolgorukii of Suzdal, and lived with a concubine, Nastasia, of a *boyar* descent. The nobles won the conflict by capturing Nastasia and burning her as an assumed witch. Yaroslav could not save his love and was broken in spirits. He had to yield to the *boyar* oligarchy, although the merchant class tried to give him all the support it could.

Yaroslav maintained well-developed foreign relations, which certainly contributed to his otherwise considerable international prestige. He remained in close relationship to Friedrich I Barbarossa, whom he recognized as his suzerain. Friedrich subsequently loyally assisted Yaroslav's son, Volodymyr, in his bid for the Galician throne.[2]

Yaroslav by his testament gave the throne of Halych to his illegitimate son, whom he had with Nastasia Chahriv, but the arrangement met a very resolute opposition, from the side of the boyardom in particular, and his legitimate son, Volodymyr, seized power, having ruled in Galicia from 1187 to 1199. Volodymyr was a weak personality, who also immediately spoiled his relations with the *boyars,* though they supported him initially. He could not manage the affairs and went to Hungary to seek help. In 1188, Bella, the Hungarian king, came to Galicia as an invader; declared himself the king of Galicia with consent of a few treacherous *boyars,* while imprisoning Volodymyr, the true ruler who asked him only for assistance. The foreign invasion produced a violent reaction in all Ukraine-*Rus',* and the voices were heard from all over the land to free Galicia "from the foreigners," including that of the Metropolitan Matvii of Kiev.

Eventually the Galician *boyars* themselves called various princes of the Ruryk house to come and to rule in Galicia, of whom Rostyslav of Berlad was the most serious contender. However, he was defeated by the Hungarians and subsequently poisoned. Then, Volodymyr received the assistance from Friedrich I Barbarossa, and with the support of his vassalage Polish troops, the former was able to regain the Galician throne. He remained the ruler of Galicia until his death. With Volodymyr, who left no successor to the throne, the Rostyslav branch of the princes of Galicia came to an end, under whose leadership West Ukraine experienced actually impressive political, and in particular, economic growth, with such commercial-urban centers as Peremyshl, Halych and Terebovla, where also architecture and the arts flourished.[3]

The Galician-Volhinian Principality; Prince Roman. Prince Roman of the Mstyslav branch of the Ruryk house in Volhinia tried to acquire Galicia in 1188, when Volodymyr left Halych, but he did not succeed, because of Barbarossa's intervention. Yet, he never gave up hope to settle in Galicia and for that reason kept in close touch with the Galician boyardom and the grand merchants, and having gained in that respect the support of Poland and Hungary. Volodymyr's death realized his dream. With the consent of the population he became the prince of the united Galician-Volhinian principality, having also started a new Roman branch of the ruling house, which ruled there for one hundred and fifty years.

Volhinia was an economically and commercially developed province of Ukraine. At first, it was divided into a great many small principalities, but subsequently the unification process went under way, so that Roman not only ruled over most of the land, but extended his domination over Kiev and a part of the right-bank Ukraine, right of the Dnieper river. Nevertheless, he had no ambition to be the Kievan prince, but rather ruled over that city, while having stayed in Volhinia. While attempting to strengthen his principality, he had to conduct wars against the Lithuanians and incorporated some of their lands. Roman was the prince of Volhinia from 1173, and the prince of Galicia and Volhinia from 1199 to 1205. The unification of these two principalities under Roman's scepter resulted in the creation of a powerful, essentially Ukrainian in the ethnical respect, statehood of a strong economic foundation, backed up by an efficient farming and well-developed domestic and foreign commerce, the commercial routes of which ran from the West and East, and from the Baltic to the Black Sea.

In order to maintain, and even to raise the power and prestige of his principality, Roman was constantly involved in complicated foreign affairs. He intervened in the Polish political matters by supporting sons of Prince Casimir against Prince Mieczyslaw in their rivalry for the supremacy in Poland; and in the Hungarian affairs by supporting King Andrew against his brother in their rivalry for the rule in Hungary. Since his favorites won the contest in both cases, Roman was able to create for himself an advantageous political situation, at least for a while. Prince Roman became an unquestionable victor in the quest for Kiev in the contest with Prince Ruryk, who was at first even a contender for Halych. Since that time, as it was mentioned above, he became a suzerain of all Right-bank Ukraine, practically speaking. It has been recorded in some historical sources that Pope Innocent III, apparently desirous to gain for himself a powerful ally, offered him a royal crown, which was refused by Roman. It was possible, that the proposal was connected with a suggestion of a Church union of the Ukrainian Orthodox Church with the Roman See. Yet, some historians assume that the whole affair of offering the crown to Roman has been a legend, connected with Roman's involvement in the Hohenstaufen-Welfs strife, which resulted in his premature and tragic death.[4]

In domestic affairs, Roman sought support of the townspeople and was very stern with the *boyars,* and in particular with the *boyar* clique, no matter, that with the latter's help, to some extent, he was able to acquire the Galician throne. He definitely aspired to an absolutist rule, vehementally objected to by the nobles, whose political power in Galicia and Volhinia was traditional. Roman exterminated many of the *boyar* oligarchs and expelled or banned many from Galicia, like *boyar* Kormylchych.

Prince Roman was definitely on his way to establish himself as an autocrat, according to the trend which was shaping itself in West Europe, and he apparently would have established his state for many decades or centuries to come, but his untimely death threw his country into a turmoil for a great many years. It weakened the principality very considerably. Being involved in the West-European political affairs, he undertook a military expedition, but the political scenery has not been as yet clarified. He either wanted to participate in the Hohenstaufen-Welfs struggle in Germany by helping Barbarossa's son, Philip, directly, or to pacify some Polish princes, who were involved on the other side of the same struggle. Moreover, he had some unsettled account with Polish prince, Leszko of Crakow. Having been not cautious enough, Roman was ambushed near the town of Zavykhost, close to the banks of the Vistula river, and killed in the battle by the Poles.[5] It opened the deplorable era of unsettled and often chaotic developments in the Galician-Volhinian principality for some thirty years.

Danylo and Vasyl. With the death of Prince Roman, the *boyar* oligarchy immediately rose against the minor sons of the deceased to protect themselves against the possibility of an absolutist and hereditary system to arise in Galicia, which would right away reduce their political power. Princess Mother Anna, cognizant of the fact, and energetic and devoted to the well-being of her sons, Danylo being three years old and Vasyl one year, called Andrew II of Hungary, a supposed friend of Roman, to come and to protect the rights of the two princes. However, Andrew occupied Galicia and proclaimed himself "King of Galicia and Lodomeria."

Andrew's move produced a reaction. The *boyars,* including those who were driven out of Galicia by Roman, did not want the Hungarians, but continued to oppose Danylo's and Vasyl's return to the throne, and called the sons of Prince Ihor, the hero of the famous Ukrainian medieval poetic creation *Slovo o polku Ihoreve,* to come and to rule in Galicia. Princess Anna with her sons had to flee to Volhinia, where she was received in a friendly way and where she soon succeeded in establishing herself and her sons as legitimate rulers.

Meanwhile in Galicia, the *boyars* became unhappy with the rule of Ihor's sons. The pro-Hungarian party got the upper hand and called on the Hungarians to come and to reign. Yet, in a while the political mood changed again in Galicia, and the *boyars* called Ihor's sons to come back and to assume the throne. The *Ihorevychi,* upon their return, acted very unwisely, and cruelly executed some five hundred *boyars* for assumed treason. The *boyar* oligarchic clique had now no choice any more, and asked the Hungarian King Andrew II to put Princes Danylo and Vasyl on the throne. This was accomplished with the support of the Hungarian armed forces. The *Ihorevychi,* Prince Ihor's sons, were hanged by the oligarchs.

Soon a conflict developed between Anna, princess-mother, who wanted to rule in the name of her sons, and the oligarchic clique, which pretended to establish an aristocratic democracy, having a prince as a figurehead only. Anna had to flee with her sons again, while the princely authority was assumed by a *boyar,* Volodyslav Kormylchych. It was the only case in the whole Ukrainian medieval history, in which the princely authority was assumed by somebody who was not a member of the Ruryk house. It was high treason in the eyes of the contemporaries, and of the princely members of the Ruryk house, in particular. The Polish-Hungarian intervention, instead of protecting the interest of the rightful Galician princes, Danylo and Vasyl, resulted in the agreement of Spish, by which Polish Leszko and Hungarian Andrew divided Galicia among themselves. The accord did not last long, and soon Mstyslav Udatnyi of the Smolensk branch of the Ruryk house was introduced to the Galician throne with Polish assistance. Yet, Mstyslav was a weak ruler, completely under the influence of the *boyars* of the pro-Hungarian political orientation. His struggle against the over-powering might of the Hungarians, which lasted for eight years, in order to keep the Galician throne, was not conclusive, and he finally resigned in 1227 in favor of the Hungarian prince, Andrew, son of King Andrew II of Hungary. Mstyslav's death opened a new chapter in the history of the Galician-Volhinian principality.

Effectively supported by the loyal Volhinian boyardom, largely inspired by his mother, Princess Anna, Prince Danylo began to achieve some successes. Having taken one town and one province after another, he dominated in reality all of Volhinia and mastered the political situation there. Yet, the opposition of the Galician boyardom was still too tough, and Danylo still had to wait a little. In his favor was the instance that the Galician townspeople supported him enthusiastically, which eventually enabled him to regain the throne of his father on a permanent basis. He was a skillful diplomat and a statesman of format. Danylo got involved by purpose in the Polish dynastic war and went with his armies deep into the Polish territory. When he was supporting the aspirations of Kondrat of Mazovia, he negotiated a treaty with Lithuania, which was growing in power, and strengthened the dynastic ties by marrying his sister to another Polish prince, Sviatopolk of Pomerania. All these measures were undertaken by him to set the international stage for his coming back to Galicia.

Danylo resumed his active campaign to regain Galicia in 1230, still having been bitterly opposed by the pro-Hungarian faction of the Galician boyardom. Although for tactical reasons he recognized the Hungarian protection, Bela IV, the new king of Hungary, yet supported Mykhailo of Chernihiv in the quest for the Galician throne. The struggle between Danylo and Mykhailo of Chernihiv, and continued by his son, as well, the latter supported by the Galician nobles, lasted again for some four years. Yet, the Galician townspeople remained faithful to Danylo and Vasyl, and that enabled them to achieve their goal, no matter that the struggle received an international projection, having been participated in a major or lesser extent by Lithuania, Hungary, Poland, the Teutonic Order and Austria. Finally, in 1238 Danylo dominated the capital of Galicia, the city of Halych, while his rival, Mykhailo's son, Prince Rostyslav, escaped to Hungary. The war for Galicia with Rostyslav, assisted by Hungary, still lasted for a full five years, eventually being terminated by the battle at Yaroslav, a decisive victory for Danylo and Vasyl, in 1245. Meanwhile, after having established himself in Galicia, Prince Danylo dominated Kiev, the ancient capital of all *Rus'*, but he continued to rule from his father's capital of Halych over the city, as also Roman did.

Of course, Danylo had to carry out a punitive action against the rebellious boyardom of Galicia; many nobles were executed, their landed estates were confiscated; some were banned, others escaped abroad, while in their place the servitude *boyars,* loyal to the prince were put in charge and endowed with those formerly confiscated properties. Then, Prince Danylo proceeded with erecting new towns, settling their colonists and protecting the townspeople to compensate them for their lasting loyalty. He also began some action to improve the social position of the peasants, who were abused by the *boyar* landowners.[6]

Yet, after forty years of victorious struggle and after having finally established himself in Galicia, another calamity was forced upon Danylo and Vasyl. The Tartar invasion followed. Kiev was soon lost, courageously defended by *voyevoda* Dmytro. Although Galicia was at first avoided by the devastating blow of the Mongol assault because of the death of Great Khan Ugedey in distant Mongolia, the delayed impact of the invasion was not, however, less cruel. The Mongols, as it was pointed out before, established a state on the lower Volga river, the Khanate of Kiptchak or the Golden Horde, with the capital of Sarai. Then, Batu began to order one Ukrainian or Muscovite prince after another to come to Sarai, to pay homage to the khan, to receive a confirmation of his right to rule in his principality from the khan on the vassalage basis, and to promise to pay a tribute to the Mongol suzerain. Various princes reacted to that demand in different ways; some complied immediately, some tried to delay the unpleasant experience, others refused and were quickly eliminated by the Mongols, as it was discussed above.[7]

Prince Danylo was deeply offended by the Mongol demand and tried to postpone his journey to Sarai in order to receive the *yarlik,* the confirmation of his rights to rule in khan's name. Nevertheless, he finally had to yield, and in 1246 he went to Sarai, where his rights to Galicia were sustained by the khan under the condition that he acknowledged himself to be a Mongol vassal. Although Danylo felt humiliated by becoming a Mongol vassal, in fact his prestige because of the Tartar protection increased. The Hungarians were quite impressed by Danylo's new position and stopped to interfere with the Galician matters, though the Hungarian king continued to call himself the ruler of "Galicia and Lodomeria."

Danylo could not come to terms with his vassalage status, and he soon began to undertake certain measures to rid himself of Mongol protection. He initiated new contacts with Rome and the Pope, hoping that the latter would be able to organize the Christian rulers of the West and lead a crusade against the Mongols. In exchange for military assistance from the Pope and the Christian rulers, Danylo was ready to join the Catholic Church in an ecclesiastic union and recognize the Pope's supremacy. Actually it is not clear whether the idea of an anti-Mongol crusade was initiated by Pope Innocent III, and suggested to the Ukrainians by his envoy, de Plano Carpini, when Danylo travelled to Sarai, and then planted in Danylo's mind, or Danylo himself developed the thought. The matter was preceded by a lengthy correspondence between the Pope and Danylo. The practical organization of a crusade did not progress far beyond planning, but to boost Danylo's prestige among the Christian rulers, the Pope sent him a royal crown, which the latter hesitated to accept. Maybe, Danylo was hesitant in order not to irk the Mongols.

Also, in order to strengthen his political position, Danylo was developing his connections with the neighboring lands. He involved himself in the Austrian succession war, participated in by Galicia, Bohemia, Poland, Bavaria and Lithuania. Then, he waged war in the Polish succession struggle, during which he occupied the ancient Polish city of Lublin in 1243. Subsequently, he established friendly relations with two Polish princely branches, the Crakovian and Mazovian ones, strengthened by dynastic intermarriages.

A separate chapter of Danylo's politics constituted his relations with Lithuania and the Lithuanian princes. At first these relations were friendly, but then, with the growth of the Lithuanian power under Prince Mendog, war erupted between the Galician-Volhinian principality and Lithuania, resulting in Danylo's occupation of several Lithuanian towns and regions, having extended his domination in the north, including the regions of Black Rus' and the towns of Horodno, Novhorodok, Slonim, Volkovyisk and others. Soon, however, peace was restored, and it was also strengthened by dynastic intermarriages. Prince Shvarno, Danylo's younger son, married Mendog's daughter, and as a result of that marriage Shvarno became prince of Lithuania for a short while after Mendog's death and after Voishelk, Mendog's son, resigned from the throne and became a monk.

Soon after the Mongol invasion and establishment of the Khanate of Kiptchak, Danylo had to face a very difficult problem, which he did not hesitate to attempt to solve, although it was a very dangerous issue, namely, the issue of the so-called "Tartar people." Certain regional communities in Volhinia and Kyiv regions refused to submit to their princes according to the dynastic tradition in *Rus'*, and preferred to organize themselves as self-governing or autonomous territories under direct Mongol protection. It was a rebellious act according to Danylo and other princes of the ruling house, undermining the political structure of the land. Hence, Danylo, as perhaps the most powerful ruler at that time in Ukraine, decided to liquidate the rebellion. He was joined by all members of the princely Roman branch in Galicia and Volhinia. Danylo, Vasyl, Lev and Shvarno assaulted the "Tartar people" in various regions, destroying their towns and villages. The most celebrated was the resistance of the so-called Bolokhiv land. The struggle was very cruel. Of course, the Mongol suzerain did not like suppression of the communities under his immediate supervision. Finally, Kuremsa, a Mongol military leader, came with a Tartar armed force to assist those communities and to pacify the princes. Yet his force was too weak to do the job, and he had to withdraw. The relations between Danylo and the khan were badly strained, after the submission of the "Tartar people" communities to the rule of the princes by force.

By this time the royal position of Danylo was well established. In 1253, he let himself be crowned king with the crown sent to him by the Pope, in the town of Dorohichyn during a war expedition against the Yatvingians. The chronicle underscored the event by the following statement: "He accepted the crown from God, from the Church of the Holy Apostles, from the altar of St. Peter, from his father, Pope Innocent and from all his bishops." Danylo's record was quite impressive. He was able to preserve his actual independence from the khan; he transferred to the west, to his capital of Halych, the traditions of the Kievan *Rus'* of being the continuation of the Ukrainian-*Rus'* statehood; for a while he dominated Kiev to underscore that continuation of the tradition; he expanded his realm territorially to the west, north and south, as well; he also pacified the "Tartar people," the threat to the medieval constitution of *Rus'* and its monarchal principle. Doubtlessly, King Danylo was one of the most outstanding rulers of Ukraine-*Rus'*, and he has been so evaluated by later historiography. His attempt to dominate Kiev again in 1257-1258, and his continuous interest in the Kievan affairs and interference with them, including the matters of the Orthodox Church there, in particular the appointment of Cyril (Kyrylo) to the Metropolitan seat for Kiev and all of *Rus'*, had proven the instance of his intention to preserve the unity of the Ukrainian south and to uproot the attempts of the Suzdalian north to interfere in nationally Ukrainan matters.[8]

Danylo's Galician-Volhinian kingdom was well administered; new urban centers, like the city of Lviv and Kholm, with fortresses were built to strengthen the defense of the country in the approaching encounter with the Mongols; defense and politically oriented colonization of the borderlands continued; economically the land was growing in wealth and opulence; crafts and industries were effectively developing; architecture reached new heights; the *boyar* oligarchy was overcome and King Danylo established himself as an indisputable ruler.

Nevertheless, toward the end of Danylo's reign a great deal of his achievements was annihilated by the Mongol intervention. Having been irked by Danylo's bold plans and undertakings, especially his negotiations with the West, his resolute handling of the rebellious "Tartar people," his attempts to strengthen the Galician-Volhinian defenses and maintenance of his sovereignty, the Tartars, led by an able strategist, Burundai, forced Danylo and Vasyl to join the Mongol war expedition against Lithuania. This disturbed the otherwise good relations between Ukraine and Lithuania. Subsequently, Burundai enforced by his threatening military power and the prospect of a complete ruin of the whole country by the Mongols that all fortresses and fortifications, constructed by Danylo and Vasyl, were to be demolished, such as Kremianets, Lutsk, Lviv, Volodymyr and others, largely by the hands of the Galicians and Volhinians themselves. The European crusade did not materialize, and consequently Danylo lost all interest in the Church union with Rome. Pope Alexander II threatened Danylo with excommunication for not having remained faithful to the Holy See in 1257.[9] All those developments broke Danylo's spirits, and he died embittered in 1264, having been called by the chronicle "as wise as Solomon himself."

Prince Vasyl remained all that time the ruler of Volhinia, having stayed always in the shadow of Danylo's great personality. Brotherly love prevailed among them, and they harmoniously administered their respective principalities, which represented one common state organization. After Danylo's death, Vasyl assumed the senior position, while various members of the Roman house, Danylo's sons, Lev, Shvarno and Mstyslav, and Vasyl's son, Volodymyr, received different provinces and towns into their respective administrative authorities. The historians of that era have not been in agreement, which lands exactly were administered by whom.[10] Vasyl died in 1270.

The Last Galician-Volhinian Rulers. Although the harmony, which prevailed between Danylo and Vasyl, was disturbed after their deaths, the unity of the Galician-Volhinian was largely preserved. Prince Lev I ruled at first in Galicia only, and then, in Volhinia, as well, from 1264 apparently until 1301; Volodymyr stayed in Volhinia, from 1270 to 1289; Mstyslav became prince of Volhinia for three years only, from 1289 to 1292. Subsequently, Lev's son, King Yuirii, reigned over the entire Galician-Volhinian "kingdom" from 1301-1315, and his sons, princes Andrei and Lev II, from 1315 to 1323. The last two princes of the Roman branch of the Ruryk house were apparently killed when waging a war against the Mongols, as a reference of a Polish prince, Wladyslaw Lokietek, in his letter to the Pope indicated. After a relatively long *interregnum,* finally in 1325, Yurii II Boleslav, only by his mother related to the Ruryk house, was called to be the prince of Galicia and Volhinia. He was poisoned in 1340, and that event started a new and troublesome era in the history of Ukraine-*Rus'*. It was probably a historical tragedy that the Galician-Volhinian branch of the Ruryk house came so suddenly to an abrupt end. Another unfortunate development marked itself by the very instance that the personalities of the last princes lacked proper stature, and that they were not able to lay firm poli-foundations under the state structure of the Galician-Volhinian principality that would have enabled it to exist for a long time. The things evolved differently in the Muscovite-Russian north, where also a branch of the Ruryk house ruled. There the branch continued to occupy the throne for more than two centuries longer and many outstanding, though infinitely ruthless, personalities, one after another, such as Dimitrii Donskoi, Ivan III the Great, Vasilii II, and Ivan IV the Terrible, aggressively worked toward the unity, political preservation and territorial expansion of their statehood of the Vladimirian-Muscovite Grand Principality.[11]

Lev I, was certainly the most able man from among all the princely brothers and cousins. With Danylo's death, he received only one part of Galicia, most probably the Halych, Peremyshl and Kholm provinces, while Shvarno and Mstyslav received other regions and towns. In 1267, as it was mentioned, Mendog's son, Prince Voishelk, gave up the throne and entered a monastery, while transferring his principality to Shvarno, who for a while became the prince of Lithuania. Lev was greatly irritated that Shvarno and not he became the ruler of most of Lithuania. Two years later he let Shvarno be killed treacherously during the latter's visit at Vasyl's court, and afterwards occupied all of Shvarno's provinces. The consequence of that political crime was very unfavorable for Ukraine, in general, since then the Lithuanian throne was ascended by Troiden, hostile towards the Galician-Volhinian realm and towards the Ukrainian-*Rus'ian* culture on the whole.

At one time, during the Polish *interregnum,* Prince Lev became a contender for the Polish throne, though unsuccessfully. Supporting then the bid of the Mazovian branch for the Polish throne, Lev waged a few years' long war with Polish Leszko the Black, captured and incorporated the city of Lublin for a while again. In result of the participation in the Hungarian succession wars, Lev was able to dominate and incorporate a part of the Carpathian Ukraine-*Rus'* with the city of Mukachevo in 1281. This was the time of the widest expansion of the Galician-Volhinian principality. He also took active part in the Czech-Austrian conflict, having been the ally of the Hapsburgs, while later on his relations with Bohemia were friendly. Lev's political might was well known abroad, and so his name was often mentioned in the West-European historical records of that time.[12]

As a shrewd statesman, in his relations with the Golden Horde, he followed approximately the same submissive pattern of policy as the Vladimirian-Muscovite princes in the north did. In this respect, he was different from Danylo. Cooperating with the Mongols, he participated even in their war expeditions against Poland and Lithuania. He regularly paid the contribution to Sarai. Nevertheless, that submissiveness did not save his country from occasional Mongol destructions, as it happened in the Muscovite North, too. Yet, it must be agreed, that the Mongol domination in Ukraine was less oppressive than in the Muscovite north, as Hrushevsky asserted.[13]

Meanwhile in Volhinia two princes, Volodymyr and Mstyslav, ruled one after another, without having distinguished themselves as statesmen to any extent. Volodymyr was a peaceful and learned man, who liked books and the construction of beautiful buildings and churches more than waging wars and attending the state affairs. He built towns, castles, churches and fortresses, bought books and copied them himself, respected common people and cared for the welfare for all. Still in his lifetime he gave his principality to Mstyslav, and not to Lev, whom he despised for killing Shvarno. Mstyslav succeeded in unifying central and eastern Volhinia, received the region of Volkovyisk from Lithuania, but soon died, surrounded by the love and respect of all. With his death, the Galician-Volhinian principality was once again united under the scepter of prince Lev, soon being inherited by his son, King Yurii.

After working with his father for a long time on state affairs, Yurii was well prepared to assume the throne. In contrast to his father, Prince Lev, Yurii tried to preserve peace and to avoid war. Although he lost Lublin, his realm achieved tremendous economic growth and prosperity, fully recognized by foreigners. He apparently was crowned as a king, and consequently he used officially on his documents and seals his royal title. This certainly increased his prestige on the foreign courts. In 1303, Yurii succeeded in establishing a separate Metropolitan seat in the city of Halych for his principality to make the Orthodox Church there fully independent of the Metropolitan, residing in the North, who had assumed the authority of being the head of all Church in East Europe, and who continued the tradition of being the Metropolitan ''of Kiev and all of *Rus'*,'' meanwhile becoming a willing tool of the Vladimirian-Muscovite political interests. That was not along the interests of the Ukrainian South, and that is why the Galician-Volhinian princes wanted to have their own, also extending its authority to Kiev, independent Metropolitan province. In order to protect his country against the Lithuanian assaults, since Lithuania meanwhile became a very strong and very aggressive nation, King Yurii negotiated an alliance with the Teutonic Order in Prussia, which since that time continued to be the Rus'ian ally against the growing threats of Poland and Lithuania until the Galician-Volhinian principality ceased to exist as a sovereign political entity of the Ukrainian people.

176

After Yurii's death, his two sons, Andrei and Lev II, who were born of Yurii's marriage with Yevphimia, daughter of the Polish King, Wladyslaw Lokietek, inherited the throne and apparently ruled harmoniously and jointly, though they might have assigned to themselves separate provinces for their separate administration and income. Otherwise, they called themselves "Princes of all *Rus'*." In order to protect their country against Poland and Lithuania, and in order to support the growth of its well developed foreign trading, Andrei and Lev continued their alliance with the Teutonic Order and the commercial connections with the Pomeranian towns. Their international prestige must have been substantial. At one time one of them was a candidate for the Hungarian throne. Their domination over the Carpathian *Rus'* continued until Carl-Rober acquired the Hungarian crown, and later on annexed Mukachevo and the Carpathian regions to Hungary.

Apparently the Mongol raids harassed Galicia and Volhinia greatly, and consequently, Andrei and Lev waged wars against the invader, and amidst the warfare they must have perished, as can be implied from Lokietek's letter to the Pope. In what particular way they died, it is not certain.

The said two princes left no male successors to the throne. For about two years there was an *interregnum* in Galicia and Volhinia with no prince, though there were a few pretenders to the said throne. Finally, in 1325, the *boyar* oligarchs called Yurii II Boleslav, son of the Mazovian prince, Troiden, and the sister of the two last princes, Maria, to assume the Galician-Volhinian princely authority.

Yurii II, originally a Catholic of the name Boleslav, became Orthodox and ascended the Galician-Volhinian throne under unfavorable conditions. The Hungarian and the Polish courts were already developing plans of in some way dominating the Galician-Volhinian principality. The Hungarians had traditional aspirations to Galicia, and several Hungarian kings called themselves rulers of "Galicia and Lodomeria." The Poles desired an

177

annexation of those territories from time immemorable, since the tenth century on. Only the power of Kiev and, then, of Halych, on the one hand, and the weakness of Poland, divided into numerous warring principalities, on the other, made those dreams not possible. Now, it was time to do something about it. Yurii-Boleslav was not a real member of the Ruryk house; the *boyar* oligarchs wanted to have him for a figurehead, while the prince had other ideas; his Catholic origin amidst the Catholic-Orthodox rivalry was regarded suspiciously; and the strained relations were getting more and more intense. It was soon apparent that Yurii could not expect a male heir. The Hungarian and Polish courts were getting ready to assume an initiative at the right time.

Yurii was fully aware of the situation. His relations with Poland were not friendly at all, and in alliance with the Mongols he tried to recapture the city of Lublin, which was Ukrainian before. On the other hand, his relations with the Mongols, Lithuania and the Teutonic order were good and cooperative. He honored fully the alliance agreement with the Teutons, made before. In the area of domestic affairs, Yurii supported and assisted the towns, brought German, Polish, Czech and other colonists, and granted them the autonomous home rule of the Magdegurg legal system and additional privileges. Several princely decrees of that kind have been preserved to illustrate Yurii's doings in that respect.

Although he sought the *boyar* advice, his Catholic background, perhaps his too independent conduct, his friendly attitude towards the townspeople, and his protection of the colonists, who were largely Catholic, brought him at odds with a powerful clique of the *boyars,* who organized a plot, and poisoned him, supposedly for his being partial towards the Catholics, the Poles, Germans, Hungarians and others, and having been planning to return to Catholicism himself. That major tragedy, which caused the termination of Ukrainian-*Rus'* statehood, happened in 1340. With the prince's death, anti-foreigners' broils were arranged in Halych and some other towns, where some foreigners and Yurii's followers were killed and injured, and their properties damaged.[14]

The Polish-Lithuanian Take-Over. Before Yurii's assassination in 1339, the Polish king, Casimir, and the Hungarian king, Carl-Robert, reached an agreement in the town of Vyshehrad with respect to the succession of the Polish throne and the future of the Galician-Volhinian principality in case of Yurii's death without an heir. It was clear then than Casimir, because of his distant blood relationship with the previous rulers of the Galician-Volhinian realm, planned to dominate that land. Curiously enough, two days after Yurii's violent death, the Polish troops were on the march for Galicia. The news was scarcely able to reach the Polish court when Casimir invaded Galicia, supposedly to "revenge" Yurii's death and the slaughter of the foreigners. Hence, some historians assumed that perhaps Casimir had an advanced knowledge of or even was taking a part in the plot on Yurii's life. Soon also, the Hungarians marched on Galicia, too, either to claim it or to support the Polish invasion.

After having put aside the hated prince, the Galician *boyars* did not dare to establish directly a *boyar* oligarchic rule, which would have been to their liking, but called Prince Lubart, a son of the Lithuanian Grand Duke, Gedymin, who also was related to the Galician-Volhinian dynasty through intermarriage, to assume the throne in their land. Volhinia accepted Lubart, Dymytrii by his Christian name, wholeheartedly, while Galicia, having recognized him as her prince, was never enthusiastic about him nor gave him much support. With Yurii's death, of course, the Lithuanians also moved to claim Galicia and Volhinia. Having faced the danger of a bloody struggle on their soil among the Poles, Hungarians and Lithuanians, the *boyars* under the leadership of Dymytrii Dietko allied themselves with the Tartars, and having been backed by their authority, were able to stop the invaders. Galicia remained autonomous under Dietko until his death in 1349, recognizing Lubart's nominal authority, while the latter ruled in Volhinia, according to the convention reached by the *boyars* with the pretenders to the Galician-Volhinian throne.

Although Dietko succeeded in preserving for nine more years a relative political independence of Galicia, yet Casimir of Poland continued to nurse his long-range plans of her occupation and ultimate annexation. He negotiated the matter with the Tartars, who initially supported *boyar* oligarchy under Dietko's leadership. He promised the Tartars to pay the annual tribute, and in exchange received the Mongol *yarlik* on Galicia, which Casimir invaded anew immediately after Dietko's death, and adopted the title of "Lord of Galicia." Lubart, who considered himself a rightful ruler of that land, began a war with Poland, in which the local population participated, largely opposing the Polish usurpation, but not energetically enough. As a result of that inconclusive war, the old Galician-Volhinian principality was divided; Poland retained Galicia and the Kholm region, while Volhinia was left under Lubart's domination. The political existence of the Western *Rus'* realm was terminated, although Casimir paid a rather high price for it. He became nominally a vassal of Sarai.[15]

According to his long-range plans, Casimir proceeded rather cautiously. He preserved at first the name of the "Rus'ian Kingdom," the usage of the old Ukrainian language as the official tongue of the land, and many state offices left in the hands of the *boyars,* in order not to antagonize the local population, and in particular, the local aristocracy. On the other hand, however, he was intentionally bringing many foreign settlers, Poles, Germans, Hungarians and others, to Galicia, settled them as self-governing communities according to the Magdeburg law, granted them privileges and treated them with favors, supported the growth of Catholicism, and was busy about introducing the Roman Catholic Church organization. He considered all these measures as means of strengthening the Polish rule in Galicia.

Neither Casimir nor Lubart was happy with the temporary solution of the Galician question. Casimir was very unsure of himself, and consequently, he arranged another meeting with the Hungarian king, Ludvig, to renew and expand the Vyshehrad convention in 1350. Accordingly, Galicia was supposed to remain under Polish rule until Casimir's death, and in the case of his childless death, Ludvig of Hungary would ascend the Polish throne and also assume the rule in the Rus'ian kingdom of

Galicia. Soon after the convention was reached, Ludvig hastened with his army to assist Casimir in his new quest for the Galician-Volhinian heritage. Long drawn-out warfare between Poland and Hungary on one side and Lithuania, on the other, was undertaken, which was waged with interruptions and with changing luck. In 1351, Lubart and Keistut, his brother, defended Volhinia against the Polish-Hungarian onslaught. Meanwhile Casimir fell sick, while Ludvig, not enthusiastic about the whole affair, arranged for a temporary settlement. In 1352, the fighting was resumed. Ludvig and Casimir tried in vain to capture the fortress of Belz, but were defeated. Polish-Hungarian losses were too great. A truce was negotiated, and the situation remained somehow like it was before. Poland held Galicia and Lithuania held Volhinia. During all these skirmishes, Casimir was morally and materially assisted by the Pope, to whom he promised a conversion of Galicia to Catholicism, the Teutons, who were urged by Rome to support the Polish quest, and the Tartars, who were bribed by Casimir. The warfare of 1353, during which time the Teutonic Order supported the Lithuanians, was a defeat for the latter. The Teutons abandoned Lubart, having been urged by the Pope to do so.

In 1366, Casimir resumed the war with great force in order to acquire Volhinia. On his side, there were this time again the Teutons and the Mongols, which forced the Lithuanian princes to submit. An ''Eternal peace'' was arranged by two separate agreements, which gave Casimir western parts of Volhinia, while the eastern regions remained with Lubart. The peace proved to be much less than an eternal one. Casimir's death motivated Keistut and Lubart to attack Poland anew to vindicate Volhinia and Galicia. Ludvig of Hungary assumed the Polish throne and undertook a war expedition against the Lithuanians in 1377. The latter were defeated for two reasons; first, the Great Duke Olgerd of Lithuania died, which caused internal confusion in this country; and second, Lithuania was suddenly attacked by the Teutons, which weakened her defenses. Ludvig retained Galicia and western Volhinia. Later on, after Ludvig's death, Lubart succeeded in revindicating western Volhinia. The Polish-Hungarian hostilities against Lubart and Lithuanian meanwhile came to a temporary lull.

Ludvig, after becoming king of Poland, assumed Galicia for Hungary, and made Volodyslav Opilsky, his loyal lieutenant, the vassal-ruler of that land. Volodyslav assumed his authority in 1372 and titled himself "by God's Grace Lord and Heir of Rus' Land." Nevertheless, he was not interested in that country's welfare at all. Having been loyal to Ludvig, he made all the effort to strengthen the Hungarian grip by bringing many foreigners to Galicia and granting them privileges. He supported the Catholics and began to establish the Roman Church organization in Galicia, having received authority from Rome to introduce Roman Catholic dioceses in Halych, Peremyshl, Kholm and Volodymyr.[16] Ludvig took away Galicia in 1378 from Opilsky, having found another assignment for him, while the land was more directly incorporated to Hungary. In the late 1380s, Volodyslav again returned to Galacia for a while, where he wanted to established himself permanently. Yet, the fate of Galicia was finally sealed by the Polish invasion in 1387.

The ultimate incorporation of Galicia into Poland, while Volhinia remained Lithuanian for many decades to come, was accomplished by Queen Jadwiga of Poland. It happened as follows. The accord of Vyshehrad provided that Ludvig and his sons would be kings in Poland, but the former died without leaving any son; only two daughters, Mary and Jadwiga. Soon, a great deal of wheeling and dealing was going on behind the scene of the Polish throne succession. There was a substantial opposition of the Polish nobility and gentry to accept Jadwiga, Ludvig's younger daughter, as the legitimate throne successor. Finally the accord was reached to accept Jadwiga, but among the many conditions, there was the Polish demand to incorporate Galicia to the Polish Crown. Jadwiga agreed. No matter that the Hungarian Queen Mary restored Opilsky as a Hungarian vassal-ruler of Galicia, and tried to establish there the indisputable Hungarian rule; that Opilksy called on all Galician people not to surrender to

Jadwiga's Polish invasion, Queen Jadwiga soon succeeded in dominating Galicia. Peremyshl, Lviv and other towns, and after feeble resistance also Halych, recognized Jadwiga's authority. Subsequent diplomatic measures to revindicate Galicia to Hungary were to no avail. Thus, after the Polish invasion in 1387, Galicia remained under the Polish occupation until the first partition of Poland in 1772.[17]

1. S. Tomashivsky, *Istoria Ukrainy, Starynni viky i seredni viky,* Munich, 1948, p. 78, 103; M. Hrushevsky, *Istoria Ukrainy-Rusy,* New York, 1954, Vol. II, pp. 407-504; Vol. III, pp. 1-142; P. Hrytsak, *Halytsko-Volynska derzhava,* New York, 1958.

2. Tomashivsky, *op. cit.,* pp. 74-76; Hrushevsky, *op. cit.,* Vol. II, pp. 446-447.

3. N. Polonska-Vasylenko. *Istoria Ukrainy,* Munich, 1972, Vol. I, p. 166.

4. J. Abraham, *Organizacia kosciola lacinskiego na Rusi,* Lwow, 1904, pp. 99-100; also Tomashivsky, *op. cit.,* p. 88; *Chronica Alberici Trium Fontium,* year 1205; B. Wlodarski, *Polityka ruska Leszka Bialego,* Lviv, 1925, p. 21.

5. Roman's rule: Hrushevsky, *op. cit.,* Vol. III, pp. 3-17; Polonska-Vasylenko, *op. cit.,* Vol. I, pp. 192-194.

6. V. Pashuto, *Ocherki po istorii Galicko-Volynskoi Rusi,* Moscow, 1950, pp. 224-226; also Polonska-Vasylenko, *ibid.,* p. 197.

7. N. Fr.-Chirovsky, *A History of the Russian Empire,* New York, 1973, Vol. I, pp. 185-192.

8. Polonska-Vasylenko, *op. cit.,* Vol. I, pp. 204-207; the same, "Korol Danylo na tli istorychnoi doby," *Vyzvolnyi Shlakh,* London, 1954, Bk. IX; Pashuto, *op. cit.,* p. 272.

9. Yu. Fedoriv, *Istoria tserkvy v Ukraini,* Toronto, 1967, pp. 100-104.

10. Polonska-Vasylenko, *Istoria Ukrainy,* Vol. I, p. 207; Pashuto, *op. cit.,* pp. 289-290; Hrushevsky, *op. cit.,* Vol. III, p. 92.

11. Chirovsky, *op. cit.,* Vol. I, pp. 185-317.

12. Evaluation of Lev as a ruler according to the Hipathian chronicle: "Lev was a wise prince, courageous and bold during a war; he exhibited courage in many warfares:" *Ipatievskaia letopis;* 1871 ed., p. 615.

13. Hrushevsky, *op. cit.,* Vol. III, p. 102-103.

14. Original sources about Yurii-Boleslav's assassination: *Monumenta Poloniae historica,* I, No. 566, also the same, II, pp. 620-621 and 629: relations by Janko z Czarnkowa; Hrushevsky, *op. cit.,* Vol. III, pp. 529-530 and 534-535.

15. Casimir promised apparently to the Khan to pay an annual tribute to get the Tartar neutrality in his struggle for Galicia: "Nuncii Tartarorum venerunt ad regem Poloniae;" *Monumenta Poloniae historica,* II, p. 885; also, Polonska-Vasylenko, *op. cit.,* Vol. I, p. 213.

16. *Ibid.,* p. 214.

17. The historical mission of the Galician-Volhinian realm: Tomashivsky, *op. cit.,* p. 103; D. Doroshenko, *Narys istorii Ukrainy,* Munich, 166, Vol. I, pp. 94-95: "Having torn apart the dynastic and ecclesiatic-political ties with Suzdal, it stopped the assimilation process of the Ukrainian ethnic element with the Russian, with the prevalence of the latter, on the other hand" (p. 94). On the history of the realm: Hrytsak, *op. cit;* Pashuto, *op. cit.;* J. Barwinski, *Pieczęcie ksiąząt halicko-wlodzimierskich z polowy XIV w.,* Cracow, 1909; I. Linnichenko, *Cherti iz istorii soslovii v zapadnoi (Galickoi) Rusi XIV-XV v.,* Moscow, 1894; D. Zubrytsky, *Istoria drevvnevo Galichesko-Russkavo kniazhestva,* Vols. I-III, Lviv, 1852-1855.

CHAPTER SEVEN

THE GOVERNMENT IN THE KIEVAN-GALICIAN TIMES

The political structure and law — The legal status of the individual — The prince — The people's meeting — The council of nobles — The general administration — The judiciary — The military.

The Political Structure and Law. It has been long assumed that the development of the Kievan *Rus'* realm was a result of a prolonged evolution of the seven Ukrainian-Rus'ian tribes. From the modest beginnings of family life, through the stage of clan organization with considerable authority of the clan chieftain and the clan elders, and the subsequent growth of the tribal constitution with the tribal leader or *voyevoda,* subsequently called prince or *kniaz',* in the old Ukrainian-Rus'ian tongue, and the super-tribal organizations or "unions," as they were referred to by such historians as Braichevsky and Hrushevsky, with a considerable power of the people's meetings, the *viche,* the *Rus'* realm or Kievan state came into existence. It began with the Polianian tribal organization, which from earliest times was referred to as *Rus'*. The *Rus'* rapid and full-blown territorial and political growth had received a powerful shot in the arm by the military and organizational genius of the Normans-Varangians, who arrived in Ukraine in a steady stream throughout the ninth and tenth centuries and were steadily hired and used by the Kievan rulers in their empire building process.[1] The Norman impact on the *Rus'* realm was on a continuous decline in the eleventh century, although the Norman warriors were hired by Volodymyr the Great and Yaroslav the Wise.

At the end of the tenth century, the *Rus'* realm was structured, although not yet fully completed as a political-constitutional entity, which was subject to subsequent evolution. The instance gave rise to several and rather different theories about the constitution of the realm, while none of them could be fully substantiated because of the inadequacy of the historical sources and their vague relations. Hence, Soloviov, or Solovev, thought that the Kievan *Rus'* represented a clan communal property of the Ruryk dynasty, rather of a private or civil legal character than of a public law nature. He thought that it was not supposed to be divided among the individual members of the dynasty at any time; that the territorial parts of it, the *udily,* were not supposed to be hereditarily claimed by individual princes or individual branches of the Ruryk house at all; and that that clan communal realm was supposed to be jointly ruled according to the principle of the *seniorate,* under the supreme authority of the eldest member of the dynasty at all times.[2]

Kostomarov made another theoretical assertion. He stressed the public law nature of the realm, where the confederate character of six lands, Ukraine, Muscovy, Byelorus'ia, Siversk land, Pskov land and Novgorod the Great land, prevailed, where the individual lands were subordinate to the interests of the whole of the realm, having been something like a relationship between an ''upper-state'' authority, on the one hand, and the ''lower-state'' authorities, on the other. If that kind of constitution of *Rus'* ever prevailed, then a correction must be introduced here, since the realm consisted rather of eight or nine, and not six individual lands. Galicia, Volhinia and the Chernihiv land must have been added to the list of the confederative components.[3] Karamzin also stressed the public law nature of the Kievan *Rus'*, and concluded that the disintegration of separation process of the realm into the individual principalities came about in the consequence of the factual weakness of the Kievan "Great Princes" and Kiev itself. Doubtlessly, it seems that later on factual development became the constitutional principle for the autonomous status of the individual lands. The case of the separation of Galicia had been the most pronounced proof of that structural change in the Kievan *Rus'* realm in the Ukrainian south.[4]

Pogodin, like Soloviov, stressed rather the private law character of the *Rus'* political structure, which, as he said, was an expression of the family legal arrangements of the Ruryk house. That, it might be concluded, then projected in the area of the customary semi-public legal relations. Presniakov still supplied another and a very specific theoretical explanation of the question. He asserted that the constitution of *Rus'* was an original one throughout, having reflected the specific Rus'ian developments. *Rus'* was, he maintained, neither a federation nor a monolithical monarchy, but a state organization of its own, where the individual princely land, the *volost'* or *udil*, became the main constitutional pillar of the realm, which was evolved from the old clan community. Finally, Hrushevsky and Kluchevskii came forward with two opposite explanations. The former thought that *Rus'* since the second half of the eleventh century was a group of independent lands, kept together by the old tradition of one Rus'ian realm of yesterday and one Ruryk dynasty, where the principle of seniorate was valid at varying degrees at various times. The latter, on the other hand, maintained that the *Rus'* realm consisted of various lands which were only administrative districts, governed by appointed princes as caretakers of public law and order.[5] Of course, among the list of historians who had their particular theoretical explanations of the constitution of *Rus'*, only a few were named.

There is no doubt that each and everyone of these theories or hypotheses has some elements of truth in describing the Kievan-Rus'ian constitution, in particular, the relationship between the capital city of Kiev and the individual lands, including Galicia. Their correctness must be qualified by the element of timing, however. No doubt, Soloviov's assumption about the clan community relationship was correct for the earliest days of the *Rus'* realm including the times of Volodymyr the Great and Yaroslav the Wise, when also Kluchevskii's belief, that the individual princes of the provinces were the caretakers of law and order in the name of senior prince in Kiev, would substantially add to the clarification of said problem. The clan communal property, the *Rus'*, was jointly owned and administered by the dynasty under the supreme authority of the senior prince of Kiev. Yaroslav's testament of 1054 and the establishment of the principle of seniorate had clearly indicated the family or clan background of the constitution of the *Rus'* realm with its private law character. The things were, however, rapidly changing. The phenomenon of the princely outcasts, the *izgoii,* unleashed the new development. The *izgoii* were the princes who for some reason were not able to get hold of their territorial share, the *udil,* as it was explained before, but never came to terms with the arising situation and continued their, often bloody, struggle to recapture their lands. The phenomenon was of a particular importance in the history of Galicia and her emancipation from Kievan supremacy. The continuous warfare among the members of the Ruryk house either to acquire the throne of Kiev or the individual *udily* brought about the convention of Lubech of 1097, the factual abolition of the seniorate principle, that the eldest in the clan was the senior prince of Kiev with the authority of a suzerain over the other, territorial princes, and replaced it with the principle of patrimoniate, that each prince had a claim on the territory ruled by his father or his branch of the dynasty. The convention initiated actually a new chapter of the history of the *Rus'* constitution. The commonwealth was progressively becoming a federation in the sense of Kostomarov's approach to the question, where still a feeling of the dynastic and traditional community prevailed. However, in the second half of the twelfth and the first half of the thirteenth century the constitutional trend progressed towards a loose confederation of the semi-independent principalities of the Ukrainian south, while the Suzdalian-Muscovite north drifted away from the Kievan center completely as a sovereign northern, and ethnically alien state federation of its own, with its later development in the direction of complete centralism and absolutism.[6]

As far as the constitution of the Galician-Volhinian principality was concerned, then in its early stage of growth, it followed the Kievan constitutional evolution, while later on, it continued as a closely knit federative state of the Roman dynastic branch, dominated by the personalities of princes Danylo, Lev and Yurii.

The constitutional process in Ukraine-*Rus'* was dominated by a continuous struggle among the three constitutional elements of government; the monarchistic, the democratic and the aristocratic ones. Of course, at times, the oligarchic element was present, but strongly interwoven with the *boyar* aristocratic trend. The tyranny and the ochlocracy, the dictatorship and the mob-rule, the inferior forms of government were scarcely present in the government structure of medieval Ukraine-*Rus'* at any time.

It seems that the democratic principle, represented by the people's meeting, the *viche*, was the oldest constitutional element in the political organization of the Ukrainian Slavs, which organically and gradually developed from the family blood ties, through the clannish and, then, tribal relations, giving to the family's grown-up men the authority of running the community affairs. Progressively, from the tribal leaders, authorized by the people's meetings to command and lead on a temporary basis, who were probably at first called the *voyevody*, the monarchistic principle began to take over, and the permanent institution of the prince, the *kniaz'*, evolved, at first with a highly limited authority, almost dependent upon the *viche*. With the formation of the upper crust of the society, the *boyar* class, these *muzhi peredni*, the better men, began to aspire to assume more political and government authority. They thought that their "blue blood," personal importance and large properties entitled them to more constitutional power, and that they could govern better than the common people or the prince. Furthermore, they wanted that power to advance themselves even more.

With the growth of the institution of the prince and of the nobility, each social factor wanted to assume more and more authority and to reduce the power of the other, including that of the ancient people's meeting, and none of these three wanted to yield. The power-play continued through the entire history of the medieval society of Ukraine-*Rus'*; at one time the prince, at another time the *boyar duma,* and at third time the *viche* gained more constitutional government influence, according to varying circumstances. Each one tried to gain from the weakness of the other or tried to exploit the changing conditions, the social, political, domestic or international ones. In studying the historical developments during the Kievan and the Galician-Volhinian times, one cannot help but notice that steady power-play among the three constitutional principles. The personalities of the princes, *boyar* leaders or the popular leaders were of great importance. The *boyars* acquired, for example, at times a great power in Galicia, while the phenomenon of the "Tartar people" in the Volhinian and Kievan regions was the manifestation of the trend towards the "people's democracy," though under the khan's protection.

No society can live and develop without law and order, and the society of the medieval Ukraine-*Rus'* was no exception. Yet, the first legal regulations came about by the way of religious and social customs and constant and habitual usage, which subsequently established the legal traditions in the form of common and unwritten laws. In that way the original constitutional or public and private or civil legal principles and institutions developed in old *Rus'*, which at times were expressed in symbols and proverbs to be more easily remembered. Also the original criminal law developed by customs and tradition and with a great deal of symbolism, as well. The customary and traditional "Rus'ian law" had existed already for a very long time and had a long evolution behind itself at the time, when the first written legal documents were drawn in the tenth century in the form of the international agreements between the *Rus'* princes, Askold, Oleh, Ihor and Sviatoslav, and the Greek or Byzantine emperors. In those documents, the references were made to that law. The said agreements, having been international treaties, contained the legal provisions in the fields of private, criminal, public and international law, as well. It was a typical feature of the old legislation, where normally the legal matters of different character were lumped together. Also other princes of Kiev must have concluded international conventions during their reigns, which affected the formation of the Rus'ian legal norms and institutions, though neither their original documents nor their contents were preserved in any written form, in the chronicle or otherwise. Then, from the late Galician-Volhinian era international agreements were preserved in some rendition, in particular the convention of princes Andrii and Lev with the Teutonic order from 1308 and 1316, and that of Yurii II with the same Order from 1325-1327. The conventions had a defensive-offensive military character and were directed against Lithuania, Poland and the Tartars. It must be underscored here that those agreements were signed, along with the signature of the prince, with those of some outstanding *boyars*. It only proved a considerable constitutional significance of the council of nobles in international affairs.

The princely conventions, the *snemy,* such as these at Lubech, Horodok, Vytechiv and Kiev at various times, had a great impact on the formation of the constitutional and legal structure of the Ukrainian-Rus'ian society and nation. They regulated the relations among the princes of the Ruryk house and coordinated their common actions against the deadly enemies of *Rus'*, such as the Cumans and Tartars.

The conventions between the princes, on the one hand, and the people of the individual principalities, theoretically speaking, and the townspeople or *boyars,* practically speaking, the *riady,* resembled the *pacta conventa* in other lands, regulated the relationships between the ruler and his subjects, having imposed certain limitations and obligations on the prince, and guaranteed certain rights to the people. It meant the free strata of the society. For example, the *riady* demanded that the prince would personally preside over the court procedures and not delegate the authority of his officials, the *tivuny;* that the prince would not commit any unjustices; and that the guilty or unfair *tivuny* would be removed from office. The *riady* were affirmed regularly by cross-kissing by the parties involved.

Princely testaments, like that of Yaroslav the Wise, and pre-testamentarian legacies, appointing the heirs to the throne or transferring the principalities to other princes, like that of Yaroslav *Osmomysl,* making his illegitimate son, Oleh, his successor, or princely grants, giving landed properties to towns, monasteries, the Church or the *boyars,* granting all kinds of privileges, such as tax exemptions, to the Church, the *boyars,* individual towns, or merchants, domestic or foreign, such as the privileges for the merchants of the cities of Cracow and Thorn, normally with the approval of the *boyar duma,* and princely *ustavy* and *uroky,* issued by Volodymyr the Great, Yaroslav the Wise and some other princes, regulating the ecclesiastic and civil matters, were the examples of the positive, and prevailingly written, legislation of that era, which either directly or indirectly affected the public, private, and criminal sectors of legislative evolution in the Kievan-Galician realm.[7]

No doubt, the most important example of the positive, written legislation in *Rus'* there was the code of laws, referred to as the *Rus'ka Pravda,* the Rus'ian Laws. The *Rus'ka Pravda* as a book of laws, had been the product of a long legislative evolution itself. Apparently the first codification of some seventeen articles originated in the eleventh and twelfth century, and it had been generally connected with Prince Yaroslav the Wise. The legal regulations might have been written down and promulgated by Yaroslav between 1016 and 1054. Then, the princes Iziaslav, Sviatoslav, and Vsevolod, with their *muzhi peredni,* had added some twenty six new articles, with new matters having been regulated, sometimes before 1068. The third installment of articles was apparently added to the code by Volodymyr Monomakh around 1113, where a prominent place had been taken by the

regulation of credit and interest rate, which followed heavy riot-
ing in Kiev and other cities as a violent reaction to the financial
abuses committed by capital owners.

According to historical sources, Yaroslav had used force to
make his *Rus'ka Pravda* be generally accepted as law. Although
initially there might have been difficulties with the enforcement
of the code, later on, however, it became a very popular piece of
legislation, a real basis for the legal process of the society, since
over 300 written old copies of the code have been uncovered. It
indicates its extensive use throughout the Ukrainian south, in
particular. The *Rus'ka Pravda* has been considered by many historians as an important factor in the unification of the Ukrainian
nationality. Some copies of the code have been the so-called
"short" and other, the so-called "expanded" versions, and so
classified in accordance with what legal material, earlier or later,
and in what form, abbreviated or comprehensive, they covered.

An analysis of the code and its comparison with the contemporary legislation in Europe disclosed some Byzantine influences
on the early Rus'ian judicial principles and concepts, while the
Scandinavian influence, in spite of a rather large number of Normans in *Rus'*, was not extensive there at all. Yet, on the other
hand, the *Rus'ka Pravda* generally embodied more humane and
more progressive ideas, along with the common law of *Rus'* in
those days, than the contemporary legal documents and legal
practices in the West or Byzantium. The penalties in *Rus'ka
Pravda* were more humane. It did not recommend capital
punishment, and corporal penalties for the free people were unknown. The corporal penalties were applied to the half-free and
slaves and with limitations. Killing and murder were punished by
monetary penalties, the so-called *vyra* and double *vyra,* under
specific circumstances, but the principle of revenge by the family
was upheld. Personal insults were heavily punished. This indicated a high conception of personal respect and honor among the
ancient Ukrainian-Rus'ians. The code also reflected a high social
position of the woman and mother in *Rus'*. In some respects,
women had equal rights with men, as, for example, with respect

to the property rights, inheritance and guardianship of the children. Ukrainian women, in particular, among the princes and nobles, participated in politics, were active in Church affairs, organized schools and promoted education, managed and disposed of their properties, studied philosophy, rhetoric and languages and achieved high levels of intellectual development.[8] Chubaty, furthermore, underscored that a progressive character of Rus'ian law was also evident with respect to the maritime law concerning the wreckage of ships, which according to most Western laws became the property of the owners of the river or sea banks. According to Rus'ian law, the state took over the protection of wreckage until its legal owner could be found, and then, after a proper procedure of identification, he would assume his ownership. In addition, in the case of crime, the circumstances, the background and motivation were taken in account in the court proceedings in *Rus'* in sentencing the guilty. This was not the case in other societies in Europe at that time.

Nevertheless, from the formal point of view, the *Rus'ka Pravda* left a great deal to desire. Similarly, like other codes of that time, there was a complete lack of any proper separation among different areas of legislation. The code covers indiscriminately the aspects of civil, criminal and procedural laws, all of them lumped together, and individual articles, following one another, at the same time refer to different and completely unrelated legal matters.

At one time, historians and jurists were involved in a discussion: was the code of *Rus'ka Pravda* an official codification of laws, undertaken by princes together with the council of nobles, or only a private compilation of generally binding common law and princely legislation, promulgated at various times? The problem might be hard to answer. Luckily, from the historical point of view, the question has not been of paramount importance. It was quite possible that Yaroslav the Wise really ordered the early code of a few articles to be compiled, and that some other prince did the same with respect to his legislation, but overall, the copies of the code uncovered and found later must be rather private compilations. Yet, the *Rus'ka Pravda* had a considerable impact on the judicial evolution of *Ukraine-Rus'* at the late Kievan-Galician era, as well as later on, since the later Polish *Statut Wislicki,* the Wislica Statute, and the Lithuanian *Statut Litewski,* the Lithuanian Statute, had drawn heavily on the *Rus'ka Pravda.* Both later laws affected the legal life of various provinces of Ukraine in the later periods of her history.

At the end of the Galician-Volhinian era the privileges of granting autonomy rights of the Magdeburg law by the princes to various towns and, later on to some villages, as well, completed the legal framework of Kievan-Galician society. The real legal impact of the Magdeburg law in Ukraine was first felt, however, in the subsequent centuries.

The Legal Status of the Individual. Not all individuals and not the entire population in the Kievan realm and the Galician-Volhinian principality were equally treated by the law and had the same legal status. First of all, the entire population was divided and separated into two large segments, the free and the unfree, and then these two segments were internally and thoroughly differentiated into specific classes of people, each having been differently treated by the law, though initially unwritten and customary, based on tradition only, but then by written princely acts and decrees and their private compilations. In that way the rights and responsibilities of these different classes developed over a period of time. In fact, only the free, according to the unwritten constitution of the realm, were the true subjects of the prince and the state authority, the citizens in the medieval sense of the term. Hence, if one wants to talk about the legal status of an individual or about "the people" as the subject of the law and the direct state authority, he must immediately exclude from the coverage of the subject matter the huge stratum of the slaves and, perhaps, the half-free, who, according to the medieval world-outlook, in general, and according to the Rus'ian legal concepts, as well, were not subjects but only objects of the law. The slaves were a "property" of the free people, void of most or any individual rights, in whom the state and government, the prince, were not directly interested, and who were scarcely protected by the law. They were within the authority of their lords. Yet, under the impact of Christianity the conditions in that respect were gradually changing. This can even be detected in some provisions of the *Rus'ka Pravda*.[9]

Only the free people in the *Rus'* realm were subjects of the law and had certain rights and responsibilities, but they were not equally treated by the law and the state authority. The free people were socially greatly differentiated and categorized in several social strata or classes, the nobles, the princes of the Ruryk house and the *boyars,* the peasants, the townpeople and the "church people." A detailed discussion of the social stratification in the Kievan and Galician realms follows in one of the later chapters, and at this point it is only mentioned in reference to the legal status of the individual. Consequently, any free individual in the *Rus'* state derived his legal status first from his membership in the particular class. A member of a higher class, such as the nobility, had a higher legal status, a more direct relationship to the prince and the state, more and quite different rights and responsibilities, than the members of the lower classes had.

Yet the very fact that the social stratification in *Rus'* was much "looser" or "more free" than in other lands and other societies, including the West-European ones, at that time was of a great legal consequence. The Rus'ian social classes were not frozen or tightly locked-in. The transition of an individual or whole families from one class to another, upward and downward, was quite easy. It was not a rigid caste system which prevailed there, but substantial social fluctuations were taking place. The relative ease, by which an individual in the Kievan state, including a slave, could change his class, and by so doing, change also his legal status, considerably "softened" the class stratification there and made life, especially of the lower classes, much more tolerable than elsewhere, obviously according to the standards of those times. The real peculiarity of the Kievan era was the fact that most individuals could even abrogate and give up their subjection to a particular prince and principality and establish themselves somewhere else.

The Prince. In the Kievan-Galician *Rus'* realm only a member of the Ruryk dynasty, by his birth, heritage and blood, could have been a prince. The honor constitutionally belonged to a *Rurykovych,* descendent of Ruryk only, and nobody else could be a prince. When in 1213, during the Galician turmoil, a *boyar,* Volodyslav Kormylchych, seized authority, and declared himself to be the prince, he caused a real furor among the Ruryk princes. They literally organized a crusade against him and his conspirators, whose deed was considered high treason, and who paid with their lives for the crime.

The princes were not only a political factor of authority, they were also an upper social stratum, with special rights and privileges, supposedly all equal ''grandchildren of the same grandfather.'' The prince of Kiev consequently did not have the title of a ''Grand Prince,'' which was given to him by some later historians. At first, he was according to the constitutional tradition a ''senior'' prince, but later on, all princes of an older generation, or those holding larger territories or principalities, or more prestigeous princely towns, like Kiev, Chernihiv, Turiv or Halych, were referred to as ''senior'' princes, who *de facto* enjoyed more prestige and power, who *de iure,* however, were equal to the so-called ''junior'' princes. Of course, according to Yarsolav's testament, which established the principle of seniorate and, by so doing, became an important constitutional act, all ''junior'' princes were supposed to respect and owed obedience to the ''senior'' prince of Kiev, ''like to their father.'' Although that principle soon lost its validity to some extent with respect to Kiev, because of the principle of patrimoniate, as introduced by the Lubech convention, it continued its force partially in the individual lands of the Kievan realm; and in Chernihiv, Preyaslav, Volodymyr, the senior princes of the given branches of the Ruryk house used to have more power and prestige *de facto* and perhaps *de iure,* as well. The personality of the prince was here, however, of a decisive importance.

In addition to the above principles, which had the consitutional or public bearing, but which also regulated the private or family relations of the Ruryk dynasty, there was a third principle of some constitutional meaning, namely, the principle of primogeniture, that the first born, the oldest son, had a first claim on his father's throne. Yet, this principle was also not fully carried on, as the previous ones, because of abuses, use of power and other unconstitutional or illegal measures, as well as by the intervention of the council of nobles, the *duma,* and the people's meeting, the *viche.* On the other hand, the prince had the right to divide his principality among his sons. That led to two opposite developments; some senior princes represented the centralist tendency, having attempted by some lawful and unlawful means to gather under their authority as many lands as possible toward building strong state organizations; on the one hand, many junior princes stood for the centrifugal tendency, having attempted to preserve their small principalities as autonomously as possible from Kiev or another territorial center, as well, on the other. Of course, it led to continuous dynastic warfare, the phenomenon of the *izgoi* princes, and the general weakening of the once powerful empire.

Generally, a descendent of the Ruryk dynasty, legitimately born and raised in the Orthodox Christianity, could become a lawful prince in any territory of the huge *Rus'* land, though some exceptions could have happened, like those in Galicia with Oleh, Yaroslav Osmomysl's illegitimate son, who, however, was soon forced to resign, or Yurii-Boleslav Troidenovych, who had to accept the Orthodoxy before he was enthroned. The throne assumption was connected with some formalities and ceremonies, like the participation of the clergy and the people's meeting, and kissing the cross by all concerned to underscore the solemn responsibility to live up to the agreement, reached between the prince and the people, or the *boyars,* in some cases.

It seems, that initially the Ruryk princes, like Ihor, Sviatoslav, Volodymyr and Yaroslav, had a very comprehensive, almost unlimited monarchic authority, but they were never despotic rulers. They had to listen to the advice of the *duma* and the *viche.* It did not mean, however, that they had to follow that advice. Later on, however, with the seniorate and patrimoniate principles affecting the princely fates, the later princes, in order to strengthen their positions, either on the Kievan throne or in the given lands of *Rus'*, had to follow the *duma* and *viche* recommendations, and even subsequently, they negotiated the agreements with these two institutions, the aristocratic-oligarchic *duma* and the democratic *viche*, and also lived up to these agreements. In some lands of *Rus'*, in Galicia, in particular, where the power of the *boyars* was very extensive, those agreements, the *riady*, greatly limited the authority of the prince. The struggle between the monarchic principle of the unlimited authority of the prince, and the aristocratic one, the power of the nobles, led in some lands to violence, such as extermination of the rebellious *boyars* or their expulsion from the given principality, or killing or expulsion of the prince and calling another one, sometimes by the democratic *viche*, as well. This happened in Kiev, Galicia, Chernihiv, and other lands.

The princely authority included the functions of being the head of the government and administration, the chief military leader and the chief justice in the land. There was no division of powers at all. The prince disposed of the land, could start a war, negotiate peace treaties, carry out defense projects by building castles and fortresses, regulate court matters, levy taxes, promulgate laws, appoint and dismiss the top officials of the state, supervise and control the government process, and affect the affairs of the Orthodox Church by being its protector, influence the appointment of the metropolitan, bishops and other top offices, issue regulations, coordinating the Church matters, the *ustavy*. However, in Ukraine, the *caesaropapist* principle, of the prince being the head of the church, never prevailed. That was the case in Suzdal-Muscovy, to the fullest extent.

The relations among the princes, as far as state matters were concerned, were practically regulated, and were largely dependent upon the personalities of individual rulers; at times they were friendly, like between Danylo and Vasyl or Volodar and Vasyl; at times they were tolerable: and at times, rather hostile. In the cases, when the safety of the entire *Rus'* land or any other major problems developed, the interprincely conventions, the said *snemy,* were held, either on the nationwide scale or on a local extent, pertaining to the particular principality, Galician-Volhinian, Chernihivian, or otherwise. There were the *snemy* in Lubech, in 1097, Vytechiv, in 1100, and Kiev, in 1223, which attempted to coordinate relations among all princes, common military action against the Cumans and, then, against the Tartars. The *snemy* were definitely an internal Rus'ian constitutional institution and never an international convention of autonomous rulers of various principalities, as some authors liked to imply.[10]

The People's Meeting. The people's meeting had been the oldest government institution among the Slavs, preceding the institution of the prince for some time. It must be admitted, therefore, that the democratic principle among the Slavs was much older than the monarchal one. It was the manifestation of the people's rule and sovereignty, and its formation was more accomplished than that of the council of nobles. Subsequently with the growth of princely authority, the power of ancient institution of the *viche* declined. Yet, whenever the authority of the prince declined for any reason, or any serious trouble developed in the given land, the *viche* automatically regained its original status as an important expression of the people's will, which either supported or replaced the princely authority in order to solve the given constitutional or political problem.

All mature or grown-up men, mostly the urban and at times suburban population of the capital town of the given principality, of the Ukrainian-Rus'ian descent could legally participate in the meeting. Essentially, during Kievan-Galician times, the prince's privilege was to call the *viche* to convene to advise him. However, at times the people's meetings convened against the prince's will, either to admonish him or to dispose of him, which was, of course, an unconstitutional measure. The regular meetings, called by the prince, dealt with national defense or other important matters; especially at the time of the prince's absence or to get the people's backing for his actions. The findings of the *viche* had to be unanimous. At first the majority decisions were fully unknown, while later on, only seldom admitted. The deliberations did not follow any set procedure. The meetings which convened without the prince's approval were constitutionally irregular.[11]

In some Ukrainian lands, and in Galicia in particular, the *de facto* and *de iure* significance of the people's meeting was not only limited by the Ruryk princes, but also by the council of nobles, the *duma,* where the *boyars* succeeded in taking over the functions of the *viche* altogether. In such cases, however, the princes often appealed to the *viche* and used it to rid themselves of the influence of the overbearing *boyar* oligarchy, like Roman and Danylo of Galicia did.

Although the importance of the people's meeting gradually declined, traditionally its responsibilities included a certain influence on the enthronement of the prince, especially if there were several candidates for the given throne at the same time. Otherwise, either the seniority or the patrimoniate principles decided the issue.[12] Further, the *viche* acted as the council of the prince in significant matters. And, finally, the meeting also had certain judicial functions to perform, and it participated partially in administration by appointments and dismissals of certain officers.[13]

The Council of Nobles. *The boyarska duma,* the oligarchic element of government, was of an ancient origin, like the *viche,* with no set composition or competence. Its membership and power were exposed to wide variations. It was of course, an advisory body. At first, the Kievan princes respected and frequently called the *boyars* to come and to counsel them, and the chronicle praised those princes, who sought the *boyar* advice. It was the old Slavic and Norse tradition that the prince could not make any decisions of importance without consulting the council of nobles, although he was not really bound by its advice. The *duma* normally participated in the land's legislation, international affairs, and the judiciary, by functioning at times, together with the prince, without him or in place of him, as a supreme court in matters of importance, like the murder of grand *boyar* or high treason. In domestic administration, it could participate in levying new taxes. Volodymyr Monomakh instructed his children (sons) "to sit and to deliberate" with their *boyars,* the retainers.

The council of nobles apparently functioned in two ways: as an inner circle of a princely "cabinet," and as a plenary assembly. On the one hand, a small body of a few members of the *boyar* upper stratum, five, seven or nine outstanding people, *muzhi peredni,* who were especially trusted by the prince, were permanently consulted, even by such strong individuals as Volodymyr the Great, Yaroslav the Wise, Volodymyr Monomakh, Roman and Danylo of Galicia, and very frequently, even daily. On the other hand, the plenary assembly was called to session to discuss major state affairs, and it included the members of the princely retinue, the *druzhyna,* the city and countryside *boyars,* and some city elders, the representatives of the urban commercial aristocracy. These plenary sessions of the *boyars* were called rather infrequently to meet and to advise, and their membership felt at times that they had been neglected and discriminated against.

As the agency of the *boyar* oligarchy, the *duma* carried on in many instances the struggle against the princely principle of monarchy and against some princes who exhibited absolutist tendencies, in particular, in Galicia, like Volodymyrko and Roman. In some cases, the *boyars* and their *duma* were responsible for outright anarchist moves, like those after Roman's death, when they did not want to accept Danylo and Vasylko as their constitutional and rightful rulers, and under the leadership of Volodyslav Kormylchych allowed themselves to commit the crime of high treason by agreeing to accept him as a prince, though only a member of the Ruryk house could be one, according to the standards of that time. Further, in some instances, the boyar *duma* and the oligarchs called foreign rulers, the Hungarian kings or princes, to replace their own, Ukrainian-Rus'ian, ones. Finally, at times they assassinated their princes, and in the case of Yurii-Boleslav, they brought about the downfall of the Galician-Volhinian realm.[14]

The General Administration. The princely court was, of course, the center, at first, of the entire realm and, then, of the individual lands' administration. A number of princely officials,

202

lieutenants and appointees performed various functions, such as the over-all administration management, financial and manorial, military, judicial, foreign relations, general office and court and other managerial functions. There was for a long time a complete fusion of a strictly public and princely private administration process. Perhaps, at the very end, a notion of separation of those two segments dawned in the minds of the responsible persons.

The whole administration process was divided into the central and the provincial or territorial ones. The most important central office was that of the *dvoretsky,* the *majordomo* or *comes palatinus,* in Latin. At the beginning, he was rather a private official of the prince, yet later he developed into a public office and acquired considerable authority. He became the deputy of the prince, and at time, the leader of the *boyars.* He coordinated and supervised the entire court administration and management, to whom all private princely officials were responsible, but at the same time his jurisdiction extended over the entire administration, as well as over the judiciary, military and financial. It seems, that the office of the *dvoretsky,* the majordomo, evolved out of the ancient institution of the *tysiatsky,* the *chiliarch* or *milesius,* who was at first the right hand of the prince, but later on became a territorial officer; and then instead of one, there were a few chiliarchs in the realm.

The *dvoretsky* possessed certain general powers as the aide to the prince, but in the case that the prince for some reason was absent from the capital, he had some special powers as the princely deputy, including the top military authority. Also in his person there was the unity of complete authority with no division of powers, the legislative, executive and judicial.[15]

The *pechatnyk,* the *cancelarius* or chancellor, was the chief of the princely chancery or office, where the official documents, decrees, privileges and court findings and decisions, were prepared and issued. Also the foreign policies were conducted and certain military functions carried out there. The *pechatnyk* unified in his person the responsibilities of the state office and the ministry of foreign affairs. Because the office required education and skill, it was frequently performed by a clergyman. The *kluchnyk*, the cammerarius or chatelaine, was the third most important official at the court, the function of which could be compared with the minister of finance of today. He was the chief of the court household, and his character was more of a private princely official, rather than that of a public state officer. The chatelaine was responsible to the *dvoretsky,* and he could be also a member of a lower social class, even a half-free, a *tivun.*

In addition to those three top officials, there were other officials of a minor importance, whose functions were similar to the comparable offices in West Europe at that time, such as the *stolnyk,* the *stabularius,* the mechnyk, the sword-bearer, the court hunter, the court clergyman, and many other officials, including many court servants, the *otroky* and *ditsky,* who performed the functions of a lower order. The *tivuny* were a particular group of the princely officials-servants, who were either slaves or half-free and were completely subordinate to the prince, and carried out the general administrative functions, and were considered partially for the members of the central, and partially for the territorial, government set-up. They performed a great variety of functions at the court and in the provinces as the judges of a lower order, tax-collectors, special princely envoys, managers of different activities at the court and so on.

The territorial or provincial administration, which had to carry out the will of the prince and his court throughout the land and keep the realm together, had two origins, and consequently also, two kinds of officials. Nevertheless, with the progress of time, these two, different by their origin, kinds of administrative set-up blended together into one system. The first group of territorial officials evolved from the electoral representatives of the autonomous tribes and lands, built strictly according to the decimal system, such as the *tysiatski, sotski* and *desiatnyky,* the *chiliarchs, centurions* and *decurions,* originally the leaders of the primitive tribal military organization, who later on developed into the princely territorial officials, having been then also appointed by the prince or the court. The *posadnyk,* perhaps, the viceroy, was of the second kind. He was strictly appointed by the prince as his deputy to administer the given territory in his name, especially if the loyalty of the given territory was not certain or the territory was newly acquired. The junior princes and grand *boyars* were usually appointed as the *posadnyky* whose loyalty was proven. It must also be underscored that at times the mayors of urban communities were called the *posadnyky*, but were not the viceroys. Also important cities were exempt from the decimal system of administration and given special viceroys. The functions of the territorial officials included, of course, general administration, finances, judiciary and the military matters, without any division of powers, as at the upper levels of administration, and combining the strictly public jurisdictions with the princely private affairs, as well.[16]

The Kievan princes had already recognized the very fact that the princely administration would not be able to solve all the problems. Consequently, after the new territories were conquered and annexed to the empire, the Kievan princes preserved the self-governing agencies of those territories, which were of ancient tribal origin, and tried to use them to the benefit of themselves and their realm. Above all, the number of the appointed princely officials was too small to cope with all the complicated administrative matters of the *Rus'* realm.

The self-government was traditionally of two kinds. The urban autonomous communities were supervised by the *posadnyky*, while the village communities were built-in in the decimal system of the country's administration. The autonomous communities were led by the elective *starosty*, the elders. Several village communities might have joined an upper autonomous unit, the *verv*, also having been of an old origin. The urban and rural self-governing entities had police, judicial and financial responsibilities. With respect to the collection of taxes and pursuit of criminals, their responsibility was collective. The taxes were levied against the self-governing communities, and they then divided the tax burden among the population, collected them and delivered to the *vyrnyky*, the financial officials of the territorial administration or of the princely court.

The significance of self-government substantially increased at

the later era of the Galician-Volhinian realm with the introduction
of the autonomy of the towns and some villages according to the
Magdeburg (German) system. The chiefs of the self-governing
communities of the Magdeburg law were called the *burmistry,*
the mayors. Of course, that extension of autonomy greatly contributed to the development of economic and commercial activities of the population.

The Judiciary. There were in the Kievan realm and then in the
Galician-Volhinian principality four kinds of courts of justice: the
princely, the manorial, the communal and the ecclesiastic ones.
Actually, the manorial and ecclesiastic judiciary were not the part
of the *Rus'* judicial government, but since they were a very important part of the judicial process of the land, a kind of private
judiciary which completed the public ones, they must be included
into discussion. The instance might have been another projection
of the mixed public and private character of the realm, all-
together, as far as its entire constitution was concerned.

The official judiciary developed out of the traditional princely
court. The prince was the highest judge; and either he himself
acted as the judge, or he could authorize his high court officials to
chair the judicial procedures, like the *dvoretsky.* In that second
case, the sentence could always be appealed to the prince himself; there was no appeal for the prince's decision. The princely
court of justice initially was on the move during a certain period
of the year, travelling from one place to another, where cases
were heard and sentences reached. The prince was then accompanied by court officials, the *yabetnyky,* state attornies, the
metalynky, the secretaries, and the *istsi,* the investigators. At
times the elders of the community were called to advise the
princely courts. The cases of a minor importance were judged by
the *sudebni tyvuny,* the princely court officials, from whom the
appeal to the prince was admissable. Later on, regular princely
courts were established throughout the realm, chaired by the
chiliarchs and the viceroys in various towns and cities.

Of course, the oldest form of the judiciary was the communal
courts, which originated with the people's meetings. The *viche*

was an ancient court of justice, partially replaced by the princely court with the progress of time. There were, of course, the traditional meetings of the free members of every community; the village or town one. There the courts of justice were held, in which each free and adult man participated. The cases of minor importance were judged by the meeting of the entire community, while the cases of grave importance were judged by the assembly of the community elders. At first, the communal courts were, perhaps, of great significance for law and order, but with the growth of the central power of the prince, the significance of those courts gradually and considerably declined, especially after the standing princely courts, chaired by the *tysiatski* and *posadnyky,* were established. Subsequently, the right to appeal from the communal court decision to the princely courts and to the prince himself was introduced. At the end, the communal court had its jurisdiction only over the cases involving property rights and crimes of minor importance.

The manorial judiciary was performed by the *boyars* — landlords over the peasants, the half-free and the slaves in the landed properties, the latifundia. In these cases corporal punishments were allowed; if, however, they were applied unjustly, an appeal to the princely court was permissible. Although the prince and the state were not interested in the internal relations between the noble lords and their subjects, and the matters of justice were almost entirely left in the hands of the masters, one could see in the case of that possibility of an appeal of a manorial subject to princely justice, a progressive and humanitarian idea developing in *Rus'*.

The ecclesiastic judiciary had a very wide jurisdiction. On the one hand, it extended only over the people who were directly related to the Orthodox Church, the so-called church-people, the secular and monastic clergy, nuns and friars, free peasants, half-free and slaves in the ecclesiastic possessions and manors, people on welfare, the *personae miserables,* including the *izgoii,* who were completely exempt from princely jurisdiction and directly subject to the prevailing church authority. The social phenomenon of the church-people will be comprehensively discussed in one of the later chapters. On the other hand, all judicial matters which bore the aspect of sin, no matter whether they pertained to the church-people only or the entire population of the *Rus'* realm, were within the jurisdiction of the Church and its courts, such as separation and divorce, bigamy, witchcraft, heresy, apostasy, inheritance, conjugal infidelity, or theft of ecclesiastic property. In such cases the jurisdiction of the Church extended over the entire population of *Rus'*, with the exclusion of the princely courts. The church judiciary was based on cannonical law and completed by the legislation of the Kievan princes, their so-called *ustavy*.

There were in *Rus'* two levels of the ecclesiastic judiciary; the episcopal courts and the metropolitan court, the first having been presided by the bishops, and the second by the Metropolitan. There was an appeal possible from the episcopal sentence to the Metropolitan revision. In some rare cases the appeal might have been forwarded as far as the Patriarch of Constantinople, the head of the Orthodox Church throughout. Whenever, the juridical problems involved church-people and the subjects of the princely judiciary, the mixed ecclesiastic-secular courts were set-up. Through the ecclesiastic judiciary the comprehensive and extensive autonomy of the ruling Orthodox Church in *Rus'* was mostly evident.[17]

The Military. The national defense had been the most ancient and the most important responsibility of the government at any time. So also the Kievan princes fully took over the responsibility of the organization of the national defense and the military matters, including the offense to conquer other lands and to expand the *Rus'* realm. The matter of defense was a very important problem in the Kievan *Rus'* case, because of the continuous threat of the steppes, from where new barbarian hordes emerged, the Pechengs, the Torks, the Black Klobuks, the Cumans and ultimately the Tartars, who viciously attacked the land of the Ukrainians-Rus'ians.

Again in this instance, as in a few other cases in the administration and judicial, the organization of the armed forces had two roots, the old Slavic one and the princely, Varangian, one. The country's general militia was an older system of defense. Every adult male member of the tribe or land had the responsibility to join the militia in case of emergency. And it remained like that all the time, except that in the later era the princely retinue of Norman origin became the very pillar of the country's armed forces, and the country's militia was called to serve in cases of extreme need and danger. Originally, the militia developed out of the principle of blood relationship, the family — the clan — the tribe, where every male was obliged to defend his blood community. Then it changed into a territorial principle, to defend his territory and ultimately his country. In this way, the decimal system of military organization came into being. The militia was divided into military units, led by the decurions, centurions, chiliarchs and army leaders, the *desiatnyky, sotski, tysiatski* and *voyevody*. The *voyevody* then developed into the office of the princes, the *kniazi*. Subsequently, this military organization evolved into the country's administration, as was pointed out above. There was no division of powers then.

The general obligation of all adult males to serve in the defense of the country comprised also another duty, namely, to participate in construction of castles, fortresses, defense walls and water ditches, which could strengthen the defensibility of the land. The members of the urban and rural communities had to contribute either labor or money or both to construct these objects. The obligation was connected also with the tax system of the Kievan-Galician *Rus'*. It was mentioned in the previous chapters that various princes, like Volodymyr the Great, Yaroslav the Wise, Danylo of Galicia, were ardent builders of walls, castles and fortresses for the country's defense against the steppe nomads. Danylo, for example, was forced by Burundai, the Tartar army leader, to demolish the fortresses and towns he built in preparation of an anti-Tartar crusade, which never materialized.[18]

The military retinue, the *druzhyna,* having been of Norman origin, was introduced to the *Rus'* by the princes of Norman descent, Oleh, Ihor, Sviatoslav, Volodymyr, and others, and soon became the very foundation of the military force of the realm. Gradually every senior and junior prince maintained his own retinue, and even territorial chiliarchs and *voyevody* had the retinues of their own as the basis of their military operations. The size and the quality of the *druzhyna* was the measure of the might of the given prince. The membership of the retinue was personally selected by the prince and it was loyally bound to him on the basis of an agreement. The *druzhynnyky,* the members of the *dryzhyna,* were supposed to be faithful and obedient to the prince, and the prince was supposed to care, defend, protect and supply the proper maintenance for them. The maintenance could have been in the form of granting to the retainers landed estates on a permanent or temporary basis, paying them wages or providing them with shelter and food, dependent upon the character of the services rendered. At first, all retainers were staying with the prince at his court, but later on the conditions were changed. At the time of peace, only a small part of the *druzhynnyky* was steadily with the prince, often performing important functions of a court and government nature, having been also the members of the council of nobles. At a later period only the *boyars* were the members of the retinue. The majority of the retainers, then, lived in the provinces and the countryside, performing various public functions and taking care of their latifundia and manorial economies. Those landed grandees appeared at the court at the time of need or emergency, or when summoned by the prince to consult him in important matters. Most of these grandees had retinues of their own and rendered military services together with the armed men under their command.

Later, in the eleventh century, neither the retinue nor the universal land militia were of sufficient force to back up either the political ambitions or the defense needs of the entire realm or of the individual principalities. Therefore, mercenary regiments were hired to increase the striking power of these political organizations. At an earlier date the Normans served as mercenaries, while later, the Cumans and other ethnic elements were employed by the princes as mercenaries to fight their dynastic or foreign wars. There were also troops composed of the voluntary free men of *Rus'*. These voluntary regiments and the mercenary troops were actually the complementary force to the first two kinds of military organizations, the universal militia and the retinue.

The cavalry was the main striking force in those days, while the infantry was only a subsidiary formation. Only later did it acquire a greater military significance. A warrior's equipment included some defensive weapons, such as a helmet, a shield and a cuirass, and some offensive arms, such as a sword, a spear, a bow and arrows. The army on the march was usually not followed by a large wagon-train of supplies, because the land it passed, whether its own, foreign or hostile, had to maintain the army, willingly or unwillingly. This was the unwritten law of war.[19]

The finances and their management were another important part of the country's administration, but their discussion has been attached to the chapters on the economic life of the Rus'ians-Ukrainians at the Kievan-Galician era.[20] The court, the general administration, the judiciary, the military, the promotion of education and culture, construction of public buildings and churches had to be financed. In particular, the defense required substantial funds. Since the power and prestige of individual princes and *boyar* grandees were estimated according to the size and quality of their knightly retinue, considerable sums from the public and private, princely revenues were used to maintain and to increase a high level of the retinue's military preparedness.

1. G. Vernadsky and M. Karpovich, *A History of Russia*, Vol. I, *Ancient Russia*, New Haven-London, 1951, p. 326; also M. Braichevsky, ''The Unification of the Old Rus'ian Lands Around the Center of Kyiv,'' *On the Beginnings of Eastern Slavic Europe*, N. Chirovsky, ed., New York, 1976, pp. 53-57, and 70-74; N. Czyrowski (Chirovsky), *Geschichtlicher Abriss der staatsrechtlichen Einrichtungen in Galizien, Bis zum Wiener-Kongress 1815*, Doktor-Dissertation, Graz, 1943, pp. 27-30.

2. S. Soloviov, *Istoria Rossii s drevnieishikh vriemen,* St. Petersburg, 1894-1895, Vol. I, pp. 6-8.

3. N. Kostomarov, "Mysli o federativnom nachale v drevniei Rusi," *Sobranie sochinienii,* St. Petersburg, 1903, Bk. 1.

4. A brief summary of all hypotheses: D. Doroshenko, *Narys istorii Ukrainy,* Munich, 1966, Vol. I, pp. 49-53; also, K. Bestuzhev-Riumin, *Russkaia istoria,* St. Petersburg, 1872, Vol. I, pp. 152-156.

5. M. Hrushevsky, *Istoria Ukrainy-Rusy,* New York, 1954, Vol. II, pp. 254-255; V. Kluchevsky, *A History of Russia,* New York, 1911-1912, Vol. I, pp. 149-150; also, A. Presniakov, *Kniazhoie pravo v drevniei Rusi; Ocherki po istorii X-XII st.,* St. Petersburg, 1909.

6. N. Fr.-Chirovsky, *A History of the Russian Empire,* New York, 1973, Vol. I, pp. 218-318 and 357-362.

7. Czyrowski, *op. cit.,* pp. 46-49; also, Vernadsky, *op. cit.,* Vol. II, *Kievan Russia,* pp. 173-186, and 207-209; M. Chubaty, *Ohlad istorii ukrainskoho prava,* Lviv, 1921, pp. 3-7 and 15, also, the Munich edition 1947; Presniakov, *op. cit.;* M. Vladimirskii-Budanov, *Obzor istorii russkavo prava,* Petrograd and Kiev, 1915, pp. 1-100.

8. A. Zimin, *Pamiatki prava Kievskavo gosudarstva, Russkaia Pravda prostrannoi redaktsii,* Moscow, 1952; E. Karskii, *Russkaia Pravda, po drevnieishemu spisu,* Leningrad, 1930; evaluation: Hrushevsky, *op. cit.,* Vol. II, pp. 38-39 and 118-119.

9. The reader must be referred at this point to the chapters on the social structure of the *Rus'* national community and on the economic life of that society, where *Rus'ka Pravda* has been mentioned over and over again.

10. The prince; the monarchistic element of the constitution: Vernadsky, *op. cit.,* Vol. II, *Kievan Russia,* pp. 178-182; Czyrowski, *op. cit.,* pp. 48-53; Vladimirskii-Budanov, *op. cit.,* pp. 36-44; about the succession to the throne: S. Soloviov, *Istoria otnoshenii mezhdu russkimi kniaziami Rurikavo doma,* Moscow, 1847.

11. Chubaty, *op. cit.,* pp. 98-99.

12. The *viche* of the townspeople of Halych called in 1145 Prince Ivan (of Berlad) to assume the Galician throne in order to get rid of Prince Volodymyr (Volodymyrko): N. Polonska-Vasylenko, *Istoria Ukrainy,* Munich, 1972, Vol. I, p. 164.

13. About the institution of the people's meeting: Chubaty, *ibid.,* Vladimirskii-Budanov, *op. cit.* 51-60; Czyrowski, *op. cit.,* pp. 54-55.

14. V. Kluchevskii, *Boiarskaia duma drevnieie Rusi,* Moscow, 1909, chapters I-II; Vladimirskii-Budanov, *op. cit.,* pp. 44-51; Polonska-Vasylenko, *op. cit.,* Vol. I, p. 216-218; Hrushevsky, *op. cit.,* Vol. III, pp. 227-231.

15. Also the *tivun dvorsky;* Czyrowski, *op. cit.,* p. 60-61: The office of the *majordomo* was specific, in particular, for the Galician developments,

where Prince Danylo carried out an administrative reform. Perhaps, it was there a Polish influence: S. Kutrzeba, *Historya ustroju Polski*, Vol. I, *Korona*, Lviv, 1917, pp. 23-24.

16. On the general administration; central and territorial: Chubaty. *op. cit.*, pp. 103-107: Vernadsky, *op. cit.*, Vol. I., *Kievan Russia*, pp. 187-202; Vladimirskii-Budanov, *op. cit.*, pp. 75-80; also, A. Presniakov, *Lektsii po russkoi istorii*, Moscow, 1938, Vol. I, pp. 197-207; and Hrushevsky, *op. cit.*, Vol. III, pp. 227-260.

17. The status of the Orthodox Church in the Kievan-Galician realm is comprehensively discussed in the next chapter of this work.

18. Polonska-Vasylenko, *op. cit.*, Vol. I, p. 206; Hrushevsky, *op. cit.*, Vol. III, pp. 87-89.

19. The armed forces: Vladimirskii-Budanov, *op. cit.*, pp. 85-86; B. Grekov, *Kievskaia Rus'*, Moscow-Leningrad, 1944, pp. 187-222; Czyrowski, *op. cit.*, pp. 66-67; H. Meynert, *Geschichte des Kriegswesens und der Heeresverfassungen in Europa*, Vienna, 1868-1869, Vol. I, pp. 34-36 and 167-170; M. Levytsky, *Istoria ukrainskoho viiska*, Winnipeg, 1953, pp. 31-32, 59-60, and 81-92 and other; Polonska-Vasylenko, *op. cit.*, Vol. I, pp. 219-220.

20. Chapter eleven, section on finances, in this work.

The church of Good Friday in Chernihiv from the late twelfth century.

The Pecherska Lavra monastery in Kiev.

214

CHAPTER EIGHT

THE SPIRITUAL AND CULTURAL LIFE OF THE KIEVAN-GALICIAN SOCIETY

— The beginnings of Christianity — The status of the Church — Education and sciences — Literature — Architecture — Painting and carving — Music and theater — Other arts.

The Beginnings of Christianity. The comparative historical studies of the beginnings of Christianity in Eastern Europe, as well as the historical source materials, have indicated that Christianity was known in *Rus'*-Ukraine since the very early times; at least a couple of centuries before, it was officially adopted as the ruling and leading faith of the land. In particular, the nearness of Ukraine to the Greek Black and Azov Sea colonies, on their northern littorals, where Christianity was known from the ancient times, made it familiar to the southern Ukrainian Slavs. On the other hand, the Rus'ian merchants and traders visited Constantinople and some other Byzantine port cities at a very early date, having been exposed directly or indirectly to the Christian influence. The bishops from the Black Sea area participated in the Councils of Nice, in 325 A.D., and of Constantinople, in 360 A.D., indicating the presence of Christianity there at that time. Doubtlessly, there were Christians among the Ukrainian Slavs as early as the eighth century.[1]

As referred to in the earlier chapter, Prince Askold, after having assaulted Constantinople in 860, according to Patriarch Photius, proceeded with the Christianization of *Rus'*, and asked for a bishop and priests for his country. He himself could have become a Christian even before this time. The subsequent political developments in *Rus'*-Ukraine, the mass arrival of the Normans into the service of the Kievan princes and the great military and constitutional upheavals in *Rus'* in the course of the reigns of Oleh, Ihor and Sviatoslav, either postponed the Christianization process or caused the relapse into paganism. In any case, however, during Ihor's time there were already many Christians in Ukraine; there was the Church of St. Iliia, Ellias, and the Christian community, perhaps even a bishop in Kiev then. The prince himself was not a Christian, but some of his retainers, *druzhynnyky,* were Christian, and by their oath on the Christian God they affirmed Ihor's treaty with the Byzantinians in 941. The text of the treaty stated as follows: ". . . And if anybody on the *Rus'* side would break the agreement, then, if he is a Christian, he should be punished by God All-Mighty and condemned eternally in this and other world. . . ."[2]

Princess Olha became a Christian, and as such, she definitely influenced the subsequent spiritual evolution of her grandson, Prince Volodymyr the Great, who, according to the chronicle, from a ragged and rough pagan became a merciful and humble Christian, and introduced Christianity to his country, *Rus'*-Ukraine, made it a ruling faith and laid the foundations for its permanent organization. As it was pointed out before, the beginnings of the permanent Christianization of *Rus'* by Volodymyr have not been a historically clarified matter. At first, the historiography had fully accepted the accounts of the events, as they were described by the *Povist' vremennykh lit* with respect to the acceptance of Christianity by Volodymyr; his marriage proposal to Princess Anna of Greece, the rejection of the proposal by the emperors, Volodymyr's Korsun campaign to force the emperors to yield and his success in that respect; marriage to Anna, Volodymyr's baptism, Anna's bringing priests to Kiev, vestments and ecclesiastic books, common baptism of the Kievans in the Dnieper River and the subsequent destruction of pagan idols.[3]

Yet, the more recent historiography, in the twentieth century, has cast grave doubts as to the reliability of the *Povist's* relations, since they have not found any confirmation of such an important event as the Christianization of the huge northern empire through Constantinople's mediation in the Greek historical sources. Priselkov built his hypothesis of *Rus'* acceptance of the Christian faith from Bulgaria. To be exact, from the city of Ochrida, there was an autocephalic patriarchate of Bulgaria, independent upon Constantinople. Many historians of the Church in *Rus'* followed the hypothesis, such as Abraham, Chubaty, Shmurlo, Nazarko, Tomashivsky and Pogorielov. Close political, commercial and other relations between *Rus'* and Bulgaria, mutually understandable language of the old Slavonic, spoken by the Bulgarian priests, tradition of the Slavic Apostles, Cyril and Methodius, and the church books written there in old Slavonic and fully comprehendable in Ukraine, have made it much more worthy of believing that from Ochrida in Bulgaria, and not from Constantinople, the Christian faith was embraced by the medieval Rus'ians-Ukrainians, who could not read Greek books and could not generally understand the Greek language.[4]

Then, a question of the fantastic story, told by the *Povist' vremennykh lit,* must be resolved. Why did the *Povist'* manufacture that completely untrue account of the Christianization of *Rus'*-Ukraine, and forcefully insist on the Greek origin of the Christian faith there? This may be the most likely explanation. The antagonism between Rome and Constantinople as of two centers of the Christian world had proceeded for some time, and it became especially acute and sharp in the years of one-thousand-forties and fifties due to the schism of Michael Cerularius, which had split original Christianity into the two huge branches, the Catholic one in the West and the Orthodox one in the East. Constantinople immediately assumed the leadership of the Or-

Volhinian Mother of God, from the thirteenth or fourteenth century (a detail).

thodoxy and attempted to gather around itself all Christian countries where the Oriental ecclesiastic rites prevailed, including *Rus'*-Ukraine. The struggle for influence and domination between Rome and Constantinople was very fierce, and the *Rus'* Church for a considerable time maintained a complete neutrality, so much more because she was spiritually more attached to the Bulgarian than to the Byzantine ''caesaropapistic'' principle. The papal envoy Humbert, who went to Constantinople after the split to discuss the matters of faith, also visited Kiev to gain the *Rus'* Church for the Roman cause, and met there probably with a neutral attitude and unwillingness to get involved in the conflict. Even before, Princess Olha and Prince Volodymyr maintained friendly relations with the Holy See in Rome, trying to keep themselves apart from the aggressiveness of the Patriarch of Constantinople.[5] Hrushevsky went as far as to assume the possibility of the Pope of Rome sending a royal crown to Volodymyr. The contacts of Kiev with Rome were very much alive until 1003. According to the Western sources, two bishops, one in Magdeburg and another in Kolberg, in Germany, were consecrated for *Rus'* and were dispatched there, but their mission failed largely because of their Latin language, which nobody could understand in *Rus'*. Later on, in Kiev and in Galicia, there were Latin orders of the Franciscans and Dominicans, that brought the evidence of tolerance and friendliness towards the ''Latinians'' in Ukraine, which was by no means the case in Byzantium at that time.

Although in the one-thousand-eighties there appeared some polemic works in Ukraine against the ''Latinians,'' indicating the shift of the Ukrainian Orthodox further to the camp of the Patriarch of Constantinople, their tone, however, was not so aggressively hostile as that of the polemic works of the Greek churchmen. At the same time, Prince Iziaslav resumed Kiev's friendly attitude towards Rome. He sent his son, Yaropolk, to the Holy See and surrendered *Rus'* to its protection. Some historians called Iziaslav the most Catholic prince of old *Rus'*. The Pope granted him the title of an ''Apostolic King.'' The friendly relations of

Kiev with Rome were also continued at the time of Vsevolod. Afterwards, the Byzantine influence, either because of the nearness of Constantinople or because of the aggressive church policy of the Patriarch, who predominantly appointed Greeks for the Metropolitan seat in Kiev and managed also to appoint many Greeks as bishops for *Rus'*, caused the entire Orthodox Church there to separate itself from Rome and to join fully the Eastern Orthodoxy under the leadership of the Patriarch of Constantinople.

Hence, at the time, when the *Povist' vremennykh lit* was written down in the twelfth century, *Rus'*-Ukraine was already completely in the orbit of the Byzantine cultural influence. Thus the author, monk Nestor, or authors, with premeditation constructed the story of *Rus'* having embraced Christianity from Greece in order to establish ideologically an unbreakable tie between Kiev and Constantinople, perhaps, also, to raise the prestige of the Rus'ian Orthodoxy. Since its origin from Ochrida in Bulgaria, the Patriarchate which was then suppressed by Byzantium, would have cast doubt upon the ancient dependence of the Church of *Rus'* upon Constantinople, the whole account of the true Christianization process of *Rus'* was methodically suppressed and replaced by the picturesque story of the *Povist'*, to serve the purpose. The similar fabrication of the *Povist'* was its relations about the Norman origin of the *Rus'* state, as discussed before.

However, no matter what the real beginnings of the Christian Church in *Rus'*-Ukraine, it was accepted there at the end of the tenth century. Of course, the essentials of Christianity were not immediately understood and embraced by the whole population. In Ukraine, the southern part of the Empire of Kiev, Christianity was peacefully accepted, because it was known there for many decades back. But, in the northern provinces of the realm, it had to be introduced by force. The chronicle related that *voyevoda* Putiata had to convert the people by sword, and *voyevoda* Dobrynia, by fire. There Christianity was not known, and its sudden introduction produced opposition, especially, where the *volkhvy*, a kind of pagan priests of Finnic origin, and Finnic superstitions strongly influenced the primitive population. However, even in Ukraine, where there was no opposition to the new faith at least for two centuries, the *dvoieviria,* the two-fold faith, a mixture of the ancient pagan beliefs and rituals and the new Christian doctrines, prevailed. For a long time certain Christian institutions were considered to be good for the royalty and nobility, like the institution of Christian marriage, while the common people continued to live as they lived before, by their rituals and superstitions, including common law marriage. The full understanding of Christianity followed much later, because its full grasp was not an easy task for the traditionally pagan mind.[6]

The Status of the Church. Notwithstanding, the Church was growing in the *Rus'* realm spiritually, organizationally, in wealth and power, and it constantly expanded territorially. The princes of Kiev and other princes of various principalities and territories ardently supported the new faith in the moral and material aspects; they built new churches, aided schools, made huge material contributions, grants and last wills, in favor of the Church, established monasteries and maintained them, paid the tithe loyally, and occasionally regulated the ecclesiastic matters by their *ustavy,* decrees. The nobles, the *boyars,* out of piety, imitated the princes and lavishly endowed the churches, monasteries, and religious orders. The common people, though not wealthy, contributed also their material share to make the Church a very rich institution.

Organizationally, the Ukrainian princes, having taken care of the Church, never pressed for the ''caesaropapist'' doctrine of the princely and state authority being supreme also in the ecclesiastic matters in *Rus'*. Caesaropapism always prevailed in Byzantium, and then it was taken over by the Suzdalian and Muscovite grand-princes and tsars. Yet, since the Patriarch of Constantinople frequently abused his authority to support the political ends of Byzantium in East Europe, at times the princes of *Rus'* opposed that negative influence in order to protect the Ukrainian ecclesiastic and political interests. Moreover, the Byzantine Patriarchs simply attempted to monopolize the authority of appointing the Metropolitans "of Kiev and of All *Rus'*," which was evident by the direct fact that, since the Christianization of *Rus'* until 1250, only four Metropolitans, Ilarion, 1051-1062, Yephrem, 1089-1097, Klyment Smolatych, 1147-1167, perhaps, and Cyril, 1233-1236, were Rus'ian-Ukrainians by ethnic origin, while almost all other Metropolitans, heads of the Ukrainian Church, were Greeks, including many bishops. It was a small wonder that all those Greeks among the hierarchy of the *Rus'* Church managed to tear it apart from Rome and subordinate it entirely to the interest, ecclesiastic and political, of Constantinople. The election of Klyment Smolatych to the Kievan Metropolitan seat was actually the manifestation of the anti-Greek feelings among the Ukrainian bishops, supported by the Kievan prince, against the will of the Greeks among the hierarchy. It produced a kind of an ecclesiastic crisis in Ukraine of a lasting duration. Metropolitan Klyment was not approved by the Patriarch, who appointed a Greek again for Kiev. On the other hand, Prince Rostyslav, was ready to dismiss the Greek and to restore Klyment.[7]

Otherwise, the Church in *Rus'*-Ukraine enjoyed a very broad autononomy, having been something of a state within the state, with huge wealth and comprehensive jurisdiction over the so-called church-people, a separate class of population, the composition and the social and political status of which will be discussed in the subsequent chapter. The jurisdiction of the Church extended also, with the exclusion of the judicial competence of the state and prince, over the matters of faith and morals of all people of the huge *Rus'* empire, as it was pointed out before.

The Metropolitan of Kiev and of All-*Rus'* was the head of the Christian Church in the realm, which in its entirety built the largest Metropolis, the ecclesiastic province, within the Patriarchate of Constantinople. Jurisdictionally, the Metropolitan was responsible to the Patriarch. According to the canon laws, the Metropolitan was supposed to be elected by the bishops of the Metropolis, but the Patriarch consistently broke the law, and in most cases managed to appoint a Greek for the Kievan seat and enforce his acceptance there. Constantinople never trusted a

Rus'ian-Ukrainian to be subservient to the ecclesiastic and political interests of Byzantium. The Metropolitan had a great authority in his Metropolis; largely appointed and consecrated the bishops; led the whole Church spiritually and organizationally; was the chief ecclesiatic justice in *Rus'*-Ukraine; was the spiritual superior of all bishops who were considered for his assistants and aides, and he also performed the canonization of the saints.

At the time of Volodymyr the Great, the Kievan Metropolis consisted of five dioceses with episcopal seats in Kiev, Chernihiv, Volodymyr Volynsky, Novgorod and Bilhorod, while subsequently, the number of dioceses increased to fifteen in the thirteenth century, and to seventeen, later on. The episcopal authority was comprehensive, though a little lesser than that of the Western Catholic bishops. The bishop, managing his dioceses spiritually and organizationally, was assisted by a number of clerical officials, such as the *protopresviter,* the first diocesean priest; the arch-deacon, the chief administrator; the *apocrisarii,* the representative of the Church at the princely court; the economist, who managed the church estates and properties; the *kantseler,* the chancellor, at first the master of the ceremonies and then, the head of the episcopal office; the *khartophilaks,* who cared for ecclesiastic books and records; and some others. The councils of bishops, under the leadership of the Metropolitan, deliberated and decided important and controversial issues, some of them having been submitted to the decisions of the Patriarch himself. The parishes in the cities, towns and some villages completed the vertical organizational structure of the Orthodox Church in *Rus'*-Ukraine.

A separate and quite important place in the ecclesiastic life of old *Rus'* belonged to the monasteries or religious orders. The religious life in the framework of the monasteries began to develop in Ukraine at the beginning of the eleventh century. The chronicle mentioned one under the year 1037. Yaroslav the Wise supposedly founded two religious orders and liked very much to remain in the company of the monks, who were pious and knowledgeable. Obviously, the monastic life developed along the Oriental Christian tradition, and substantially aided the growth of the spiritual, intellectual and economic life of the Rus'ian society, since there the missionary and religious work was concentrated, the first books translated, written and copied, the first schools and libraries organized, and progressive methods in farming, cattle raising, fish breeding and craftsmanship applied. From the monasteries, the first metropolitans, bishops, theologians, writers and princely advisors were drawn.[8]

The Pecherska Lavra monastery in Kiev soon acquired fame as the outstanding center of the monastic life in all Ukraine. Venerable Antonii Pechersky, who spent some time on Athos, the holy mountain in Greece, where the monks from Greece, the Balkan Peninsula and the Near East gathered to serve God, developed the original monastic rules, which were then imitated throughout all of *Rus'*, and in the twelfth and thirteenth century there were literally hundreds of monasteries of rather small and medium sizes, existing independently, and not constituting any huge, coordinated religious order, with many branches only, and under one central authority. Thousands of people joined the monastic life, filled with prayer, religious practices, fasting and long hours of labor of all kinds, according to the rules, established by Antonii.

Thousands upon thousands of people, "white" or secular, "black" or monastic, clergy, friars, nuns, deacons, cantors, "church-people" of all sorts, were the parts of the huge ecclesiastic body of the Orthodox Church. There were several reasons why so many people were engaged in Church services. Some joined the Church out of personal piety and sanctity; others looked for security and good life, since the Church had estates, properties and wealth and took good care of its people; still others were drawn into the services, because the Church had enormous responsibilities and tasks to perform, missionary work of spreading the faith, teaching the faith, education and maintenance of schools and libraries, continuous copying, translating and writing new books, taking care of needy people, *personae miserabiles,* orphans, elderly, sick and crippled, *izgoii,* widows, managing what could be termed the "welfare program," maintenance of the churches and other ecclesiastic buildings, and administration of estates, manors and other properties, administration of church affairs and ecclesiastic judiciary.[9] In order to cope with all those responsibilities the Church drew its financial support from its huge properties, the tax of the tithe, selling the candles, court fees, the leasing of manors, hunting and fishing rights, and pious donations of the faithful.

The Church in *Rus'* governed itself by its own laws, which then regulated all Eastern Churches: the Canons of the Holy Apostles, the Canons of the first seven Ecumenical Councils, the Nomocanons or the collections of ecclesiastic laws, including some civil laws, issued by the Byzantine emperors, rules and regulations, issued by the Patriarchs and Metropolitans, and the lasting practice and tradition of the Church. The Nomocanons or collections of laws and regulations of the Church, popular in *Rus'*-Ukraine, were referred to as the *Kormcha Knyha*. In addition, the Ukrainian princes also issued the decrees, regulating some ecclesiastic matters, such as the *ustavy* of Volodymyr the Great, Yaroslav the Wise, Vsevolod, Sviatoslav and Rostyslav, and also the *Rus'ka Pravda* was used supplementarily to rule the Church in Ukraine. The organization of the Catholic Church was very feeble; there were a few Latin monasteries and churches here and there in Kiev and Galicia, having been tolerated but not looked upon with favor. A permanent Latin ecclesiastic organization never succeeded, because of the Byzantine hostility.

This was approximately the state of the Church matters on the eve of the Mongol invasion, which gravely changed the conditions of life in *Rus'*, terminated the growth of the spiritual and intellectual values and caused in Eastern Ukraine a substantial regression. Some bishops and many religious people perished, many churches and other buildings were destroyed; schools and libraries were demolished; many parishes just disappeared. Nevertheless, after a few decades, things began to improve slowly. Yet, the most lasting and fateful consequence of the Invasion was the transfer of the seat of the Metropolitan "of Kiev and All-*Rus'* '' to Vladimir, and then to Moscow, in the North. Metropolitan Josyf was missing after the destruction of Kiev in 1240, while his successor a few years later, Cyril, went north, at first on a temporary basis, which turned to be a permanent change. Andrei Bogolubskii sought to establish a separate Metropolitan seat in the North, but the Patriarch opposed that plan, and did not permit the division of the Kievan Metropolis. Once the Metropolitan arrived in Vladimir, the grand-prince did not allow him to leave anymore. He had his far-reaching plans in that respect.

Soon enough, having retained the title of the ''Metropolitan of Kiev and All-*Rus'*,'' the Metropolitan was forced to yield to the northern ''caesaropapism'' of the grand-princes, and became somewhat a tool of their state and Church policies, in general, and as far as the Ukrainian south was concerned, in particular.

As it was mentioned above, after the Mongol invasion, the Galician-Volhinian principality took over the tradition of the Ukrainian statehood, where the Western influences were much stronger, than in Kiev. There the Church matters acquired great importance. At the reigning time of Prince Roman, the papal envoys arrived in Galicia and supposedly offered him a royal crown and proposed the Church union with the Holy See. They met, however, with Roman's rejection, while he was at the very height of his power. On the other hand, the political situation of Prince Danylo was quite different after he suffered a defeat from the Mongol hands, and was forced to become the Khan's vassal. Hence, either by Rome's initiation through his envoy to the Khan, John de Plano Carpini, or Danylo's own initiative, the plans for an anti-Mongol crusade of the European Catholic countries and a Church union of the Galician-Volhinian realm with the Holy See developed. Yet, neither the idea of a crusade materialized nor the union with Rome established itself permanently. Only the coronation of Danylo as the king of *Rus'* in Dorohichyn, in 1253, underscored the instance of close relations between the prince of Galicia and the pope of Rome and the constant leanings of Western Ukraine towards the West. It may be also here indicated that the whole incidence with the planned Church union might have been an intuitive undertaking to protect the West-Ukrainian Orthodoxy from the growing pressure of the Metropolitan of Vladimir, no matter what his title was, and his ecclesiastic policies, subservient as they were to the interests of the Vladimirian, and also soon, to the Muscovite grand-princes.

In order to rid the Galician-Volhinian principality of the bothersome interference of the Metropolitan from the North, Prince Lev undertook some measures in preparation to establish a separate Galician Orthodox Metropolis. Finally, in 1303, during the reign of King Yurii, such a Galician Metropolis came into being with the consent of the Patriarch, and against the will of the grand-prince of Vladimir. The Galician Metropolis included six dioceses with the episcopal seats in the cities of Halych, Peremyshl, Volodymyr Volynsky, Kholm, Lutsk and Turiv. The jurisdictions of both Metropolitans, of Halych and of Vladimir, were never clearly marked. The existence of the new Metropolis was rather uncertain from its very beginning, because of the opposition and the intrigues of the northern grand-princes. The first Galician Metropolitan was a Greek again, but the second to be elected for the high office, Petro or Peter, was a Ukrainian. However, due to the political maneuvers of the Vladimirian grand-dukes and the Patriarch, he actually became the Kievan Metropolitan with the obligation to live in Vladimir. Practically speaking, the Galician Metropolis ceased to exist, through the intrigues of the grand-princes of Moscow, and grand-prince Simeon, in particular, who sent envoys and substantial sums of money to Constantinople in 1345 to persuade the Patriarch to abolish the Galician Metropolis. A very important and indicative instance took place in 1352. The Metropolitan Theodoryt, consecrated by the Bulgarian Patriarch of Turnovo, came to Kiev to assume the office. He was either a Ukrainian or Bulgarian. Yet, soon he was prohibited by the Patriarchal Council of Greece to perform his duties. The particular occurrence had indicated, perhaps, the subsequent attempt to assert the ecclesiastic independence of Kiev from Moscow by means of the Bulgarian

Church, which might have been instrumental in introducing Christianity to *Rus'*-Ukraine. The consecration of Theodoryt might have been reminiscent of that important detail, so eagerly suppressed by Constantinople.

After Galicia was dominated by Polish King Casimir, the Polish government did not like any probability of Moscow's interference with the Orthodox Church there. In 1370, Casimir demanded from Constantinople to appoint a Metropolitan for Galicia, threatening otherwise an introduction of Catholicism in that newly acquired land. The Patriarch yielded to the threat and agreed to elevate Antonii of Galicia to the reactivated high office. The lack of care for distant lands by Moscow's Metropolitan Aleksei was given as an excuse.[10]

Education and Sciences. Whatever aspects of the spiritual or cultural life of the Kievan-Galician society were concerned, they were either totally or in their most part either Church- and faith-sponsored or oriented, while pious princes and *boyars* were their sponsors to a substantial degree. The Byzantine spiritual and cultural influence was visible there all-over, beginning with the education and sciences of Kiev.

It is impossible to ascertain when the first school was established in Ukraine. It is probable that, because of the nearness of the Hellenic colonies, some old Rus'ians acquired the mastery of writing and reading at a very early date, as the agreements between Oleh, Ihor and Sviatoslav, on the one hand, and the Byzantine emperors, on the other, might have let one to deduce. Perhaps, there was some school at the St. Ilia Church in Kiev, at Ihor's time, while other schools might have been established as the time progressed. Maybe some Rus'ians acquired the knowledge of writing and reading, when they remained in Constantinople while attending their commercial interests there.

The historical records first credited Volodymyr the Great for establishing schools in the ninth century, immediately after the introduction of Christianity. He certainly organized a school for the children of the nobles at the Church of Tithe, and it is reasonable to assume that he did not stop there, but promoted the organization of other schools, church affiliated, later on as well.[11] Yaroslav, the Wise, founded schools in Novgorod and Kiev, and other towns, primarily for the children of the elders, clergy and nobles, where the religious were the teachers. It seems that soon the schools existed in all major cities, affiliated with Cathedral churches and monasteries. Apparently, other princes did not neglect that responsibility either, since even some princesses, like Yanka and Yefrosina, established schools for girls, affiliated with the monasteries they had entered. Those things not only indicated a drive for education in Kievan *Rus'*, but also the elevated position of women there.

Tatishchev, an historian of the eighteenth century, who apparently was able to use some historical sources, which were lost since, gave a rather very favorable picture of the educational level of the Kievan society, while other historians were rather too supersceptical in that respect, like Golubinskii.[12] However, the findings of private letters from the eleventh and twelfth centuries, inscriptions on church walls—prayers, names, loose sentences, all kinds of "graffitis," at times frivolous, made largely by young people—brought an evidence of a wide-spread knowledge of writing and reading, based on schooling. Moreover, certain crafts, like ceramics and *icon* painting, required literacy, since on such works, according to the customs of that time, inscriptions were made, obviously by people who were literate. It cannot be doubted, therefore, that elementary education and schooling were widely developed, relatively speaking, and for the upper brackets of the society, the children of princely families, nobility and clergy, were even at times compulsory. The Church and the princes sponsored education for two different reasons; the Church needed educated clergy to continue the missionary and preaching work, while the courts needed educated clerks for state and princely administration. No doubt that capable young men from the noble and clerical circles were sometimes sent to Constantinople to complete their education there.

How far back education went into past history in *Rus'*, can well be illustrated by the fact that in the years 860-861 St. Constantine found in Chersones, in Crimea, a Bible and a Psalm book, written in the "Rus'ian lettering." Later on, some kind of an ''Ivan lettering'' was used in southern *Rus'*, and subsequently two different writing styles, the *hlaholytsia* and *kyrylytsia*. The first was originated by St. Cyril, Kyrylo, and did not become popular and, hence, was rarely used. The second was developed by St. Cyril's and Methodius's disciples, and it soon replaced the *hlaholytsia,* having become the leading lettering type among many Slavic countries, including *Rus'*-Ukraine.

No doubt the circle of the highly intellectual people was constantly growing and widening in the framework of the Kievan-Galician society. Many people knew a few languages, in particular Greek, Latin, Bulgarian and German, due to the vital ecclesiastic, cultural and commercial relations. The members of the intellectual elite of the society read Homer, Plato and Aristotle and were acquainted with the classical literature. Also, women joined the elite, coming from the princely and noble strata, who knew languages, philosophy, rhetoric and grammar. Princess Yefrosina, after having become a nun, copied books and established a library at St. Sophia Cathedral. Libraries were established, according to the chronicle, by princes Yaroslav, Sviatoslav, Volodymyr of Volhinia, and, doubtlessly, by some others. Sviatoslav and a certain monk Hrihorii, who had many books, gave their book collections to monasteries, in order to protect them against the thieves, visibly interested in the intellectual exploit.[13]

In the twelfth century there was a fair number of schools throughout the land, where mathematics, astronomy, geography, reading and writing, languages, Holy Bible and the writings of the fathers of the Church were taught. Apparently, there were some schools of a lower and others of a higher educational level. Obviously, the Byzantine example, where education was on a high level, did much to spur the intellectual growth of *Rus'*.

Due to the growing number of schools and libraries, and the travelling abroad to further the education, various branches of knowledge and science began to develop from their very humble inceptions. Philosophy and theology began with the translation of the Greek works. Then, in the eleventh and twelfth century, the

Rus'ian theologians, such as Metropolitan Ilarion, Metropolitan Klyment and bishop Cyril, began on their own to contribute to the development of two said disciplines. Ilarion wrote the celebrated *Discourse on Law and Grace;* Klement was referred to by the chronicle as so far the greatest philosopher ever living in *Rus';* Cyril became famous by his sermons. Otherwise, the Rus'ian philosophical thought evolved on the basis of the Platonian and Aristotelian patterns. The *Pchela,* the Rus'ian translation of the Greek collection of philosophical quotations of Democritus, Plato, Aristotle, Philo and others, was popular in the realm.

Actually, the jurisprudence was rather well developed in *Rus'*-Ukraine, having been based rather on the Slavic tradition more than the Roman legal patterns. Later, the Byzantine jurisprudence began to affect the Rus'ian legal evolution by the way of the ecclesiastic law of the Eastern Church, the nomocanons, in particular, reflected in the *Kormcha Knyha,* as it was mentioned above. Furthermore, the legal manual, the *Zakon sudnyi ludiem,* compiled in Bulgaria and based on a similar Byzantine manual, called *Ecloga,* influenced the evolution of the Rus'ian law in the same direction.

Otherwise, the Slavic legal tradition, which indicated some similarities with the German law and German jurisprudence of the time, received its splendid expression in the *Rus'ka Pravda.* The compilation of the Rus'-ian common law into a book of laws certainly brought witness to the exceptional abilities, interests and even training of the Rus'ian-Ukrainian mind in the area of jurisprudence, developing since the time of Yaroslav the Wise, and throughout the later period under the later princes, credited with later codifications. Also, the issuance of the *ustavy,* to regulate the ecclesiastic matters, and the *uroky,* to regulate the civilian and state matters, indicated the growth of the science of jurisprudence in the Rus' realm.

Another scholarly endeavor, which developed rather effectively for its time, was the historiography. The chronicle, the

Povist' vremennykh lit, was not only an account of the historical events, but it included some interpretation of those events, some ideas from the area of political thought and philosophy, and geographical information. The first version of the chronicle was written down, perhaps by 1039, but then it was revised several times, in 1073, 1095, extended, and finally completed in 1113, when it was given its name, the *Povist' vremennykh lit.* Although it was earlier referred to as the work of monk Nestor, in reality, the *Povist'* was a joint effort of many learned historians of the time, while its final version was, perhaps, completed under Nestor as its chief editor. The authors of this historical work gave it a specific conceptual framework, dominated by the patriotic feeling of the unity of all *Rus'* lands under one dynasty of Ruryk and the *Rus'* mission of greatness. In order to support this conceptual framework, the *Povist'* developed the "Normanist" theory of the political beginning of *Rus'* and its Christianization derived from Byzantium, though both assumptions have proven to be rather problematic. Yet, the Normans or Vikings were famous at that time in the West, and Byzantium was then the greatest and most civilized land in the East. It was worthwhile, from the point of view of the authors or editors of the *Povist',* to connect the political and cultural beginnings of *Rus'*-Ukraine with these two powers.[14]

The chronicles were compiled not only in Kiev, where the *Povist' vremennykh lit,* originated, but in Chernihiv, Pereyaslav, Halych, Novgorod, and other princely capitals. In the twelfth century, the Kievan chronicle was compiled from various earlier sources, the lietmotif of which was the biblical idea that all misfortunes represent divine punishment for sins. *The Ipatiivska and Lavrentiivska Litopysy* (Hipatian and Laurentian Chronicles) were subsequently compiled and extended their contents over wider time periods. A separate place belongs here to the Galician-Volhinian chronicle, the *Halytsko-Volynska litopys',* which covered the historical developments in West-Ukraine until the twelve-hundred and eighties.[15]

Out of the chronicles, literary writings and other written source material the inceptions of the early Rus'ian-Ukrainian political thought may be deduced. One can easily detect from these sources a support for the monarchal system of rule with mild approval of the aristocratic element of government; it means the *boyar* participation in the country's legislative and administrative process. Also at times the democratic element is mentioned; it means the role of the *viche*. Yet, the chronicle rather mentioned the fact of the people's participation in the government in various cities of the realm, without coming to its support. Nevertheless, again, one may detect the notion that, if the prince was not living up to his responsibilities, the people have the right to replace him by another one.

According to the concepts of that time, the prince was not an autocrat above the law, but bound by the law. Monk Yakiv in his letter to Prince Iziaslav pointed out that the prince was bound by Christian moral principles, and should not tolerate any arbitrariness in his government. The *Povist' vremennykh lit* praised the good princes and reprimanded the bad ones for neglecting their responsibilities in administration, for letting their agents to exploit or plunder the people; for not respecting the tradition; for surrounding themselves with inept advisers and assistants; and other improper conduct. It pointed out that the mismanagement of state affairs may ruin them and their people. Otherwise, bad deeds and sins may bring, according to the chronicles and other documents of the time, God's punishments in the form of famines, wars and other misfortunes.[16]

The first geography works in *Rus'* were the translations of the earlier Greek works, describing foreign lands and places, while the first original Rus'ian work of geographical character was the *Life and Journeys of Danylo, the Abbot of the Rus' land*. Abbot Danylo travelled to the Holy Land in 1106-1108, and then described his experiences and places visited. His work soon became a very popular reading in Ukraine. Some contribution to the geographical science was made by the *Povist' vremennykh lit*, having described the *Rus'* land and the territorial locations of its original Slavic tribes, and some other writings.

Arithmetic was taught in the schools as an important subject for figuring out the calendar, in particular to ascertain the dates of

Easter, and for running the manorial economies of royalty, nobility and Church, as well as for proper management of the fiscal matters of the state. Four rules of arithmetic, addition, subtraction, multiplication and division, were well known. Also, some basic geometry, useful for architecture and construction, was developed. Only one worthwhile mathematical treatise was written in *Rus'*. Natural history was very little developed. Only the translation of the antiquitated *Physiologus* was available for the Rus'ian literate public. On the other hand, medicine seemed to be rather well developed in *Rus'*. There were good physicians practicing medical science in the princely courts and monasteries. Volodymyr Monomakh had his own physician; there were renowned physicians in the Pecherska Lavra monastery; a certain Petro was at first a princely physician, and then he moved to Kiev and there "he healed many people." The legal records asserted that in the case of injury the offender had to pay a compensation to the injured and also cover his medical expenses.[17] The physicians were foreign and native and they trained assistants for the profession. Mostly herbs and weeds were used in medicine, especially the so-called *narodnia medytsyna,* the people's medicine.

Technology was progressing in Kievan and Galician realms. The Rus'ians-Ukrainians were acquainted with navigation, chemical warfare, in particular the "Greek fire," used against them by the Byzantinians in 941, the arrow-throwers, used by the Khoresmians; and they knew how to construct sawmills, driven by water. Their civilization was of a rather high level.

Literature. Doubtlessly, literature is one of the most outstanding indicators of the spiritual and cultural growth of any society. The literature of the Kievan-Galician era was rather well developed by comparison with other European countries at that time. Its beginnings must be sought in the old Slavic folklore; the ancient songs, legends, fairy tales, proverbs, riddles and other forms of the oral literary creativity, the origin of which was related either to the pagan religious rites, or the seasonal circle of changing weather conditions throughout the year, or social events and customs, such as birth, wedding and death, or outstanding achievements of some "heroes," who gave rise to the historical epics. In this way the *kolady,* the songs at the time of the winter holidays, the *hailky* and *vesnivky,* the songs at the time of the spring holidays, wedding and funeral songs, songs for various social occasions, legends and the historical epics, the *bylyny* and *staryny,* and legends came into being. They were all created by common people, but of exceptional artistic abilities, and transmitted by them from one generation to the other.

The introduction of Christianity, which brought *Rus'* into the circle of the civilized nations of the time, also initiated the development of the literature in the true sense of the written word, since it brought with itself the *hlaholytsia* and *kyrylytsia* alphabets to enable writing and reading, at first of the religious books. Yet, soon enough, the folklore of yesterday was penetrating into and being absorbed by the new kind of literature of the secular slant. The ecclesiastic books, the Holy Bible, the Letters of the Holy Apostles, the Psalmbooks, and other liturgical books, already translated into the old Slavonic and written in the *hlaholytsia* or *kyrylytsia* alphabets, were the first to arrive in *Rus'*-Ukraine. The popularity of the ecclesiastic books, written in Greek, was rather limited, since that language was not broadly known there. The writings of the Fathers of the Church followed.

The first literary works, either brought to *Rus'*-Ukraine from abroad or done there, were largely translations from the Greek, such as the apocryphal writings, the life-stories of the saints, and the secular stories. The apocryphal writings represented the religiously motivated tales, where the canonically established facts in the Christian faith were intermingled with fantastic and make-believe stories, related either to the Old and New Testament, or the lives of the saints or life beyond the grave. Some of the apocryphal stories originated in the Orient, and then, having been adopted by Byzantium, they were there remodeled, and subsequently communicated to *Rus'*. The Church was at first hostile toward the apocryphas, since they frequently misconstrued the matters of faith and even included some pagan elements, but subsequently it accepted them, only trying to make them as Christian as it was possible, since their impact upon the people's beliefs was great. The apocrypha *Virgin Mary's Journey Through Inferno* was, for example, exceptionally popular in *Rus'*-Ukraine.

The life-stories of the saints aided the moral and religious growth of the society, and because of that, they enjoyed a widespread acceptance by newly Christianized and religiously over-zealous *Rus'*. Various kinds of the collections of life-stories of the saints were in circulation there. The *Prology* were arranged according to the calendar, discussing in brief the lives of the saints for each day of the year; the *Mynei* were arranged according to the months of the year; while the *Pateryky* described the lives of the saints of a given country.

The stories of a more secular character, and being either translations or original Rus'ian writings, which were the inception of the Rus'ian-Ukrainian literary creation, were the *Story of Varlaam and Ioasaf,* where the vanity of the earthly life was presented, *Aleksandria,* a largely fantastic story of Alexander the Great, the *Indian Empire,* the *Trojan War,* and many others.

The marvelous political and economic growth of the Kievan *Rus'* realm at the time of Volodymyr the Great and Yaroslav the Wise in a most natural way sponsored and facilitated its overall cultural development, including the development of its original literary writing. Metropolitan Ilarion wrote the *Discourse on Law and Grace,* a theological treatise on the Old and New Testaments, the *Glorification of Prince Volodymyr* for making *Rus'* Christian, the land known all over, and other works. Metropolitan Klyment Smolatych and bishops Cyril of Turiv and Serapion wrote original sermons in the twelfth and thirteenth centuries. Meanwhile the life-stories of the Rus'ian saints, churchmen and monks were written, like those about St. Theodosii, the organizer of the monastery of Pecherska Lavra in Kiev, the martyr-princes Borys and Hlib, composed by monks Nestor and Yakiv, and the *Patericon of Pecherska Lavra,* a collection of life-stories, frequently fantastic and unbelievable, of the monks of the said monastery, originated in the thirteenth century and soon became one of the most popular readings in Ukraine.[18]

Then the *bylyny,* the epic songs, the older ones, the *staryny,* and the newer ones, about the heroes such as Dobrynia, Illa Muromets', Diuk Stepanovych, Volha Sviatoslavych and others, were partially written down. They praised the bloody struggle of *Rus'* against her enemies to preserve her greatness. Yet, during the Mongol invasion and Mongol domination over Ukraine during the second half of the thirteenth and the fourteenth centuries, the *bylyny* were largely forgotten in the Ukrainian south, which was about to initiate its new heroic era of the Cossack struggle against Tartar steppes.

The Life and Journeys of Danylo, the Abbot of the Land of Rus', written down by Abbot Danylo, was an outstanding piece of literary creation, as mentioned above. In addition to giving some reliable geographical description of the Holy Land, in particular of the city of Jerusalem and the Jordan River, which he visited in 1106-1108, he gave the expression of his patriotic feeling, by telling how he prayed for *Rus'* and her princes. The literary value of the work was greatly increased by the inclusion into its content of various legends and apocryphas to brighten his descriptions of the journey.

A separate place in the early Rus'ian-Ukrainian literature had been taken by the *Advice for the Children,* written by Prince Volodymyr Monomakh, the first notable secular author, not a bishop, priest, monk or other religious person, though his work continued to be permeated by moral and religious sentiments. In that semi-biographical work of literary value, Volodymyr advised his sons what kind of princes they should be. They were supposed to be just and charitable, defend the weak, never to punish by death either the guilty or the innocent, respect a guest, love their wives but never let their wives prevail over themselves, attend to important matters personally and never rely upon others to do their work, since laziness "is the mother of all evil," and to pray. The work fully illustrates the moral atmosphere which inspired the medieval Rus'ian-Ukrainians, since the *Advice* was not written by a clergyman, whose job was to preach, but by a worldly person, a prince, who believed in these high principles. It meant that the culture of *Rus'* in the twelfth century was thoroughly

Christian. According to the literary experts, Volodymyr Monomakh followed in this work some Byzantine and English literary patterns.

Another example of the literary work completed by a layman, an anonymous minor retainer, *druzhynnyk,* was the *Petition of Danylo Zatochnyk,* which also reflected the cultrual milieu of *Rus'.* It was a collection of various aphorisms, quotations, and statements, frequently in the form of satire, put in the framework of a petition according to Greek literary prototype, resembling to some extent the collection of the *Pchola,* the *Bee.* It contains quotations about the rich and the poor, wisdom and stupidity, good and bad princely advisors and lieutenants, good and bad wives and so on. ''The author's fiery opposition to the 'black clergy' and the *boyars''* gave, as Vernadsky asserts, some political significance to the work, written probably by a commoner or even a former slave.

The historical aspect of the chronicles, the *Povist' vremennykh lit,* the *Kyivsky litopys',* the *Halytsko-volynsky litopys',* the *Chernivivian chronicle,* and others, was discussed above, while at this place only their literary value must be underscored. They all were permeated by great love of and attachment to the fatherland; written in a vivid and often poetic and at times dramatic style, richly interwoven with legends, narrations, proverbs and fragments of folklore songs, such as the legend of St. Andrew, the legend about the beginnings of the city of Kiev, about Oleh's horse, and *yevshan* herbs; and all historical developments having been evaluated from the point of view of the Christian religion and ethics.[19]

Doubtlessly, however, the historical epic, *Slovo o polku Ihoreve,* the *Lay of Ihor' Campaign,* had been the most outstanding literary creation of medieval *Rus'*-Ukraine, of the great artistic and ideological values, narrating the unfortunate campaign of the Rus'ian armed forces against the Cumans, led by Prince Ihor in 1185. The author of the masterpiece did not reveal his name, but it can be assumed that he was a princely *druzhynnyk* at that time, or perhaps, even a participant of the said anti-Cuman expedition. He must have been a highly educated man of outstanding poetic abilities who passionately loved his country, *Rus'*-Ukraine, and dreamt of her greatness. The original of the epic poem was not preserved, while its copy was first discovered in 1795.

The *Slovo* resembles to some extent the Western *Roland' Saga,* the epic poem praising knighthood and chivalry, the knights who were able to stand in defense of the honor and fame of their fatherland, not being frightened by any dangers, having accepted defeat with dignity. The leitmotif of the epic was the unity, the honor and fame of the *Rus'* realm; hence the author reproached Princes Ihor and Vsevolod, the main instigators of the campaign, for having undertaken the step without thinking it through, and having not considered the probability of defeat and the risk of damaging the interest of the realm.

The literary and artistic value of the *Slovo* consists of its perfect composition, beautiful descriptions of the troops on march and of the battle, introduction of powerful emotional elements, deep reflections of the author himself about the campaign as a whole and its component parts, as well as bringing into the action the vital participation of the powers of nature, affecting human fate. The poetic language of the work is very rich and close to the Ukrainian national folklore of that time. The *Slovo o polku Ihoreve,* because of its richness and beauty, has been translated into all Slavic languages, as well as into German, French, English, Dutch, Hungarian, Swedish, Danish, and other tongues. The Ukrainian poets, such as Shevchenko, Shashkevych, Shchurat, Hordynsky and Rylsky, gave numerous poetic versions of the epic in modern Ukrainian, while Ukrainian and foreign linguists and literary experts continuously study the masterpiece, and always find in it still undiscovered yet artistic values.[20]

With the Mongol invasion and the Mongol domination, the marvelous growth of the Rus'ian-Ukrainian literature came to an abrupt and violent end in the middle of the thirteenth century, which was an enormous loss for the entire Western-Christian civilization.

Although for many centuries, as Jakobson asserted, the Rus'ian-Ukrainian literature remained almost entirely ecclesiastic, almost entirely concerned with lives of saints, pious men, morals and ethics, yet the laity at that time apparently possessed ''a copious, original, manifold, and highly artistic fiction, but the only medium for its diffusion was oral transmission.'' It seemed that using letters for secular writings was alien to the Rus'ian-Ukrainian tradition, and that was apparently the reason why so much of that copious secular fiction, including the *bylyny,* was lost in course of the centuries, and especially, in the wake of the Mongol devastation.[21] Only a few and more outstanding ones survived.

Architecture. The Ukrainian Slav developed his own architecture and construction industry on his own from the most humble beginnings of a dug-house and a wooden shack up to the level of building wooden and stone houses and wooden churches in the so-called *narodnyi styl,* the Rus'ian popular style. The huts were about 50 per cent wooden, about 34 per cent clay, and the remainder, stone constructions, normally divided into three parts, the living chamber, the corridor, and the storage. The hut was in most cases fenced and with a small garden, a yard and some household buildings. The wooden churches in the villages and towns in the Rus'ian popular style were also constructed in the three-divisional manner, with three towers. Some living quarters and most churches were decorated by wooden carving from inside and outside, in particular, their window frames, door frames and doors, as well as some furnishings. The living quarters, the *teremy,* of the princes and *boyars* were, of course, more spacious, more impressive, and better constructed than those of the commoners.[21]

In the area of architecture, the Hellenic and then Byzantine cultural impact upon *Rus'* was enormous. Since the times of antiquity, the ancient inhabitants of southern Ukraine must have gotten acquainted with the classical Hellenic architectural styles, the Ionian, Dorian and Corynthian ones, amply represented by the structures and edifices in the Greek colonies on the banks of the Black and Azov Seas. Twice the nomad steppe hordes gravely ruined the Greek civilization there by their recurring waves, in the second century B.C., and about the sixth century A.D. The archeology subsequently retrieved ruins of many ancient temples, chapels and other buildings from both eras of the flourishing Hellenic colonies in that region.

The architecture of the Kievan-Galician period must be divided into three sectors: the defense, the civilian and the ecclesiastic ones. The construction of churches was probably the most important with respect to artistic values. The acceptance of Christianity introduced the Byzantine architectural style in *Rus'*. It has been asserted by many, as Vernadsky stated, that in that respect *Rus'* was but a province of Byzantium.[22] The first architects, who built the first Christian churches in that country and who introduced there the said Byzantine style, must have been Greeks and Bulgarians, and the first local Ukrainian builders who learned the skill and began to construct edifices in that style probably in the twelfth century. The first Byzantine church, constructed in Kiev, was the Church of the Tithe, or of the Holy Assumption, built according to the patterns of the churches in Ochrida, in Bulgaria; an instance which again seemed to imply the acceptance of Christianity by *Rus'* from Bulgaria, and not from Byzantium, as suggested by the *Povist' vremennykh lit.*

It seems that the Church of Tithe or Holy Mary's Assumption, built at the time of Volodymyr the Great, was the oldest church in Ukraine, particularly referred to by the historical sources. It consisted of three naves, beautifully ornamented with frescoes and mosaics, marbles and artistic carvings, encrusted floors, and having on top one large *copula,* semi-oval top. It was ruined by Batu's invasion, and never reconstructed. Another outstanding example of the Rus'ian architecture of the early time was the Church of Lord's Transfiguration in Chernihiv, taken under construction by Prince Mstyslav and completed by Yaroslav the

Wise. It has been considered to be one of the most beautiful architectural creations of the Kievan era.

The real boom in constructing churches and other edifices developed during the reign of Yaroslav the Wise. He built many beautiful structures in the Byzantine and mixed Byzantine and locally popular styles, but the edifice which brought real fame to his name was the Cathedral of St. Sophia. A huge construction of five naves, five apses, a gallery and thirteen *copulas,* built with thick walls, and ornamented, like the Church of Tithe and other churches, but with much grander and elaborate, mosaics, frescos and artistic paintings. A huge painting of the Holy Mother, the *Oranta,* attracted the most attention. The Church of St. Sophia, which had enchanted many in the past, as well as today, being of the Byzantine style, bore the elements of local originality and genius, but it incorporated also some components of the Armenian, Syrian and Romanesque architectural influences. Enormous literature arose in the course of time evaluating the artistic aspects of the Cathedral.[23]

Prince Yaroslav erected a great many other churches, among them, the Church of St. George and Irene and the Annunciation, in Kiev and other cities, as well. All other later princes continued with the architectural construction of churches and chapels in Chernihiv, Pereyaslav, Halych, Peremyshl, Ovruch, Volodymyr Volynsky, Kholm and other places, since in that way they wanted to manifest their greatness and leave an impression upon later generations. The chronicles reported that at one time in Kiev there were four hundred churches, probably including chapels, while six hundred of them perished by fire sometime later. The number must have been an exaggeration, but then their number must have been considerable. The churches were built by princes, *boyars,* rich merchants and various communities, while princes and grand *boyars* had private churches and chapels of their own to pray in, in private. There were churches and chapels erected also at the monasteries to assist the religious in their pious practices.

In most cases, these churches were built in the form of squares, with three apses, the naves, topped with one, two or three *copulas* or towers. Because Ukraine was on the crossroads between the Occident and the Orient, one could detect in the Ukrainian churches all over of that time the admixtures of the Eastern architectural elements with the Western Romanesque, while the structural elements of the latter were getting ever so much pronounced in West Ukraine, the Galician-Volhinian principality, where even the German, Polish and Hungarian influences were visible. There the Roman Catholic churches of the German, Polish and Hungarian settlers, brought by the Galician princes, were erected mostly in the Romanesque style prevailing, along with the buildings of the Catholic orders.

The civilian architecture was used for erecting the palaces and public buildings, which were first wooden and then brick and stone ones. At the time of Ihor and Olha, there existed in Kiev an impressive stone-structured palace of two stories, beautified with paintings, mosaics, frescos and marble, as excavations have indicated. The richness of the palace had indicated that the upper class of the *Rus'* society lived well at that time, and that it was not primitive at all. Volodymyr the Great erected three grand edifices, while Yaroslav's activity in that area was quite extensive. He constructed many palaces and public buildings throughout his huge empire. Later princes and *boyars* continued with building palaces and expansive living quarters, mostly brick and stone structures, with many parts, connected by long, and at times even hidden, corridors, and many rooms, large halls for meetings and social gatherings or official functions. Metropolitans and bishops also lived in palaces, while religious orders possessed large monastic structures for their communal living. These civilian buildings were usually connected with the private churches and chapels for their religious activities.

The towns and cities in *Rus'* must have been impressively built, since the Hungarian king, arriving at the walls of Volodymyr Volynsky in 1231, exclaimed with amusement, "Such a city I did not see even in the German lands"; as the *litopys'*, the chronicle, asserted.

The defense construction was extensive; the deep, 18-20 yards wide ditches filled with water; wide stone or brick walls surrounding the town; high towers; strong gates with the drawbridges were built to defend the inner city or town, where churches, palaces, public buildings, market places and living quarters of the very townspeople were located.[24]

Painting and Carving. The arts of painting and carving developed in connection with the religious life of the ancient *Rus'* society, and long with the growth of architecture. Yet, primitive man aspired to decorate his cave or even dug-house by carving or painting, this being his natural drive for beauty. Painting was quite developed at the time of the Tripillian culture. Then, the art of painting, frescos and mosaics, radiated again over southern Ukraine from the Hellenic colonies. The introduction of Christianity brought to *Rus'* Byzantine painting, which developed very well. Of course, the first artists of that painting style were Greeks, who imitated the Byzantine patterns, but when a little later the local Ukrainian artists took over the profession, they substantially deviated from the Byzantine style by introducing some national elements of the Ukrainian folklore art, and by having been somewhat influenced by the Western artistic patterns of painting, especially in Galicia and Volhinia.

The Byzantine art of painting was a departure from naturalism in contrast to the earlier style, which attempted to imitate nature as closely as possible. Having been thoroughly ecclesiastic, Byzantine painting attempted to reflect holiness and sanctity. Hence, picturing Jesus Christ, Holy Mary and the saints of the Old and New Testament as realistic human figures seemed to the pious Byzantine painter to be highly improper. So he developed the skills of stylization of the human figure in order to reflect piety and spirituality of the images of God and of the saints by distorting naturalism. These images and figures were made unnaturally tall, skinny and ascetic; with small and narrow lips, which implied their complete restraint from sinful speech; and small ears, which implied their restraint from listening to sinful talks; and unnaturally large eyes, through which the divine soul was seeing the world. Specific colors were prescribed to present certain ideas, and the images were always identified by abbreviated inscriptions. The churches of the Kievan era were decorated with grand and beautiful wall paintings and mural frescos of Divine providence, Jesus Christ, Virgin Mary and of all kinds of saints, of which St. George, Yurii, St. Demetrius, Dymytrii, and some others, were most popular. The frescos in the St. Sophia Cathedral, combined with the mosaics, represent one of the highest artistic achievements of the medieval Rus'ian-Ukrainian culture. Their greatness suggests that they were completed by a collective of artists-painters according to a well-conceived plan, and under a central leadership. Nothing seems incidental there, but well-patterned, including the impressive painting of the *Oranta,* of the Virgin Mary. The combination of the mosaics and frescos unfolds originality. Not less beautiful were the murals and mosaics in the Church of the Tithe. It is only a pity that they were not preserved for posterity. The colors and the figures in the Church of the Tithe were lighter and more gentle and mild in their expression than those in the Cathedral of St. Sophia.[25] Other churches in Kiev and in other cities and towns were similarly decorated and ornamented by mosaics and frescos, such as the Church of St. Dymytrii and the Church of the Holy Assumption at the Pecherska Lavra monastery, demolished by the Russian Bolsheviks in the nineteen-thirties and forties in the course of their atheistic and anti-Ukrainian drives. The Church of St. Cyril in Chernihiv also amazed the spectator by the artistry of its murals, illustrating the scenes from the life of the said saint.

In the twelfth and thirteenth century, the local Ukrainian artists began to depart and deviate from the rigor of the Byzantine style of painting and mosaic development, by giving to their works more life and motion, and attempting to unite external beauty and internal emotions of the personages and scenes presented by the murals and mosaics. They made themselves artistically more independent of the Byzantine standards of artistry and introduced into their creative paintings some motive of national art, although the painting remained essentially Byzantine.

Parallel with the mural frescos and the mosaics, also the *icon* or holy picture, painting developed in *Rus'* and it was continued even after the Mongol invasion, while other forms of arts were then declining. The *icons,* first of the Greek origin and subsequently painted by the Ukrainian artists, were prepared according to some rigid standards of Byzantine art and its long tradition. By the eleventh century, the *icons* were beautified, ornamented and enriched by silver or gold vestments, richly decorated with pearls and precious stones. Two oustanding examples of the *icons* in *Rus'*-Ukraine were the *icon* of Holy Mother of Belz, which was transferred in 1382 by the Polish government to Częstochova, in Poland, and soon became the most revered image of Virgin Mary in that country, and the *icon* of Holy Mother of Vyshhorod, taken by Andrei Bogolubskii to the northern city of Vladimir in 1155, and later on became a sacred picture of Russia. Both *icons* were most probably originated in Greece, then given by the Greeks to the Ukrainian princes, and finally either by force or by trickery taken away out of Ukraine.[26]

The miniature paintings to decorate ecclesiastic and other books represented still another form of painting art, which anticipated future engraving. Their artistic quality was very high, as for example the miniatures in the Gospel, copied by deacon Hryhorii in 1057, or in the *Izbornyk,* the Collection, of Prince Sviatoslav from 1073.

Carving, and especially wood carving, was traditional in *Rus'*-Ukraine. The old Rus'ians decorated window and door frames, the doors, benches and other furniture pieces with wood carving. In the same way the wooden churches were decorated, including the altars, pulpits, crosses, and the *ikonostasy,* the icon-stands, and candlesticks. The stone was carved in pagan times to make idols of the deities.

This national tradition was continued throughout the Kievan and Galician era, although the Byzantine version of Christianity was against wood and stone carving, having been afraid that it would promote the pagan beliefs and superstitions either to return or to persist. The Bulgarian and Western influences, however, encouraged and facilitated the development of the art of carving in *Rus'*, where those influences were clearly visible.

Excavations disclosed marble carving, having been used to decorate Ihor's and Olha's palace in Kiev, the Church of the Tithe, and the churches in different parts of *Rus'*, in particular, in Western Ukraine, where material for carving was amply supplied, and Western cultural influence especially strong. The chronicles mentioned carved figures of Jesus Christ and John the Baptist in the churches of the city of Kholm. Carving was used also to decorate tombstones and sarcophaguses of princes and grand *boyars*, such as the sarcophagus of Yaroslav the Wise, made from white marble, in the Cathedral of St. Sophia, and that of Princess Olha, made of red slate, in the Church of the Tithe. Yet, most of those artistically carved tombstones and sarcophagi were destroyed and lost forever during later tumultuous times.[27]

Music and Theater. The pagan ritual and religious songs, folk songs for various family and social occasions and ancient epic songs, praising heroes and their heroic deeds and exploits, initiated the evolution of the musical art in old *Rus'*. Masudi, an Arab writer in the tenth century, pointed out that a traveler, passing by pagan temples in the lands of the Slavs, could hear musical melodies sung there. Solo and choral singing was known by the ancient Slavs, while often a leader was singing the main theme, accompanied by other singers, who modulated and embellished the song to create a beautiful whole. The songs were melodic, harmonious and very rhythmic.

Very early the professional singers-rhapsodists were already known in Ukraine. They travelled from one court to another, from one palace to another, to public places and public and religious festivities, and market places, and sang there, accompanied by some instruments, like the *kobza*, or recited the old *staryny* and *bylyny*, the heroic ballads and sagas, to entertain the royalty and nobility at the banquets and the common people at other occasions. The *Slovo o polku Ihoreve* mentioned Boian, one of those rhapsodists, in the twelfth century, while according to another source, Mytusa, was apparently an outstanding singer-rhapsodist in the thirteenth century. Those singers, called sometimes *skomorokhy,* must have been many and very popular, since there was scarcely any other entertainment of that kind available. At the princely courts there were already some simple musical bands in existence, which used such then commonly known musical instruments as the ancient *kobza,* the *husli,* the lute, the harp, the horn, the flute, and some other minor ones.[28]

With the introduction of Christianity, the Byzantine church singing came to Ukraine, where there was no instrumental music, according to tradition, but where choral singing reached a very high level of artistry. The monastery of Pecherska Lavra was certainly the very center in the development of the church or ecclesiastic music. The so-called *Kyivskyi rozspiv,* the Kievan book of notes, was prepared there to assist church singing, the notes of which were not as yet properly deciphered and interpreted.

From the ancient pagan singing, the *koliady, hailky, vesnianky, kupalni,* the ritual dancing, and rhythmic dialogues, elaborate wedding and funeral ceremonies, all with the elements of theatrical art, the beginnings of the theater in Kievan *Rus'* developed. Soon professional travelling actors, called *skomorokhy, shpilmany* or *svystilnyky,* emerged, while some princes organized primitive theaters of their own. The Byzantine example certainly facilitated the development. Although the church-oriented Byzantine culture at first scorned theater as a pagan custom, after a while it reconciled itself to the art and aided its growth. From there the appreciation of theater came to *Rus',* where there were already its humble beginnings. Also in Ukraine the Church at first was hostile, especially towards the travelling *skomorokhy* as supposedly continuing the pagan tradition, but following the Byzantine example, it gave up its opposition. The early theater at the princely courts promoted high ideals, since its interest was centered on heroism, loyal service to the prince, defense of the fatherland, aid to the weak and needy, and chivalry. Of course, the Mongol invasion and domination largely terminated the development of arts in *Rus'*-Ukraine, for the struggle for physical survival was so straining that scarcely a moment was left to care for any cultural and artistic values.[29]

Other Arts. The archeological excavations have given ample proof of a well developed art of jewelry making in *Rus'*-Ukraine in the period of the eleventh to the thirteenth century. The tradition of the art was very old, going back into ancient history as far as the Scythian era. Then, of course, the Hellenic, Oriental and Byzantine influences facilitated the growth of the art, which reached a high level of development in Kiev. The local masters of jewelry-making produced crosses, rings, earrings, chains, necklaces, necklets, bracelets, sword-handles, and other varieties of jewelry from gold and silver, using precious stones and pearls for decorations. Several techniques were used by the jewellers, who used engraving and oxydizing, either on gold or gold-plated items. Artistic binding and decorating church books and making church vessels from gold and silver completed that artistic craftsmanship which served the ecclesiastic and secular needs. The local craftsmen introduced in their art local patterns, which enriched the art, along with the foreign influence.

The art of ceramics, of producing and artistically decorating the clay dishes and pots, also had an old tradition in Ukraine, going back for thousands of years, to the era of the Tripillian culture. In the Ukrainian ceramics local patterns were found along with the foreign, Byzantine, and other ones, being either geometric, plant or animal motifs, in painting the dishes and pots largely in green, red, white and black colors.

Embroidery was developing very impressively during the Kievan-Galician period. It definitely indicated the deep-rooted conservativism in the patterns and colors used in embroidery over the centuries, while a great many things were ornamented and decorated with embroidering, female and male shirts, towels, belts, various pieces of female clothing, in particular, tablecloths, bed-covers, and church vestments. Skilled embroiderers worked in convents and princely and *boyar* palaces. Princesses and noble women especially patronized embroidery as a very popular art,

among the common people as well. Embroidering was definitely
an art, developed by women, and there was scarcely a Ukrainian
woman who did not master the art at least to some extent. Apparently embroidering also went back to the Scythian and Sarmatian
times as a traditional art on Ukrainian soil.[30] The students of the
old Ukrainian-Rus'ian arts generally have agreed that all the arts:
painting, carving, engraving, ornamentation of books, embroidering, and ceramics, have proven beyond any doubts the great
artistic abilities of the Ukrainian people and their great artistic
individualism.

1. Yu. Fedoriv, *Istoria tserkvy v Ukraini,* Toronto, 1967, p. 28.
2. *Ibid.,* p. 29; also, *Povist' vremennykh lit,* by P. Adrianovaia-Perets and D.
   Likhachev, Moscow-Leningrad, 1950, Vol. I, p. 39, year 945.
3. *Ibid.,* Vol. I, 81, year 988; E. Golubinskii, *Istoria russkoi tserkvi,* Moscow, 1901 I, part 1, pp. 163-182.
4. M. Priselkov, *Ocherki po tserkovno-politicheskoi istorii Kievskoi Rusi X-XI
   st,* St. Petersburg, 1913; N. Polonska-Vasylenko, *Istoria Ukrainy,*
   Munich, 1972, Vo. I, pp. 117-118: "All that speaks in favor of the argument, that the Bulgarians were the first teachers and ecclesiastic leaders of
   Rus' ".
5. Fedoriv, *op. cit.,* p. 41; Polonska-Vasylenko, *op. cit.,* Vol. I, p. 119; L.
   Vynar, "Pereizd Bruno z Kverfurtu cherez Kyiv chasiv Volodymyra,"
   Rozbudova derzhavy, Denver, 1955, Book 1.
6. G. Vernadsky and M. Karpovich, *A History of Russia,* Vol. II, *Kievan
   Russia,* New Haven, 1951, pp. 263-264; M. Hrushevsky, *Istoria
   Ukrainy-Rusy,* 1954, Vol. III, pp. 402-404.
7. Fedoriv, *op. cit.,* pp. 52, 77-81; H. Luzhnytsky, *Ukrainska tserkva mizh
   Skhodom i Zakhodom,* Philadelphia, 1954, pp. 115-117; J. Abraham,
   Powstanie kosciola lacinskiego na Rusi, Lviv, 1904, p. 112.
8. Monasteries and the monastic life: Fedoriv, *op. cit.,* pp. 60-63; Polonska-
   Vasylenko, *op. cit.,* Vol. I, pp. 235-236; Ilarion, Mytropolyt, *Blyskucha
   zoria v ukrainskii dukhovii kultury.* Winnipeg, 1960, pp. 26 and following;
   Hrushevsky, *op. cit.,* Vol. III, pp. 413-421: *chernetstvo;* on various aspects
   of the monastic life: *Kievo-Pecherskyi Pateryk,* Kiev, 1931; I. Nazarko,
   "Kyivski monastyri domonholskoi doby," *Logos,* Vol. III, 1952.
9. Churchpeople: the reader is referred to the next chapter, covering the social
   structure of the Kievan realm.
10. Fedoriv, *op. cit.,* pp. 109-110.
11. Vernadsky, *op. cit.,* Vol. II, pp. 277-280; A. Wanczur, *Szkolnicktwo w
    starej Rusi,* Lviv, 1923; M. Pogodin, "Obrazovanie i gramotnost' v drev-

niem periodie russkoi istorii," *Zhurnal Ministerstva Narodnavo Prosvieshchenia*, 153, 1871, pp. 1-28.

12. V. Tatishchev, *Istoria rossiiskaia*, Moscow, 1768-1774, Vol. II, p. 138; Golubinskii, *op. cit.*, I, part 1, p. 873; also Vernadsky, *op. cit.*, Vol. II, p. 278.

13. Polonska-Vasylenko, *op. cit.*, Vol. I, pp. 239-244; D. Chyzhevsky, *Istoria ukrainiskoi literatury*, New York, 1956, pp. 99-103.

14. Chyzhevsky, *op. cit.*, pp. 113-122; Hrushevsky, *op. cit.*, Vol. III, pp. 486-488; M. Priselkov, *Istoria russkavo letopisania XI-XV viekov*, Leningrad, 1940.

15. V. Pashuto, *Ocherki po istorii Galitsko-Volynskoi Rusi*, Moscow, 1950, pp. 68-100 and 101-133; Polonska-Vasylenko, *op. cit.*, Vol. I, p. 250.

16. M. Shakhmatov, *Uchenia russkikh letopisei domongolskavo perioda o gosudarstviennoi vlasti*, Prague, 1927, 2 volumes; Vernadsky, *op. cit.*, Vol. II, pp. 287-290.

17. *Mediavel Russian Laws*, ed. by A. Evans, in *Records of Civilization*, No. 41, New York, 1947, pp. 27 and 39.

18. Chyzhevsky, *op. cit.*, pp. 23-212.; V. Radzykevych, *Istoria ukrainskoi literatury*, Detroit, 1955, Vol. I, pp. 1-70; Polonska-Vasylenko, *op. cit.*, Vol. I, pp. 239-250.

19. Radzykevych, *op. cit.*, Vol. I, pp. 49-53, and 64.

20. *Ibid.*, pp. 53-60; Chyzhevsky, *op. cit.*, pp. 181-197.

21. Polonska-Vasylenko, *op. cit.*, Vol. I, pp. 256-258; Vernadsky, *op. cit.*, Vol. II, pp. 302-303.

22. *Ibid.*, p. 256.

23. V. Sichynsky, *Arkhitektura starokyivskoi doby X-XIII st.*, Prague, 1926; P. Kurinnyi, "Arkhitektura Desiatynnoi Tserkvy," *Ukrainskyi samostiinyk*, 1953, No. 16; O. Povstenko, "Katedra sv. Sofii v Kyivi," *The Annals of the Ukrainian Academy of Arts and Sciences in the U.S.*, 1954, Vol. III-IV; V. Sichynsky, *Istoria ukrainskoho mystetstva*, Vol. I-II, *Arkhitektura*, New York, 1956.

24. M. Levytsky, ed., *Istoria ukrainskoho viiska*, Winnipeg, 1953, pp. 70-75; M. Braichevsky, *Kyiv—tsentr drevnierus'koi derzhavy*, *Istoria Kyieva*, Kiev, 1960, Vol, I, pp. 55-70.

25. Povstenko, *op. cit.*, pp. 124-141; the same, "Fresky i mozaiky sv. Sofii," and "Fresky i mozaiky Mykhailivskoho (Dymytriivskoho) monastyria v Kyievi," in *Ukrainske mystetstvo*, Munich, 1947, Vol. I, pp. 5-12; Vol. II, pp. 6-10; briefly: Polonska-Vasylenko, *op. cit.*, Vol. I, pp. 261-264.

26. V. Yaniv, *Narys ukrainskoi kultury*, New York, 1961, pp. 55-57: painting; *The Ukrainian icon of the XII to XVIII centuries*, ed. by S. Hordynsky, Philadelphia, 1973; *Ukrainskyi seredniovichnyi zhyvopys*, eds. H. Logvyn, L. Miliaieva and V. Svientsitska, Kiev, 1976.

27. Yaniv, *op. cit.*, pp. 49-50; Polonska-Vasylenko, *op. cit.*, Vol. I, pp. 264-265.

28. Vernadsky, *op. cit.*, Vol. II, pp. 251-253; N. Findeizen, *Ocherki po istorii muzyki v Rossii*, Moscow and Leningrad, 1928, Vol. I; Yaniv, *op. cit.*, p. 71; N. Nyzhankivsky, "Folk music" and "Folk instruments," in *Ukraine, A Concise Encyclopedia*, Vol. I, Toronto, 1963, pp. 371-383.

29. Vernadsky, *op. cit.*, Vol. II, pp. 253-256; Yaniv, *op. cit.*, pp. 77-78; B. Malnick, "The Origin and Early History of the Theater in Russia," *Slavonic and East European Review*, 19, pp. 203-227; I. Mirtschuk, *Geschichte der Ukrainischen Kultur*, Munich, 1957, pp. 181-182.

30. Vernadsky, *op. cit.*, Vol. II, pp. 262-263; Yaniv, *op. cit.*, pp. 17-18, 22-23; D. Horniatkevych and L. Nenadkevych, "Embroideries," *Ukraine, A Concise Encylopedia*, Toronto, 1963, Vol. I, pp. 395-403.

CHAPTER NINE

THE SOCIAL STRUCTURE DURING THE KIEVAN-GALICIAN TIMES.

Social classes of *Rus'ka Pravda* — Nobility — Peasantry — Townspeople — Slavery — Churchpeople — Foreigners — The issue of feudalism in Ukraine.

Social Classes of the Rus'ka Pravda. Concurrently with the political and cultural progress of medieval Ukraine, her social differentiation and social structure grew more complex and more elaborate. The oldest Ukrainian code of laws, *Rus'ka Pravda,* which was a product of at least two centuries of evolution of the legal and social concepts of the Ukrainian people, gives us an approximate insight into the social constitution of the Kievan-Galician period. Of course, it does not matter here whether *Rus'ka Pravda* was an official or unofficial legal compilation. The social differentiation of that period, according to the code, advanced so far as to become a class differentiation in the sense of public, as well as civil, law. Prior to the Kievan era, the social stratification of the Ukrainian Slavs was primarily a creation of the private law. The code provided the legal framework for those social classes. But according to Vladimirskii-Budanov, a reliable student of the history of Ukrainian and Russian law, the social concepts of *Rus'ka Pravda* did not represent any advanced product of the evolution of medieval Ukrainian society, but only a certain evolutionary stage of its social and legal growth.[1]

Of course, the individual lands of the empire exhibited certain social peculiarities of their own, which were not adequately evaluated by the code. It seems, however, that the legal concepts of *Rus'ka Pravda* were intended to have a universal character, that is, to contribute towards imperial unity by overcoming regional individualism. At the same time, parallel efforts were made towards consolidation by the newly introduced Christianity. The code of *Rus'ka Pravda* continued basically to differentiate among three classes, the princely people, the common people, and the slaves. All three classes, including the princes, were placed in a differentiated relation to the sovereign. The princely people, the aristocracy or, as they were later called, the *boyary,* were directly and individually subordinated to the duke. Consequently, each and every princely man had certain individual rights and obligations toward the state and the prince. The relationship between the common people and the prince was also direct, but on a collective basis, so that villages and towns had certain rights and bore certain obligations toward the state and the prince. The common free man had his individuality and personality in the sense of the civil law; his local or professional community, however, was the subject of public affairs. The slaves were in no direct relation to the prince—they were the property of the free citizens, and were regarded as such by law. According to the code, war prisoners, criminals, and debtors in default were to become slaves, and of course, there were also the slaves by birth. *Rus'ka Pravda* also recognized slavery that arose in consequence of an individual agreement between the master-to-be and the slave-to-be. This peculiarity will be discussed later. The slave was a thing and had no public rights, although he enjoyed some civil rights (limited property). Killing a slave was punished only by a monetary compensation paid to his owner.

Later developments brought new forms of social differentiation, already initiated by the principles of *Rus'ka Pravda,* namely: the aristocratic upper class, peasantry, townspeople, slaves, church people, and the separate group of the foreigners. Since each and every class then became considerably stratified in itself, there resulted a very complex Kievo-Galician society. These classes not only were socio-political phenomena, but they also originated as separate occupational and economic groups, and continued as such throughout the entire medieval period. Each class had a distinct economic function to perform, as well. Social stratification continued to prevail in the projections of the public and private law. Individuals acquired their social positions primarily as members of their classes, and their rights and obligations toward society as a whole and toward the state could change only by a change in their class membership, as pointed out above.

The transition from one class to another was relatively easy in the Kievan-Galician era, as Yaniv pointed out in his analysis of the history of the Ukrainian social constitution. He found certain internal and external forces which rendered that flexibility in the social structure so different from the West European patterns. Even the closest neighbors of Ukraine, Poland and Muscovy, later on developed more drastic and more rigid class distinctions. Poland effected these distinctions by following more closely the West European developments, while Muscovy's social stratification was more of Oriental origin. The internal force which eased social differences in Ukraine was the tradition of individualism. The Ukrainian Slavs followed an instinct to let human beings grow individually rather than to subordinate them to the interest of the class or the state. A natural result was the reduction of class antagonism. The external contributions to the structural flexibility of Ukrainian society of that era were even more powerful. Yaniv explained them as follows: "The borderland character of Ukraine always exposed her to the constant attacks and raids of the steppe nomads, and this required a defense preparedness of the entire population, and not only a particular class or caste. Military duty was imposed on all social strata, although to a different extent, and the continuous threat produced a feeling of social solidarity of the whole nation, and minimized social contradictions and opposing class interests.''[2] Furthermore, this continuous threat and permanent warfare required a great deal of individual initiative and individual responsibility to face and to resist the dangers. In this way also, the individualistic features of the Ukrainian national character were intensified and magnified by the external developments, while the rigidity of the social stratification was considerably softened.

Nobility. The ethnical, racial, and national composition of the Ukrainian upper class of the Kievan-Galician era was heterogeneous, since it originated in three distinct social and ethnical processes. First of all, the Northmen introduced into the Ukrainian national constitution the institution of the princely retinue (*druzhyna*), which originally was the basic military unit, assisting the prince permanently in both war and peace. By the time of the arrival of the Varangians in Ukraine, the retinue was exclusively Germanic, and it represented the core of the military power of the adventurous princes. Later on, after having completely lost its Normanic ethnic character, the institution remained in medieval Ukraine as the foundation of the military power of individual princes and individual federative lands. The relationship of service between the prince and the warriors was based on individual agreements which established far-reaching social ties, rights, and obligations, and necessitated a close dependence of the knights upon the prince. But the military nature of the retinue was soon widened. Having tested the fidelity of their warriors, the princes began to use them as their deputies and officials in administration and government, both on the central and on the local levels. Yet the appointment of the knights to governmental and administrative positions was associated, according to the medieval custom as in Western Europe, with the latifundia grants of landed estates, soil meadows, and woods, and undersurface mineral resources, as compensation and reward for the services rendered or to be rendered.

After the knights acquired wealth and prestige and became interested in local affairs, the personal ties between them and the princes were subject to a gradual weakening so that these retainers slowly developed into the fairly independent stratum of landed aristocracy. Their obligation to public service, including military and administrative functions, remained, but at the same time they assumed new economic functions, especially after having amalgamated with the old Slavic upper class. This Slavic plutocracy, originating from the ancient merchant-warriors, had already become the land-owning class prior to the Kievan period. In the course of an overall assimilation, these native members of the upper class were soon absorbed into the governmental and administrative machine by the Kievan princes. In this way these nobles acquired additional wealth and prestige. Land ownership, wealth, government service, and public prestige became the common denominators for the Normanic adventurer-knights and the Slavic nobility, resulting in the growth of a new special class, commonly called *boyary*. Within the class a rapid naturalization tended to produce a prevailingly Slavic ethnic alloy, solidly cemented to the Kievan society. It should be pointed out that the Slavic plutocracy, being the second component of the Kievan-Galician *boyar* class, was originally an ethnical mixture of Slavs, Avars, Khozars, and other peoples, who willingly subordinated themselves to Slavic rule. The third human element constituting the Kievan noble class was the continuous influx into the *boyar* or grandee class of the "new men," descendants of the common people, such as children of the orthodox churchmen, the aristocracy of the towns, and the various foreigners in the service of the prince, including Poles, Czechs, and Hungarians. This vertical mobility was a very important element in preventing the development of a rigid class system in medieval Ukrainian society, and retaining a fluctuating and flexible system of social stratification.

The evolutionary process which resulted in the formation of the *boyar* class was an interesting phenomenon. For example, the Normanic warriors acquired wealth, prestige, and status from their outstanding services. The Slavic upper class was admitted to the public service because of their wealth and prestige, and, eventually, became the *boyary*. Commoners could improve their status only through their faithful service to the prince. This advance was possible even without such racial and traditional ties as existed between the Ruryk house and its Scandinavian warriors.

All three branches of the class of grandees soon developed mutual interests, opposed to the lower classes and antagonistic to the princes. While the *boyar* council, the duma, gradually acquired more and more power in determining the domestic and foreign affairs of their lands, the authority of the princes declined because of the continuous wars among themselves, during which each and every prince solicited by favors the aid of the nobles. The *boyars* exploited the situation to their advantage. In certain lands, and especially in Galicia, the grandees engaged in open conflict with the princes. They instigated and organized palace revolutions, expelled princes from the country, called others to rule, even murdered them, and in all cases considerably limited the princely authority. Once, in 1213, the *boyary* seized power, and one of them, Kormylchych, proclaimed himself the prince. This act was, of course, regarded by the Ruryk dynasty as high treason, and the traitor was eventually punished by death. But it distinctly indicates the social influence and the political strength that the Galician grandees managed to obtain for themselves.

The *boyar* class was greatly differentiated internally. Of the highest rank were the so-called hearth friends (the *ohnyshchany*), the nobles who held the most elevated offices and were so very close to the prince that they almost became members of his household. Oddly enough, however, the princely slaves *(tivuny),* who also performed important governmental and administrative functions, were included among the hearth friends. This circumstance directly helped to confuse the social barriers even between the nobles and the socially elevated slaves. Then came the social stratum of the grand *boyary,* rather few in number but very wealthy and powerful provincial aristocrats, especially in Galicia. They were the main opponents of the extensive authority of the prince. Some Galician rulers, like Prince Volodymyr and Prince Roman, did not hesitate to use violence and bloodshed in order to confirm their own power by reducing that of the rebellious *boyary*. The third *boyar* stratum was the country gentry—the knights in the Western European sense—larger in number, less powerful than the grand *boyary,* but holding closely together. All members of the entire *boyar* class were endowed with full personal freedom, complete rights to hold private property, unlimited inheritance, equality in consideration among male and female beneficiaries, freedom of business and initiative, and exemption from certain taxes such as inheritance taxes. They were protected by law against violence. Killing or injuring a nobleman was punished by fines twice as high as a commoner. The status of nobility was acquired either by birth or as a reward for faithful service to the prince, and it was lost by conviction for major crimes, such as murder, robbery, military desertion, and treason.

The grandees were economically very important since they owned a great deal of the country's land, productive resources, forests and minerals, the majority of the slaves, who were a substantial portion of the labor force, at least in the early Kievan era. They enjoyed freedom of initiative and private property rights to an extent that no other social group had, and they were, along with the princes and a few wealthy merchants, the main capitalists who had the opportunity and facilities to contribute to the country's production and economic growth. Agriculture was the most important sector of the Kievan-Galician economy, and the *boyars,* owning latifundia, produced a major share of the income of that sector. Being wealthy "capitalists," the *boyars* supplied capital also for certain other ventures, and participated sometimes directly and openly, and sometimes indirectly and secretly, on a partnership basis in various mercantile propositions. They owned mines, produced potash and tar, exploited iron ore and manufactured iron, and were extensively engaged in foreign trading and many other business activities. Ukrainian aristocracy was very business-like, without those prejudices against trades which existed in West Europe. Some *boyars* were in direct service relations to the city communities. This business-like attitude of the Ukrainian gentry was another factor tending toward smoothening the social stratification of the Kievan-Galician period.[3]

Peasantry. The peasants formed the second most important social class in the Kievan Empire and the Galician-Volhinian state. They made up the majority of the population, the stock of the nation. Socially, they were also considerably differentiated into a number of strata, ranging from the common free peasants, through the group of the half-free agricultural workers, down to the serfs, whose social standing differed little from that of the slaves. The peasantry was not, of course, racially and ethnically homogeneous, since it consisted of the prevailing Slavic element with a substantial addition of the conquered ancient natives of Ukraine who populated the country at various historical epochs, such as the Cimmerians, Scythians, Goths, Avars, and others, plus the numerous immigrating ethnical groups, such as the Khozars and steppe nomads. Also, by the way of liberation of the slaves to the status of the free peasants, the ethnic heterogeneity of the Ukrainian peasantry was intensified, since a substantial portion of the slave population was composed of prisoners of war, coming from various lands and peoples. In the earlier era, the free peasants were split into two strata: those who had full property rights on soil, and those who had only the rights of possession of soil owned by princes, gentry, or the village communities. Cultivation of the soil was their business, and some of them were legally bound to the soil *(glebae adscripti).* Yet Hrushevsky denied the existence of any soil-bound peasantry in Kiev and Galicia, and was inclined to accept the presence there of only the free peasants who enjoyed full property rights.[4] Kluchevskii, on the other hand, believed that there were no fully free peasants in Ukraine, but only the soil-bound tenants of the ducal and boyar estates.[5] It seems, however, that both classes existed for some time, while soil-bound peasants represented a transitional social phenomenon, the result of the gradual development of peasant individual property out of the village communal ownership of land. In the Galician-Volhinian state, the soil-bound peasantry no longer existed, but probably the entire

260

peasant class was included in a somewhat feudal system of the West European type. Later, still another group of relatively free peasants emerged, having originated from the stratum of the very poor who voluntarily accepted material dependence upon the royalty or boyardom. They were restricted to some extent in their personal freedom, including features of some contractural soil-boundage.

But all segments of the free peasantry enjoyed relative fullness of personal property rights. The inheritance rights of the peasants were somewhat restricted, however, since female descendants were excluded from inheriting real estate. Chubaty explained the situation as follows: ownership and inheritance of real estate were insolubly interrelated with the obligation of military service for the country. Thus, the sons of the free peasants, by performing their military obligation, established their full inheritance rights, while the daughters, being unqualified for service, forfeited their unlimited right to inherit soil and personal property, unless they married able young men who could guarantee to perform military service.[6]

Politically, peasants were full citizens, with the right and obligation to participate in the peoples' councils and their own self-governing institutions in the village and *verv* organizations, in the local police and judicial powers, and in collective tax responsibilities. The status of peasant was acquired by birth, by social and material elevation of the half-free and by legal emancipation of an agricultural slave. The peasant could forfeit his social standing and become a slave, as a consequence of a crime, bankruptcy, indebtedness, or marriage with a slave, or by way of a voluntary slavery contract.

The second distinct sub-class of the Kievan-Galician peasantry was the half-free, *zakupy*. The half-free were the poor peasants who worked for others, free peasants or gentry, and for others' account, on their soil and with their tools. *Zakupy* did not own or possess any soil or any working implements, but were rather a kind of farm labor. The half-free relationship was established on a contractual basis, with the distinct contractual agreement of

261

remaining personally free despite becoming a hired and materially dependent laborer. But the lord accepted also some contractual obligations toward the half-free, such as furnishing them with working tools, food, some money, and some personal property. Personal freedom of the *zakupy* was, of course, restricted in many respects. They did not participate in the village and *verv* self-government. They were subject to the judicial authority of their lords, and could not be witnesses in important cases. They could be whipped for punishment, a penalty never imposed upon free peasants. The half-free could be easily turned into slaves, especially for default in payment of debts. Nevertheless, they were extensively protected by the princely authority against the abuses committed by their lords and employers, a fact which considerably strengthened their social position. Full freedom of the *zakupy* could be restored by their improved material status and the termination of the contractual agreements. The peasant class was, economically speaking, a result of the progressive specialization in production of medieval societies in general. In Ukraine the peasants contributed substantially to the national income, primarily by farming but also by partially processing food and raw material. They also engaged in fishing, hunting, and cattle raising. The productive efficiency of the peasant class was motivated by private property rights and personal freedom for the majority of that class; facts which contributed to individual initiative.

The enormous wealth of the Kievan Empire astonished contemporary foreigners and modern historians. Kluchevskii and his followers erroneously attributed it to trade. But the real source of this wealth was agriculture, both *boyar* and peasant, founded on private ownership and individual initiative, and consequently a much more efficient system than that of Muscovy and Poland, where freedom did not exist to any great extent. At the same time, the peasants, including the half-free, were the most important labor power and productive agent of the medieval economy. However, since peasant capital ownership was rather negligible, peasant farming remained confined to small-scale enterprise.

Townspeople were the free bearers of the commercial and trading activities in the economic life of medieval Ukraine, just as in the West European socio-economic patterns of that time. Along with acquiring considerable wealth as a result of their commercial business, they also gained considerable political importance in the Kievan Empire. Their situation, however, changed in the Galician-Volhinian state, where the class of townspeople was politically suppressed by the nobility, and eventually prevented from any active role in current state matters. Actually, the merchant-townspeople lived only in big cities like Kiev, Chernihiv, Pereyaslav, Halych, and Terebovla, while the inhabitants of the small towns and villages were occupied primarily with agricultural activities.

As far as the national character of the medieval city people of Ukraine was concerned, Pogodin tried to prove that this class, at least in the Kievan era, was Normanic. However, historical evidence seems to contradict Pogodin's hypothesis, and proves the prevailingly Slavic nature of the Ukrainian town. The influx of the Varangians in Kievan society was never large enough to make even the Kievan noble class primarily Normanic. And to claim any Normanic origin of the town population seems to be a very artificial historiographical speculation. Much more untenable is Pogodin's idea of Galician conditions.[7] The Northmen were first of all warriors and administrators, secondarily merchants, and never craftsmen. Moreover, the Ukrainian townspeople in the course of the medieval centuries experienced a continuous influx of foreign ethnic elements as a result of a permanent assimilation process. Many foreign immigrants, Poles, Germans, Jews, Armenians, and Wallachians, came in considerable numbers to the medieval Ukrainian towns, settled there, and in the third or fourth generation, became Ukrainian. The Galician princes often invited the foreigners to come, and attracted them by granting special privileges for settling in Ukrainian towns. Their civilization, commercial abilities, and the Ukrainian connections seemed to be very advantageous for the growth of domestic economy.

The townspeople were composed of merchants and craftsmen, and their professions gave to the medieval town its specific character. These classes were internally differentiated, as were the nobility and the peasantry. Leadership was in the hands of an upper group of city patricians, especially rich and influential individuals and families. The second group was much more numerous, the social segment of the city plebs. Among them, material well-being, wealth, and capital ownership were the criteria of social stratification, rather than blood relationship or family traditions. The wealthy merchants were large capital owners, and as such, they financed many large-scale trading activities, both domestic and foreign, and not infrequently in an open or silent partnership with the business-minded *boyary* and princes. Upward social mobility for them was not difficult because, from a legal point of view, they were held to be equal to the *boyary*. They also could be called to perform services in the princely courts in the capacity of hearth-friends, a position which was held in high esteem.

The acquisition of wealth, therefore, permitted a city man to become a noble. In the Galician-Volhinian state, however, the social development was rather detrimental to the townspeople since the *boyary* acquired a more dominant political position, and successfully resisted the upward mobility of the townspeople despite the frequent intervention of the princes on their behalf.[25]

From a very early era, the town enjoyed the privilege of extensive self-government. Since it was immune from the regular ducal administration pattern, this administrative freedom and autonomy aided greatly in the economic growth of the city. Indeed, the wider and more comprehensive the autonomy of the individual town, the more prosperous it usually was, while any infringement upon that freedom brought in its wake an economic decline. The later Galician-Volhinian princes introduced into some of their cities the Magdeburg system of municipal self-government, having hoped in this way to increase the prosperity of the towns. Among the first towns to receive the Magdeburg law were Volodymyr, 1324, and Sanok, 1339, but the full development of that new German system of government of the townspeople took place later following the collapse of Ukrainian statehood.

The urban patricians were the cornerstone of municipal self-government which, at the time of the old *verve* system, included police authority, judicial power, and cooperation with the princely tax collectors within the city limits. Although Vernadsky refers to the townspeople as a middle class, they actually formed a social stratum somewhat more privileged than the free peasants. In general, summarizing the over-all significance of the medieval town for the socio-economic evolution of the Ukrainian people, the townspeople as a class performed a secondary role in the growth of the nation, a role subordinate to that of the nobility and the peasantry.

Slavery. An ancient institution in Ukraine, slavery developed partially under the influence of trade relations with the Orient, as has been indicated in the previous sections of this treatise. Slavery was very important in the medieval economy for two major reasons. Above all, slaves were a significant source of labor power, almost indispensible in the period of a primitive economy and a relative shortage of labor in relation to the rather vast supply of land, especially in the large-scale, latifundium-based economies of the royalty and boyardom. Secondly, at least in the earlier Kievan era, the slave trade was highly profitable.

As a social phenomenon slavery was equally important. The racial composition of the slave class was heterogeneous. Therefore, in later years as the institution of slavery gradually withered away, manumission of slaves resulted in another infusion of non-Slavic blood into Ukrainian society which, however, still remained predominantly Slavonic in contrast to the Muscovite or Russian people, whose Slavic character was lost to a greater extent as a result of the process of assimilation of the Mongol element.

The slaves were also socially stratified. At least two sub-classes of the unfree could be differentiated. The higher of these classes, the *tivuny,* served as administrators, tax collectors, real estate managers, princely officials, and in other similar offices. Their social position was rather close to that of the half-free. In fact (although not in the theoretical terms of the law), it was even higher than the position of the common free princely subjects. In their capacity as princely officials, the *tivuny* enjoyed legal privileges as far as being protected by a double death-money indemnity when killed or murdered. Some of them were even considered to be the hearth-friends of the prince, and in this capacity they could associate with the grand *boyary*.

Another, a lower group of the unfree, were the common slaves performing menial labor in the service of the gentry and common people. In the legal sense, the common slaves, *kholopy,* lacked legal personality; they were considered the property and possession of their lords and masters. As such they were left fully in the power of their masters, who originally had complete authority of the *domini vitae necisque.* The common law took no interest in the slave. Later, however, under the influence of the Christian religion, first by reason of custom, and eventually by the evolution of legal concepts, the slave was treated more humanely. His master could be forced by court sentence to give him up, merely on sufficient proof of the master's cruelty. Although the lord was principally liable for the illegal deeds of his slave and had to compensate any material losses caused by the slave, the latter himself was held responsible in the case of murder, and was immediately punished by the death sentence. The unfree, of course, could not own any real property; they were unable to inherit; and they could not be witnesses in court proceedings. Yet those limitations were seldom applied to the *tivuny*.

Ultimately accepted by the Ukrainian people in 988 or 989, Christianity had a favorable influence on the social position of the unfree. Most conspicuous was the development of a number of new forms of manumission. The status of slave was acquired by birth, capture in battle, conviction for a crime, marriage with a slave, purchase contractual agreement, bankruptcy, and indebtedness. All of these methods were reminiscent of ancient pagan customs. But the pagan era knew only a few grounds for the liberation of a slave. The Christian religion introduced, first of all, compulsory liberation of a slave, in due course of law, in the event of cruel and inhuman treatment. In addition, a prisoner of war could easily secure his freedom through ransom. Furthermore, the unfree concubine and her children by her lord obtained freedom automatically upon the latter's death. A sexually abused female slave received freedom at once according to new Christian principles. No doubt, under the impact of the Church and Western civilization, the lot of the slave was eased, his status improved, and his manumission facilitated. The abolition of the institution of slavery began, but it was not completed until much later. The gradual elimination of slavery continued after the collapse of the Galician-Volhinian state, within the political frameworks of the Lithuanian-Ukrainian realm and the Polish-Lithuanian commonwealth, through the fifteenth and sixteenth centuries. The process was finished earlier in the West than in East Ukraine.[8]

Churchpeople. Another segment of the population, the churchpeople, developed in an essentially Ukrainian manner at the time of the Kievan-Galician period; only to a certain extent was this group analogous to the West European clergy. The main difference in the social status of these two groups was in their different relationship to the state authority. The West European clergy was just another privileged class with its specific rights and obligations. The Ukrainian churchpeople were not a homogeneous class of people, but rather a highly heterogeneous alloy of differentiated social elements, which, for one reason or another, were exempt from the legal authority of the state, and were fully subordinated to the ecclesiastic administrative and judicial processes.

There were three subdivisions of churchpeople: the clergy, both secular (white clergy) and religious orders (black clergy), the people in the service of the Church, and the needy, *personae miserables*. The churchpeople, constituting these social elements, retained at the same time their respective class characteristics as *boyary,* townspeople, peasants, or slaves, regardless of whether they were in the service of the Church or in its care, like the widows, the aged, the crippled, the orphans, or the so-called *izgoii*. The churchpeople were inhabitants of the towns and villages owned by the Church, the peasants cultivating the ecclesiastical landed estates as tenants, along with those *boyary* who were in a vassalage relationship to the Church. In the Galician-Volhinian realm there were, however, no more church-owned towns, but there still were the Church *boyary,* peasants, and slaves.

The insitutions of the churchpeople indicated the enormous authority and wide autonomy of the Church, which was at that time "a state within a state." As a matter of fact, a very large number of people were directly exempt from the regular princely administration and court power, and constituted another comprehensive group of indirect citizens, or princely subjects. Certainly, the churchpeople were supposed to perform military duty for the country's defense, but they did it under the command of separate officers, appointed by ecclesiastical authorities, probably jointly with the princely military commanders. Only the ecclesiastical courts of the bishop and metropolitan were competent to judge the church wards. Kluchevskii believed, for example, that in the Kievan Empire there were actually two different species of social stratification: the species of the civic (secular) social classes, as discussed in the preceding sections, and the parallel species of the Church classes.[9]

This parallelism, if existing, was not recognized by the public law, however, which always considered the Church wards only under their common name of the churchpeople. A very peculiar social phenomenon were the above mentioned *izgoii,* under the protection of the Church. They were the people who, because of unfavorable circumstances or extraordinary developments, lost their previous social status. Thus, a prince who lost his land, or forfeited his princely rights of inheritance; a priest's son who, having failed to master the arts of reading and writing, could not succeed to his father's vocation; a merchant who lost his business, but left no debts—all these became *izgoii.* There were also many other forms of izgoism as a consequence of various other developments. The temporary izgoism of the princes or princely descendants was a cause of permanent political turmoil in medieval Ukraine, because the princely *izgoii* in due process of law usually declined to submit, and, taking their fortunes into their own hands, attempted to reestablish their previous political positions by force.[10]

From the point of view of the economic development of the Ukrainian people, the social phenomenon of the churchpeople was rather insignificant since they did not perform any specific economic or productive function of their own. Individual classes of Church wards participated in the national economy according to the medieval pattern of class specialization and their established functions as owning *boyary,* trading townspeople, and toiling slaves. On the other hand, the church as a legal person and the clergy as an owning social group were highly significant economic factors because of their large-scale land ownership and considerable capital accumulation. Especially significant were the religious orders, male and female, located in all major cities and towns, being of a large number in the Kievan Empire. These orders amassed wealth in lands and riches, both from donations and from their own hard work. They pioneered in progressive agriculture by developing intensive farms of fruit orcharding and vegetable gardening; they financed and managed many commercial and industrial enterprises, such as mills, distilleries, textile factories, and mines; and they also participated in the export business. The religious orders also contributed toward colonization and founded some new settlements in sparsely populated areas. This expansion, however, took place in the later periods to a much greater extent than during the Kievan-Galician era.

Foreigners were always well received in Ukraine, and they always enjoyed the friendly protection of the Ukrainian rulers. This privilege was a direct consequence of the very ancient and well developed foreign trade of the Ukrainians and their acquaintance with foreign lands and peoples. Since time immemorial, foreigners traveled, settled, and traded in Ukraine, just as the Ukrainian merchants undertook their business journeys to distant countries and places. Arabs, Iranians, Greeks, Armenians, Wallachians, Jews, and Khozars were well known. No doubt, the medieval Ukrainians were aware of the fact that there was a great opportunity to learn something advantageous and profitable from strangers, either in the way of business or culture.

At first, the wealth and prosperity of the Ukrainian economy attracted foreigners to settle among the Ukrainian Slavs. Indeed, the Northmen came to Ukraine, lured by her wealth. They soon settled there. The Varangians were scarcely ever treated as foreigners, in Ukraine; rather they joined the upper class of medieval Ukrainian society. The Khozars, Jews, Bulgars, Greeks, Germans, Poles, Hungarians, and later, the Armenians, Wallachians, and others, came into Ukraine in a continuous stream of immigration. Then things changed fundamentally. At the end of the thirteenth century and in the course of the fourteenth century, the great attraction of Ukraine declined because of continuous warfare and the Mongol danger. Yet, in this later period, the Galician-Volhinian princes especially called on foreigners to settle in their towns and villages, and granted them the privileges of the extensive Magdeburg self-government, exemption from taxes and military service, and the special protection of the state. It was also not difficult for the foreigners, particularly the Poles and Hungarians in Galicia, to be admitted to boyardom and to the princely retinue. The Germans and the Poles were called to advance the colonization and development of new settlements in Galicia and Volhinia according to the progressive methods of either the German or Polish patterns, which seemed to be more alluring and more efficient than colonization on the traditional Ruthenian basis *(ius Ruthenum)*.[11]

The Jews were put directly under the protection of the princes, as the so-called *servi camerae,* and were allowed to trade without restrictions. The Cumans also settled among the Ukrainians, and were rapidly assimilated. Another great national minority, which lived in the framework of the Kievan Empire, were the Ugro-Finns, who over a long period of time amalgamated with the Northern Slavs to form the ethnic group known as the Muscovite-Russians. They were certainly considered at the beginning, probably the ninth and tenth centuries, as enemies or second-class citizens, but eventually became the full-fledged co-creators of the later Muscovy-Russia.

In Ukraine all foreigners enjoyed full religious and national tolerance, as well as the privilege of self-government which directly contributed to their gradual Ukrainization. Foreigners usually lived in towns and villages, concentrating within certain city quarters, such as the German quarter, the Polish quarter, and the Jewish quarter, where they were able to develop their national customs and traditions freely. Accordingly, they were able to avoid immediate assimilation, a process which was then postponed for several generations. Because of the prevailing institutions, foreigners were somewhat restricted by law. Such restrictions were accepted, however, as natural. Thus, foreigners could not freely buy or sell or inherit real estate. They were severely punished in the case of sex crimes committed against native females.

This particular provision of Ukrainian criminal law might have been founded on the general high social position of and esteem for women in Ukraine since ancient times. The important role of foreigners in the economic growth of the country, especially in its commerce and industry, cannot be overemphasized. They contributed skill, labor, and capital to the economy. At first the Iranians and Greeks introduced their progressive business skills and spiritual values. In the later period, the Poles, Germans, and Jews concentrated in their hands the major part of the trade and commerce in Galicia and Volhinia. These foreigners brought into Ukraine their Western civilization; they were one of the channels through which Western culture conquered Ukraine.

The Issue of Feudalism in Old Ukraine. The older Ukrainian historians paid little attention to the issue of feudalism in the *Rus'* state. The whole question did not seem to them important enough nor worthy of any detailed analysis. And if they came across the problem, as did Kostomarov, Hrushevsky, or Kluchevskii, they simply denied the existence of feudalism in medieval Ukraine.

Modern Soviet historians, however, take a diametrically opposite stand in this matter. After accepting dialectical materialism and the Marxist economic interpretation of history, they had no other choice but to admit uncritically a feudal era in Ukraine-*Rus'*. Thus according to Marxism, the permanent, somewhat standard, evolutionary changes of the "mode of production" from a slave to a feudal society, and feudalism to capitalism have been going on for centuries. Following indisputably the Marxist historical pattern, the Soviet scholars did everything possible to gather evidence of the feudal character of the Kievan economy and social constitution. The compulsory nature of that official Marxist interpretation of the medieval history of *Rus'* was corroborated by Lyashchenko, when he opened the relevant chapter of his celebrated work with a quotation from Marx: ". . . the character of the evolving feudal conditions and the emergence of the feudal state were a natural result of the primitive organization of the Norse conquests—the vassalage without fief relations, and fiefs consisting solely of tribute!"[12] And in another place, Lyashchenko continued: "Marx dates the beginning of the feudal period of the Kievan state, with its accompanying dispersion and feudal wars, from the middle of the eleventh century. . . . Naturally this process of assimilation consumed more than one century."[13] To prove the presence of feudal characteristics in the *Rus'* economy and society was considered by the Soviet scholars as a most important task of a dogmatic nature, which would establish the validity of Marx's and Lenin's historical speculations as applied to Eastern Europe. For the communist student it was an article of faith.

From the point of view of objectively well established historical studies such as those of Vernadsky and Florinsky, the existence of feudalism in the Kievan Empire seems to be at least a very dubious matter. Particularly excellent is Vernadsky's treatment of the subject in his "Feudalism in Russia" and "On Economic and Social Feudalism in Kievan Russia."[14] After having analyzed the concept of "pure" feudalism, he showed that feudalism in the strict sense of the term, "a manorial system with the restricted status of the peasants, . . . and a complete fusion of the political and economic authority," did not exist in medieval Ukraine at all. What the Marxists called "feudalism" was not feudalism, but was a form of natural economy with the essentially Ukrainian system of developing appanage.

The condition of the free peasantry in Kiev with full property rights as well as the absence of any elaborate social ladder of vassal relationships denied the existence of West European forms of feudalism in medieval Ukraine. Furthermore, the authority of the grand *boyars* over the tenant peasants, who were the minority of the peasant class, was still less comprehensive than that of the Western barons. And finally, there was in the Kievan Empire no developed pattern of a fusion of the political and economic authorities. *Rus'ka Pravda* permitted individual landownership to the peasant as late as the twelfth century, and the Kievan latifundia, as Vernadsky pointed out, did not prove *per se* the presence of feudalism.

As far as the general characteristics of the Kievan social and economic constitution were concerned, they might be described as a specifically Ukrainian, early commercial capitalism, combined with an agriculturally motivated appanage. Mavor supplied the following definition of the institution of appanage: "Subjection to it was voluntary. If one who served a prince chose to do so, he could leave his service and enter the service of another prince without forfeiting his estate, if he had any. There was thus no relation between the prince and his subjects corresponding to a feudal relation. Their relations were not obligatory, but were the result of consent, and they could be broken at will."[15] And then, the economy of medieval Ukraine was no longer based exclusively on agriculture, for it had become a semi-commercialized economy of money, with advanced credit and marketing, and with the essentially capitalistic institutions of individualism and freedom, in both large-scale and small-scale enterprises, as much in farming as in trading. Feudalism was never like this. Historians agree in this respect rather on the terms "early capitalism" or "pre-capitalism." Furthermore, the flexibility of the Kievan class structure would argue against the feudal theory. So far, the Kievan economic system was more advanced than that of its Western European counterparts.

On the other hand, the prevalence of slavery in the Kievan state indicated a certain backwardness in its social relations, being in this respect not much further advanced than a primitive slave society. In the West at that time slavery was no longer known. This mixed but certainly not feudal character of the Kievan economy is explained by the situation of Ukraine as a borderland between the Occident and the Orient, influenced by both Eastern and Western institutions, and particularly by the Arabic and Byzantine, which clashed against each other on Ukrainian soil. Nevertheless, feudalism was beginning to develop in medieval Ukraine. The Mongol invasion interrupted the process, but it resumed in the Galician-Volhinian state where, under the impact of Western civilization, feudalism took on much more definite forms. The Polish and Hungarian patterns especially influenced the feudal evolution of Ukrainian society. This evolution continued in the political framework of the Lithuanian-*Rus'* state and the Polish-Lithuanian commonwealth of the fourteenth and fifteenth centuries, parallel with the liquidation of slavery in westernized Ukraine.

1. M. Vladimirskii-Budanov, *Khristomatia po istorii russkavo prava*, Petrograd-Kiev, 1908, Vol. I, p. 23; also, V. Kluchevskii, *Istoria soslovii v Rossii*, Moscow, 1913, pp. 41-48.
2. V. Yaniv, "Suspilni vestrvy," *Entsyklopedia ukrainoznavstva*, Munich, 1949, Vol. I, Book III, p. 1137.
3. The boyardom of the Kievan-Galician period was rather plutocratic than aristocratic; hence the descendents of the clergy, merchants or even peasantry could become *boyars,* the nobles, if they only managed to acquire considerable wealth. M. Chubaty, *Ohlad istorii ukrainskoho prava*, Munich, 1947, pp. 51-56; G. Vernadsky and M. Karpovich, *A History of Russia,* Vol. II, *Kievan Russia,* New Haven, 1951, pp. 137-140.
4. M. Hrushevsky, *Istoria Ukrainy-Rusy*, New York, 1956, Vol. III, pp. 316-317.
5. Kluchevskii, *op. cit.,* p. 49.
6. Chubaty, *op. cit.,* p. 54-55.
7. Hrushevsky, *op. cit.,* Vol. I, pp. 601-624.
8. Kluchevskii, *ibid.,* pp. 55-60.
9. *Loc. cit.,* p. 58.

10. Especially in the second half of the eleventh century, the princely *izgoii* became a very grave social and political problem in Kievan *Rus'*. As a result of the seniority principle, established by Prince Yaroslav the Wise, at least nine junior princes of the Ruryk house were immediately deprived of their lands, and of course, they tried all available means in order to reestablish themselves, thereby creating futher political chaos. Compare: N. Polonska-Vasylenko, *Istoria Ukrainy,* Munich, 1972, Vol. I, pp. 133-147.

11. *The Hipatian Chronicle,* under the date 1259, related that Danylo of Galicia invited the Poles and the Germans to settle in Kholm, the newly erected town: J. Abraham, *Organizacia kościola lacińskiego na Rusi,* Lviv, 1904, Vol. I, pp. 91 and others.

12. K. Marx, *Secrete Diplomatic History of the Eighteenth Century,* London, 1899, pp. 76-77.

13. Lyashchenko quotes Marx, and dogmatically accepted feudalism in Kievan *Rus',* but he still makes some reservations, basing his views on the reports of the *Laurentian Chronicle:* P. Lyashchenko, *History of the National Economy of Russia,* New York, 1949, pp. 96-99.

14. G. Vernadsky, "Feudalism in Russia," *Speculum,* 14 (1939), pp. 300-323; also the same, *A History of Russia,* Vol. II, *Kievan Russia,* as quoted above, pp. 163-172 and 209-213. An opposite view: B. Grekov, "Rabstvo i feodalism v drevniei Rusi," *Academy of the History of Material Culture,* 1932, Issue 86.

15. J. Mavor, *An Economic History of Russia,* London, 1914, Vol. I, pp. 23-24.

CHAPTER TEN

ECONOMIC LIFE; THE EXTRACTIVE AND MANUFAC-TURING INDUSTRIES

The over-all economic development — Hunting and Fishing — Cattle raising — Agriculture — Mining — Towns in Ukraine — Crafts — Metallurgy, carpentry, and the construction industry — Ceramics, textile, tanning and the fur business.

The over-all economic development of Kievan Ukraine did not start from nothing. The previous period had already witnessed the development of great economic traditions in all areas, especially in agriculture and trading. This high level of material culture was the result of commercial intercourses with advanced foreign cultures such as those of the Arabs and the Greeks. The political unification of Ukraine by Kiev into a single, powerful state organization also had its economic impact. It brought together areas diversified and geographically specialized but richly endowed with natural resources, diversified climatic zones, numerous minerals, fertile soil, and many navigable rivers teeming with fish.

The Kievan Empire, especially in its early period of political centralization, encouraged the successful growth of a large-scale national economy based on a territorial division of labor, specialization of production by the various provinces, and the mutual exchange of their products. Vast southern steppes, producing meat, hides, and grain, exchanged their produce for furs, wax, and honey of the northern forests. The small-scale tribal economies of the Polianians, Derevlianians, Dulibians, Khorvatians, Siverianians, Tiverians, and Ulichians merged into a progressive and wealthy national economy.

The growth of this national economy was also facilitated by the single and fairly unified legal system of *Rus'*, which received expression in the code of *Rus'ka Pravda,* and by princely legislation, especially that of Volodymyr the Great, Yaroslav the Wise, and Volodymyr Monomakh. It is true that the historian Sergeievich doubted the practical validity of *Pravda*. According to him, in that primitive era nobody actually cared to read the code, because only a few knew how to read at all. Therefore, he continued, the influence of the code on the development of legal concepts and relations was very limited, or perhaps even nil. But he failed to stress one significant circumstance, namely, that the codification was rather a written compilation of the binding principles of the customary common law, with only a few original contributions of individual princes and codifying authors.[1] And as a document of the common law, *Rus'ka Pravda* doubtlessly did have a unifying effect.

Within the framework of the Kievan economy an important evolutionary process was accomplished. The individual tribal economies had been based primarily on hunting, fishing, and cattle raising. Although agriculture was fairly developed at that time, it was not the leading industry. Between the tenth and thirteenth centuries, however, the Ukrainian economy became decidedly agricultural-commercial, while the extractive industries of hunting and fishing were reduced to subsidiary and secondary roles. These industries retained their dominant roles only in the southern and eastern borderlands of the empire. Moreover, within the political framework of the *Rus'* state, the crystallization of the early Kievan capitalism based on money, credit exchange, and developed commercial activities had been accomplished, and enormous wealth accumulated. The riches of these princes frequently amazed the foreign visitors. For instance, the Nestor chronicle related under the date of 1075 the wondering reflections of the envoy of Emperor Henry IV about the princely treasures he had chanced to see. It was expressly pointed out before that the principles of economic individualism achieved a fairly mature form in the Kievan-Galician era, being considerably more advanced than in Western Europe. The Roman and Byzantine social, legal, and economic institutions certainly had a great impact on the growth of the Kievan economic constitution, especially the acceptance of Christianity by Kiev.

The Byzantine influences in Ukraine continuously grew in strength and aggressiveness. However, the Greek *Nomacanons* and Greek legal concepts, which could be directly traced back to the ancient Roman individualistic legal and economic institutions, had a much older tradition in Ukraine than the year 988, the date of her Christianization. Ukraine of the tenth and thirteenth centuries was in fact a northern borderland of the Byzantine-Roman civilization, and as a result it was the Roman and Byzantine capitalistic forms which molded the Ukrainian economy. Concerning this Vernadsky said, ". . . we are obliged to connect Kievan Russia sociologically not only with a type of commercial empire—that of a 'capitalistic' formation based on slavery."[2] The democratic constitution of the Orthodox Church also contributed to the capitalism of Kievan Rus', while in the West the more democratic constitution of the Orthodox Church also contributed to the capitalism of Kievan Rus', while in the West the more absolutist constitution of the Roman Catholic Church was instead conducive to the growth of feudalism.

The forms of business organization in the Kievan state were also advanced far beyond the simple partnership. The "merchant associations" in Kiev and Novgorod rather reminded one of modern limited partnerships or corporations, motivated exclusively by profit, and considerably preceding in time similar West

European forms of business organization. Still another advanced feature of Kievan economy was social legislation, including protection of the poor, orphans, and the widows, and regulation of the interest rate, which could easily have developed into a form of exploitation. The feature of ''absentee capitalism'' might have occurred in Kiev, but the princes, Volodymyr Monomakh in particular, made an attempt to curb possible abuse.

Hunting and Fishing. Throughout the entire Kievan-Galician period, hunting and fishing continued to be very important industries, although at this time they were relegated to a secondary position, following agriculture and trade.

As a result of socio-economic evolution, the Ukrainian Slavs, after having undergone phases of hunting, fishing, and cattle raising, attained, during the Kievan period (from the tenth to the thirteenth century) and the Galician era (from the twelfth to the fourteenth century), an agricultural-commercial economy. This important fact was stressed in the previous sections of this historical analysis. But, traditionally, even at that time, all social classes—royalty, boyardom, townspeople, and peasantry—were vitally interested in hunting and fishing as a supplementary way of earning a living. As far as hunting was concerned, animals were still abundant in all the forest and steppe regions. As a matter of fact, the same kinds of small and large animals, such as squirrels, martens, foxes, lynxes, sables, beavers, deer, wolves, bears, bulls, and ureoxes, began to disappear in the sixteenth century as a result of indiscriminate hunting practices.

Hunting provided food, and also hides and fur for boots and clothing. Fur and hides were also important articles of trade and a medium of paying taxes. Fur, especially, was exported from Ukraine, in the Kievan-Galician period, to every part of the civilized world. Large-scale hunting projects were also organized to acquire necessary reserves of food and animal raw materials to supply warriors during their campaign. Hunting techniques improved only slightly in contrast to the pre-Kievan era of tribal economies. The common people, who produced actually the great portion of their income from hunting, used old and traditional methods such as setting up traps, spreading nets and snares between the trees to catch small beasts and birds, and hunting with bows and arrows, knives, hatchets, and spears. But the royalty and boyardom developed a new approach to hunting, holding regular seasonal hunts, employing professional whips and falconers hired from among the slaves and peasants to scare the animals and to drive them directly against the armed hunters, and using properly trained hawks, falcons and dogs. The princes sometimes raised hounds for their favorite sport-like occupation.

Hunting having been mainly a way of earning a living, the institution of the professional hunter developed. Hunting was also a favorite sport and a form of elegant social activity for the upper classes. Great occasions, like the birth of a first son or receiving state honors and offices, were celebrated by hunts. Rare and distinguished guests were always honored by great hunting expeditions for large animals such as bears, bulls, and ureoxes. By way of example, the chronicle relates a grand hunting expedition organized by Prince Yaroslav of Galicia to honor Andronikos, the Byzantinian heir to the Emperor's crown. Prince Volodymyr Monomakh regarded hunting as a most noble occupation for princes and their sons, comparable to that of making war.[3] Not infrequently, female royalty also participated in the sport. Because hunting was generally thought to be a noble occupation, the children of the aristocrats were trained from a very early age to appreciate and to master the art of hunting. Skill and courage exhibited during the hunt were praised highly and esteemed almost as acts of heroism.

Although fishing was relegated to the lower classes, fishing rights were also owned by the *boyary,* monasteries, and religious orders, and were carefully protected. With the introduction of Christianity, the demand for fish considerably increased because of lenten and other abstinence regulations of the Church. But apart from that, fish was generally consumed. Fishermen were a separate occupational group. They fished on rivers, lakes, and the sea, to get food not so much for their own consumption, but rather to sell to others. Their settlements extended along the river banks. The Galician fishermen undertook fishing trips down the river Dniester, as far as the Black Sea and the mouth of the river. Danube.[4] Their fishing tools were nets, harpoons, and angling rods. Angling and barring the small rivers with wooden pails were practiced by the common people in order to supplement their usual diet with fish, while the commercial fisherman preferred boats, nets, and harpoons. In the northern areas, Volhinia, Polisia, and Chernihiv, where the poverty of the soil required the people to resort to occupations other than farming, fishing was vital as a means of subsistence. The abundance of their rivers pointed to fishing as a way of making a living.

The economic importance of hunting and fishing in the Kievo-Galician society is proven by the comprehensive legislation for the protection of the private hunting and fishing rights of the princes, *boyars,* monasteries, towns, villages, and other individual owners. Hunting and fishing areas were regulated by law as early as the tenth century under Princess Olha. Then, *Rus'ka Pravda* provided penalties for the violators of private hunting and fishing rights, or for destroying and damaging hunting and fishing equipment, such as nets, snares, and traps. Monasteries were most anxious to protect their fishing rights, since fish was a highly important item in the diet of monks. On the other hand, princes were also interested in protecting their hunting areas and hunting regalias. Where a specific law or princely grant could not safeguard hunting and fishing rights they were regulated by private agreements and arrangements.

Cattle Raising. Slavonic linguistic studies confirm the ancient raising of cows, oxen, calves, sheep, hogs, horses, mules, donkeys, dogs, and even camels. This traditional industry, the origin of which goes back as far as the remote Indo-European era, developed successfully throughout the Kievan-Galician period, but its secondary status in the country's economy was self-evident. Numerous fowl, such as chickens, geese, ducks, pigeons, and swans, were also known in the pre-Kievan era, but they did not come into wide use until considerably later. According to Hrushevsky, this did not happen until the Kievan era or the period immediately preceeding it.[5] Cats were the first domestic animals to be introduced into the Ukranian household; they were unknown before the historical period. Ibn-Fadlan, the Arab traveller-merchant, related about an extensive cattle-raising and bird-raising among the Slavs, and Ibn-Dasta said that the Slavs "kept hogs as they were sheep," by which he meant in great numbers and under the open sky.[6]

Cattle and fowl production was mainly for food; very few were sold. No cattle exportation, but rather horse importation, was reported by the historical documents of the time. The archaeological excavations proved for the ancient period, and the *Laurentian* and *Hipatian Chronicles* for the Kievan-Galician period, a very great consumption of meat, such as lamb, pork, beef, veal, poultry, and even horse, and of milk and milk products, like butter, buttermilk, eggs, and various kinds of cheese. Besides, hides and wool, as animal by-products, were widely used for shoe and clothing manufacturing within individual households, and were also sold in the domestic market. Horses, oxen, and mules were widely used as draft-animals in their field work.

The chronicle, relating, as of the year 1103, the preparations for a large-scale joint expedition of the Ukrainian princes against the Cumans, pointed out also that the dukes discussed a proper timing for their military expedition, planning to arrange matters in such a way as to avoid depriving the peasants of workhorses. Furthermore, Prince Volodymyr of Volhinia, before his death in 1288, ordered his horses to be distributed among the poor peasants, to assist them in working their farms more efficiently.

Such specialized occupations of herdsmen as shepherds, cowboys, horse-herdsmen, and swine-herdsmen existed during that period. They offered their services to the princes, boyars, and village communities as well as to individual peasants of the higher income brackets. The princes and grand *boyars* often owned large cattle and horse breeding estates. These sometimes included thousands of mares and stallions. No doubt, horse-breeding was of great military importance in furnishing mounts for the knights and warriors.

When cavalry was needed, the Ukrainian princes hired the Norman horseback warriors if they were unable to furnish enough horses for their own troops. Special kinds of horses were imported from the Cumans, the Torkman nomads, and the Hungarians. The administration of the princely horse-breeding estates was in the hands of special officials, *koniushi,* and the menial work there was done by specially trained slaves and hired employees, *koniukhy.*

As mentioned previously, the princes were also vitally interested in breeding special kinds of hunting hounds, while dogs were customary in the households of the *boyars* and commoners. Property rights with respect to horse breeding and cattle raising were regulated and protected by law. For example, the code of *Rus'ka Pravda* provided rules for cattle-trading and penalties for cattle and horse theft.

Along with cattle, horse, and fowl production, bee-keeping continued to be important to the economy. It produced wax and honey for domestic uses and for export. Wooden beehives were built in the form of pitchers, or were arranged in the holes of old trees in the forests. Bee-keeping was a separate occupation, although some peasants and even some townspeople kept bees to supplement their incomes. *Rus'ka Pravda* and other documents often mentioned bee-keeping and provided regulations and penalties for violations of hive rights, such as damaging hives, stealing honey and wax, and destroying the conventional ownership signs. The princes often kept their exclusive rights on beehives in the forests, or made grants to the monasteries, which were extremely interested in apiculture.

In general, the monks were good bee-keepers, since honey and wax were important to the communal life of the religious orders. Apiculture was a profitable business because everybody, from the prince to the slave, ate honey and drank honey-drink and burned candles. Moreover, honey and wax were the most important Kievan exports. They were generally accepted as money. The state even accepted them as the means of payment of taxes and duties. The commercial significance of honey and wax from Ukraine was stressed by Sviatoslav, the Kievan prince. According to the *Laurentian Chronicle,* Sviatoslav planned to conquer and to transfer his capital from Kiev to Pereslav on the Danube, which was a commercial center at that time. There the Greeks sold gold, textiles, fruits, and vines, the Czechs and Hungarians supplied silver and horses, and *Rus'* supplied honey, wax, fur, and slaves. The same chronicle again mentioned honey, wax, and fur as the gifts of Prince Ihor to the Byzantine envoy.[7] Although of secondary importance like fishing and hunting, apiculture must be regarded as highly significant to medieval Ukrainian society.

Agriculture was indisputedly the foundation of the national economy, and by the same token, the major source of the national income. In the course of the tenth and eleventh centuries, the Ukrainian peasant and tradesman still penetrated new regions, having pushed their frontiers even further into the southern and eastern steppe borderlands at the price of continuous frictions with the steppe nomads, the Cumans and Torkmans. Nevertheless, the Slavonic ethnic stock was in this area in the earliest times and its plows conquered new acres of unoccupied land and absorbed it into the national territory of *Rus'*.

In the twelfth century, however, circumstances changed fundamentally and unfavorably. The southeastern colonization had not only been halted by the opposition of the nomads, but some land in this area was gradually lost to them. The Ukrainian ethnic element began a slow retreat to the north. The "black soil" of the fertile steppes grew scarcer, as they moved north and west to Kiev, Cherniv, Polisia, Volhinia, and Galicia, where they introduced their form of intensive colonization. Because only poorer soil was available in this region, farming techniques had to change. Cultivation became more intensive.

The gradual retreat of the Ukrainian people from the southeastern borderlands also had its influences on their internal political structure. Civil wars among the individual princes and separate branches of the Ruryk dynasty wasted much of the national energy which might have been used to retain the southern regions. Yet the historical fact is that the bulk of this population movement from the southern steppes to the northern forests was confined to Ukrainian territory. Russian historians, such as Pogodin and Kluchevskii, were not justified in deducing from this migration a theory of mass migration of the population of Ukraine to the northern Russian principalities of Suzdal, Rostov, and Vladimir as it was pointed out before.

During the Kievan-Galician period various kinds of grain were cultivated throughout the country. Among these were wheat, rye oats, millet, barley, spelt, and even buckwheat. Winter and spring seeds were also to some extent developed at that time. Farming in the north differed somewhat from that in the south. In the south, because of soil and climate, the principal grains were wheat, buckwheat, and spelt. In the northern regions rye, oats, and barley were the leading crops. This distribution of crops is deduced from the chronicles. They relate, for example, that Prince Volodymyr of Volhinia introduced in the city of Berest a tax on oats and rye, presumably because these grains were the leading farm products in his northern principality. Prince Danylo of Galicia, on the other hand, supplied Prince Mykhailo of Chernihiv with wheat to help him and his people in time of distress, wheat being the chief farm product in the Galician-Polodian districts.[8]

Moreover, farm technology in the north differed from that employed in the south. In the southern steppe areas there was much fertile and easily accessible soil, permitting extensive farming without hard labor. The growing population in the forest areas, due to both natural increase and to the continuous influx of harassed southerners, resulted in an increasing shortage of land, forcing upon the people both the hard work of clearing more and more inaccessible wooded regions, and the introduction of the two-field and three-field systems. Moreover, the poor soils in the northern sections demanded intensive and regular plowing and fertilizing. Actually, the political developments of the floating frontiers sponsored a gradual progress in agricultural technology

in the politically safer northern regions, and resulted in the de-
population and economic primitivism of the politically unsafe
steppes.

In the northern sections, such as Polisia and Volhinia, there
were found some iron mines, resulting in the gradual adoption of
iron farming implements, or at least, implements with some iron
parts. Among these were the iron plow, iron hoe, harrow, shovel,
fork, sickle, and scythe. Ancient documents time and again refer
to these implements, throwing considerable light on the farm
techniques of the era.

Oxen and horses were introduced and extensively used as draft
animals in the field and forest work, providing at the same time
animal manure, now more widely used for fertilizer. These im-
provements in agricultural technology resulted in enormous agricultural production. The chronicles and other written documents, such as the literary creations of the time, afford ample
evidence of the huge stores of grain available all over the country,
and the large-scale exports of grain, especially to Novgorod the
Great, the Suzdal-Vladimir principalities, Lithuania, and the
German cities and principalities. For example, the Novgorodians
suffered famine in 1141 when no exports of grain arrived from
Ukraine because of bad weather. In the year 1270 the Yatvingians, a tribe in southern Lithuania, having suffered a famine,
sent their envoys to the Galician-Volhinian prince asking for grain
and food. Volodymyr of Volhinia dispatched grain by way of the
rivers Buh and Narev to assist the Yatvingians, but the shipment
was attacked and robbed by the Poles, and never reached its
destination. This incident resulted eventually in a Ukrainian-
Polish war.

Lay of Ihor's Host, Patericon, chronicles, and other literary
works from the time of the Kievan-Galician era supplied abundant information about the agricultural economy of medieval
Ukraine: ordinary field work, implements used, the kinds of crops
raised, plowing, sowing, harvesting, threshing, and even
methods of crop processing, such as storage, milling, and bread
baking; the use of free and slave labor, as well as the growing

usage of draft animals. This information not only indicates how important farming was—that it was indisputably the main and leading industry of the Kievan-Galician economy—but it also shows clearly that Ukraine was the center of agricultural progress of the time.

The continuous although slow progress in medieval farming in Ukraine has been admitted by Aristov, Kulisher, Grekov, Bahalii, and other students of the socio-economic history of Eastern Europe, and only this progress could explain the agricultural opulence of the country. Compared to our standards, of course, agricultural productivity was rather low, but compared to that of the Russian north at that time it was quite high. As Lyashchenko rightly said, "The technique was indeed primitive [here he meant the whole European East] but in some districts, along the Dnieper in particular (Ukraine), it was quite advanced for its time."

On the other hand, Ukrainian agriculture frequently suffered grave losses in productivity because of natural catastrophes like droughts, overabundant rainfalls, floods, and excessive cold. Often local famines followed such events. The *Patericon* of the Kievan monastery and the tales about the lives of the saints mention the so-called "hungry years." Since the tenth century, locusts also plagued the southern regions, leaving nothing behind but hungry people.

The cultivation of gardens and orchards progressed in Kievan-Galician times in an impressive way. Among the vegetables, onions, garlic, peas, beans, carrots, parsley, lentils, cabbage, turnips, beets, pumpkins, and poppies were continually cultivated. Apples, pears, plums and cherries were the leading fruits. At that time a modest beginning was made in the cultivation of nuts and grapes. Gardens and orchards were developed primarily in the vicinity of large cities, such as Kiev and Halych. That the professional gardeners had their own organizations with their own leaders and laws indicated the relatively advanced standing of the profession as well as the economic importance of the business.

Vernadsky was rather dubious about the considerable development of gardening in Kiev, but numerous references to gardening and raising vegetables made by the above mentioned *Patericon,* the story of the saints of the Kievan monastery, seem to disprove these doubts.[9] The monasteries were especially interested in gardening and the monks were true pioneers in the intensive and skilled work required. On the *boyar* estates and the peasant farms, cultivation of vegetables and fruits was also widely known, a tradition inherited from the ancient era. Prince Danylo developed in the new city of Kholm a beautiful garden, the chronicle relates, one which displayed the advanced state of horticulture in his realm. Vegetables and fruit were important to the diets of the royalty, boyardom, and the wealthier townspeople and peasantry.

The growth of agriculture as well as the wealth derived from it in Kiev and Galicia was facilitated by the system of private enterprise. Although some authors, like Rozhkov, denied that the peasant in the Kievan state held any extensive rights to private property, such a view seems to lack any justification, since the code of *Rus'ka Pravda* and numerous copies of deeds give ample and sufficient proof of the prevalence of such rights. In these deeds the boundaries of the private estates and landholdings are described and their unilateral violation prohibited. *Rus'ka Pravda* provided penalties for plowing a field beyond its boundaries. Certain historical references imply the prevalence of private ownership in farming for all East Slavic tribes as early as the tenth century. For instance, *Lavrentiivska litopys'* (chronicle) relates for Princess Olha's time that "the Derevlianians make their own fields and their own lands," and *Ipatiivska litopys'* says that the Viatichians pay the tribute from the plow. Of course, farms differed greatly in size in the Kievan period, since the tradition of private property was old. Ample time had already passed for differentiated skill and industry to result in considerable differences in individual land holdings. The princely estates were huge, including many villages and thousands of acres of land. The estates of the great *boyars* were also large, while the holdings of the country gentry and the monasteries were somewhat smaller. The peasant farms were even smaller.

The princely estates already had at that time an elaborate management, being divided into a number of administrative units under separate management and separate officials. Special personnel were in charge of the different parts of the business. Some officials supervised the field work, others cattle and horse raising, still others were in charge of sheepherding, gardening, and orchard cultivation. These special officials were generally called *tivuny,* and were often elevated from the slave class. Cattle raising was often in the hands of herdsmen of Turkish extraction, as Vernadsky indicated. The manual work and the tilling of the fields were done either by slaves or the half-free, of whom there were hundreds on the princely and *boyar* lands. This work was also done by hired, indentured laborers. Some portions of land meadows and woods were leased by the princes and grand *boyars* to the tenant-peasants. Sometimes the half-free, *zakupy,* were also made farm tenants.

Grain was stored either in the fields or in the barns, or in holes in the ground, properly arranged and protected. Hay was mowed and stored for the feeding of animals. The peasant farm was managed by the family, cultivated primarily by free labor and the extensive use of draft animals. Rarely did the peasants store their grain and hay in barns.

Initially, the bulk of agricultural production was done by free people on small farms. Later, as Hrushevsky has explained, the free peasant declined in importance because of the attrition due to continuous civil wars. Peasants could not survive these conditions for long, and either they voluntarily gave up their farm ownership and accepted tenant relationship together with boyar protection, or through spoliation and abuse by the nobles, peasants were forced off their farms and gradually reduced to the status of half-free or slaves. This phenomenon accounts for the growing importance of unfree labor in agriculture, on the one hand, and the rise of semi-feudal relations and the decline of the traditional farm system, on the other. The peasants could not endure requisitions, ruin, disturbances in field work, and other hardships of war, while the latifundia system could progress only if cheap labor were secured to cultivate the enormous land areas.

War supplied slaves in the form of war prisoners and impoverished peasants and half-free who had to adjust their labor to the extensive farm lands of the now depopulated country. At the end of the Kievan-Galician period, even the institution of the *glaebae adscripti* peasants appeared in Ukraine. These soil-bound peasants were a result of military developments and the wars with the Cumans, while in western Ukraine (Galician and Volhinia) the peasant was bound to the soil as a consequence of semi-feudal institutions copied from Hungary and Poland. Thus, the latifundia system slowly replaced the peasant farm in Ukraine's agriculture, but this development should be regarded, from the historical-philosophical point of view, as the beginning of the socio-economic processes of the next period of the evolution of Ukrainian agriculture. It was never an essential feature of the Kievan-Galician economy as some historians have claimed.

Mining. While the processing of mineral resources was fairly well developed in the Kievan and Galician eras, and considerable quantities of ores were imported for that purpose, mining occupied a modest place in the economy of the times. It was limited primarily to the extraction of iron ore for the manufacture of arms and tools, the extraction of clay for ceramic production, and the mining of salt for direct consumption. Mining of ores is directly related to the metallurgic industries, but the discussion of the latter will be reserved for one of the next sections. Here only a brief description of the medieval Ukrainian mining and smelting business will be given.

In the swamps and woods of northern Ukraine, in Polisia and Volhinia, there were abundant reserves of near-surface iron ores which could be mined by primitive techniques. Archeological excavations supplied ample evidence of extensive iron extraction by the Derevlianians and the Polianians since early historic times. Certainly, during the Kievan period, mining and smelting continued, and perhaps, progressed. The rich southern reserves of iron and other metallic ores in the steppes, however, were not yet accessible to the early Slavs for two reasons. First of all, those regions were either occupied or continually harassed by the Cumans and other nomads so that no industry could emerge there. Secondly, the Slavs at that time were not yet able to master the method of extracting the rich but deep veins of ore. For two reasons the iron industry was highly important to the Ukrainian Slavs. In the first place, they could produce arms and weapons for their needs, and, second, they could manufacture indispensable farm implements and household utensils from their own iron. Extraction of iron ore was done by the peasants, as well as on royal, *boyar,* and ecclesiastical domains. Proof of the existence of foundries and smithies is to be found in the chronicles and other early literature and in archeological discoveries.[10] Special artisans, miners, boilermen, and smelters were employed in the business of extracting and smelting.

Salt mining prevailed in the pre-Carpathian districts of Galicia, from which the entire Ukraine was supplied with salt. When during a civil war in 1097 the Galician rulers prohibited any export of that commodity to the other provinces of the country, Kiev and the rest of Ukraine suffered a shortage of salt, and were compelled to import it from the Crimean Peninsula and the Don-Volga region in a much larger quantity than before.

Clay was extracted and processed in various regions of the Kievan and Galician states, to produce pots, jugs, dishes, and other ceramic ware for the home. The domestic extraction of all of the above minerals, especially of iron ore, as well as the considerable importation of such metals as copper, bronze, lead, silver, and gold, constituted the basis for the growth of medieval Ukrainian metallurgy, and must be regarded as a very important component of the material culture of the Kievan-Galician society.

Towns in Ukraine. It has been mentioned earlier that archaelogical excavations disclosed the existence of hundreds of fortified ''towns'' in ancient Ukraine. There are convincing indications that about 450 towns existed in the Kievan province, some 350 in Volhinia, and over 100 in Galicia. Since all these ''towns'' were situated in the northern forest belt of Ukraine, these forest areas were really the original cells of ethnical growth as well as the most densely populated part of the country.

From there, colonization was usually started in an attempt to conquer by sword and plow the southern and eastern steppes which were richly endowed with natural resources. Strategic and commercial considerations produced in the course of centuries these magnificent fortified towns. On the one hand, the ancient inhabitants of Ukraine—the Scythians, Roxolianians, Goths, Sarmatians, Antes, and later the Slavs—desired to protect themselves by erecting fortified places against the continuous threat of repeated surprise attacks by the steppe nomads. On the other hand, they also established commercial centers in the borderlands and on the trade routes, chiefly along the main and navigable rivers, in order to take full advantage of the location of the Ukrainian country as the crossroad of Eurasia. Erecting towns was instinctive for almost all the races and tribes which populated Ukraine at various times in its earliest periods. Some towns, like Kiev, were ancient, the origin of which might be traced back as far as the Gothic period, or even earlier. Other towns were the creation of the Ukrainian Slav, and the chronicles enumerate some of the more important, such as Cherven, Red-Towns, in general, Turiv, Iskorosten, Lubech, Peresechen, Chernihiv, and Peremyshl, although the exact date of their establishment cannot be ascertained. They doubtlessly originated as the political centers of Slavic tribal organizations. When Ukraine was still organized into tribes, the townspeople, as the common people in general, were an important political factor of a democratic constitution. The wealth of the townspeople contributed considerably toward their significant political position. But the growth of the Kievan Empire and the power of the first rulers of the Ruryk house reduced tribal particularism and the political role of the townspeople, making the people's meetings, *viche,* almost meaningless.

Then, Ruryk, Volodymyr the Great, Yaroslav the Wise and Danylo of Galicia in particular, as well as some other princes to a lesser degree, initiated a third phase in Ukrainian urban history. They began to erect new towns along the river banks or on the traditional trade routes, or in places strategically favorable from a commercial or political point of view. Frequently small towns and villages expanded into large cities. Soon the princely administrative apparatus, following this trend, moved into such cities, making them the capitals of local administration. Thus, the *Laurentian Chronicle* related, in the year 988, that Volodymyr the Great "began to erect towns along the rivers Desna, Vorskla, Trubezha, Sula and Stuhna."[11] Volodymyr's son, Prince Yaroslav, emulated his father by establishing, among other towns, Yuriiv (later called Dorpat and then, Tartu) in Estonia. All these towns and fortresses were customarily located in the borderlands of the Empire for two reasons: first, to protect the nation against the permanent threat of foreign attack, especially against the steppe nomads in the east, and secondly to create commercial centers for trading with neighboring lands and peoples. Still a third reason might be added with respect to the Kievan princes, namely to strengthen in this way their central authority in newly acquired territories.

Wherever necessary new towns were established as the sites of the Kievan deputies and of the military government. It was done in order to bind those areas more closely to the Kievan capital and the Ruryk dynasty. During the second half of the tenth century and during the eleventh century, the political importance of the city diminished somewhat, and it did not matter any more whether it was an old center of the tribal or clan organization or a new administrative unit of the central government. The democratic principle of the people's meeting was greatly weakened at the same time by the overwhelming authority of the Kievan grand princes; hence the town lost its original significance.

Economically, however, the town experienced a new growth under the protection of the centralized and pacifying rule of Kiev. Commercial activities continually expanded. Relative political peace, and the opportunity of a large-scale interprovincial and international trade added extensively to the growth of the medieval city, and, as a direct result of these developments, the townspeople accumulated wealth and enjoyed relative prosperity. Savitsky made an interesting study of economic fluctuations in the Kievan state, and, on the whole, it seems that between 980 and 1092—throughout the era of Kievan supremacy—there were approximately 22 years of depression, and the rest, some 90 years, were prosperity, near prosperity, or revival.

Later, in the course of the twelfth century, these conditions were reversed. After 1092, depressions became longer and more frequent, and their ratio to periods of prosperity prior to 1237 was 50 years of depression and 70 years of relative prosperity.[12] Obviously, the pattern of business cycles in the Kievan Empire was determined by political developments. Political growth resulted in a prosperous economy; political decline initiated an economic depression. The reigns of Volodymyr the Great, Yaroslav the Wise, Volodymyr Monomakh, and Mstyslav in the eleventh and the first half of the twelfth centuries were periods of greatest prosperity, for these were the greatest of the Kievan princes.

Growing political chaos, continuous civil war, frequent changes in the person of the ruling prince, and the decline of the central authority of the Kievan capital produced, however, a revival of the political influence of the town and the townspeople. The people's meeting began anew to play a significant role in political developments, calling and expelling the princes, acquiescing in or limiting their authority, and thus the democratic principle began to supersede the monarchic one once more. From that time on, princes were dependent upon the will of the townspeople and had to pay close attention to the recommendations of the meetings. Apropos of this fact, Kluchevskii said, "The new order of phenomena represented by these conventions between princes and *viche* continued in force throughout the eleventh and twelfth centuries, and introduced into Rus'ian political life an important change. . . . Even the suzerain of Kiev retained his throne for himself only by keeping on good terms with the local *viche*, lest his *boyary* and townsmen should address to him the reminder: 'Thou remainst here only so long as thou dost hold with the people of Kiev'."[13]

The heights in the development of the democratic institution of the *viche* (people's meeting) and of the political role of the townspeople were reached in the latter half of the twelfth century, and lasted as long as the city retained its economic position despite nationwide unfavorable political conditions. But when the deterioration of law and order became almost intolerable to merchandising in the thirteenth century, the city began to decline politically as well as economically, and soon the aristocratic *boyar* council overrode both the monarchal princely authority and the democratic people's meeting. This development was, *nota bene,* manifested most distinctly in the Galician-Volhinian state, as discussed above.

The wealth, opulence, and beauty of the medieval Ukrainian town often astonished the eyes of foreigners. The Scandinavians called Ukraine "the land of towns."[14] Tietmar of Merseburg related that the city of Kiev had 400 churches, eight market places and a very large population. Adam of Bremen who was in Kiev around 1072, said that Kiev was so prosperous that it might be considered a rival of the Greek Constantinople, and when Andrew of Hungary moved with his troops into the Galician-Volhinian territories and saw the city of Volodymyr, he exclaimed in astonishment, "Such a city I did not see even in Germany." At that time the German Empire was the mightiest in Europe.

The impressive monuments of the Ukrainian architecture of that era, the churches, monasteries and palaces, as well as city gates and bridges, definitely indicate the prosperity of these towns. St. Mary's Church of the Tithe, built by Volodymyr the Great in the years 986-996, the Cathedral of St. Sophia, the "Golden Gate," and the Church of the Annunciation, erected by Yaroslav the Wise between 1017 and 1037, the two St. Michael's monastery buildings with churches built between 1088 and 1188, and various city buildings—all in Kiev; and then, the Church of the Transfiguration of Our Lord, 1024-1036, the Church of Sts. Borys and Hlib, 1120-1123, and the Assumption Monastery erected around 1160, in Chernihiv; and the architecture of the Galician-Volhinian realm of the later epoch, such as St. Basil's Church in Ovruch, twelfth century, the Church of the Assumption in Volodymyr, erected by Mstyslaw around 1160; St. Panteleymont's Church in Halich, 1200; and the buildings and churches of the cities of Kholm and Lviv, established by Danylo and Lev of Galicia in the fourteenth century—all afford ample proof of the opulence of the fourteenth century Ukrainian town, as Doroshenko noted.

No doubt, the princes and *boyars* contributed greatly to the splendor of these buildings and towns, either by their donations or by their constructive activity, but this contribution confirms the over-all wealth of the people and the significance of the town as the center of the cultural growth of medieval Ukrainian society. When the princes built new towns they encouraged foreigners to come from all over, and to contribute their genius and skill to Ukrainian economic and cultural development.

Kluchevskii and Pokrovskii, impressed by the medieval growth of the town, called the entire period the "commercial" or "urban" *Rus'*. But they were too enthusiastic in this respect. Dovnar-Zapolski, Grekov, Lyashchenko, and some others found proof enough that the era was still a period of relative agricultural primitivism.[15] It was rather an emergence of a new capitalistic commercialism which was not permitted by political developments to ripen fully.

The town was populated largely by merchants and artisans. *Rus'ka Pravda,* however, gave but little legal protection to the artisan, a fact indicative of his low legal and social status which was comparable to that of the half-free and the hired servant. This low status might be a direct result of the artisan's low earnings and his rather modest contribution to the national income. The real economic significance of the city was based on its traditional commercial activities and its merchant class.

The medieval town was engineered in such a way as to serve both the military and commercial needs of the country. Since time immemorial the towns were erected on the banks of navigable rivers which afforded the best trade routes. If a town was not situated on a river bank, its defense was usually given first consideration. Castles and fortresses always occupied the central position, around which the town and the suburbs emerged and grew. The castle and the town buildings, churches and market places were defended by strong stone and wooden walls, sometimes running in triple parallel lines, and surrounded by earthen walls and moats. Usually several gates, strongly built and heavily defended by drawbridges, permitted ingress and egress. Outside the city gates the suburbs extended, sometimes for miles, and here lived the townspeople, merchants, and artisans. The medieval Ukrainian town afforded distinct proof of the high level attained by the contemporary construction industry.

Crafts. Having emerged from relatively scanty beginnings, restricted largely to the self-sufficient household economy, the trades developed to the level of medieval craftsmanship by the Kievan-Galician period. The code of *Rus'ka Pravda,* the *Laurentian Chronicle,* the *Hipatian Chronicle,* the Kievan *Patericon,* and the foreign written documents, such as the Emperor Constantine Prophirogenitus' *De Imperio Administrando,* and the narrations of Arabic travelers, frequently referred to various artisans and their works, while archaeological excavations confirm the existence of such trades in Kiev and Galicia. Among these were tanners, furriers, weavers, fullers, basket weavers, carpenters, woodcutters, fence-makers, builders, bridge-makers, shipwrights, saddlers, shoemakers, foundry workers and blacksmiths, coopers, jewelers, fur dressers, and tailors. This list is far from complete. Hat makers, bakers, and millers could easily be included.

Some trades admitted women as well as men, although there was considerable discrimination among the sexes. Heavy work, such as carpentry and metallurgy, was reserved for the male. Weaving, tailoring, knitting, embroidering, and, to some extent, ceramics were the crafts for women. The freemen as well as the unfree and the slaves were engaged in crafts and trades. Especially in large manufacturing establishments operated by princes, *boyary,* and monasteries, the unfree artisans were employed as weavers, fullers, carpenters and builders, working for the enrichment of their masters. Their products, like those of the free and independent craftsmen, ranged from the crude to the artistic. *Rus'ka Pravda* recounted various categories of the unfree artisans whose wages were very low, not exceeding one *hryvna* a year, when the earnings of free artisans for similar jobs were from 18 to 20 *hryvnas* for the same period of time.[16]

The craftsmen and artisans organized partnerships and corporations, and otherwise joined various organizations to foster their businesses. Some of these associations were, perhaps, similar to the Western trade guilds, and others resembled modern producer cooperatives. There were in Kiev associations of shippers who shipped wood to the river harbors and of carpenters, gardeners, coffin makers, wood workers, and builders. A building association had at one time great significance, for its chairman was a close friend of the prince himself, and was also invited to join the commission for codifying the later phases of the *Rus'ka Pravda.* The Kievan *Patericon* and the *Laurentian Chronicle,* as well as other sources, mention these associations.

Although the trades were fairly well developed in the Kievan-Galician period, Lyashchenko warned against overrating their economic significance when he said, "In any event, the share of all these urban industries and handicrafts in the national economy of the tenth and twelfth centuries was rather negligible since the overwhelming part of the population within the framework of a natural economy was engaged in tillage, and in the primary processing of agricultural materials."[17] It seems, however, that Lyashchenko and those who shared his views rather underestimated the relatively high level of material civilization among the medieval Ukrainians. In general, archaeological findings, including metal tools and household articles, pieces of clothing, and arms, are indicative of a considerable material culture at that time. Kiev was certainly inferior to Byzantium in its cultural achievements, but it was not inferior to the West.

Metallurgy, Carpentry, and the Construction Industry.
The main classification of the crafts at that time would be approximately as follows: metallurgy and metal processing, carpentry,
construction industries, ceramics and glass production, the textile
and garment industries, tanning and furriery. Metallurgy and
metal processing must be regarded as the foundation of the material culture of the *Rus'* society. Metals were used in every sector
of the Kievan economy. Iron ore had been mined in northern
Ukraine from time immemorial. Iron extraction and smelting
were carried on for civilian as well as military purposes. Historical references point to a developed armament industry particularly among the Polianians. The chronicle related, for example,
an interesting instance in the political developments in Kiev. The
Khozars defeated the Polianians and demanded a tribute. The
Polianians sent them two-edged swords, previously unknown to
the Khozars, an alarming kind of tribute.

Ibn-Khordadbeh also reported an export of swords from the
land of *Rus'* to Byzantium. These two references seem to indicate
skills in the production of arms and weapons.[18]

On the other hand, excavations and linguistic studies have
proven extensive manufacturing and usage of iron and copper
implements and utensils among the early Ukrainians. Among
these were plow shares, shovels, spades, hoes, harrow teeth,
wheels, axes, sickles, frying pans, candlesticks, nails, needles,
knives, hammers, forks, spoons, drills, pots, ladders, saws, and
chisels. Cast iron was used for manufacturing fences and stairways. For military purposes there were swords, spears, helmets,
and shields produced by specialized craftsmen. As a matter of
fact, archaeological excavations led the modern historian to re-
construct the state of the metal industries in Kiev and Galicia
much more fully than the scanty written documents of the time.
Smelting and smithing were the most important phases of
medieval Ukrainian iron processing. Thus, in Kiev, for example,
a special section of the city was inhabited exclusively by smiths,
and the city gate nearest to this section was called ''Smith Gate.''

The smiths were mentioned in Theodosius' *Life Story,* in the Kievan *Patericon.* Besides the smiths there were also special arms makers, shield makers, tool and appliance makers, and other specilaized trades engaged in the processing of iron.

Other metals were also extensively processed in Ukraine from ores imported from foreign lands. Processing copper and the manufacture of various copper products were, no doubt, the second most important metal industry in the Kievan Empire. It included such activities as the production of church bells, coinage of copper coins, the manufacture of copper stairways, fences, and roofs for churches and palaces, and the production of such kitchen wares and household utensils as kettles, wash basins, pans, candlesticks, and similar items. Cyril of Turiv, for example, mentioned in his writings a copper axe. Probably other tools were also made from copper, but the practice was soon abandoned since iron tools were more efficient.

Church bells were mentioned in the chronicles in the year 1146, in Putivl. But no doubt they existed in the Kievan Empire much earlier, and were brought to Ukraine soon after the introduction of Christianity. It is impossible to say when the Ukrainians began to make church bells, but doubtlessly this industry did develop and there were skilled artisans in this field. The Galician-Volhinian chronicle related (as of the year 1259) that "some bells were brought from Kiev and others were cast here." The statement refers to the newly established city of Kholm, of which Prince Danylo of Galicia took special care, and where he built city walls, gates, and churches, provided market places, and developed industries. In Kholm, as in other large towns, smelting iron, smithing, and processing copper and silver took place. Copper was imported from Caucasus and Asia Minor to supply the extensive domestic needs.

Lead and tin (the Slavic language of that time was not very clear in differentiating between these two metals) were imported principally from Bohemia, and out of them, fences, roofs for churches, palaces and official buildings, some tools, and princely and government seals were manufactured by the domestic craftsmen. Jewelry was made and fine silver and gold work was also done in Kiev and Galicia. The art was learned from Greece and the West; the precious metals were imported from Bohemia, the Ural areas by way of the Suzdal and Rostov principalities, Caucasus, Byzantium, and the Cuman territory. Among the medieval fine silver and gold work one might find jewels, dishes, and especially plates, bowls, spoons, and chalices for secular use of the wealthy; chalices, crosses, gold-covered gospels, vessels, gold and silver ornaments for the inside walls and roofs of churches; and other things for religious and ecclesiastic uses. Rich gold and silver ornaments had plant, animal, and human motifs, and were strongly influenced by Byzantine art.[19]

Carpentry and the construction industries, which were considerably developed in the Kievan period, evolved from primitive home construction by the ancient family commune. Then, the communal clearing of the forests was followed by primitive woodcraft providing for both agriculture and the production of some primitive tools and household articles. Woodworking was a very old craft. At first forests were cleared by means of rather primitive tools. By the time of the Kievan era, tools, including axes, saws, hammers, drills, and pliers, contained at least some iron parts. Also used by the carpenters were chisels, level-arms, and wooden and iron nails. Carpentry produced a variety of household and farm appliances, such as wagons, carts, wheels, barrels, benches, slides, tables, chairs, beds, other home furnishings, spoons, jars, cribs, cattlesheds, ladders, and baskets. These articles of carpentry ranged from very crude forms to artistic masterpieces for the princely, boyar, and wealthy merchant households. Coffin makers and shield makers were specialized carpenters.

Since the earliest times, wooden dwellings, houses, huts, stables, barns, and grain elevators were built in Ukraine. In some parts of the North, probably in the lands of the Derevlianians, sodhuts were built. Holes were dug into the earth and wooden roofs were built over them and covered with earth and clay. Ibn-Dasta said that sod huts were built by the Slavs in order to protect themselves against the cold.

During the Kievan era wooden huts covered with straw were commonly erected by the country people. In the towns wooden houses were covered with tin or shingles. Later, with the growth of wealth among the upper classes, princes and *boyars,* wooden palaces were also constructed. With the acceptance of Christianity, wooden churches were built. Palaces and public buildings had deep basements, and frequently two floors. Those wooden constructions were sometimes very luxurious, with marble floors, artistically painted ceilings, and walls covered with domestic and oriental carpets.

Town builders and bridge builders constituted special occupational groups. Originally, city walls and bridges were of wood; they were strongly constructed and provided defense and security. In this connection, one historical reference is rather interesting. In 1016 the armies of the Kievan prince, Sviatopolk, facing the approaching cohorts of Yaroslav of Novgorod, shouted to them, "You carpenters! We shall put you to work on our own houses." *Rus'ka Prvada* provided legal regulations controlling the wages of the bridge builders.

Wooden construction was a Ukrainian art, while stone construction was an imported one. Foreigners were called by the princes to erect stone and brick buildings, churches, palaces, and public buildings. The skill of masonry was also brought to Kiev from abroad. But soon both brick and stone construction were equally popular in Ukraine, and Ukrainian artisans excelled in both.

A stone building was first mentioned by the *Laurentian Chronicle* as early as the year 945.[20] Beautiful must have been the palace of Princess Olha. But in other instances luxury and beauty were also stressed in construction and ornamentation. In the eleventh century stone city-walls and stone fortifications were known all over the Ukraine. Beginning with the eleventh century, town churches were predominantly of stone and brick construction, while in the countryside they remained exclusively wooden. Prince Yaroslav the Wise called in foreigners to do the masonry around St. Sophia Cathedral. Foreign masons migrated to Ukraine throughout the tenth and eleventh centuries, until domestic craftsmanship began to compete against foreign skill.

Constantine Porphyrogenitus, in his *De Imperio Adminis-trando,* described the subjects of *Rus'* who cut wood, built boats, went to the city of Kiev, loaded their vessels with various goods, and then sailed down the river Dnieper to the Black Sea and to the capital of Constantinople, to trade with the Greek merchants. The reference indicates that besides the construction of wooden houses and carpentry, shipbuilding also developed very early as an important industry until the Cumans barred the Ukrainians from the Black Sea.

But the industry continued during the Galician period to supply boats for fishermen still fishing at the mouths of rivers Dniester and Danube, and on the sea. Thus various types of boats and vessels were manufactured by local craftsmen as commercial vessels for trade along the river banks and the littorals of the Baltic and Black Seas, as fishing vessels, and as warships. Commercial vessels were so common on the Black Sea that it was named by some ancient travelers as the *"Rus'* Sea."[21]

Boat builders were a class much in demand. At first the primitive method of burning out a hole in a large block of wood was employed. Later, however, a more complex and elaborate method came into use. Prices for boats were fixed. A small river boat was priced at one "hrivna," while a large seaworthy vessel commanded as much as three "hrivnas."

Ceramics, Textiles, Tanning and the Fur Business. Ceramics developed in Ukraine from the earliest times. First, wooden utensils were used by the ancient nomadic population. Clay and ceramic products were breakable, and therefore impractical for nomads. Archaelogical excavations furnished very few examples of ceramics from the nomadic eras, indicating that in those days wooden dishes were generally used. But when the Slavs settled permanently they developed the ceramic art. At first the crosses, chalices, and drinking cups they made were the clumsy work of unskilled and usually female hands. The *Hipatian Chronicle* and the Kievan *Patericon* also mentioned clay pots and dishes. The excavations from the time of the Kievan era, however, revealed examples of fine and artistic ceramics. There was, no doubt, a direct connection between the ancient Greek ceramics and the Ukrainian by way of the Tripillian culture and the Greek colonies on the northern littorals of the Pontus Euxinus (Black Sea), although the Ukrainian ceramics were inferior to those of the Greeks. Fine Greek ceramics (Ionian and Athenian) were therefore imported. Along with ceramics, brick production also developed in Ukraine. Bricks were used very early for the construction of churches, palaces, and urban official buildings.

According to Sichinsky, the old Ukrainians produced very good and exceptionally strong bricks and tiles, better than those made today. These bricks were furnished with manufacturers' trade marks, and exported to Poland and elsewhere. Bricks, tiles, and other ceramic products were made in Kiev, Chernihiv, Korsun, Halych, Zvenyhorod, Belz, and Terebovla. The craftsmen in the ceramics industry were organized into business collectives. The first craftsmen were Greeks. Later on, however, the trade became Ukrainian, but the artisans were doubtlessly trained either in Greece or at least by Greek masters. The builder's trade was largely organized as journeywork. The craftsmen travelled from place to place, accepted orders, established brick and tile works, and erected brick buildings.

There is some historical evidence of glass manufacturing in the Kievan Empire. The terms "glassmith" and "glassmithy," used in the old Ukrainian language, lead us to assume the existence of at least a small glass industry in Kiev and Galicia. But fine glassware was imported, primarily from Byzantium, but also from the West.

Naturally, the textile and garment industries were very important since clothing is required to protect people in a harsh climate. In the written documents of the time—the chronicles, life stories of the saints, legal acts, fables and other stories—numerous references were made to weaving and spinning, and garment procurement. Hemp and flax were the primary raw materials, processed by women and men with spinning wheels, usually of the handwheel type, and hand looms. During the Kievan era, spinning was still done in homes by women, while weaving and fulling developed into special crafts and were done in separate shops. Also a great deal of spinning, weaving, and fulling was done by the monasteries, not only for their own use but for the market as well. Like members of other crafts, the weavers and fullers were organized into strong guild associations.

Various types of kinds of linen were manufactured at that time. Coarse, bleached, refined, dyed, and ornamented linens were all available in the markers of the Kievan state. Their production required professional skill and experience. Linen was needed not only as clothing material, but also for sailcloth for commercial and naval vessels. *Rus' ka Pravda* took special note of the stealing of linen, and provided penalties for such theft. As in all cases of special interests covered by the old code of laws, this law clearly indicates the economic importance of linen production and consumption.[22]

In direct relation to linen manufacturing was the production of cordage, which had its traditions from prehistoric time. Cordage was indispensable for manufacturing of hunting and fishing nets, as well as for ships. Canvas was also manufactured into tents for the army.

Wool production and processing also progressed in the Kievan Empire. Sheep raising was quite extensive, mainly for wool. Crude woolen materials were produced domestically. On the other hand wool was used, mostly by women, for knitting socks, stockings, and caps for winter, and for civilian as well as military needs. But linen and woolen materials, especially those of fine qualities, and silk and silk products for consumption of the upper classes of the Kievan-Galician society, were largely imported from Byzantium, the West and the Orient.

Tanning and furriery were both among the leading trades of the medieval Ukrainian economy. Agriculture, cattle raising, and hunting supplied large quantities of hides and skins for processing, and for the manufacture of clothing, shoes, boots, saddles, sacks, and belts. Leather was also extensively used for military purposes, such as shields, harnesses, and other things. Tanners, furriers, shoemakers, saddlers, and other leather craftsmen enjoyed such wealth that tanners and furriers were subject to a special tax. Probably their riches caused the princes to look to them for another convenient source of additional public revenue.

The social prestige of these two occupations may be demonstrated by the story told by the chronicle of tanner Kuzhumiaka, who saved the capital of Kiev from the Cuman invasion. The historical episode was mentioned already in another place. Of course, tanning was done in a rather primitive way, as the *Povist' vremennykh lit* informs us about the process of leather production in the year 992. Some kind of tanning acid was used, but the bulk of the process was accomplished by human hands alone. That leather footwear was used by the Slavs is undoubtedly admitted by the chronicle. However, according to the chronicle, probably the residents of the wealthier regions or the upper classes wore leather boots and shoes, while the poor could afford only footwear made from bast.[23] Especially in the northern sectors of Ukraine there were famous and expert furriers, and furs, like leather boots, were an indication of opulence and power.

1. About the unifying effects of the *Rus' ka Pravda:* M. Chubaty, *Ohlad istorii ukrainskoho prava,* Munich, 1947, p. 28; also, V. Sergeievich, *Russkaia Pravda v cheteriokh redaktsiakh,* St. Petersburg, 1904, pp. XIX-XX. A comprehensive analysis of the code: V. Kluchevsky, *A History of Russia,* London, 1911, Vol. I, pp. 128-143.
2. G. Vernadsky and M. Karpovich, *A History of Russia,* Vol. II, *Kievan Russia,* New Haven, 1951, p. 172.
3. D. Chyzhevsky, *Istoria ukrainskoi literatury,* New York, 1956, pp. 105-107.
4. Vernadsky, *op. cit.,* Vol. II, p. 107: "In the same time" he said, "fishermen from Galicia established themselves on the lower Danube River."
5. M. Hrushevsky, *Istoria Ukrainy-Rusy,* Munich, 1954, Vol. I, p. 256.

6. A. Garkavi, *Skazania muzulmanskikh pisatelei o slovianakh i russkikh*, St. Petersburg, 1870: relations of Ibn-Dasta, Ibn-Hawqual and others, pp. 221, 268, and other; also P. Lyashchenko, *History of National Economy of Russia*, New York, 1959, p. 65.

7. A. Zimin, *Pamiatki prava kievskavo gosudarstva, Russkaia Pravda prostrannoi redaktsii*, Moscow, 1952, arts. 71-72, 75-76, 79-80, pp. 130 and subsequent; *Povist' vremennykh lit*, years 883, 912, 945, 969, 992.

8. I. Krypiakevych, "Pobut," *Istoria ukrainskoi kultury*, Winnipeg, 1964, p. 41: "Hunting the forest animals was done also to get meat, especially before military expeditions in order to provide food for the armies."

9. *Paterik kievo-pecherskavo monastiria*, ed. by D. Abramovich, St. Petersburg, 1911; for example, the chapter on St. Theodosius' life mentioned several times gardening and orcharding, vegetables and fruits. The references to the above occupations were also made by the *Lavrentiiska litopys'*.

10. G. Vernadsky, "Iron mining and iron industries in Medieval Russia," *Etudes dediés á la mémoire D' André Andreadés*, Athens, 1939, pp. 361-366.

11. Various towns and places mentioned in the Medieval written sources: *Povist'*, under the years 882, 947, 988 and other; also, in Lyashchenko's, *op. cit.*, pp. 71-75, 110-112.

12. P. Savitsky, "Podiiem i depressia v drevnie-russkoi istorii," *Yevraziiskaia khronika*, II, 1936, pp. 65-100.

13. A general coverage of the role of the *viche:* Kluchevsky, *op. cit.*, Vol. I, pp. 116 and following. Vernadsky and Karpovich, *op. cit.*, Vol. II, pp. 185-186; Chubaty, *op. cit.*, Vol. I, pp. 45-70.

14. Gardariki, a Scandinavian, identified the land of *Rus'* as a land of towns or forts: Hrushevsky, *ibid.*, Vol. I, pp. 361-362.

15. Lyashchenko, *op. cit.*, pp. 99 and 110-111: "The most important factor in the dissolution of the old social forms . . . was not the development of trade and the military-commercial town . . . but the most profound regeneration of the social activities arising from the main production basis of the national economy, its agriculture." (99). One should bear in mind, however, that Lyashchenko was a Marxist, and that he had to insist on the feudalism (agriculturally oriented) in Kievan *Rus'* in order not to deviate from the Party line. Hence, he had to minimize the significance of commercial activities there, no matter whether he believed in that or he did not. The same argument goes for Pokrovskii, too. M. Pokrovskii, *Ocherki istorii russkoi kultury*, Moscow, 1923, pp. 50-65; Also to the point: M. Dovnar-Zapolsky, *Istoria russkavo narodnavo khaziaistva*, Kiev, 1911, Vol. I, p. 266, in particular, and also chapters 3, 4, and 6; in addition, V. Kluchevskii, *Boyarskaia duma drevniei Rusi*, Moscow, 1909, p. 13.

16. Zimin, *op. cit.*, arts. 97; also, *Russkaia Pravda,* Karamzinskii spisok, arts. 12 and 69; Hrushevsky, *op. cit.,* Vol. III, pp. 340-344.

17. Lyashchenko, *op. cit.*, p. 113.

18. Garkavi, *op. cit.*, p. 47; V. Sichynsky, *Narys ukrainskoi promyslovosti,* Lviv, 1936, pp. 85-88; also, S. Cross and O. Sherbowitz-Wetzor, *The Russian Primary Chronicle,* Cambridge, 1953, pp. 143-144.

19. W. Zaloziecky, "Byzantinisch-ruthenische Kunst," *Deutschtum und Ausland,* Notebook 28/29, Münster, 1930; M. Holubets, "Mystetstvo," *Istoria ukrainskoi kultury,* Lviv, 1937, p. 466; also Vernadsky, *op. cit.,* Vol. II, pp. 256-263: V. Sichynsky, *Istoria ukrainskoho mystetstva,* New York, 1956, Vol. I.

20. Cross, *op. cit.*, year 945: ". . . the princely palace was in the town . . . and there was there a stone hall"; compare: Chapter Eight, on architecture.

21. Masudi related, "In the upper part of the Khozar (Volga) River there is a connection with the Naitas (Black) Sea which is called 'Rus' Sea,' since there nobody but Rus' navigates, which lives on one of the littorals:" Garkavi, *op. cit.*, p. 130.

22. In one of the early acts, issued by Yaroslav the Wise, sometime prior to 1051, penalties were introduced for stealing "white pants or linen or petticoats."

23. *Povist' vremennykh lit,* under the year 985 quoted the following: "And Dobrynia said to Volodymyr, 'Look, those people wear boots. They will give no tribute. We have to look for those who wear only the bast footwear (the *lapti*).'"

CHAPTER ELEVEN

TRADE AND FINANCE

Domestic trade — Foreign trade — The Byzantine and Oriental trade — The Northern and Western trade — Finance.

Domestic Trade. Trading activities, both domestic and foreign, contributed greatly to the income of the Kievan-Galician society. Their importance was widely recognized by the people themselves from the earliest times, since the time the Ukrainian Slavs engaged extensively in trade. Whole families, not only among the city population but also among the peasants, were either fully or partially occupied with trade. For centuries merchant caravans traveled across Ukraine in all directions. Many of these crossed its borders into foreign countries.

The caravans met the need for protection in those uncertain times. Distances were great; roads were poor and dangerous; wild animals, thieves, and robbers threatened constantly; and there was literally no police protection. Therefore it was impractical to travel alone or in small groups. Usually these caravans were jointly organized by a number of merchants, or by one or more merchant associations. They were well armed when they traveled the traditional trade routes.

This caravan trading system of the merchants was known later on as *Chumatski valky,* and it prevailed in Ukraine until the end of the eighteenth century. The salt caravans traveled to the salt mines in Galicia, Transylvania, and Crimea, and from there carried the precious salt to all parts of the Kievan Empire. Metals and metal articles, either produced domestically or imported, iron, copper, zinc, and other metals were important items of domestic trade. Grain caravans traveled continuously from the South to the North, where grain was scarce. According to historical sources, it would seem that salt, metal, and grain distribution presented the greatest problems of domestic commerce and exchange, and occupied a leading position in the internal marketing organization of the Kievan Empire.[1] At that time the major part of domestic distribution of imported articles consisted of luxurious merchandise, in particular, gold, silver, jewelry, ceramics, glassware, carpets, fine textiles, silk, and spices—articles usually destined for the upper classes.

Besides the overland caravans, a well developed system of waterways provided channels for domestic trade. The river Dnieper was the most important commercial water route, not only because it was, for the most part, navigable, but also because its system was extensive, connecting regions of the country which differed greatly in their economies. It linked the southern grain-producing areas with the northern bread-consuming districts. It was connected to the river Vistula and the Baltic Sea by the river Prypet. By the river Desna, it joined the river system of Oka in the North; by the river Seim it was linked to the river system of the Don and the Azov Sea in the East and South-east. As a matter of fact, the commercial routes and the waterways most naturally extended the country's domestic trading and the interprovincial exchange of the Empire into a large-scale foreign trade of intercontinental character.

The river Dnieper did not represent any hindrance to large-scale exchange between those who lived on its right and left banks, since numerous bridges crossed it, and, as Bahalii said, a number of trade routes connected these two parts of the Kievan Empire. Kiev ranked first, Chernihiv and Novgorod second, as commercial centers of trade.

Goods and merchandise from various provinces of the empire and from abroad were displayed for sale in the public market places of towns and cities. In some cities there were several market places, frequently specialized as to types of merchandise. Market places were large spaces, with booths and stands for private merchants, and approved scales operated by city officials and available for a small fee to sellers and buyers alike. Business was always being transacted in the market place. It was supervised by city clerks, who were also witnesses to credit transactions and contractual arrangements.

On certain days of the week, usually on Friday or other days sanctioned by custom and tradition, the market places were turned into fairs. Peasants came in great numbers to sell their produce, merchants displayed newly arrived merchandise, and artisans brought their manufactured articles. The entire affair became a social event. The weekly, monthly, and yearly fairs were regularly attended by the monks, who were sent by their respective monasteries to sell their output of vegetables, cloth, honey, and appliances, and to buy whatever was needed for their communal way of life.

The small towns held markets within an exclusively local trading radius, while in the big cities the radius was almost nationwide. Already at the time some advertising was used by the Ukrainian and foreign merchants in the form of displaying and announcing merchandise available for sale. Also at that time, some specialized mercantile professions existed, exclusive sellers of coffins, for example.

The market place, moreover, was the center not only of medieval commercial life, but also of significant social and political activities. Important announcements were made by the town crier. Losses and thefts had to be first of all announced in the market place by a city officials before any action to prosecute the thieves could be initiated in the courts. And there also thieves were tried and sentenced. Finally, the market place was the site of the peoples' meetings, the *viche*.

Of course, commercial life was not equally developed in all sections of medieval Ukraine. The city of Kiev and its vicinity traded most extensively and must be considered the heart of the commercialized economy of the Empire. This commercialization was so striking that some foreign observers, like Emperor Constantine and Ibn-Dasta, erroneously associated the term ''Rus','' especially applicable to Kiev and the country of the Polianians, with the class of merchants and traders.[2]

On the whole, domestic trading owes its origin to two highly important factors. First, it was caused by the great diversification in the distribution of the natural resources, and in particular, by forest economy of the North and the steppe economy of the South. Here geography pointed to the mutual advantages of reciprocal trade. Secondly, domestic marketing was a most logical and automatic consequence of economic specialization, by which the countryside exchanged its produce for the manufactured goods of the town.

Foreign Trade. The grand scale of foreign commercial activities was, perhaps, the most distinctive feature of the economic life of medieval Ukrainian society from the time of the Kievan Empire. It demonstrated, on the one hand, the considerable commercial skills and abilities of the Ukranian Slavs which were due to geographic factors, and, on the other hand, it indicated their relatively well developed material culture. Foreign trade naturally evolved as an extension of domestic trade since domestic commercial routes, whether by land or water, were simply extended into foreign territories.

For the same reason Kiev became the center of foreign trade, as it was the heart of domestic trade because of its location at the commercial crossroads of the nation. Naturally, this pattern of international trade was subject to continuous fluctuations and to major and minor changes. Some sectors developed earlier. For example, the Oriental Arabic-Iranian trade was succeeded upon its decline by the Byzantine trade. Finally, the Byzantine trade was superseded by the growth of trade with the West. Thus from the eighth to the tenth century, the eastern part of Ukrainian international commerce was highly important. Ukrainian merchant caravans went as far as Baghdad, Derbent, Iran, Syria, and perhaps Turkestan, while Arab merchants came to Kiev, Volhinia, and Novgorod, and beyond that, to Central Europe, as far as Cracow in Poland and Prague in Bohemia. Ukraine not only exported to, and imported from the Orient, but also gained enormously from the transit trade by serving as a middleman between the Orient and Western Europe on the one hand and the Orient and European Northeast on the other.

After Prince Sviatoslav the Conqueror put an end to the flourishing Eastern trade by destroying two major commercial centers of the European East, Ityl and Great Bulgar, the ancient Byzantine trade became increasingly important. But territorial advances made by the nomadic Cumans in the Steppes of the Black and Azov Seas finally undercut the Ukrainian-Greek commercial ties. The liquidation of all worthwhile Greek trade began with the First and was completed with the Fourth Crusade (1096-1099 and 1204), which opened new avenues for the East-West trade via the Mediterranean, bypassing Ukraine and excluding the Ukrainian middleman.

The importance of the transit trade to the medieval Ukrainian economy cannot be overemphasized, since Ukrainian territories linked East and West, and North and South by land and water. Naturally the Ukrainians were anxious to retain their economic advantages. In the twelfth century, with the growth of Western civilization and the decline of Byzantium, Ukraine became more and more interested in trade connections with the West. The Galician-Volhinian Ukraine was already vitally and progressively engaged in trade with Poland, Hungary, Bohemia, and Germany. There is no doubt that these commercial relations represented also the most important avenues for cultural influences. Having been exposed to a cross-pollination of ideas, Ukraine developed a culture and civilization which embodied, to a great extent, those of other peoples.

Naturally, as long as the Kievan Empire and the Galician-Volhinian state were at the peak of their political power, the growth of commerce continued. With the collapse of the Kievan realm, commercialism declined, and for a long time little trade took place in eastern Ukraine.

Although Ukraine, and Kiev and its vicinity in particular, was the heart of the Dnieper trading system, curiously enough, archaeological findings of foreign coins were much fewer in Ukraine than in the Russian north, where trading was considerably less advanced. Hrushevsky gave three reasons for this historical paradox. First of all, the credit system was well developed in Ukraine. It was especially useful for financing large-scale commercial transactions, which included both Ukrainian exports and foreign imports. To a great extent imports were paid for by exports to Greece and the Middle East. The extensive use of credit, of course, involved little transfer of cash. This fact, together with the considerable lapse of time, accounts for the relatively few foreign coins found.

In the Russian north, however, the conditions were reversed. The North-Eastern tribes were impoverished, their economy poor and under-developed. Imports were negligible and exports were paid for in cash, a fact which explains the large quantities of foreign coins—Greek, Arabic, Roman, and German—in the Muscovite-Russian north.[3]

The Ukrainians fully appreciated the value and importance of foreign trade, calling foreign merchants ''guests'' and according them great respect. *Rus'ka Pravda* gave to the ''guest'' special legal protection, particularly in bankruptcy cases where local merchants defaulted. The foreigner had a legal claim against the property of the bankrupt person second only to that of the prince. The position of a foreign merchant was quite different in the latter Muscovite principality where legal restrictions and suspicions enveloped the foreigner. This difference is still further evidence of the erroneous assumptions of Russian historians in associating Kiev and Moscow spiritually. Also, commercial credit was cheaper and easier to obtain, and more leniency was granted in the execution of the claims. For negotiating a regular loan, three witnesses were required, while for a commercial loan one witness sufficed. An oral contract was permissible. A bankrupt individual was usually sold into slavery to cover the claims of the lender, while a bankrupt merchant, if the bankruptcy occurred evidently without his personal fault, had a legal right to an extension of time to allow him to adjust the difficulties.[4]

To cover the problem of Ukrainian ancient and medieval trade satisfactorily, it is essential to discuss it in its individual territorial segments. These were the southern or Byzantine-Oriental trade, the West European trade, and the Northern trade. It would seem most logical to begin with the traditional Greek-Ukrainian commercial relations.

The Byzantine and Oriental Trade. The "Route from the Varangians to the Greeks" was an extremely important commercial avenue, running along the river Dnieper. Via this route the Kievan economy obtained a great many things from abroad, both for domestic consumption and for reshipment to other countries. The Kievan merchants wanted this trade to be as large as possible and they must have been rather aggressive in their attempt to maintain commercial relations with the Greeks, since historical sources furnish enough proof of Greek antagonism toward the northern barbarians. By orders of the Emperors, the Ukrainian merchants were required to live in only one sector of the city of Constantinople, to move about the city only in small groups, without any arms, and then only under the supervision of Greek officials, to pay a special tax and to leave the country by autumn. Since these merchants always arrived in spring, this rule meant that they could remain in the city no longer than six months.[5] Presumably, there were some adventurers and scoundrels among the Kievan-*Rus'* merchants who, by harassing the local population, largely justified these harsh regulations.

The later agreement between the Greek emperors and the

Kievan princes required that each group of incoming Ukrainian merchants bring with them a letter from a prince listing the names of all members of the group and their authorization to trade in Constantinople, in order to protect the Greek population from abuses by undesirable elements. But on the other hand, the Greeks were jealous and did not want to share their business with foreigners. For this reason the Greek authorities denied the right of permanent residence to Ukrainians in Byzantium. Probably the *Rus'* were not even admitted to the other Greek cities, except perhaps Alexandria. There are no historical references indicating their presence in any other part of the Byzantine Empire. Of course such restrictions infuriated the Kievan princes, the more so because the Greek trade was a traditional source of wealth for Ukrainians in general, since the *boyars* and the royalty vitally participated in these commercial activitics.

Greek discriminatory practices caused a number of wars between Kiev and Constantinople. The first Kievan campaign against the Greeks, in 860, led by the "Varangians" Askold and Dir, was perhaps a commercially motivated expedition for booty, while Oleh's campaign in 907 was concluded by a commercial treaty clearly indicating an economic motivation. Among other things, the treaty provided for the liberalization of trade relations. The Ukrainian merchants in Constantinople no longer had to pay the tax designed for them. They received more freedom when moving within the city limits. They were supposed to get gratuitous board and meals for six months when in Greece, as well as tools and naval appliances, such as linen and cordage, and also food for their journey home.

The Greeks, on the other hand, received, according to the agreement, the assurance that the Ukrainian merchants would not damage their property, would not carry arms within the city, would live only in their own section of the city, and would leave the country after a six-month period of transacting business. In addition, no merchant would be permitted to come from Ukraine without being authorized by the Kievan prince. The treaty was solemnly sworn to by both parties involved. However, the agreement may not have been detailed enough, or perhaps some new conflicts developed soon after. Perhaps, in 911, a new treaty was negotiated and executed, although this is not fully proven: it seems to be either only a more elaborate amendment to the treaty of 907, or only another version of the original pact. It confirmed again the willingness of both parties, the Ukrainians and the Greeks, to keep peace and friendly relations. It also regulated the punishment of criminals and the personal liabilities of the Ukrainian visitors and the Greek natives.

By the year 940, the relations between Kiev and Constantinople worsened, and their commercial problems became so acute that Prince Ihor planned a new war against Byzantium. He probably waged two wars, one ending in shameful defeat in 941, and the other resulting in a new treaty in 944. The new agreement was supposed to restore peace and unhampered trade, and to secure undisputed Greek fishing along the nothern shores of the Black Sea. Furthermore, the parties involved promised not to destory each other's vessels. The Ukrainian merchants also promised not to import any fine cloth from Greece. However, things were not settled permanently even this time. Prince Sviatoslav the Conqueror, the son and successor of Ihor and Olha, again became involved in an economically motivated war with Byzantium. In fact, it had an even broader commercial background. Sviatoslav desired not so much to continue commercial relations with the Greeks as to conquer major commercial centers which, until that time, were under Greek domination, and to incorporate them into his empire. Thus, the later wars of Volodymyr the Great in 984 and of Yaroslav the Wise in 1043 were due predominantly although not exclusively to commercial motives. As the Ukrainian empire grew, its leaders sought all the more to extend the Byzantine trade. The Greeks became all the more suspicious and fearful. This atmosphere contributed to quarrels and antagonism and almost continuous frictions—an indication of the importance of this trade to the Ukrainian national economy.

In its early history, Ukraine exported to Greece furs, wax, honey, and slaves, but in the twelfth century the exports changed.

First of all, technological progress and the growth of agriculture progressively introduced various kinds of grain into the trade, replacing to some extent the exports from the forest economy. Secondly, with the introduction of Christianity, the slave trade rapidly declined and finally disappeared.

A far greater variety of items was imported from Greece, including silk and silk products, fine cloth, textiles, fabrics, carpets and rugs, gold and silver articles, brocades, glassware, ceramics, religious articles, icons, articles of art, wine, fruits, and spices. The archaelogical excavations of that time definitely indicate that the Kievan-Galician era was clearly under the cultural dominance of Byzantium, especially after the year 988. Following the collapse of the Kievan Empire in 1240, the Ukrainian-Byzantinian commercial exchange continued, but to a much lesser degree. The list of items imported from Greece was similar to that of the earlier periods. Among these some grain must be included. However, at that time trade with Western Europe occupied the leading place as the Greek trade continued to decline.

Commercial relations with the Crimean cities may rightly be considered both a branch of Ukraine's southern foreign trade, and an extension of the Greek commodity exchange via Crimea. Its most important article was salt. The Ukrainian merchant caravans came again and again to the Crimean peninsula to buy this precious item which they transported to all parts of their country. Furthermore the merchants in Crimean cities served as important middlemen for the Ukrainian-Byzantine commerce. It was especially important in those instances where the export from Greece of the articles in question was forbidden.

The Oriental or Eastern trade was no less ancient and no less important to the Ukrainian Slavs, although its leading role was soon terminated. As early as the tenth century, Sviatoslav the Conqueror destroyed the two centers of Oriental trade in East Europe, Great Bulgar and Ityl. For a while, Great Bulgar, which was the center of the European Northeast, did recover from the blow, but Ityl, the commercial center of the European Southeast, never regained its economic position and the Khozars disappeared entirely as a nation.

The radius of Kievan Oriental commerce reached as far as Bagdad, Teheran, and Turkestan. In the ninth and tenth centuries, the caravans of Ukrainian merchants were seen in these places, while Arabs and Khozars came to Kiev and Novgorod. At first, the Arabs traded directly with the Ukrainian Slavs, traveling by land and water along the Volga-Don and Dnieper river systems, and even farther west. Numerous written documents of that time were left behind by the Arab and Jewish travelers and merchants, such as Masudi, Ibn-Dasta, Ibn Jacob, Ibn-Khordadbeh, Ibn-Fadlan, and others, in the form of memoirs, travelogues, and narratives.[6] The Arab merchants purchased a great deal in Ukraine and in neighboring countries, and imported from those areas costly furs, such as beavers, sables, foxes, martens, and even rabbits, leather, fish, sheep, oxen, honey and wax, caps, arrows, nuts, fish teeth, fish-oil, and slaves. The Arabs brought into Ukraine such things as jewelry, precious stones, rugs and carpets, weapons and swords of Damascan steel, silk and silk materials, satin, metal goods, articles of art, fruit, and spices. Some Oriental goods were also imported through Byzantine middlemen.

In the ninth and tenth centuries, Ityl in the Khozar land and Great Bulgar in the Bulgar land progressively took over the role of monopolistic middlemen in the trade with the Arab world, Turkestan, and the Ural mountain areas, on the one hand, and between *Rus'* and Western Europe on the other. Ityl and Great Bulgar became the chief commercial centers because of their key positions on the Volga river system which, through the river Kama, connected the North and South, and the East and West as well. The Ukrainian merchants traveling to Ityl and Great Bulgar, either by the river routes of Dnieper-Seim-Don-Volga, or by land, supplied those two centers with all the articles of the Ukrainian eastern trade mentioned above, and bought Oriental merchandise, including cotton, from the Middle East and metal and costly furs from the Ural mountains. According to Masudi and Ibn-Fadlan, the Slavic merchants, including the Ukrainian, occupied half of the city of Ityl, engaging in business there. They had to pay a special tax to the city amounting to a tithe of their proceeds. Ibn-Fadlan related that those Ukrainian merchants operated in groups, which may indicate that their activities were operated by partnerships and mercantile associations, similar to those existing in Ukraine.[7]

To secure the benefits of that lucrative eastern trade, the Kievan princes, not underestimating their Black Sea commercial interests, several times attempted to dominate the shores of the Caspian Sea and the commercial routes to the East. For example, in 909 and 910, and again in 913, Oleh undertook a campaign, going by water routes of the Don and the Volga to plunder the wealthy cities and commercial centers on the littorals of the Caspain Sea, as far down as the Baku region. This operation was initially successful but finally turned into a bad defeat. His successor in Kiev, Prince Ihor, again organized a large-scale campaign in the years 944 and 945, in order to establish Ukrainian interests in the Caucasian and Caspian regions, as far as Derbent and Berdah. Although he did not succeed in dominating those areas, his armies returned victorious with great quantities of booty, according to the chronicles.

The commercial routes actually directed the Kievan rulers in their political and strategic moves. Sviatoslav continued with the tradition, and planned to dominate the avenues and centers of the Oriental trade directly. He completely ruined Ityl, plundered the littorals of the Caspian Sea, and conquered the cities of Sarkel and Semender, opening the way for direct trade with the East, Asia Minor, and Central Asia. Politically, however, this conquest proved to be a very poor achievement, for the destruction of the Khozars liquidated an important buffer state which had effectively protected *Rus'* from the continuous attacks of Asiatic tribes as pointed out before. Consequently, in the middle of the thirteenth century, the Mongol hordes struck with full force against the Kievan state, and the latter, having been exposed directly to the attacks of Genghis Khan, collapsed.

Trading with the steppe nomads, the Cumans in the Black and Azov Sea areas, must be considered a segment of the Ukrainian-Oriental commercial relations, since these nomads were primarily middlemen for the exchange of Eastern goods, and, secondly, middlemen for the Ukrainian-Greek trade as well. Emperor Constantine Porphyrogenitus related how the Slavs purchased oxen, horses, and sheep from the Cumans.[8] The city of Oleshi was one of the centers of the Cuman transit trade. It was situated at the mouth of the river Dnieper. The steppe nomads, as a matter of fact, eventually put an end to any extensive trade between the Ukrainians and the Black and Azov Sea areas. Vernadsky emphasized the interest that the Kievan princes had in the city of Tmutorokan, located on the Kerch Strait between the Black and Azov Seas. No doubt, this city was an important center for the Oriental trade as late as the eleventh century. But the Cumans soon blocked Ukrainian trade with the Caspian areas as well, and the economic significance of Tmutorokan declined.

The Northern and Western trade. In its first phase, Ukraine served simply as a middleman for the transportation of Greek products to those northern regions, and to a much lesser degree, for the exportation of northern products to Greece. The ancient ''route from the Varangians to the Greeks'' owed its commercial importance to its transit character. Kiev captured the key position in this commerce in earliest times, attracting the attention of the Scandinavians, who invaded the city and its vicinity, and laid, to some extent, the foundation for the future empire of *Rus'*.

Ibn-Khordadbeh indicated this transit nature of the Ukrainian northern trade. Later on, however, beginning probably with the eleventh century, the Ukrainian exportation to Scandinavia, Novgorod, the Northern principalities, and Lithuania was initiated and began to play an increasingly important role in this already essentially Ukrainian foreign trade. From the Suzdalian north, the Ukrainians imported but little: some furs, especially costly furs, lumber, and wooden articles.

The Ukrainian trade with Central and Western European countries at first also bore extreme characteristics of transit commerce, supplying Europe with such Oriental and Byzantine articles as silk and silk fabrics, satin, brocades, rugs, and carpets. Ukrainian merchants traveled to Poland, Bohemia, Hungary, and even farther, to Germany. German custom laws from 904 mention the Slavic visitors trading in German towns. Polish, Czech, Hungarian, and German merchants visited Ukraine. Gallus Anonymous, the first Polish chronicler, said that Poland was known only to those western travelers who visited *Rus'*. Certainly, those Westerners were primarily missionaries and merchants, who had either religious or commercial interest in Ukraine-*Rus'*.

From the West, Ukraine imported raw materials, such as tin, bronze, iron, and copper, and some manufactured goods, such as fabrics from Flanders, swords from France, helmets from Italy, some arms even from Spain, finished articles such as woolen and linen materials, needles, glassware, wines, salt, and others. She exported to Europe furs, wax, honey, flax, hemp, hops, skins, hides, and other raw materials, in addition to the resale of Oriental and Byzantine products. Later, with the growth of agriculture, more and more grain was exported to the West, to Scandinavia and to German cities in particular.[9] The Galician merchants owned vessels on the Baltic Sea in order to trade more effectively and more profitably with the West. Of course, the transit through Polish territory had to be taken into account, since the Cumans, and later, the Tartars closed tightly all access to the Black Sea.

There existed some commercial agreements between the Galician and the Prussian cities, as far as economic interests were concerned. In the later Galician period, cloth, textiles, metals, and manufactured goods composed most of the Ukrainian imports from the West. Commercial relations with the German towns were intensified after more Ukrainian cities had been granted the Magdeburg legal system. At the time of the Polish-Lithuanian occupation of Ukraine, the Western trade attained a predominant place, while other segments of foreign commerce either shrank to almost nothing or disappeared altogether.

Finance, comprising currency and credit systems and methods of private and public financing, is an essential element of any developed economy. A well developed monetary and credit system, mature credit institutions, and a properly managed public economy are indications of an advanced state of economic evolution. Such indications were present in Kievan-Galician society. Some aspects of medieval Ukrainian finance have not been explained satisfactorily by historians. For example, the monetary system of Kiev is not fully understood. The language of medieval legal documents, such as *Rus'ka Pravda,* is often inexact, contributing to the confusion. It is not clear what the *hryvna*—the Kievan monetary unit—means: a "silver hrivna" or a "hrivna of martens." On the other hand, the relation and ratio of various monetary units were neither stable nor consistent. Their values changed frequently, according to economic needs and the pattern of foreign trade. These circumstances substantially confuse the study of financial problems, and leave some detailed questions unanswered and open to discussion.

There is no doubt that since ancient times furs were used by the Ukrainian Slavs as a medium of exchange, a form of commodity money. The names *kuna* (marten skin), and *nogata* (sable skin), and *veksha* (squirrel skin), were the ancient nomenclature of money in Ukraine.

During the hunting and fishing phase, wealth was measured in skins and furs. These items became generally accepted as a medium of exchange, replacing simple barter, and facilitating the exchange of goods. Rubrik reported the presence and circulation of fur money in Ukraine as late as 1253 as a supplementary medium of exchange employed in domestic trade.[10]

As a result of commercial relations with many foreign peoples, numerous foreign coins—Roman, Greek, Arabic, Iranian, and German—were found in ancient Ukraine, circulating along with furs as a medium of exchange. Foreign coins also became a means of storing value, as accumulations of ancient money indicate. Gold and silver coins were thus introduced to the Ukrainians in this manner. The outstanding princes of Kiev, Volodymyr the Great, Sviatopolk the Sinner, Yaroslav the Wise, and, perhaps a few others, coined their own Ukrainian money in the tenth and eleventh centuries. Later, coinage was discontinued and foreign money was used in foreign and domestic trade. These were predominantly Polish, German, and Hungarian coins.

The largest monetary unit of the Kievan currency system was the "Silver hrivna," the value of which fluctuated widely from time to time, depending upon the changing patterns of foreign trade. Traditionally, the *hrivna* was associated with the Orient, since the term originally meant a heavy necklace or neck ring worn by the Iranian and Allan chieftains in the remote past. At first, the *hrivna* was a unit of weight, approximately half a pound. Later it was associated with the value of about one-half pound (troy) of silver, similar to the Byzantine monetary unit, while in the North, it was more, being adjusted to the German monetary system. With the decline of the Ukrainian-Byzantine trade and the increasing importance of that of the West, the value and silver content of the *hrivna* was raised to correspond with the new financial needs.

In the Kievan period, the silver standard prevailed, and the code of *Rus'ka Pravda* and other documentary sources employed terms of silver, although a gold *hrivna* was known, a unit weighing approximatley six troy ounces. The valuation ratio between gold and silver was approximately one to twelve. Since the value of the silver *hrivna* had a tendency to rise above one-half troy-pound of silver, the initial price of twelve silver *hrivna* for one golden *hrivna* must have dropped to ten or even less. Eventually, silver became relatively more expensive and the silver content of the *hrivna* gradually dropped to one-third, and finally to one-fourth troy-pound of silver.[11] The *hrivna* took the form of silver or gold bars, rather than that of coins.

There were also smaller monetary units, primarily silver coins with princely seals and heraldic figures, the names of which vividly reminded one of fur commodity money. One silver *hrivna,* primarily reserved for large-scale and foreign trade operations, was equal to four *hrivna of kuna* (of martens), which were generally used in domestic trade and daily business, and frequently translated into terms of marten skins. One *hrivna of kuna* was equal to 25 *kuna* (martens), although it was not always so, for the ratio rather fluctuated from 20 to 30 martens per *hrivna,* according to commercial needs. One *rizan* (cut-off) was one-half of a *kuna* (marten). This meant that one *hrivna* of martens was equal to 50 *rizans*.

On the other hand, there was also another set of currency units derived from the silver *hrivna*. One silver *hrivna* equaled 20 *nohat* (sables), and one sable equaled about 30 *veksha* (squirrels). The *veksha* was the smallest coin in the Kievan monetary system; approximately 600 of them equaled a silver *hrivna*. A small church candle sold for a *veksha,* according to an ancient narrative.[12] There is no doubt that in domestic trade of a local character fur money was still in circulation as a secondary and supplementary medium of exchange until the end of the thirteenth century.

Probably there was a relative shortage of money in the Kievan Empire in relation to the enormous needs for financing foreign trade. An even greater shortage existed in the Galician-Volhinian state where, because there was no domestic coinage, reliance was placed exclusively upon foreign coins and furs. Consequently, credit developed on a wide scale. Although historians exaggerated its costs, it certainly was not cheap. The interest rate depended upon the maturity factor. For very short-term credit (less than six months), the legal rate of interest exceeded 50 percent. This was also the rate for a year. In long-term credit, the legitimate interest rate was considerably lower, approximately 10 per cent per annum, or ten martens on each silver *hrivna* borrowed, according to Vernadsky's interpretation.

Thus, when the code of *Rus'ka Pravda* refers to one *hrivna* in this connection, it is not clear which *hrivna* is meant, the silver *hrivna* or the *hrivna of kuna*. In long-term and large-scale credit transactions, frequently international in scope, it would seem that the silver *hrivna* would be the basic unit of account, similar in its value and content to the Byzantine and German monetary unit. The 40 per cent rate for long-term credit, as accepted by Hrushevsky, Kluchevskii, and others, is a confusion resulting from the misinterpretation of the term *hrivna*. Moreover, a 5.5 to 8 per cent rate, depending upon the terms of the credit, was a legitimate rate of interest in Greece at that time, a fact indirectly influencing the Ukrainian legal rate. Hence long-term Ukrainian credit could not be entirely out of line in comparison with Greek terms, since long-term credit was used primarily in international transactions.

Actually, it was in short-term consumer credit where there were so many and such drastic abuses that they eventually led to the rebellion of 1113. This was clearly a revolt of the common people against exploitation by money-lenders who charged usurious interest rates, exploiting employees by turning them first into debtors and finally into slaves. These developments finally forced Prince Volodymyr Monomakh to regulate the most pressing social problems, including the interest rates, in order to protect the common people. Interest rates exceeding 40 to 50 per cent were declared illegal, and penalties were imposed on usury, reducing although by no means eliminating the practice. The Church vehemently opposed usury, regarding it as a mortal sin. But the growing need for capital caused many to disregard both Church and State in this matter, and the cumulative results inflicted great hardship on the poor.

Short-term consumer credit was the core of the problem. It was formally negotiated in the presence of three witnesses, and rigorously executed. Defaulting or bankrupt debtors were sold into slavery. Commercial credit was legally privileged. No witnesses were required, and in the case of bankruptcy without contributory guilt of the debtor (drunkardness, crime, or hazardous speculation), the borrower always received an extension of time to repay. In addition, his long-term interest rate was considerably lower.

Capital accumulation at this time was considerable, in particular among the princes who owned large landed estates and participated in commercial activities, and among the grand *boyars* and merchants. Money accumulated by the upper classes ran into thousands of gold and silver *hrivna,* more than enough to finance the large-scale business operations of the time. Princes, *boyars,* and merchants were so wealthy that they could afford not only private palaces, but also beautiful churches for the use of the people. Partnerships and corporate associations were organized to finance ventures too vast for any one person. But the merchants were still too undercapitalized (even when organized) to corner any market; therefore competition universally prevailed. An exception to this condition existed when the salt merchants organized a cartel in an attempt to corner the salt market for Prince Sviatopolk of Kiev.

As far as public finance was concerned, there was no distinction between state property and the private properties and finances of the ruler. According to medieval political theory, however, individual principalities were the *patrimonium* (property) of the ruling princely families, and not a popular commonwealth. This instance may explain why it was considered unnecessary to separate public revenues and expenditures, on the one hand, from the private financial affairs of the prince, on the other. The whole principality was held to be the private property of the prince or duke. Nor was there any elaborate financial administration, any systematic control of income and outlay, receipts, and disbursements, or any accounting system whatsoever. The prince merely paid his bills, both public and private, from what revenues he could collect regardless of source, a system similar to that employed in the West at that time.

Public revenue was collected from many sources: from princely properties in the narrow sense of the term, from the booty of successful wars, in the form of tributes from subjugated and vassal tribes, by the levy of direct and indirect taxes on the people, and from the collection of such non-tax monies as court fees, penalties, fines, and other charges. The princely properties included, first of all, large landed estates which in many cases were well administered. On these grain was produced, and cattle, horses, and sheep were raised. It may be interesting to note that the ruling prince could own land in other principalities under the supremacy of other princes. This seems to indicate a slight difference between the concepts of strictly public affairs and the private property of the princes. However, the principle was largely ignored.

The prince also held certain rights, such as mining, fishing, hunting, and bee hiving, which constituted the exclusive right to exploit these resources.[13] In addition, the dukes regularly participated in profitable commercial ventures, and sometimes attempted to establish and exploit monopolies.

The most ancient form of tax revenue of the Kievan prince was the collection of tribute from Slavic and non-Slavic tribes which remained in vassalage. These tributes were paid in kind, honey, wax, fur, and grain, or in gold and silver. The chronicles record such payments. Ihor, Olha, and Sviatoslav undertook military expeditions for the purpose of imposing and collecting tribute. Dobrynia, a knight and nobleman, sought tribute-paying tribes in the name of his suzerain. Once the tributes were imposed, they were delivered by the vassal tribes rather than collected by the officials of Kiev. If any tribes were stubborn and unwilling to pay, the princes themselves undertook punitive expeditions against them.[14]

The tributes, an important princely source of revenue in the early Kievan era, declined in significance, and, in the Galician-Volhinian state, disappeared altogether. Instead, Galicia and Volhinia were obliged to pay a tribute to the Mongol suzerain and at times to the German Emperor.

In the earliest period, booty and plunder also constituted a considerable source of revenue for the state and the duke. Thus, Askold and Dir, Oleh, Ihor, Sviatoslav, and other early princes organized numerous military expeditions for the purpose of plundering. This practice declined under such outstanding Kievan sovereigns as Volodymyr the Great and Yaroslav the Wise.

Among the so-called direct taxes collected regularly, the most important were the capitation, *poliudia,* and the service obligations owed to the sovereign duke. Initially collected either from the individual homesteads or individual tilling units (acreage), the capitation was imposed upon the entire free rural population. Cities, towns, and the upper classes were exempt. Collection was organized on a regional basis. Thus the *verv,* a territorial administrative unit, was collectively responsible for gathering the tax as well as for the performance of the service obligations, and the payment of other financial burdens owed to the prince.

In the thirteenth century, the capitation was made a strictly personal tax on both property and income, levied against the entire rural population. The first Kievan princes traveled personally from October to April of each year in order to collect the capitation. Meanwhile a tax collection system was developed with officials called *vyrnyky*. Cities and towns, exempt from the capitation, were obliged to pay a special tax called the "town contribution," *pohorodia*. The capitation and the town contribution were paid either in produce, such as fur, skins, honey, wax, fruit, meat, or grain, or in currency.

Another type of tax was the service obligation borne by the working classes, who were obliged to labor on bridges, roads, castles, forts, city walls, and other public projects. Often the princes abused the custom, forcing people to work on jobs not authorized by tradition. At the end of the Kievan period, peasants were compelled to work a few days in the princely fields. People attempted to evade these burdens in numerous ways. In his *Descriptions of Kiev,* Zakrevsky wrote that Prince Yaroslav could not get workers to build St. George's Church because the builders and helpers believed they would not be paid for their labor. The prince was compelled to make it quite clear that their work would not simply be considered a service obligation.

In general, it seems that there was not much certainty as far as tax rates and methods of collection were concerned. Among the service obligations, the duty to feed, house, and transport the prince and his retine on their journeys must be included. Later this obligation developed into a separate form of burdensome tax.

Business taxes and excise taxes were very numerous in the Kievan era. Among these were taxes on storehouses, market places, taverns, shipments across rivers, sales transactions in salt, honey, and other articles, portages, and many other mecantile and marketing operations. Also prevalent were tolls and duties at the approaches to towns and cities, or for the use of ferries and bridges.

Another very large souce of public revenue was such fees and charges as death money collected by the prince as a penalty for murder or killing, other court fees raised for various occasions and frequently abusive in their rates, and special fees for weighing and measuring goods sold in the market places. Especially the court fees were high, at times so excessively high that they contributed to the pauperization of the people.

The public expenditures included, first of all, the maintenance of the princely court, and the retinue and other forms of the armed forces, particularly in national emergencies. Considerable amounts were spent on the judicial system, while policing was inadequately provided by the younger members of the princely retinue as a secondary function, or organized on a local, municipal, or communal basis. A portion of the fees and charges collected was used to pay the officials. Maintenance of the administrative establishments, central and provincial, including those of various clerks and officials, constituted another important item in the national budget.[15]

Finally, public welfare, charities, education, and assistance to the Church can be included. The administration of the public and princely finances was in the hands of a majordomo and remained under the supervision of the chancellor. Matters concerning the internal revenues were taken care of by officials, called *vyrnyky*, and tolls and tariffs were administered by the *mytnyky*. Otherwise, no rational accounting of receipts and expenditures was kept. In case of need, money was borrowed from private capitalists just as it is done today.

1. M. Hrushevsky, *Istoria Ukrainy-Rusy*, New York, 1954, Vol. I, p. 302: "In the domestic trade, salt and metals must have been particularly important, since as far as the consumer's needs were concerned, they were largely covered by local production." Some trading routes received their names from the chief articles which were handled through these channels. Thus, one was called "the salt route," another, "the iron route," since the time immemorial in Ukraine-Rus'. The reader is requested to compare the section on commerce in Chapter Four of this very work.
2. Domestic trade in the Kievan Ukraine: I. Kulischer, *Russische Wirtschaftgeschichte*, Jena, 1925, pp. 103-105; M. Dovnar-Zapolsky, *Istoria russkavo narodnavo khaziaistva*, Kiev, 1911, Vol. I, chapters 3 and 4; N. Polonska-Vasylenko, *Istoria Ukrainy*, Munich, 1972, Vol. I, pp.

228-230; Hrushevsky, *op. cit.*, Vol. I, pp. 278-305, and P. Lyashchenko, *History of the National Economy of Russia,* New York, 1949, pp. 72-74, 102-110, and other.

3. Hrushevksy, *op. cit.*, Vol. I, p. 304.
4. About the favorable treatment and the favorable economic and legal position of foreign merchants in Kievan Rus': A. Zimin, *Pamiatki prava kievskavo gosudarstva, Russkaia Pravda prostrannoi redaktsii,* Moscow, 1952, arts. 54 and 55; also, *Russkaia Pravda,* Karamzinskii spisok, arts. 44-45, 47-48, 66, 68-69.
5. *Povist' vremennykh lit,* under the year 945.
6. A. Garkavi, *Skazania muzulmanskikh pisatelei o slovianakh i russkikh,* St. Petersburg, 1870, pp. 49, 63-69, 85, 221, 267 and other reports of foreign merchants and travellers.
7. *Ibid.,* pp. 85-102: "They come from their land, anchor on the Ityl, which is a great river, and build large houses on its bank; and in one house they live ten, twelve, or even more men together."
8. Constantine Porhphyrogenitus, *De Administrando Imperio,* Patrologiae Cursus Completus, Series Graeca, ed. by J. Migne, CXIII, Book IX; also, I. Krypiakevych, "Pobut," *Istoria ukrainskoi kultury,* Winnipeg, 1964, p. 42.
9. V. Vassilevskii, "Drevnia torgovlia Kieva s Regensburgom," *Zhurnal Ministerstva Narodnavo Prosveshchenia,* 1898, pp. 121-150; also, L. Goetz, *Deutsch-Russische Handelsgeschichte des Mittelalters,* Lübeck, 1922.
10. W. de Rubruqui, *Rescueil des vojages publie par la societe de geographie,* IV, 1839, 329; the coverage of the Crimean trade: pp. 215-219.
11. D. Prozorovskii, *Moneta i ves* v Rossii, St. Petersburg, 1865.
12. A good coverage of the monetary system in Kievan Rus': Hrushevsky,*op. cit.,* Vol. III, pp. 347-352.
13. M. Chubaty, *Ohlad istorii ukrainskoho prava,* Munich, 1947, Vol. I, p. 60: At that time the princely income was not separated from the public income of the state; revenues from the private estates of the prince and the tax collections were kept in the princely treasury, and from that source the prince covered also his private as well as public expenditures. . . . Also, M. Vladimisrskii-Budanov, *Obzor istorii russkavo prava,* Petrograd-Kiev, 1915, pp. 82-89.
14. *Povist' vremennykh lit,* under the years 883, 885, 945, 946, 985; Vernadsky erroneously identified the tribute, *dan,* with the capitation,*poludia;* G. Vernadsky and M. Karpovich, *A History of Russia,* Vol. II, *Kievan Russia,* New Haven, 1951, p. 190, while the concepts should be strictly differentiated: Vladimirskii-Budanov, *loc cit.*
15. The people of Kiev complained about these excessive fees, for example in 1093: Hruskevsky, *op. cit.,* Vol. III, p. 258.

BIBLIOGRAPHY

I. *General works on history.*

Andrusiak, M., *Istoria Ukrainy,* Prague, 1941.

Bestuzhev-Riumin, K., *Russkaia istoria,* St. Petersburg, 1872.

Bobrzynski, M., *Dzieje Polski w zarysie,* Warsaw, 1927-1931, 3 volms.

Chase, T., *The Story of Lithuania,* New York, 1946.

Chirovsky, Fr.-, N., *A History of the Russian Empire,* New York, 1973, Vol. I.

Chirovsky, Fr.-, N., *An Introduction to Russian History,* New York, 1967.

Dlugosz, J., *Historia Poloniae,* Warsaw, 1902, Volms. I-IV.

Doroshenko, D., *Narys istorii Ukrainy,* Munich, 1966, Vol. I.

Halecky, O., *History of Poland,* New York, 1942.

Hrushevsky, M., *A History of Ukraine,* New Haven, 1970.

Hrushevsky, M., *Istoria Ukrainy-Rusy,* New York, 1954-55, Vol. I-IV.

Istoria Ukrainskoi RSR, I. Artemenko, ed.-in-chief, Kiev, 1977, Vol. I.

Kholmsky, I., *Istoria Ukrainy,* New York-Munich, 1948.

Kluchevsky, V., *A History of Russia,* London-New York, 1911-1914, Vol. I-II.

Krypiakevych, I. and Dolnytsky, M., *Istoria Ukrainy,* New York, 1966.

Lelevel, J., *Polska, Rzeczy i Dzieje Jej,* Poznan, 1863, Volms. I-IV.

Nahayevsky, I., Rev., *History of Ukraine,* Philadelphia, 1975.

Pokrovskii, M., *Brief History of Russia,* London, 1933, Vol. I.

Polonska-Vasylenko, N., *Istoria Ukrainy,* Munich, 1972, Vol. I.

Presniakov, A., *Lektsii po russkoi istorii, Kievskaia Rus',* Moscov, 1939, Vol. I.

Soloviov (Solovev), S., *Istoria Rossii s drevnieishikh vriemen,* St. Petersburg, 1894-1895, Vols. I-X.

Tomashivsky, S., *Istoria Ukrainy, starynni viky i seredni viky,* Munich, 1948.

Vernadsky, G. and Karpovich, M., *A History of Russia,* Vol, I, *Ancient Russia,* New Haven-London, 1952: Vol. II, *Kievan Russia,* New Haven-London, 1951; Vol. III, *The Mongols and Russia,* New Haven-London, 1953.

II. *Monographic works and special subject matters.*

Abraham, J., *Powstaine organizacji Kościola lacińskiego na Rusi,* Lviv, 1904.

Arkas, M., *Istoria pivnichnoi Chornomorshchyny,* Toronto, 1969.

Bahalii, D., *Narys istorii Ukrainy na sotsialno-ekonomichnomu grunti,* Kharkiv, 1928, Vol, I.

Braichevsky, M., *Istoria Kyieva, Kyiv-tsentr drevniorus'koi derzhavy,* Kiev, 1960, Vol. I.

Braichevsky, M., *Koly i yak vynyk Kyiv,* Kiev, 1968.

Braichevsky, M., *Pokhodzennia Rusi,* Kiev, 1963.

Chirovsky, Fr.-, N., *The Economic Factors in the Growth of Russia,* New York, 1957.

Chirovsky, Fr.-, N., *Old Ukraine, Its Socio-Economic History prior to 1781,* Madison, 1963.

Chubaty, N., *Ohlad istorii ukrainskoho prava,* Munich, 1947, Vol, I.

Chubaty, N., *Rus'-Ukraina ta vyneknennia triokh skhidnioslovianskykh natsii,* New York, 1964.

Chyzhevsky, D., *Istoria ukrainskoi literatury,* New York, 1956.

Czyrowski, Fr.-, N., (Chirovsky), *Geschichtlicher Abriss der Staatsrechtlichen Einrichtungen in Galizien (Bis zum Wiener-Kongress 1815),* doctor-thesis, Graz, 1943, (manuscript).

Fedoriv, Yu. Rev., *Istoria tserkvy v Ukraini,* Toronto, 1967.

Findeisen, *Ocherki po istorii muzyki v Rossii,* Moscow-Leningrad, 1928.

Goetz, L., *Deutsch-Russische Handelsgeschichte des Mittelalters,* Luebeck, 1922.

Golubinskii, E., *Istoria russkoi tserkvy,* Moscow, 1901-1904, Vol, I.

Grekov, B., *Kievskaia Rus',* Moscow, 1953.

Hensiorsky, A., *Halytsko-Volynskyi litopys;* Kiev, 1956.

Hordynsky, S., ed. *The Ukrainian Icon of the XII-XVIII centuries,* Philadelphia, 1973.

Hrytsak, P., *Halytsko-Volynska derzhava,* New York, 1958.

Ilarion, Metropolitan (Ohienko, E.), *Blyskucha zoria v ukrainskii dukhovii kulturi,* Winnipeg, 1960.

Ilarion, Metropolitan (Ohienko, E.), *Slovo pro Ihoriv pokhid,* Winnipeg, 1949.

Ilarion, Metropolitan (Ohienko, E.), *Vyzantia i Ukraina,* Winnipeg, 1954.

Kluchevskii, V., *Boiarskaia duma drevniei Rusi,* Moscow, 1909.

Kluchevskii, V., *Istoria soslovii v Rossii,* Moscow, 1913.

Kulischer, J., *Russische Wirtschaftsgeschichte,* Jena, 1925.

Levytsky, M., ed., *Istoria ukrainskoho viiska,* Winnipeg, 1953.

Linnichenko, A., *Cherty iz istorii soslovii Galitskoi Rusi XIV-XV v.,* Moscow, 1894.

Logvyn, H., Miliaieva, L., and Svientsitska, edts., *Ukrainskyi seredniovichnyi zhyvopys,* Kiev, 1976.

Luzhnytsky, H., *Ukrainska tserkva mizh Skhodom i Zakhodom,* Philadelphia, 1954.

Lyashchenko, P., *History of the National Economy of Russia,* New York, 1949.

Mansikka, V., *Die Religion der Ostslaven,* Helsinki, 1922.

Meynert, H., *Geschichte des Kriegswesens und der Heeresverfassungen in Europa,* Vienna, 1868-1869, Vol. I.

Mirtchuk, I., *Geschichte der Ukrainischen Kultur,* Munich, 1957.

Nazarko, I., *Sviatyi Volodymyr Velykyi, volodar i khrystytel Rusi-Ukrainy,* Rome, 1954.

Ohienko, I. (Ilarion, Mytropolyt), *Ukrainska kultura,* Prague, 1923.

Ohienko, I. *Ukrainska tserkva,* Prague, 1942, Vols. I-II.

Pashuto, V., *Ocherki po istorii Galitsko-Volynskoi Rusi,* Moscov, 1950.

Pasternak, Ya., *Arkheolohia Ukrainy,* New York, 1961.

Pasternak, Ya., *Korotka arkheolohia zakhidnio-ukrainskykh zemel,* Lviv, 1932, Vols. I-II.

Pokrovskii, M., *Ocherki po istorii russkoi kultury,* Moscow, 1923.

Povstenko, O., *Istoria ukrainskoho mystetstva,* Nuerenberg-Fuerth, 1948.

Presniakov, A., *Kniazhoie pravo v drevniei Rusi; ocherki po istorii X-XII st.,* St. Petersburg, 1909.

Priselkov., M., *Istoria russkayo letopisania, XI-XIV v.,* Leningrad, 1940.

Priselkov, M., *Ocherki po tserkovno-politicheskoi istorii Kievskoi Rusi X-XII st.,* St. Petersburg, 1913.

Radzykevych, V., *Istoria ukrainskoi literatury,* Detroit, 1955, Vol. I.

Rostovtsev, M., *Skytia i Bospor,* Moscow, 1925.

Rostovtsev, M., *Yellinstvo i iranstvo na yuge Rossii,* Petrograd, 1918.

Rybakov, B., *Remeslo drevniei Rusi,* Moscow-Leningrad, 1948.

Rybakov, B., *Skazania, bylyny, letopisi,* Kiev, 1963.

Sergeievich, V., *Drevnosti russkavo prava,* St. Petersburg, 1908-1911, Vols. I-II.

Sergeievich, V., *Russkaia Pravda v cheteriokh redaktsiakh,* St. Petersburg, 1904.

Shakhmatov, M., *Ucheniia russkikh letopisei domongolskavo perioda o gosudarstvennoi vlasti,* Prague, 1927.

Shcherbakivsky, V., *Formatsia ukrainskoi natsii,* Prague, 1940.

Shcherbakivsky, V., *Kamiana doba,* Munich, 1947.

Shelukhin, S., *Ukraina,* Prague, 1936-1937.

Sichynsky, V., *Arkhitektura starokniazivskoi doby,* X-XIII st., Prague, 1926.

Sichynsky, V., *Istoria ukrainskoho mystetstva,* Vol. I-II, *Arkhitektura,* New York, 1956.

Sichynsky, V., *Narys ukrainskoi promyslovosty,* Lviv, 1936.

Sichynsky, V., *Ukraine in Foreign Comments and Descriptions, from the VIth to the XXth century,* New York, 1953.

Slabchenko, M., *Orhanizatsia khaziaistva Ukrainy,* Kharkiv, 1925, Vol. I.

Soloviov, S., *Istoria otnoshenia mezhdu russkimi kniaziami Rurikavo doma,* Moscow, 1847.

Spuler, B., *Die Goldene Horde,* Leipzig, 1943.

Tomashivsky, S., *Istoria tserkvy na Ukraini,* Philadelphia (the year of publication not indicated).

Tretiakov., P., *Vostochno-slavianskie plemena,* Moscow, 1953.

Trubetskoi, N., *Nasledie Jinghiskhana,* Berlin, 1925.

Tikhomirov, M., *Drevnierusskie goroda,* Moscow, 1956.

Tikhomirov, M., *Krestianskie i gorodskie vozstania na Rusi XI-XIII vv.,* Moscov, 1955.

Vladimirskii-Budanov, M., *Khristomatia po istorii russkavo prava,* St. Petersburg-Kiev, 1908.

Vladimirskii-Budanov, M., *Obzor istorii russkavo prava*. Petrograd-Kiev, 1915.

Vlasovsky, V., *Narys istorii ukrainskoi pravoslavnoi tserkvy*, New York, 1955, Vol. I.

Vozniak, M., *Istoria ukrainskoi literatury*, Lviv, 1920, Vol. I.

Wanczura, A., *Szkolnictwo w starej Rusi*, Lviv, 1923.

Winter, E., *Byzanz und Rom in Kampf um die Ukraine*, Leipzig, 1942.

Wlodarski, B., *Polska i Rus' 1194-1340*, Warsaw, 1966.

Wlodarski, B., *Polityka ruska Leszka Bialego*, Lviv, 1925.

Yaniv, V., *Narys ukrainskoi kultury*, New York, 1961.

Zubrytsky, D., *Istoria drevnievo Galichesko-russkavo kniazhestva*, Lviv, 1852-1855.

III. *Articles, chronicles and documents.*

Abramovich, D., ed., *Kievo-pecherskii Pateryk*, St. Petersburg, 1911; second ed., Kiev, 1930.

Annales Bertiniani in usum scholarum, Hannover, 1883.

Bidnov, V., "Hroshi", *Zahalna ukrainska entsyklopedia*, Lviv, 1936, Vol. III.

Bidnov, V., "Pravoslavna tserkva", *Ibid*.

Braichevsky, M., "Starodavni skhidni sloviany", *Narysy z starodavnioi istorii URSR*, Kiev, 1957.

Braichevsky, M., "The Unification of the old Rus' Lands around the Center of Kyiv", *On the Historical Beginnings of Eastern Slavic Europe*, N. Chirovsky, Fr.-, ed., New York, 1976.

Chubaty, N., "The Meaning of 'Rus' and 'Ukraine'", *On the Historical Beginnings of Eastern Slavic Europe*, N. Chirovsky, Fr.-, ed., New York, 1976.

Constantine Porphyrogenitus, "De Administrando Imperio", *Patrologiae Cursus Completus*, Series Graeca, CXIII, cols. 157-422.

Cross, S. and Sherbowitz-Wetzor, O., edts., *The Russian Primary Chronicle*, Cambridge, 1953.

Dombrovsky, A., "The Spiritual Trend of Ukraine in Antiquity", *Proceedings*, Historical-Philosophical Section, Shevchenko Scientific Society, New York, 1951.

Evans, A., ed., "Medieval Russian Laws", *Records of Civilization*, New York, 1947.

Garkavi, A., *Skazania muzulmanskikh pisatelei o slovianakh i russkikh*, St. Petersburg, 1870.

Grekov, B., "Drevnieishie sudby slovianstva v Prykarpatskykh oblastiakh", *Izbrannyie trudy*, Moscow, 1955, Vol. II.

Grekov, B., "Rabstvo i feodalizm v drevniei Rusi", *Akademia Istorii Materialnoi Kultury*, Moscow, 1932, Issue 86.

Herodotus, *Historiae*, ed. by H. Stein, Berlin, 1884.

Holubets, M., "Mystetstvo", *Istoria ukrainskoi kultury,* Lviv, 1937.

Horniatkevych, D. and Nenadkevych, L., "Embroideries", *Ukraine, A Concise Encyclopedia,* Toronto, 1963, Vol. I.

Hrushevsky, M., "Ethnographic Categories and Cultural-Archeological Groups in Contemporary Studies of Eastern Europe", *On the Historical Beginnings of Eastern Slavic Europe,* N. Chirovsky, Fr.-, ed., New York, 1976.

Hrushevsky, M., "Some Debatable Questions in Old Rus'ian Ethnography", *ibid.*

Hrushevsky, M., "The Traditional System of 'Russian History' vs a Rational History of Eastern Slavs", *ibid.*

The Hypatian Chronicle, Ipatievsk litopys', see: *Polnoi sobranie russkikh letopisei.*

Karskii, E., *Russkaia Pravda po drevnieishemu spisu,* Leningrad, 1930.

Kedrenus (Cedrenus) Georgius, *Historiarum Compendium,* ed. by J. Bekker, Bonn, 1838-1839.

Kortchmaryk, B., "Russian Interpretation of Ukrainian Historical Source Materials", *On the Historical Beginnings of Eastern Slavic Europe,* N. Chirovsky, Fr.-, ed., New York, 1976.

Kostomarov, M., "Mysli o federatyvnom nachale v drevniei Rusi", *Sobranie sochinenii,* St. Petersburg, 1903, Vol. I.

Kotkovskii, J., *Letopis Nestora.,* Kiev, 1860.

Krypiakevych, I., "Pobut", *Istoria ukrainskoi kultury,* Winnipeg, 1964, Vol. I.

Kurinnyi, P., "Arkhitektura Desiatynnoi tserkvy", *Ukrainskyi Samostiinyk,* Munich, 1953, No. 16.

The Laurentian Chronicle, Lavrentiiska litopys', See: *Polnoie sobraine russkikh letopisei.*

Leo Diaconus, *Historiae Libri decem.,* B. Hase, ed., Bonn, 1828.

Manning, C., "Kremlin's New Theses on Ukraine", *On the Historical Beginnings of Eastern Slavic Europe,* N. Chirovsky, Fr.-, ed. New York, 1976.

Mirchuk, I., "The Basic Traits of the Ukrainian People", *Ukraine and Its People,* I. Mirchuk, ed., Munich, 1949.

Monumenta Poloniae historica, Lviv, 1864 and the following, Vols. I-II-III.

Nazarko, I., "Kyiivski monastyri domonholskoi doby", *Logos,* 1952, Vol. III.

Petrov, V., "Obriadovyi folklor narodno-kalendarnoho tsyklu yak metodolohichna problema", *Naukovyi zbirnyk Ukrainskoho Vilnoho Universtetu,* Munich, 1948, Vol. V.

Photii epistolae, E. Miller, ed., *Fragmenta Historiae graecae,* 1870; also, *Photii epistulae,* ed. by Valetta, London, 1864.

Pogodin, M., "Obrazovanie i gramotnost' v drevniem periodie russkoi istorii", *Zhurnal Ministerstva Narodnavo Prosveshchenia,* 1871, Vol. 153.

Polnoie sobranie russkikh letopisei: Lavrentievskaia letopis', Leningrad, 1926, I: *Ipatievskaia letopis',* Petrograd, 1923, II.

Polonska-Vasylenko, N., "Korol Danylo na tli istorychnoi doby", *Vyzvolnyi Shlakh,* 1954, London, 1954, Book IX.

Povist' vremennykh lit, edts. V. Adrianovaia-Perets, and D. Likhachev, (commentary), Moscow-Leningrad, 1950, Vols. I-II.

Povstenko, O., "Fresky i mozaiky Mykhailivskoho (Dmytrivskoho) monastyria v Kyievi", *Ukrainske mystetstov,* Munich, 1947, II.

Povstenko, O., "Fresky i mozaiky sv. Sofii", *ibid.,* I.

Pritsak, O. and Reshetar, J., "Ukraine and the Dialectics of Nation-Building", *On the Historical Beginnings of Eastern Slavic Europe,* N. Chirovsky, Fr.-, ed., New York, 1976.

Procopius, *History of the Wars,* H. Dewing, ed., Loeb Classical Library, 5 volms.

Rudnytsky, Ya. and Sichynsky, V., "Nazva 'Ukrainia'", *Entsyklopedia ukrainoznavstva,* Munich-New York, 1949, Vol., I-III.

Rybakov, B., "Znaky sobstvennosti v kniazheskom khaziaisvi Kievskoi Rusi", *Sovietskaia arkheologia,* Moscow, 1940, Vol. 6.

Savitsky, P., "Podiem i depressia v drevnie-russkoi istorii", *Yevraziiskaia Khronika,* 1936, II.

Shcherbakivsky, V., "Ukrainska praistoria", *Nasha kultura,* Warsaw, 1935-37, Vol. I.

Sherekh, Yu., "Nazva 'Rus'", *Entsyklopedia ukrainoznavstva,* Munich, 1949, Vol. I.

Tietmar of Merseburg, *Chronicon,* F. Kurze, ed., Hanover, 1889.

Tretiakov, P., "O proiskhozhdenie slovian", *Voprosy istorii,* Moscow, 1953, Book II.

Vasmer, M., "Wikingenspuren in Russland", *Sitzungsberichte,* Phil.-Hist. Klasse, Preussische Akademie der Wissenschaften, Berlin, 1931, XXIV.

Vassilevskii, V., "Drevnia torgovlia Kieva s Regensburgom", *Zhurnal ministerstva narodnava prosveshchenia,* 1888, Vol. 258.

Vernadsky, G., "Feudalism in Russia", *Speculum,* 1939, 14.

Vernadsky, G., "Iron Mining and Iron Industries in Medieval Russia", *Etudés dédieés á la mémoire d' André Andreadés,* Athens, 1939.

Viazmitina, M., "Sarmaty", *Narysy z starodavnioi istorii URSR,* Kiev, 1957.

Vynar, L., "Pereizd Bruno z Kverfurtu cherez Kyiv chasiv Volodymyra Velykoho", *Rozbudova natsii,* Denver, 1955, No. I.

Yaniv, V., "Suspilni verstvy", *Entsyklopedia ukrainoznavstva,* Munich, 1949, Vol. I.

Zaloziecky, W., "Byzantinisch-ruthenische Kunst", *Deutschtum und Ausland,* Munich, 1930, Book 28-29.

Zhdan, M., "Ukraina i Zolota Orda", *Ukrainskyi istoryk,* New York, 1964, No. 2-3.

Zimin, A., *Pamiatki prava Kievskavo gosudarstva, Russkaia Pravda prostrannoi redaktsii,* Moscow, 1952.

INDEX OF NAMES

Edmund, of England, 127
Ellias, St., 98
Engels, F., 42
Ermenrics, King, 55
Estonians, the, xi
Esugay Bagatur, 146
Evans, A., ed., 251

Fairbank, J., 68
Fedoriv, Yu., 101, 157, 183, 250
Ferguson, W., 67
Findeisen, N., 252
Florinsky, M., 272
Franciscans, the 219
Franks, the, 56, 61
Friedrich I, Barbarossa, 163-164

Gallus Anonimus, 322
Gardariki, Scandinavian, 307
Garkavi, A., xvi, 101,
    307-308, 331
Gedeonov, S., 108
Gedymin, of Lithuania, 179
Germans, the, 88, 96, 108, 178,
    180, 263, 270-271, 275
Getes, the, 49
Genghis-Khan (also, Ginghis-Khan)
    Temudzhin, 5, 15, 146, 320
Gita, of England, 137
Goetz, L., 331
Golubiev, S., 16
Golubinskii, E., 229, 250-251
Goths, the, see Ostgoths, the
Great Russians, the, see Russians,
    the, also, Muscovites, the,
Greeks, the, 47, 52, 88, 94, 96,
    106-107, 111-112, 116-117,
    122, 216, 220, 222, 269-271,
    276, 284, 304, 315-317, 321
Gregory VII, Pope, 132
Grekov, B., 19, 156, 213, 275,
    287, 296
Gruzians (Georgians), the, xi

Guyuk, Khan, 151

Hapsburgs, the, 175
Harcave, S., 17
Harold II, of England, 137
Heinrich II, Emperor, 123, 127
Heinrich IV, Emperor, 132, 278
Henry I, of France, 128
Heraclios, 56
Herodotus, xiii, 49, 52, 59
Hesiodes, 59
Hindus, the people, 96
Hitler, A., 37
Hlib, St., 125, 138, 236
Hohenstaufen, the, 165-166
Holubets, M., 308
Homer, 230
Hordynsky, S., 239, 251
Horniatkevych, D., 252
Horak, S., xii
Hrihorii (Hryhorii), monk, 230, 246
Hrushevsky, M., xii-xiii, 16-17,
    35, 63, 65, 67-68, 95, 100-101,
    108, 115, 123, 156-157, 175,
    183, 185, 187, 212-213, 219,
    250-251, 260, 271, 274, 282,
    289, 306-308, 314, 325,
    330-331
Hrytsak, P., 183-184
Humbert, envoy, 219
Hungarians (Magyars), the, 57,
    166, 170, 178-180, 257, 270,
    283-284
Huns, the, 5, 54-56, 61

Iam, the, tribe, 66
Iazygians, the, 71
Ibn-Dasta (Rusta), xiv, 77, 96, 99,
    101, 282, 302, 307, 312, 319
Ibn-Fadlan, xiv, 99, 101, 282,
    319-320
Ibn-Hawqal, xiv, 79, 96, 101, 307
Ibn-Jakob (Jakub), xiv, 101, 319